AC  NTS

Without the support of some very fine folk, *TokyoScope* almost certainly would have been a scratchy, silent 8mm affair projected on a bedsheet somewhere. Super-sized serving of thanks and appreciation are in order:

Editor and ringside trainer Alvin Lu imparted valuable lesson after valuable lesson and was a great friend every step of the way. Designer Izumi Evers brought immense talent and experience to this project, often doing triple shifts as a translator, coordinator, and *benshi* narrator. Happy Ujihashi's constant stream of illustrations delighted, inspired, and supplied the strength to go on. Viva la Showakan! Praise be also to Tomohiro Machiyama, trusted friend and founding editor of *Eiga Hi-Ho* magazine, who selflessly provided information and analysis, supplied films, and helped open doors on countless occasions. And major indebtedness to *TokyoScope*'s crack team of translators, who include Andy Nakatani (who gave his time often, freely, and always in good humor), Akemi Wegmuller, Yuji Oniki, and Zachary Braverman.

Lots of other people, contributors, friends, folks who helped one way or another: Kinji Fukasaku, Takashi Miike, Kiyoshi Kurosawa, Risaku Kiridoshi, TDC Fujiki, J-Taro Sugisaki, Mahiro Maeda, Kiichiro Yanashita, Aki Kameda, Toshiko Adilman, Taro Goto, Anne McKnight, Jason Thompson, Carl Horn, Chuck Stephens, David Weisman, Robert Houston, Jim and Gibran Evans, Mark Walkow, Trish Ledoux, Laura Heins, Roy Wood, August Ragone, Femke Wolting and the Rotterdam International Film Festival, Chris D. and the American Cinematheque, Mona Nagai and the Pacific Film Archive, my father, the makers of *Deva Absenta*, and everyone at Tidepoint Pictures and Viz Communications.

And a final outpouring of deep gratitude in the general direction of Hyoe Narita, Seiji Horibuchi, and especially Satoru Fuji for the desk, the computer, and the chance to write a book about crazy Japanese movies.

P.M.

CONTENTS

003 **ACKNOWLEDGEMENTS**
009 **FOREWORD** BY KINJI FUKASAKU
010 **PROLOGUE**
012 **THE SHINJUKU SHOWAKAN**

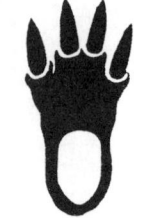

014 **GIANT MONSTERS**

016 **INTRODUCTION**

019 **REVIEWS**
　　Godzilla
　　Giant Monster Gamera
　　Godzilla vs. Monster Zero
　　War of the Gargantuas
　　Gappa
　　Godzilla vs. Biollante
　　Gamera 3—Revenge of Iris
　　Dark Soldier D

027 **ETC.**
　　Exploitation
　　How to Make Monster Movies
　　The *Dai Majin* Trilogy
　　The Making of *Godzilla vs. the Smog Monster*

038 **Sonny Chiba**

040 **INTRODUCTION**

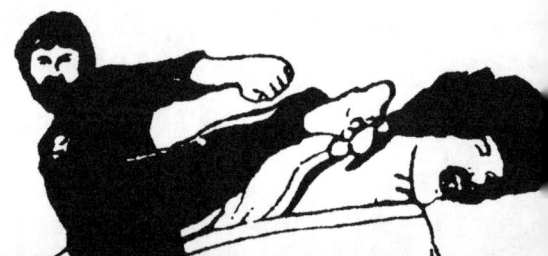

045 **REVIEWS**
The Assassin
The Bodyguard
The Street Fighter
Direct Hit! Hell Fist—Big Reversal
Champion of Death
Dragon Princess
Golgo 13: Assignment: Kowloon
Roaring Fire

053 **ETC.**
Hiroyuki Sanda
Etsuko Shihomi
The Sonny Video Round-up
Sonny's Best Screen Kills

060 **Shogun Assassin**

068 **HORROR**

070 **INTRODUCTION**

074 **REVIEWS**
Claws of Iron
The Ghost of Yotsuya
Attack of the Mushroom People
Goke, Body Snatcher from Hell
House
Tokyo: The Last Megalopolis
Mermaid in a Manhole
The Ring
Uzumaki

083 **ETC.**
Mitsugu Okura
Nobuo Nakagawa
Kiyoshi Kurosawa

090 **MANGA**
Yukio "Scissors" Oda

092 YAKUZA

094 INTRODUCTION

104 REVIEWS
Yakuza Punishment History—Lynch
The Violent Street
Escaped Murderer from Hiroshima Prison
Yokohama Underworld—Machine Gun Dragon
Noboru Ando's Chronicle of Fugitive Days and Sex
Yakuza Cruel Secrets—Arm Dismemberment
The Tattooed Hit Man

111 ETC.
Bunta Sugawara
Noboru Ando: From Gangster to Gang Star
Yakuza Movie History
Toei Co., Ltd. Hyperbole Dpt.

130 kinji Fukasaku

132 INTRODUCTION

137 REVIEWS
Greed in Broad Daylight
The Green Slime
Gambler—Foreign Force
Modern Yakuza—Outlaw Killer
Fight without Honor and Humanity
Graveyard of Honor and Humanity
Message from Space
Battle Royale

147 ETC.
Kinji Fukasaku Filmography
Behind the *BR* Controversy in Japan
Interview with Kinji Fukasaku

158 BANNED...
160 INTRODUCTION
163 REVIEWS
Half-Human
The 99th Virgin
Latitude Zero
Collected Works of Edogawa Rampo—Horrible Malformed Men
The Last Days of Planet Earth

168 ETC.
Teruo Ishii

170 Pink & Violent
172 INTRODUCTION
178 REVIEWS
The Weird Love Makers
Female Slave Ship
Ecstasy of the Angels
Tokugawa Sex Prohibition—Lustful Lord
School of the Holy Beast
Flower and Snake
Female Convict Scorpion—Jailhouse 41

186 ETC.
Nikkatsu's *Roman Porno*
Toei's "Pinky Violence"
Nikkatsu Hyperbole
How to Watch Erotic Movies

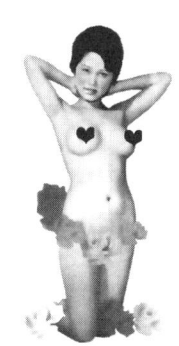

194 MANGA
Message from Space

Panic & Disaster!!!

196

198 INTRODUCTION

203 REVIEWS
- The Last War
- Submersion of Japan
- The Last Days of Planet Earth
- Bullet Train Big Explosion
- Crazy Beast
- Deathquake
- Tetsuro Tanba's Great Spirit World
- The Peking Man

211 ETC.
- Tetsuro Tanba

214

216 INTRODUCTION

223 REVIEWS
- Fudoh—The New Generation
- Dead or Alive
- Audition
- The City of Lost Souls
- Ichi the Killer
- Hardboiled

229 ETC.
- Riki Takeuchi
- Boutique Riki Takeuchi

234 EPILOGUE

236 AFTERWORD BY TAKASHI MIIKE

237 INDEX

FOREWORD

To paraphrase the titles of some of my favorite films I have made, it is with honour and much humility that I read about my work and those of my contemporaries in this book.

It is always hard to make a film no matter when and no matter in what country. When we began making the films that are mentioned so meticulously in this book you can't imagine what Japan was like. In the early 1960s when my career began, Japan was recovering from the war, but I still felt left out.

As a nation we were all still coming to grips with the destruction of our cities, our sense of nationhood and of our own psyches. It haunts us still.

So you can imagine how little we thought about making films that would appeal to Western audiences. I can certainly say that along with the other filmmakers of my generation, I thought only about trying as best I could to interest the Japanese audience and then maybe only a small part of it.

Through recent experiences, I have discovered to my delight that Western critics like our films, too. As the president of the Directors' Guild of Japan, I can also say that in this book you will find as good an analysis of what we were trying to do as I have ever read. Patrick Macias has written very keenly and with much understanding about Japanese films, mine included.

Kinji Fukasaku

PROLOGUE

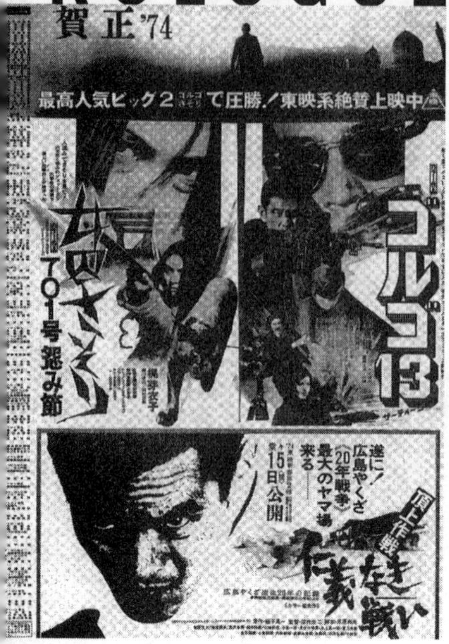
賀正'74
ゴルゴ13
遂に!広島やくざ〈20年戦争〉最大のヤマ場来る
15日公開
仁義なき戦い

Female Convict Scorpion, *Golgo 13*, and Bunta. A typically killer Toei triple feature from 1974.

This is the story of a lost chapter in Japanese film history. It is a missing reel of cutting-room-floor footage that needs to be edited back in before the Big Picture, the *dai eiga*, nears true completion.

You might already know some of the story.

From the postwar years on, Japan produced some truly amazing films and filmmakers. The works of Akira Kurosawa, Yasujiro Ozu, Kenji Mizoguchi, Kon Ichikawa, and Nagisa Oshima, for starters. Acclaimed. Award winning. Ever present. The Western perception of Japanese cinema has been dominated by them for decades now. And not without good reason.

Yet during the same period, let's say from 1950-1976, during which the big guns created their signature works, Japan's popular cinema was also at its peak. During the late fifties and sixties especially, impressive moviemaking machinery was in place: a star system, a studio system, and an audience that supported Japanese films by demanding a host of new double- and triple–features every week.

A new generation of young filmmakers had to be ushered in to grind 'em out. The rules were simple. Keep it cheap. Do it on time. Above all, make it entertaining.

Although these limitations were non-negotiable, the artists and journeymen who agreed to them were granted an enormous amount of creative freedom. As director Norifumi Suzuki (who helmed the almost unbelievably blasphemous *School of the Holy Beast*) has said in interviews, the only taboo that could not be transgressed was the Emperor. But aside from that, and a strict no-show stance on hardcore sexual imagery, the B- and C-class filmmakers could get away with anything.

Filmmakers like Norifumi Suzuki and screenwriters like Takeshi Kimura (aka Kaoru Mabuchi) sized up the situation and ran with the ball. They were progressive, free-thinking individuals who had endured the war, the subsequent American occupation, and were now working in a highly competitive and commercial mass medium.

Film studios, forever besieged with labor issues, had long held considerable attachments to the right wing and organized crime. The people who actually directed and wrote these films were frequently far more left of center. Yet these institutions and individuals needed each other. And out of the friction came both conflict and creativity.

Flickers from the late sixties and earlier seventies: yakuza movies, porno flicks, karate killers. This was the era of true Japanese exploitation films, primarily intended to rope in blue-collar types and young men who had migrated to the big city to take part in the economic miracle. The target audience got what it wanted in spades: criminals, monsters, escapism, shivers, sex and violence.

These movies, once considered so disposable by the parent studios that film prints and negatives were frequently destroyed soon after release, were often nothing less than the manifestos of the people who made them. Kinji Fukasaku's yakuza films spoke as eloquently on the turmoil of postwar Japan as any history professor could. Shunya Ito's *Female Convict Scorpion* series was a scathing critique of Japanese imperialism and patriarchy. *Godzilla vs. the Smog Monster* was a reaction to a horrific series of industrial pollution accidents. You didn't even have to dig very deep to get the message. These "trash films" proudly wore their subtext on their sleeves.

And they looked great. Although frequently made on the quick and cheap, consummate professionals handled the raw materials all down the line. Japanese aesthetics of composition and design made their genre films truly special. During this quarter-century streak of Japanese film, no one consistently made more handsome pop films, save perhaps for the Italians (God bless them).

But it is not like many outside of Japan knew about any of this when it was happening.

Japanese studios, either out of sheer laziness or by assuming that there was no audience for these films abroad, did amazingly little to promote their titles overseas. And the ones that did make it to foreign screens? They were marketed to children, drive-ins, grindhouse theaters, and other channels of distribution either beneath the contempt, or simply the radar, of both the general public and "Japanese film experts."

The people who did follow the trail saw enough to form lasting cults around. By the seventies, Japanese monsters and Sonny "The Street Fighter" Chiba could claim loyal acolytes world-wide.

During this same era in Japan, the tide went out for the film industry. Domestically produced movies had lost the lion's share of their audience to TV shows and Hollywood blockbusters. The postwar generation of filmmakers had lost their playground. They moved to television, retired, or expired. By proxy, Japanese films became cult films in Japan too.

Cut to now.

A new Japanese New Wave is currently piquing the world's interest. Filmmakers like Takashi Miike (*Dead or Alive*), Kiyoshi Kurosawa (*Cure*), Kaizo Hayashi (*The Most Terrible Time in My Life*), and Hideo Nakata (*The Ring*) have taken film festivals and international audiences by storm. They seem to have sprung from nowhere. People reach for comparisons, points of origin, and find a black hole.

The truth is that these new superstars of Japanese film sprang from the soil of the previous generation. Hideo Nakata first became a director at Nikkatsu studios during their notorious *roman porno* heyday. Kaizo Hayashi quotes freely from old yakuza films and ninja movies.

The old timers showed these future directors that there was nothing wrong with making genre films. Even the time-honored dance of time and money could give one immense artistic room to maneuver. And maybe most importantly, all of Japanese film, from A to Z, deserved to be on equal historical footing.

Take Takashi Miike. He began his film career as an assistant director to Shohei Imamura, yet he claims the work of Yukio Noda as a major inspiration.

Shohei Imamura? Sure. The Cannes-winning director of *Insect Woman* and *The Pornographers*. But who the heck is Yukio Noda? Answer: turn to page 51 of this book, for a write-up of his *Golgo 13* movie starring Sonny Chiba, which can be found on US home video without too much difficulty.

The films obtained for review in this book were found any way we got them. Mostly this meant video. English-dubbed, raw Japanese, PAL/NTSC transfers, crappy Hong Kong VCDs, you name it. Several titles were procured by trading with a Japanese pen pal in exchange for contraband tapes of *House Party 2* and *3* (perhaps he's writing *Kid 'N Play Scope*). We even hopped on a plane and went to Japan a couple of times. If we listed a movie as being "available" that means that you can get it on the internet, or bug your local video stores, or gray-market dealers, and probably come up with a copy.

If we wrote up a certain title, that means it gave us some thrills and some laughs and inspired us enough to generate a missive. This is not a book with a ratings system meant to divide things up into "authoritative" piles of Good and Bad. And to be honest, when it comes to these kinds of movies, there isn't a heck of a lot that we don't like.

After all, this book is subtitled *The Japanese Cult Film Companion*. We're not trying to be an encyclopedia, *Psychopathia Sexualis*, or the phone book. We just want to take you off the beaten path of Kurosawa, Ozu, and Oshima for a bit and show you where the wild things are. Which means our first stop is Tokyo and the Shinjuku Showakan, the greatest movie theater in the world.

And immediately following the short subject: the main feature, an alternate history of Japanese film, a cult movie, proudly presented...in TokyoScope.

Patrick Macias
Sacramento—San Francisco—Japan, 2001 東

THE SHINJUKU SHOWAKAN

Shinjuku, Tokyo. The pulsing heart of modern Japan. Electric, overwhelming, Asian chaos. Total sensory overload. The only possible comparison for the visitor, still after all these years, is *Blade Runner*.

For the natives, Shinjuku Station is a transfer point, a place to jump a commuter train and hop on the bullet. Leave the six-story station/fortress at any one of sixty exits in any direction, and your money is immediately up for grabs: dig the curbside ramen, electronic emporiums, prostitutes from around the world, video game arcades, titanic department stores. Gorge on fast food, gourmet dining. Get wild with bootleg-CD box sets. Snap up those movie tickets.

Immense billboards next to East Exit advertise what's playing at the Toei- and Toho-owned theaters in nearby Kabuki-cho. In late summer 2000, massive campaigns were in effect for Setsuro Wakamatsu's *Whiteout* and the Wayans brothers' *Scary Movie*.

Head south. Stay off the main thoroughfares. Get lost down the numerous side streets and alleys. Explore. Pass the cell-phone kiosks, the sex shops, and pachinko parlors. A grid of ancient-looking movie posters will strategically appear out of the ether: snarling faces framed by guns and knives. Yazuka. Gamblers. Tumbling dice and *hanafuda* cards.

This is how the Shinjuku Showakan announces itself, in images frozen in time from Japan's Showa era (1925-1989).

Don't sneeze at the ¥1300 admission fee. You've saved a few, compared to the ¥1800 admission for a first-run flick, and can use it on the vending machine in the lobby. Pay the nice old lady inside the box-office window. She'll tear your stub in half.

Walk inside. Look around. Try not to sniff around too much. Curious smells might give you a bad first impression. Adjust the eyes. Some two hundred seats make up the main floor, with additional seating located in a spacious balcony. There's maybe only forty to sixty or so people in there along with you. Most of them are middle-aged men.

The Japanese word for them is *oyaji*. And in a culture that worships youth and style, they are probably the most unfashionable people in the country. First and foremost, the Showakan is their place. A hardcore contingent, the Showakan Army, lines up every day before the doors open at noon. They come for all kinds of reasons. To get off of the street. To crash on the cheap. Others come because they have no stomach for Hollywood film, televised entertainment consisting of pop stars eating exotic foods, or trendy dramas about everyday life. The Showakan's films used to represent the mainstream of Japanese pop cinema. Now these old movies are as alternative as it gets. The Showakan is also a clubhouse for the local yakuza. And with movies like *Nihon no don* (The Don of Japan) and *Soshiki boryoku* (Organized Violence) constantly playing, how could it not be?

Perhaps because of the Showakan's rough-hewn clientele, a bad reputation hovers around the place. Mention it to people out of the inner circle and they'll warn you about the place as if it were a dragon's lair minus any treasure. Once inside though, the joint turns out to be down home and nearly benign. By promixity alone, simply walking through the door makes you an honorary *oyaji* or temporary yakuza.

As if to show there is nothing to be anxious about, some patrons are asleep, peacefully oblivious to whatever might be playing on the screen. Others are prone to distraction, endlessly rummaging through plastic bags, muttering to themselves or at the screen (especially when guns or breasts appear). Still others watch intently. They've been inside the theater all day. From the glazed looks of them, perhaps all their lives.

The Showakan's doors first opened in 1932, when the theater specialized in foreign films (meaning American and European fare), then during World War II it was burnt to the ground, like much of the surrounding area, by Allied fire bombings.

The Showakan rose from the ashes in 1951. Once rebuilt, it played what the major Japanese studios offered and what the public wanted to see. Mostly this meant sword films or yakuza films with period flavor. There was one major patriotic stipulation: the films would have to be Japanese. If the Showakan was going to cultivate a loyal audience, then it had to draw the line somewhere.

In the sixties, as the all-pervasive popularity of television began to shut down theaters, and domestic studios sold their property to cash in on the growing value of real estate, the Showakan managed to hang on. You can thank the yakuza for that mostly, even though they sometimes demanded free admission from the hapless staff. During turf wars, fights could break out between rowdy patrons. Toei shot scenes for movies inside. The programming switched to triple bills daily, and time marched on, at least outside the increasingly hermetically sealed Showakan.

Then as now, two genres utterly dominate the programming: yakuza films and horror movies. Sonny Chiba is a big draw here. So is anything directed by Nobuo Nakagawa. Far and away the most popular fare is culled from Kinji Fukasaku's seventies-era *Jingi naki tatakai* (Fight without Honor and Humanity) series.

The management is constantly struggling to obtain raw materials, but film prints, some of which have been in circulation for upwards of thirty years, are not always in the best of shape. The same goes for what little advertising materials the studios can be bothered to cough up. When original posters and film stills are not available, illustrator and Showakan schedule-maker Happy Ujihashi goes to work and paints smashing new interpretations all his own. He also creates a monthly *Showakan News* flyer that's distributed throughout the neighborhood.

So the place might be a little beat-up in places. (Whoa! Watch out for that bathroom.) There's still much to be proud of. Sound and projection are first-rate. So is the programming. Living history in light and shadow.

The Showakan management has made recent attempts to turn the *oyaji* onto new stuff from time to time. In 2000, recent films such as Kiyoshi Kurosawa's *Serpent's Path* and Sabu's *Dangan Runner* (aka *Non-Stop*) were screened and well received. But the crowd is picky. Takashi Miike's *Dead or Alive* seemed like a sure thing, until the English title confused the patrons. Thinking that Kinji Fukasaku could always be counted on, *Battle Royale* was booked. But it seemed that the old timers didn't want to watch a movie about high school kids. Especially one with an English title.

Give it another thirty years or so. The next generation of *oyaji* will probably need a place deep in Tokyo to call home, too. And the Showakan will be there to mop up when they do. 東

大怪獣

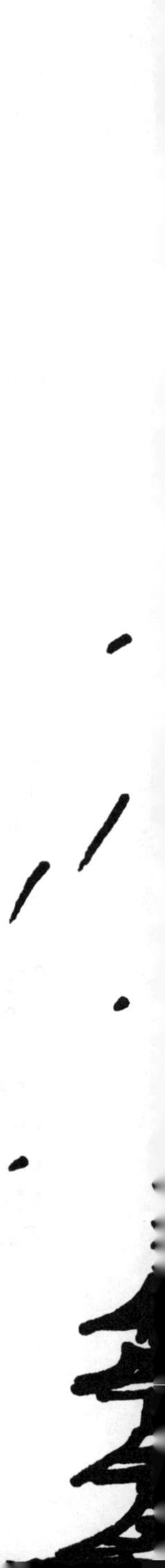

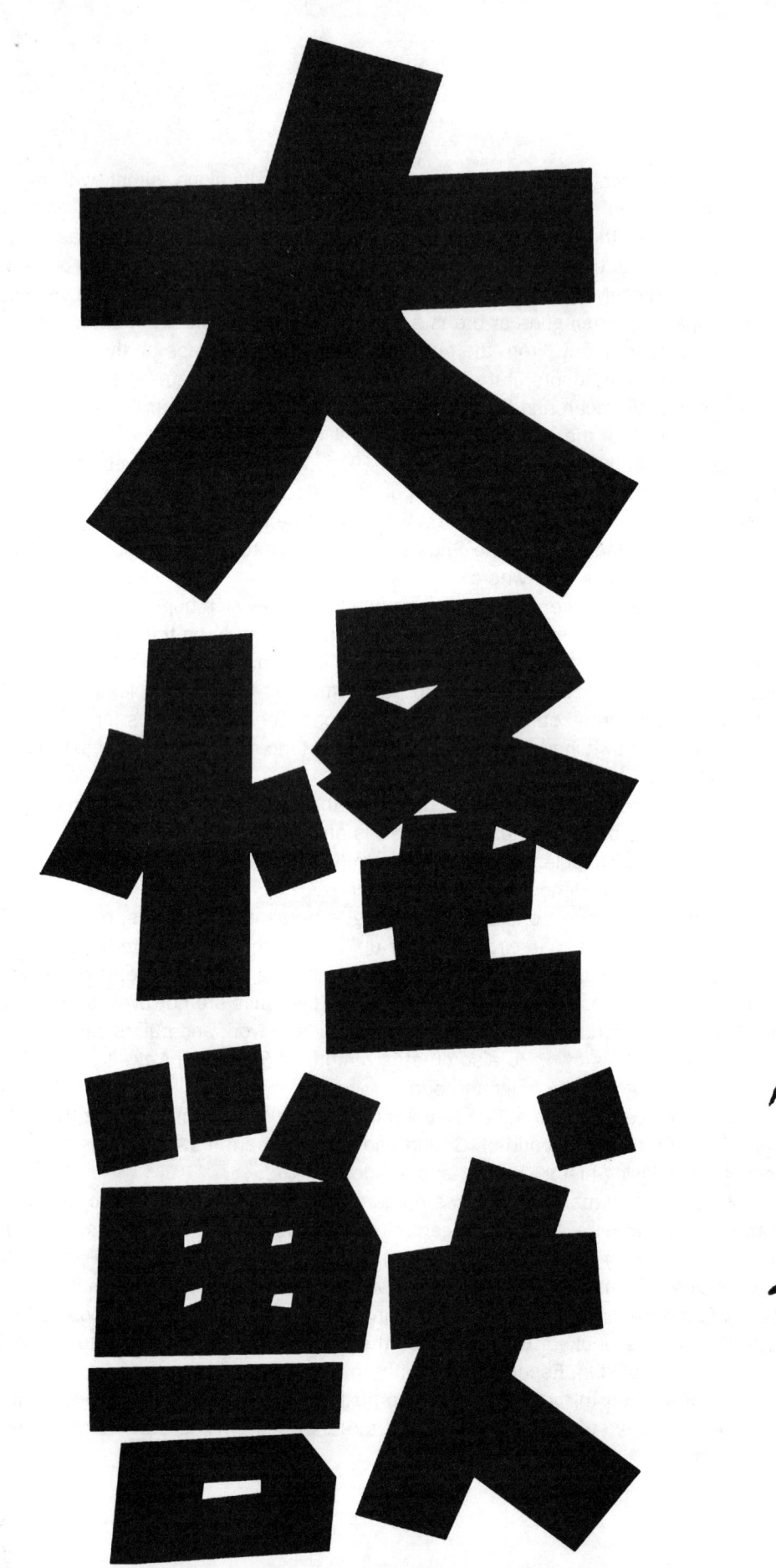

GIANT MONSTERS

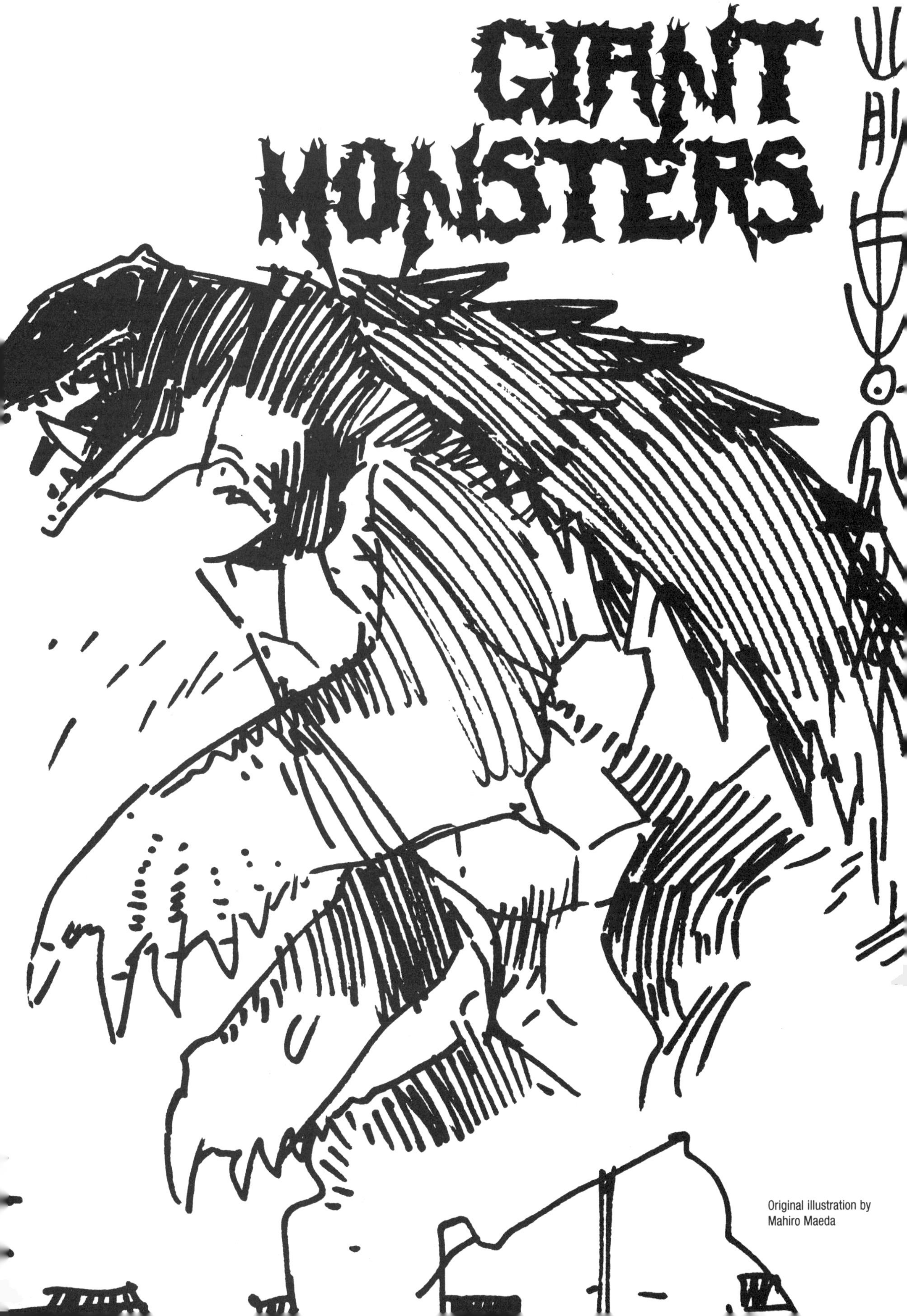

Original illustration by
Mahiro Maeda

GIANT MONSTERS

Art attempts to create the impossible with limited means. Sometimes this gives birth to works of greatness. Sometimes it leads to giant monsters.

Is the ceiling of the Sistine Chapel the actual Glory of the Almighty made manifest? No, it is more like a really good celebrity impersonation.

And whatever you feel about movies such as *Godzilla vs. the Smog Monster* or *War of the Gargantuas*, Japanese monsters are part of this noble tradition.

In addition to wielding paint and brushes, the filmmakers and technicians behind Godzilla, Gamera, and their kith and kin must keep a very big palette at their disposal, one with rubber monster costumes, optical printers, miniature cities, and computers in order to create an illusion of reality.

"KAIJU EIGA"—MONSTER MOVIES

"Film is a synthetic art form in every respect," said the late Ishiro Honda, director of 1954's *Gojira* (Godzilla) and one of the founding fathers of the *tokusatsu*, or special-effects film. "It is also a form of synthetic techniques. The filmmaker is an artist, but at the same time he must also be a scientific technician."

Michelangelo, himself a multitasking sculptor, architect, painter, and poet, would have made great monster movies.

After studying 1933's *King Kong* and 1953's *The Beast from 20,000 Fathoms*, and using special-effects skills gleaned from numerous domestically produced World War II propaganda films (such as 1942's *The War at Sea: From Hawaii to Malay*), it was the Japanese who erected the dynasty of the *kaiju eiga*—the giant monster movie.

Even if you've never heard of Gappa the Triphibian Monster or Gamera the Invincible, *everyone* knows Godzilla. From Thailand to Germany (even though, okay, he's been sold there on

ATTENTION
ITIES OF THE WORLD:
r planet may be doomed....
r earth may be devastated!
e monsters are in revolt and
ilization is in chaos. New York,
scow, London and Peking are
der attack. What city is next?
at nation can survive?
Forces of annihilation have
en massed against us.
AMERICAN INTERNATIONAL presents
DESTROY ALL
MONSTERS
OR BY BERKEY-PATHÉ
G Suggested for GENERAL audiences
HRA·GODZILLA·RODAN·MANDA
1969 American International Pictures
AD MAT 202
202 — 2 COL. x 9 3/8 — 260 LINES
ORDER

INTR

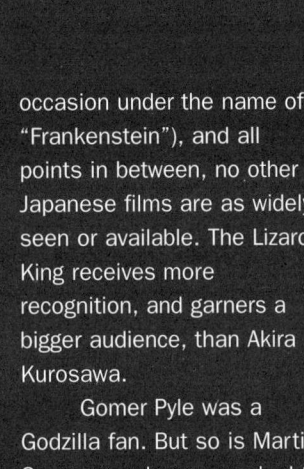

occasion under the name of "Frankenstein"), and all points in between, no other Japanese films are as widely seen or available. The Lizard King receives more recognition, and garners a bigger audience, than Akira Kurosawa.

Gomer Pyle was a Godzilla fan. But so is Martin Scorsese, who once asked to meet Ishiro Honda on the basis of the fondly remembered films he saw as a kid in a Brooklyn theater.

Kaiju eiga are the films of one's childhood, screened at matinees and on Saturday morning TV. In Japan, entire *tokusatsu* films were cobbled together and edited down just to show at kiddie film festivals. Why not? Stepping on a city and spewing atomic heat death is the ultimate temper tantrum. To criticize

GIANT MONSTERS

these films as childish is redundant.

At the other extreme, some people take *kaiju* films as seriously as sacred texts. Academics concoct overreaching theories about them regarding the state apparatus of postwar Japan. Hollywood pisses away

juxtaposition of ticking Geiger counter and dazed child its single most disturbing image.

Follow-ups would handle the primal theme either too lightly (*King Kong vs. Godzilla*), too heavy-handedly (*Godzilla 1985*), or not at all. References to reality gave way to a flood of

If the genre has long since reached its dead end and chosen to endlessly reenact the same rituals (the winking self-awareness of *Gamera 3* admits as much), *kaiju eiga* will forever function as Trojan horse—as point of entry into the less traveled woods of Japanese film and

REVIEW

Godzilla
Gojira

1954, Toho
Director Ishiro Honda
Cast Takashi Shimura, Momoko Kochi, Akira Takarata, Akihiko Hirata

A mysterious force destroys a Japanese fishing boat at sea. The families of the missing demand answers. A subsequent investigation leads to terrible revelations.

The scenario plays like a nightmare headline, the ink only beginning to dry. A collision between a US Navy submarine and a Japanese fishing vessel? No, the opening chain of events from *Gojira,* the first Godzilla movie.

The unaltered 1954 *Gojira* is a film shown so seldom outside Japan one might think it suppressed. No wonder. Half a century on, *Gojira,* a conscious exploration of unconscious fears, still taps into national traumas and anxieties.

"Behind the fear of Gojira was the fear of the atomic bomb," wrote director Ishiro Honda, in an essay. "We thought that if we were to shy away from it, even a little bit, the film would not be completely successful."

Japanese audiences witnessed scenes which directly addressed the horror and banality of life in the then newly minted atom age. Much of this aspect is absent from the 1956 Americanized re-edit of the film, *Godzilla, King of the Monsters,* which instead opts for placing the reassuring face of Raymond Burr center-screen. It's *Perry Mason vs. Godzilla.*

In the Japanese *Gojira*, a TV crew catches sight of a mutant dinosaur awakened by atomic testing and assures us that, "This is not a movie or a play." The high-contrast black-and-white footage resembles a newsreel taken at ground zero.

Honda did his utmost to give his *Gojira* documentary strength; the point of view is informed by personal experience and real catastrophe. As the principal characters watch Tokyo Bay and much of the surrounding city burn down, the feeling is far away from popcorn entertainment. You can't root for this monster or even vicariously enjoy the carnage it creates. The mood is somber and one of pure helplessness.

Gojira is the bomb. Gojira is the Great Kanto Earthquake. Gojira is the sound of thunder coming down from the mountain. Gojira is a multi-purpose symbol for destruction incarnate.

Fifty years on, Godzilla is a pop icon, but, in a new era of sunken fishing boats and mad science, the original *Gojira* still haunts the seas.

☞ **Original Japanese version available as import only**

Giant Monster Gamera

Dai kaiju Gamera, aka Gamera the Invincible

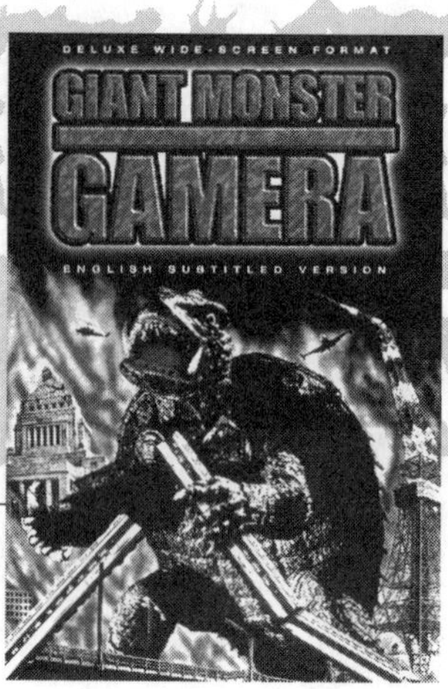
DELUXE WIDE-SCREEN FORMAT
GIANT MONSTER
GAMERA
ENGLISH SUBTITLED VERSION

1965, Daiei
Director Noriaki Yuasa
Cast Eiji Funankoshi, Junichiro Yamashita, Michiko Sugata, Harumi Kiritachi

Gamera, a giant flying jet-propelled turtle, sounds like an insane idea to base an entire movie series around. But it becomes almost pedestrian when you hear that the film *Dai kaiju Gamera* originally evolved from the ruins of a proposed swarm-of-giant-rats film, a project that was canceled when its real-life rodent stars—and indeed portions of Daiei's studio—were besieged by a plague of fleas.

Stuck with an abundance of surplus miniature city, producer Masaichi Nagata (*Rashomon*) was struck by a vision of a flying turtle and decided to make a *kaiju* quickie with second-time director Noriaki Yuasa at the helm.

Whereas Godzilla took at least half an hour to get to his very first close-up, Gamera pops up, jack-in-the-box style, five minutes after the appearance of the opening Daiei logo. The grim shadow of the Cold War looms large at the beginning, but things wrap on an upbeat note as the world unites as one to combat Gamera.

Gamera also marks the introduction of what would soon emerge as a major theme of *kaiju eiga*: the alliance between children and monsters. The soul of the film is Toshio, a troubled, motherless kid obsessed with turtles. He is convinced that his AWOL terrapin pet has somehow become the giant, indestructible Gamera.

Even as the monster blows up power plants and burns Tokyo citizens to a crisp, Toshio is convinced that Gamera is a good guy and is merely misunderstood. Meanwhile, the adults just keep trying to find a way to get rid of the monster, which at one point kills thousands in Tokyo, all the while trying to break down Toshio's imaginary world. But since Gamera functions more as psychological projection than as atom-age nightmare, simply shooting him into space won't work for long. And it didn't, as the successive increasingly childish Gamera films would prove.

At one point in the film, one of the adults asks, "When World War III breaks out, why bother with turtles?" Clearly, there's a generation gap at work here. The grown-ups don't know, but the little boys understand.

☞ **Available subbed or dubbed on VHS from Neptune Media**

☞ **More: THE DAI MAJIN TRILOGY p. 30**

REVIEW

Godzilla vs. Monster Zero
Kaiju dai senso (Great War of the Monsters)

1965, Toho
Director Ishiro Honda
Cast Nick Adams, Kumi Mizuno, Yoshio Tsuchiya, Akira Takarata

The *War and Peace* of the *Godzilla* series, a tale of star-crossed love and interstellar conflict, fraught with radio waves, light rays, personal-guard alarms, and no less than three giant monsters—Godzilla, Rodan, King Ghidorah—running amok across two planets.

A role call of stock scientists, inventors, army men, and alien invaders suggests at first that *Godzilla vs. Monster Zero* might be little different from numerous other Japanese monster films. Even the cosmos had been breached before in Honda's *Chikyu boeigun* (aka *The Mysterians*, 1957) and *Uchu dai senso* (Battle in Outer Space, 1959), both gorgeous pulp illustrations come to life.

And yet *Monster Zero* contains perhaps the most passionate and emotional moments to be found in the entire Godzilla oeuvre. It detonates from the inside with improper conduct.

Rhona Barrett-like reports from the field have suggested that married-with-children American star Nick Adams (who plays "Astronaut Glen" with all-American full-throttle ferocity) and costar Kumi Mizuno, Toho's resident sex bomb (in the part of "fetching alien spy from Planet X"), were most likely getting it on.

With the fallout from this troubled affair spilling over into the performances, *Monster Zero* is less a simple Godzilla movie and more of a prism reflecting back the dangerous liaisons of Nick and Kumi, human and alien, East and West. Few who see Nick grabbing Kumi, clad in black and gray alien fetish gear, by the shoulders and shouting something about "happiness in this world" having less worth than "a hill of beans" can forget it. Think that it's over the top? This *is* the top.

It's also a first-rate Godzilla film. In fact, it's the final hurrah for the classic core Toho staff before turning their monster over to others for inevitable downsizing and diminishing returns. Everything about *Monster Zero* is tight and crisp, designed with a snappy sense of mid-sixties style.

A sequel would have been great. Nick, who would be found dead under mysterious circumstances in 1970, surely would have gone on to become the ambassador of a defeated planet where every woman looked like his late fiancée. And perhaps then the monster movies that followed would have had as much human soul as they would men-in-suits.

☞ **Available dubbed on DVD from Simitar Video**

War of the Gargantuas

Frankenstein no kaiju—Sanda tai Gaira (Frankenstein's Monster—Sanda vs. Gaira)

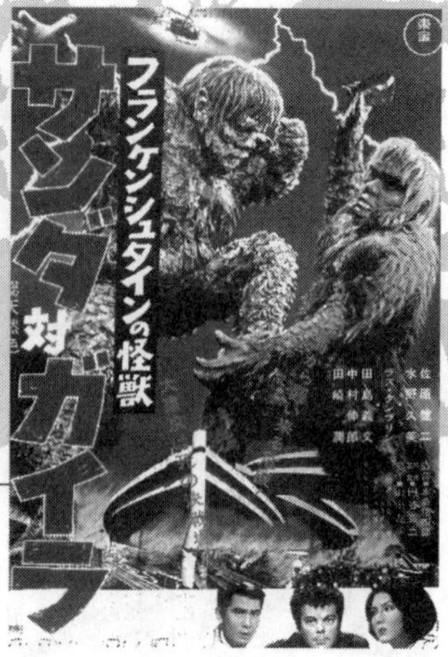
フランケンシュタインの怪獣
サンダ対ガイラ

1966, Toho
Director Ishiro Honda
Cast Russ Tamblyn, Kumi Mizuno, Kenji Sahara

This tale of two fighting mad mutant brothers spawned from the severed hand of Frankenstein's monster is as savage as a Japanese monster movie can possibly be. In addition to continually beating on each other like a pair of rowdy drunks, one of the Gargantuas pauses occasionally to snack on innocent people, spitting out their bloody clothes like watermelon seeds. All this from the pen of Toho's resident pessimist, screenwriter Takeshi Kimura (aka Kaoru Mabuchi).

The film is a semi-sequel to 1965's *Frankenstein tai chitei kaiju Baragon* (aka *Frankenstein Conquers the World*) which was, like *Monster Zero* and *Frankenstein Conquers...* before it, a co-production between Toho and Americans Henry G. Saperstein and Reuben Bercovitch.

These kinds of co-productions often featured a top-billed performance from a wayward paleface to help boost international sales. This time 'round, *West Side Story* alumni Russ Tamblyn ("a prima donna pain in the ass," according to the late Saperstein) appears in the role of "heroic doctor who studies giant animals." Although he gives a completely disinterested performance (compare Tamblyn's interaction with comely co-star Kumi Mizuno with that of human-torch predecessor Nick Adams), his psychotronic casting alone catapults *War of the Gargantuas* into the history books.

As the two warring Gargantuas pulverize each other across land and sea, they are enacting one of Japan's primal myths: that of Umihiko and his brother Yamahiko, the sea boy and the mountain boy who were themselves stand-ins for Japan's ancient warring tribes.

With one foot in the realm of myth, director Honda goes for as much realism and detail as he can, piling on the military maneuvers and hardware. By the time the fantastical anti-monster maser cannons show up, they almost seem to fit right in with the tanks, helicopters, and little green army men.

At least one scene comes completely out of left field. Second-billed "special guest star" Kipp Hamilton (rumored to be "special friend" to Mr. Saperstein) stops the movie cold so she can warble her unforgettable number "The Words Get Stuck in My Throat" (covered by Devo in concert) until a Gargantua pops around to manhandle her.

For its mix of myth and realism, black-and-blue savagery, outright surrealism, and career catastrophe, *War of the Gargantuas* must be considered the dark heart of the *kaiju eiga*.

☞ **Available dubbed on VHS from Paramount Home Video**

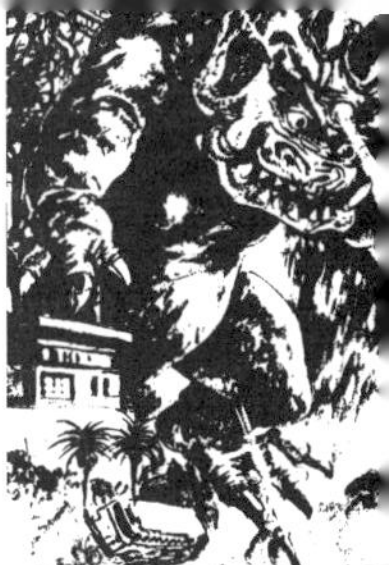

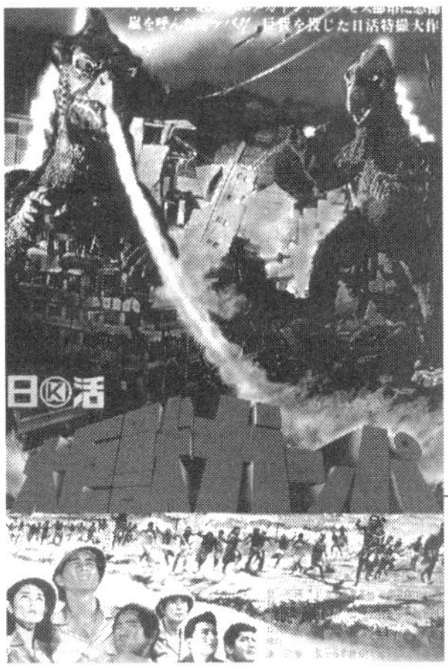

Gappa—The Triphibian Monsters

Dai kyoju Gappa (Gigantic Beast Gappa) aka Monster from the Prehistoric Planet

1967, Nikkatsu
Director Haruyasu Noguchi
Cast Tamio Kawaji, Yoko Yamamoto, Keisuke Yukioka

In their mid-sixties salad days, Nikkatsu Studios were better known for their colorful musicals, zippy action films, and (would-you-believe) Westerns featuring the top stars of the day. After all, giant monsters and special-effects bonanzas were Toho and Daiei Studios' stock-in-trade.

Gappa: The Triphibian Monsters changed all that. The film was Nikkatsu's single foray into the seas of *kaiju eiga*, a burst of family-centric whimsy before becoming one of the naughtiest (and with all that S&M in their *roman porno* films, "knottiest") film studios in the world.

What *Gappa* wasn't was very original. The story of a baby monster abducted by a greedy profitseeker was executed before by the British in *Gorgo*. *Gappa*'s screenwriters denied having ever seen the 1961 King Brothers production, but any grubby kid with an issue of *Famous Monsters of Filmland* magazine can spot the similarity. Other sequences in *Gappa*, especially those set on tropical islands, complete with singing, dancing, monster-worshipping, brown-painted natives, seem pinched from Toho films like *King Kong vs. Godzilla* and *Mothra*.

Gappa's distinctiveness does not emerge until midpoint in the film. Mother and father Gappa, acting like tourists as much as they look like stand-ins for the Japanese mythological creature known as the Kappa, are strolling through the nighttime Atami hotel district looking for Gappa Jr., doing the things that giant monsters do: smashing buildings and breathing optically printed death rays (effects overseen by former Toho employee Akira Watanabe).

Around them, neon signs dot the nighttime sky. The red, blue, and yellow names of bars and hotels radiate a mid-sixties Tokyo chic that's more akin to Pizzicato Five than *Mystery Science Theater 3000*. Maybe that's not enough to catapult *Gappa* onto the crucial list, but no other *kaiju eiga* captures quite so well the swinging vibe of nighttime Tokyo, even momentarily or unintentionally. Odd that it comes from a director whose specialty was period yakuza films.

Certainly remarkable also is *Gappa*'s gonzo theme song, which brings together disparate elements of jazz, go-go, surf rock, and sound-effects records into a wild cacophony complete with lyrics stating that the "true mystery of the universe" is not the DNA helix, or even a perfect egg salad recipe, but Gappa!

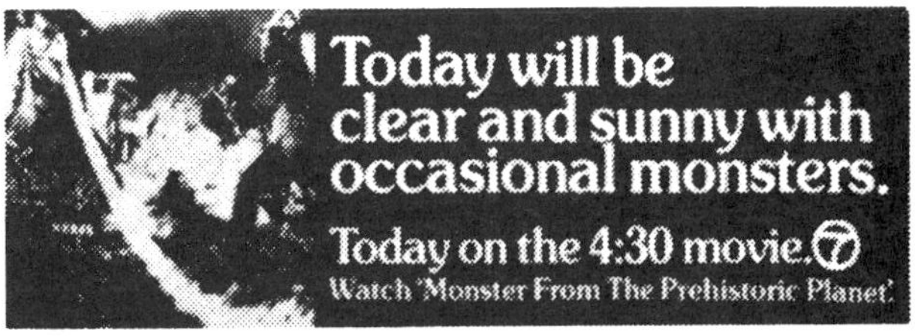
Today will be clear and sunny with occasional monsters.
Today on the 4:30 movie.
Watch 'Monster From The Prehistoric Planet.'

☞ **Available subbed and dubbed on VHS/DVD from Kaiju Productions/Media Blasters**

Godzilla vs. Biollante

Gojira tai Biollante

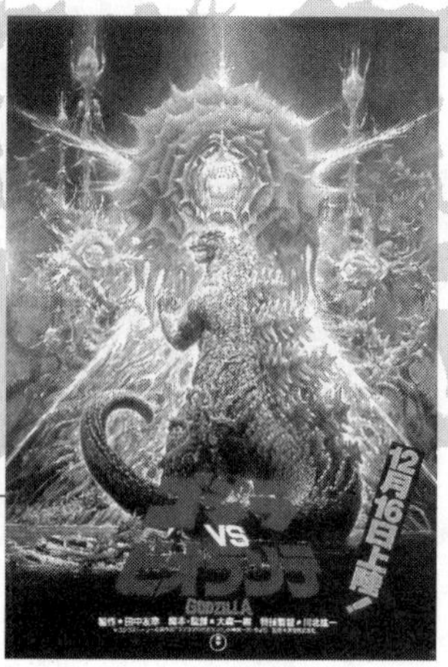
12月16日上映!
VS
GODZILLA

1989, Toho
Director Kazuki Omori
Cast Koji Takahashi, Toru Minegishi, Megumi Odaka

It is currently fashionable among Godzilla cognoscenti to poo-poo *Godzilla vs. Biollante*, the 17th film in the series. The ritual abuse goes something like this: "It's got too many characters, too many subplots, and presents a new monster who isn't as immediately memorable or pleasurable as Mothra." Heck, you'd think some people would rather complain about feast than famine.

Okay, so it's no masterpiece. Mistakes have been made, but only with the best intentions in mind.

This is the Godzilla film that works overtime to keep you entertained. And if that means focus is forsaken for an ever shifting floor show of biotechnology, psychic girls, corporate espionage, fantastic military hardware (and lots of real military hardware—the film marked the first collaboration between Toho and the Japanese Self-Defense Forces in some time), topped off by two giant monsters, then that's the way it's got to be, baby.

But when you get right down to it, *Godzilla vs. Biollante* simply features some of the best city-wrecking and monster scuffles of the modern era. Whereas conflict in the later Godzilla films often amounted to little more than two monsters standing at opposite sides of the screen exchanging optically printed beams back and forth, here the plant-derived Biollante puts Godzilla's green blood on tap and at one point almost crunches his head like a sour apple Blow Pop.

Godzilla himself rises to the challenge with renewed savagery. Thanks to the aid of a mechanical "Cybot" head used for close-up shots (originally built for 1984's *Gojira*, aka *Godzilla 1985*), he's more animal than man-in-suit now. Emerging from a volcano, he's also explicitly a force of nature with destruction as his reason for being. As the Magnificent One strolls through Osaka, there's a perfectly executed tracking shot in which the Big Guy takes a look right into the camera, as if to say "I love my job." That pretty much says it all right there.

☞ **Available dubbed from HBO Home Video**

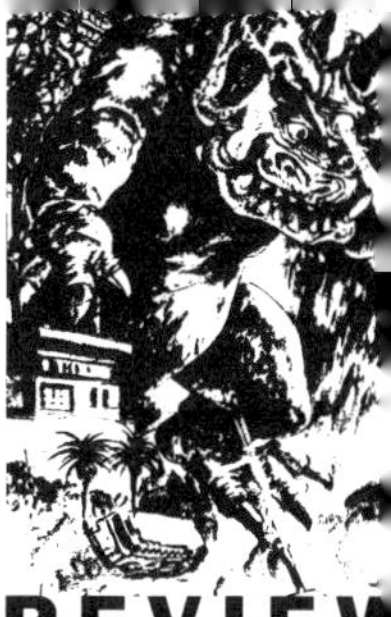

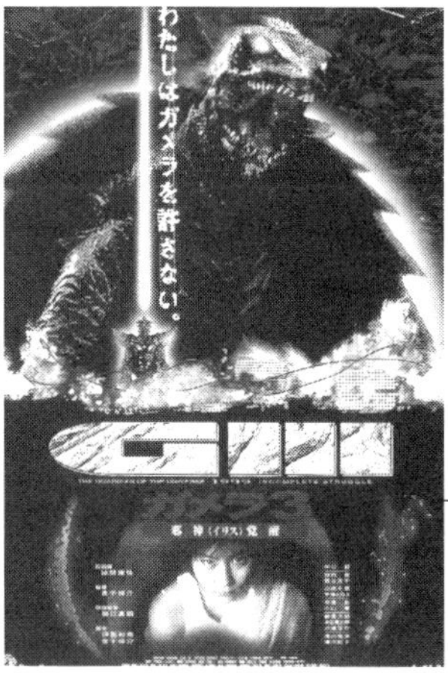
わたしはガメラを許さない。

Gamera 3—Revenge of Iris

Gamera 3—Iris kakusei

1999, Daiei
Director Shunsuke Kaneko
Cast Shinobu Nakayama, Ai Maeda, Ayako Fujitani

Smack in the middle of *Gamera 3*, a bunch of important-looking people hold a high level meeting to ask, perfectly straight-faced, "Why is Japan constantly being attacked by monsters? And what can we do to stop it?"

At long last, the *kaiju eiga* addresses one of life's great mysteries and Gamera, once the perennial *kaiju* underdog to jeer and laugh at, is now holding all the cards. How did such things come to pass?

While Godzilla remains a carefully guarded, studio-controlled property, Gamera was resurrected for his 1995 comeback by a pack of fans-turned-pros, who grew up pledging allegiance to giant monster movies. In many ways, the stylistic antecedent of the new Gamera isn't the approved *Godzilla* style, but the low-budget, high-impact 16mm amateur film *Yamata Orochi no gyakushu* (Revenge of Yamata Orochi), produced by fan company Studio Gainax. Members of Yamata Orochi's special-effects staff, (such as Shinji Higuchi, the Gen-X answer to Eiji Tsuburaya), would eventually toil on landmark anime titles like *Neon Genesis Evangelion* in addition to the new *Gamera* series.

One thing is clear. The *otaku* influence has infiltrated the *kaiju eiga* with the stuff of anime and video games. And in *Gamera 3* especially, the result is beyond anything that's been done in Japan before. The lumbering old lizard moping around on a plainly photographed set (*Godzilla 2000* for instance) is no competition for a giant turtle tripping the light fantastic.

The mix of audacity and accomplishment finally reaches full force in *Gamera 3*. Screenwriter Kazunori Ito (*Ghost in the Shell*) pushes the old monster-on-the-loose clichés—the high level meeting of important personages, for instance—into new territories of self-awareness.

Meanwhile, director Shunsuke Kaneko, always a big fan of virginal female protagonists, rails against modern Japan by turning the trendy Shibuya ward into an inferno with 20,000 people (presumably most of them horrifically dressed schoolgirls) caught in the crossfire of marauding giant monsters.

The only downside is an overreliance on mystical hoodoo. Much talk is given over to the "Gods of the North and South," all of it wasted since giant monsters like Gamera and Iris don't really need half-baked theologies to prop them up. They are monsters, abstract forces that we can paint our own fears on.

So why is Japan constantly being attacked by monsters? Because, either out of love or trauma, we can't stop making them.

☞ **Available from ADV Films**

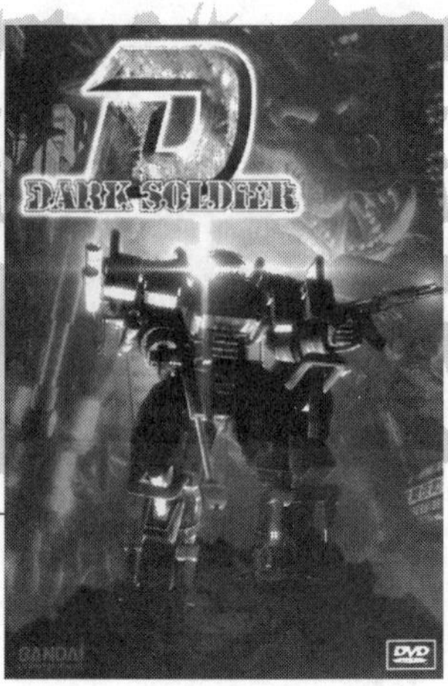
DARK SOLDIER

Dark Soldier D

Dark Soldier D

1999, Buildup/Bandai
Director Nobuya Okabe
Cast Daisuke Nagakura, Masanori Machida, Hideki Shirakuni

Macho solider of fortune Kawamata, like so many Japanese genre heroes before him, is inside of a metal suit battling a giant monster with an array of high-tech weaponry at his fingertips. The difference is that he had unwisely boozed up before he climbed into his stolen combat suit and has just barfed all over himself. Now it's hard to tell which is the greater threat to Japan, Kawamata or the giant chicken that he's been sent by the government to assassinate.

A low-budget, shot-entirely-on-digital-video wonder, *Dark Soldier D* was written and directed by Nobuya Okabe, president of the Shibuya-based special-effects house Buildup. In addition to providing computer graphics for a bounty of TV commercials, the company also designs animatronic creatures, including those used for *Godzilla vs. Biollante* (1989) and *Godzilla vs. King Ghidorah* (1991).

According to Buildup's promotional materials, "*D* has no pretentious theme, but is full of realistic images that will stun audiences everywhere."

And the story? In order to stop a series of meteor-spawned monsters, bad-tempered Kawamata gets to indulge his love of bullets and firepower via a combat suit stolen from the Russians during the collapse of the Soviet Union. Unfortunately, in the process of trying to stop a salaryman-turned-monster in Shinjuku (a wild, geographically correct scene set mere blocks away from the Showakan Theater), he blows away 43 people. Kawamata goes to jail for mass murder, but reemerges as state-sponsored killing machine, protecting Japan both from giant creatures and the Russians who want their Dark Soldier technology back.

D could have functioned perfectly well as nothing more than an effects demo reel for Buildup. But by the end of the three exciting episodes, where a living brain in a jar gives a stirring soliloquy, it's clear that the production is less about eye candy than blistering black comedy, the kind that piles on exaggeration and absurdity with poker-faced conviction.

As with *Gamera 3*, it feels like honest-to-goodness fans are at the controls of *D*. Only fitting, then, that anti-hero Kawamata (who at one point kicks someone out of their wheelchair) embodies that which unites *kaiju eiga* audiences past, present, and future: a nihilistic and simple love of mass destruction.

☞ **Available subbed and dubbed on VHS/DVD from Bandai Entertainment**

EXPLOITATION

SELL LIKE A MONSTER

Stage a Destroy All Monsters contest via newspaper or with handbills. Object is to show face shots of monsters in film, have them identified. Award passes to first fifty people who correctly identify same . . .

EXAMPLE:
KNOW YOUR MONSTERS??

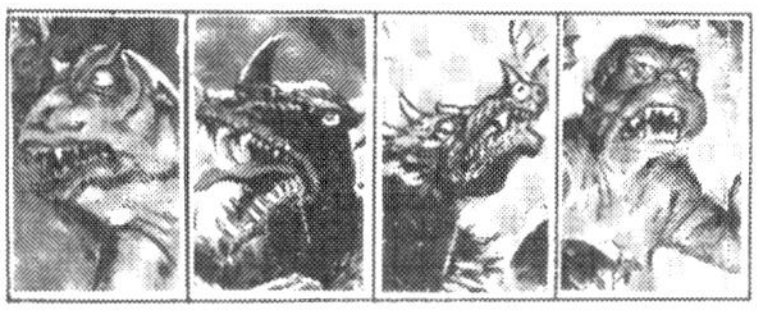

Faces of monsters without names — copy about film, space for name and address of contestant, and room for theatre logo and playdate.

EXTERMINATORS LOVE MONSTERS

Make a tie-up with local exterminators. These people constantly use newspaper and radio advertising. Example of a tie-up could be . . . "We Destroy All Monsters Too" . . . "but not the variety seen in American International's 'DESTROY ALL MONSTERS' coming to the Apex Theatre. Guess how many different kinds of monsters we destroy and win two free tickets to see 'DESTROY ALL MONSTERS' which opens (playdate)........ ....etc."

WINDOW CARDS

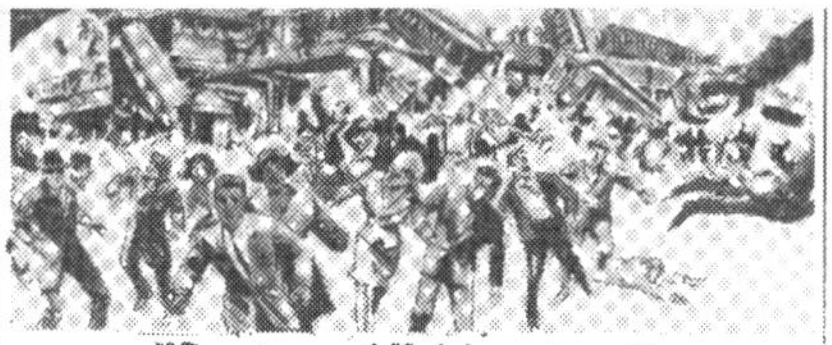

"Destroy All Monsters"
Theatre..
Playdate..

FOOT PRINTS

Make stencil prints to look like monster prints, and using washable paint, stencil city sidewalks with "DESTROY ALL MONSTERS" on stencil . . .

TOTAL WRECK

Have wrecked or totally demolished cars placed around the city and in front of the theatre with cards attached reading — "A Victim of DESTROY ALL MONSTERS" — theatre and playdate.

FREE COLOR TELEVISION TRAILERS . . .

They live on television and are more realistic than life, in color. Your campaign must include a heavy saturation schedule on "DESTROY ALL MONSTERS." Order the complete set FREE in 60/30/20 and 10 second lengths from your local American International Branch Manager.

CLASSIFY YOUR MONSTERS IN THE CLASSIFIED SECTION

Classified ads can be helpful in promoting the film. Suggested ad:

WANTED

MEN, WOMEN, OR YOUNG ADULTS
TO HELP
"DESTROY ALL MONSTERS"

Apply In Person Only After 11:30 a.m.
(or boxoffice time)

(Theatre address but not theatre name)

WANTED POSTERS

Make wanted posters using star heads of monsters and distribute around town.

EXAMPLE:

WANTED

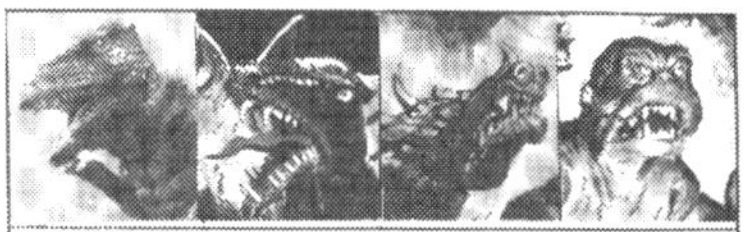

DEAD OR ALIVE WE MUST
"Destroy All Monsters"

Playdate..................................

TIEUPS

Make a tie-up with local safety council. These groups are always anxious to tie-up and promote safety, etc. The title "DESTROY ALL MONSTERS" lends itself to such a promo, i.e., safe driving, drinking, etc.

MONSTER RADIO

Radio station D.J.'s especially on Top 40 stations will be able to have fun and at the same time promote the film on the station. Have each D.J. select his favorite monster in the film, incorporate this in his name, and then have the listeners write in why they, too, like or dislike this monster from "DESTROY ALL MONSTERS" . . . The winner to receive locally promoted prizes.

ALL MONSTER HEAD SHOTS
ARE INCLUDED IN
NATIONAL SCREEN STILL SETS

FREE RADIO PACKAGE . . .

Saturate the air waves with round the clock radio schedule. Hit your action audience with the use of this powerful radio package. Order the E.T. direct from your local American International Branch Manager. They are FREE in 60 and 30 second segments.

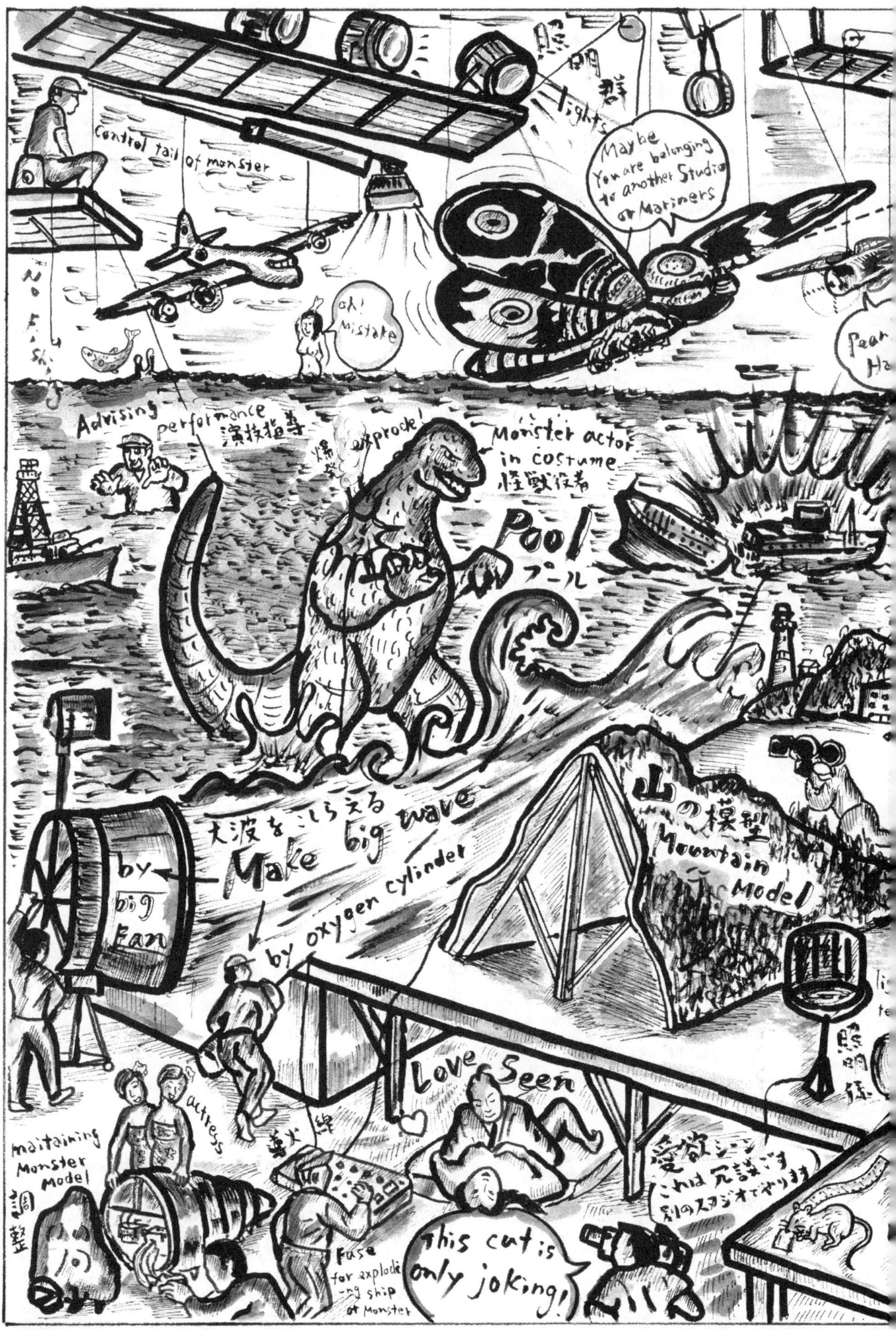
照明群
lights
Control tail of monster
Maybe You are belonging to another Studio or Mariners
No Fish
oh! Mistake
Advising performance 演技指導
爆発
exprode!
Monster actor in costume 怪獣役者
Pool
プール
大波をこしらえる
Make big wave
by big Fan
by oxygen cylinder
山の模型
Mountain Model
照明係
Love Seen
愛欲シーン
これは冗談です
別のスタジオでやります
actress
maitaining Monster Model
調整
導火線
Fuse for explodi-ng ship of Monster
This cut is only joking!

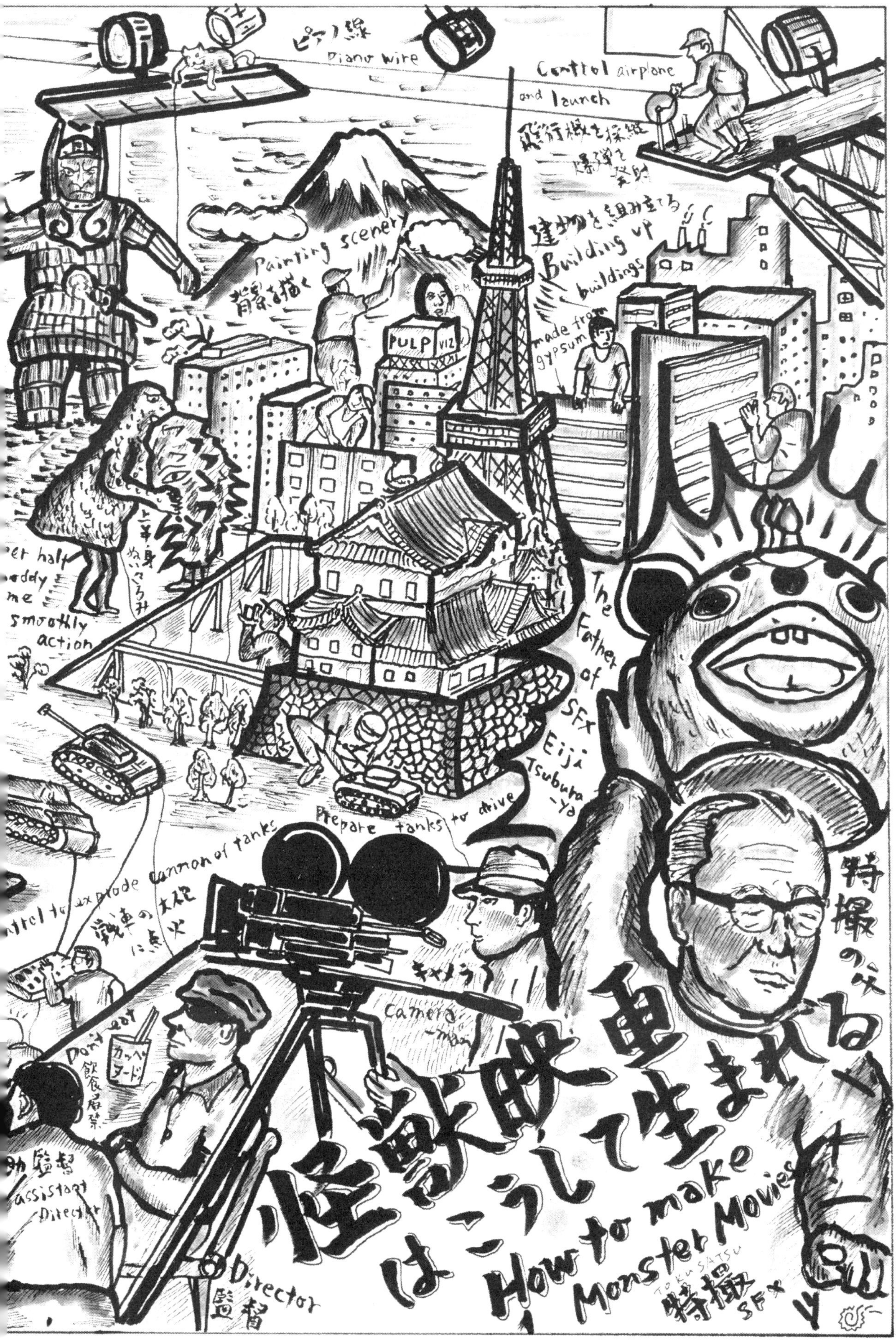

怪獣映画はこうして生まれる
How to make Monster Movies
TOKUSATSU 特撮 SFX
ピアノ線
Piano wire
Control airplane and launch
飛行機を操縦
爆弾を発射
Painting scenery
背景を描く
建物を組み立てる
Building up buildings
made from gypsum
PULP
上半身ぬいぐるみ
smoothly action
The Father of SFX Eiji Tsubura-ya
特撮の父
Prepare tanks to drive
control to explode cannon of tanks
戦車の大砲に点火
キャメラ
Camera-man
Don't eat
飲食厳禁
カップヌードル
助監督
assistant Director
Director
監督

The Dai Majin Trilogy

大魔神

After the success of Daiei Tokyo's 1965 *Gamera* film, Akinari Suzuki, the head of Daiei's Kyoto branch, was on the lookout for his own special-effects franchise. One day, he brought a picture of an ancient Japanese clay statue to a studio meeting and asked, "Couldn't we make a movie out of this?"

The result was the *Dai Majin* trilogy, three films (all released in 1966) about a giant Golem-like statue come to life to perform the duties of karma incarnate. The introductory film, *Dai Majin*, told a tale of feudal era class struggle that ended with the legendary Wrath of the Gods (adorned with a stern face said to be based on Kirk Douglas) laying waste to the stronghold of a despotic lord. Unlike the gigantic proportions of *Godzilla* and *Gamera*, *Majin* operated at a more manageable scale of two-and-a-half times the size of a human being. This allowed for a greater degree of realism, masterfully achieved by former child-star-turned-special-effects-director Yoshiyuki Kuroda and director of photography Fujio Morita, who won an industry award for his work on the film.

Former Mainichi Orions ballplayer Riki Hashimoto donned the Dai Majin costume for all three films, lending his own ferocious eyes to the character. Hashimoto later went head-to-head with Bruce Lee in 1972's *Fist of Fury*. The sequel, *Dai Majin ikaru* (Wrath of Dai Majin), helmed by legendary samurai film director Kenji Misumi (who toiled on numerous *Zatoichi* films and the *Lone Wolf and Cub* movies parts one through four) boasted an elaborate ending wherein Majin parts Lake Yagumo like Moses. After the effects-heavy third film, *Dai Majin gyakushu* (aka Return of Dai Majin) was released, Daiei decided to end the series, owing to its enormous cost of production.

Rumors of a Dai Majin comeback pop up periodically, but none more memorable than when it was reported in the late eighties that Kevin Costner had optioned the property. Where's the Wrath of the Gods when you really need it? 東

☞ **The Dai Majin trilogy is available subtitled on VHS from ADV Films**

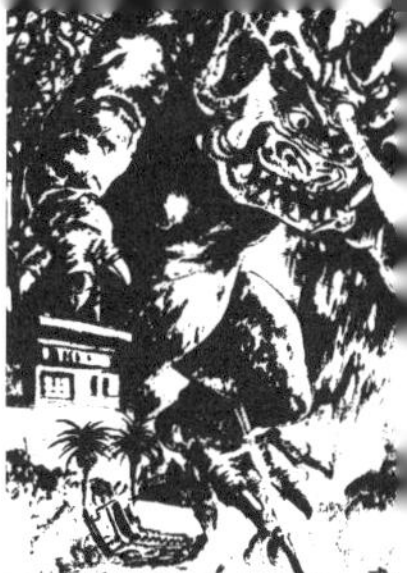

The Making of *Godzilla vs. the Smog Monster:* Interview with Yoshimitsu Banno

By Risaku Kiridoshi

This article first appeared in Japanese in *Eiga Hi-Ho* magazine. Translation by Akemi Wegmuller.

Yoshimitsu Banno: *Born 1931. Joined Toho Studios following graduation from the University of Tokyo's Faculty of Literature, Department of Aesthetics and Art History. Worked, as studio production staff and production assistant, on Akira Kurosawa's* Kumonosujo *(Throne of Blood),* Donzoko *(The Lower Depths),* Warui yatsu hodo yoku nemuru *(The Bad Sleep Well), and* Kakushi toride no san akunin *(The Hidden Fortress). Under Toho producer Tomoyuki Tanaka, was in charge of image and sound production for Mitsubishi's "Hall of the Future" at the 1970 Osaka World Expo. Directed* Gojira tai Hedorah *(Godzilla vs. the Smog Monster) in 1971. Served as associate director in charge of overseas locations for* Zankoku kiga tairiku *(Cruel Famine Continent) and* Nostradamus no dai yogen *(aka* The Last Days of Planet Earth*). Developed the "Japax System," a 70mm film projection system for the Tsukuba Science Expo in 1985. In 1991, produced the Space World theme pavilion as Toho's managing director in charge of "motion picture art." Currently planning a 70mm production of* Tobu *(To Fly), based on a script by Akira Kurosawa.*

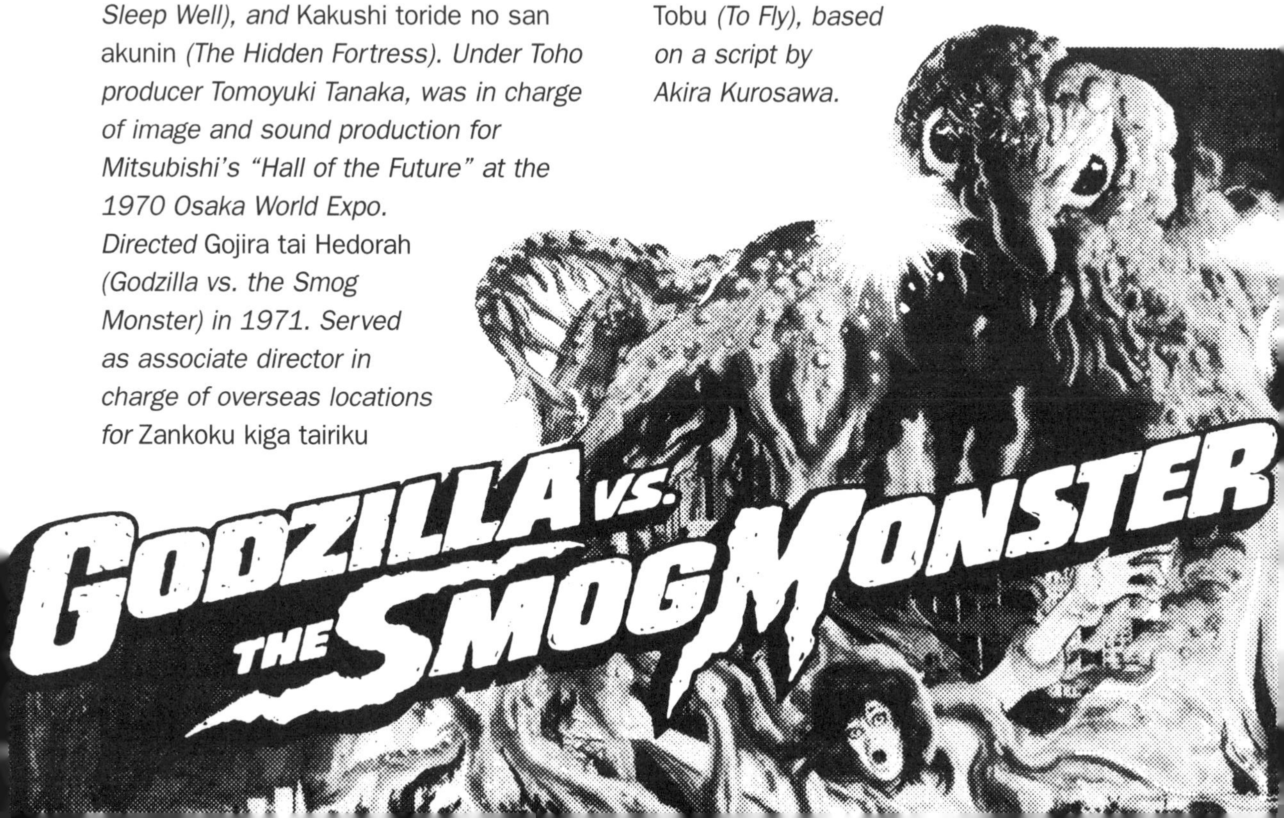
GODZILLA VS. THE SMOG MONSTER

GIANT MONSTERS

A female singer covered in psychedelic body paint reels off toxic substances while she writhes to the pulse of a rock beat. Behind her, semi-transparent red and blue liquid splashes around the screen. As she intones "Give us back the greenery, give us back the blue sky, give it back, give it back!" (lyrics reduced to "save the Earth, save the Earth" in the American version of the film), abstract shapes float around in the background like amoebae.

Who would ever have expected such images to burst forth from a Japanese monster movie? But burst they did in 1971's *Gojira tai Hedorah*, also known as *Godzilla vs. the Smog Monster*.

Out of this heady atmosphere, the pollution-spawned monster Hedorah (*hedoro* means pollution in Japanese) rises out of industrial sludge to fight Godzilla, who loses an eye and sees his left hand turned to bleached bone after it passes through Hedorah's intangible, slimy body. Thrashing around in a sea of sludge, Godzilla battles the monster with everything he's got. For this writer, who was in the second grade at the time, seeing this movie was a shocking experience. It was like getting a glimpse of the forbidden world of big boys and girls.

Twenty-seven years after *Godzilla vs. the Smog Monster* was made, I had the opportunity to interview its director, Yoshimitsu Banno. The interview was conducted in a hotel room, with the video of his movie playing in the background.

Gay bars and the avant-garde

Yoshimitsu Banno acted as both the director of the cast and of special-effects sequences, and so is responsible for the overall image of *Godzilla vs. the Smog Monster*. The most immediately striking aspect of his film is its use of glaring, gaudy, liquid light-show effects.

"At the time, there was this go-go club in Akasaka called Mugen, where crowds of young people would dance jammed together in a heaving, swirling mass, just like in the movie. There was a platform up front, on which girls in miniskirts would be writhing to the music. I modeled the set on that club. But having the girl wear body paint was my idea [laughs]."

Take a good look, though: the dancer in the film is actually wearing a body-stocking with psychedelic patterns painted on it. What a bummer! Still, I grew up harboring the belief that maybe, somewhere, there really did exist a go-go club with naked body-painted dancers.

"The red and blue liquids moving around in the background at the go-go club were recreated by one of the art people, who'd seen it in a gay bar in Chicago. You put some salad oil in a bowl of water and swirl it around with your finger in time to the music. Throw colored lights on it and project it onto a screen, and there you are."

Another unusual touch is the use of symbolic cartoon interludes in the film. These surreal pollution parables are a good example of Banno's experimental technique: the artwork has a nasty sting to it that gives it an avant-garde feel.

"At first, I asked [legendary experimental manga artist] Yoshiharu Tsuge to do the animation artwork. When I read his *Sanshouo* [Salamander], a manga in which all kinds of things come floating down a river of sewage, I sensed a connection to Hedorah. When I met with Tsuge-san, he was extremely antisocial. He said he'd never even been to a movie theater, he was so people-phobic. The reason he worked as a manga artist was because he

INTERVIEW

hated working in groups, he said. So he turned me down. Animation would be a nightmare for him. I could see his point [laughs]."

Rachel Carson vs. the Smog Monster

For those of us who had watched a lot of Toho monster movies before, *Godzilla vs. the Smog Monster* didn't seem to offer a lot of familiar faces.

"Budget considerations of course had a lot to do with deciding to use lesser-known actors instead of more established stars. For the role of the protagonist's father, a scientist who does a lot of deep-sea diving with an aqualung, we chose Akira Yamauchi because his physique was similar to that of the stand-in who'd be doing the underwater scenes. That stand-in, incidentally, was me."

In other words, Yamauchi was cast because his physique resembled the director's! Banno was involved in the establishment of Toho's underwater camera crew in 1966 and directed the underwater scenes in 1967's *Minami taiheiyo no wakadaisho* (Young Guy of the South Pacific). After *Godzilla vs. the Smog Monster*, he worked on even more marine documentaries. You could even say that photographing the sea has been Banno's life work.

"I was born in Imabari, [a port city] in Ehime prefecture, so I swam in the sea a lot as a child. Maybe because of this background, one of my favorite books is *The Edge of the Sea* by Rachel Carson, who is often called the founding figure of environmentalism in the United States. Carson's book *Silent Spring* [published 1962] was the first to raise the issue of environmental degradation in the US. Apparently, because she'd published this book, Carson feared for her life, expecting to be attacked any time. And yes, the lyrics of 'Give Us Back the Sun!' [the film's theme song] were influenced by her philosophy."

Monsters and metaphors

Among Toho's special-effects movies, the work of screenwriter Takeshi Kimura (aka Kaoru Mabuchi) provides a contrast to the lighter touch of Shinichi Sekizawa, who wrote the screenplays for 1961's *Mothra* and 1962's *King Kong vs. Godzilla*. Mabuchi's *Gasu ningen dai ichigo* (The Human Vapor) and *Frankenstein tai chitei kaiju Baragon* (Frankenstein Conquers the World) depicted the anguish of those termed "monsters" by civilization. *Godzilla vs. the Smog Monster* was Mabuchi's first screenplay in a long time.

"The best Godzilla movie was the first one, made in 1954. It had the weight of having been made directly after the 'Lucky Dragon Incident.' One reason why Japanese movies are no good anymore is that, instead of trying to get a message across, they simply pander to audiences more and more."

Banno devoted particular attention to Godzilla's appearances in the movie. In a scene where he first appears in a child's imagination, Godzilla enters the screen from the side, against a background dominated by a large, orange sun. You know immediately he is the star of the movie.

Later, when Godzilla and Hedorah go at it in a battle under Mt. Fuji, there's a nice scene where the beams emitted by Hedorah and the radioactive flames returned by Godzilla are the only things visible far away in the dark night.

"It was a way of showing [their fight] indirectly. I wanted to create a sense of distance. This movie had a budget of only 90 million yen and a shooting schedule of just a little over a month. So [special-effects director] Teruyoshi Nakano and I were splitting up to

GIANT MONSTERS

shoot Godzilla and Hedorah on the same set, but in some of the long shots we really needed to have both monsters in the same frame, with some people in the foreground. So we invited Ishiro Honda, who directed the first Godzilla movie, to view the rushes, and with a word from Honda-san, we were able to shoot some additional material. But rather than use up our small budget on crowd scenes, we tried to come up with other ways to effectively convey Hedorah's deadliness. If the result is that Godzilla sometimes appears isolated in his fight against the monster, I would say we succeeded."

A foreign reviewer's comment that the first Godzilla movie had given concrete shape to something abstract—the fear of the Bomb—caught Banno's attention. The Bomb and pollution are not just phenomena that give rise to monsters: the monsters themselves embody the horror of these phenomena. This was why Hedorah couldn't simply be a giant iguana or mutant worm caused by environmental destruction, but the incarnation of pollution itself.

There was also another inspiration.

"Hedorah's eyes were modeled on female genitalia. I drew the kind of crude picture you find on the walls of a public toilet and handed it to the modeling staff. I said, 'This is what I want Hedorah's eyes to look like.' [laughs] Well, come on, vaginas are scary!"

Even after Godzilla's hard-won victory against Hedorah at the conclusion, another baby Hedorah is born. This is a monster that multiplies.

"Ultimately, it means that not even Godzilla can defeat this monster. Because that's the nature of pollution. We're saying, if you don't do anything about it, it's going to keep on growing. Look at Minamata [a small factory town where a chemical company dumped toxic amounts of mercury into the water over a decades-long time span], where people actually died."

Another remarkable thing about this movie is the number of scenes in which Hedorah's victims graphically perish. There are scenes in which you actually see people dissolve until only their skeletons are left, while other scenes show the mounting death toll being reported on the news.

"Toho didn't tell us to change anything in the screenplay, and for me it was only natural [that people would die]. It wasn't so much that we were emphasizing the casualties. We just wanted to show that you can't run away from pollution."

I grew up in Tokyo's Suginami Ward, so I'd heard about how kids at one school in the ward had dropped like flies during P.E. from photochemical smog.

"Yes, that was an inspiration. That incident at the Suginami school in which girls collapsed from smog happened in July, and we incorporated it in the film immediately."

The scene in which girls exercising in the school yard collapse when Hedorah flies is in fact a true-to-life depiction of the times in which the movie was made.

We are powerless

In the socially concerned film *Wakamono no hata* (Flag of Youth), directed by Tokihisa Morikawa and released a year before *Godzilla vs. the Smog Monster*, there's a scene in which Saburo (Kei Yamamoto), an editor trying to publish an exposé on environmental pollution, is told at a planning meeting that "trying to educate the public at a time when corporations are conducting their own

INTERVIEW

specialized research is passé." Saburo insists that this very attempt to profit from the pollution-control industry—the Japanese tendency to act as an "economic animal"—needs to be probed. In response, a colleague says, "Okay, okay, so how about this? Throw in some super-psychedelic manga, and probe the 'animalism' that way."

Godzilla vs. the Smog Monster does just that. It was born bearing the karma of its times on its shoulders. Let's not forget that when the Liberal Democratic Party finally joined the chorus, saying "pollution is bad," this helped open the door to allow this movie to be made.

At one point in the movie, the screen splits up into a mosaic of smaller screens as people talk about pollution from a variety of standpoints. The montage builds in intensity until all the voices merge into a mad cacophony, and the split-screen starts to flash in prismatic colors. Banno's experience in creating multiple split-screen images for Mitsubishi's "Hall of the Future" at the 1970 Osaka World Expo came in handy for this scene, which cost a lot of money to create.

"It was imperative that we make graphic the accumulation of numbers of everyone shouting their piece at the same time...to show that, actually, this is futile in fighting pollution."

Ken's uncle, played by Toshio Shiba, is also a leader of the young people who hang out at the go-go club. When the Hedorah panic sets in, he forms the "Japan Youth League" and tries to organize a million-man protest against pollution, but ends up changing it to a million-go-go-dancer party instead. These actions of the young people in the movie are reminiscent of the Japan Communist Party and Democratic Youth League of Japan, which withdrew from the Narita Airport controversy and started folk dancing instead.

"Our screenwriter, Kaoru Mabuchi, was a local delegate of the JCP. He spent World War II in jail for his activities in the [leftist] New Theater movement. He quarreled with [JCP leader] Kyuichi Tokuda over the use of Molotov cocktails and quit the party. At the age of 40, he paid a visit to [Toho and *Godzilla* series producer] Tomoyuki Tanaka, who'd been two years his junior at Kansai University, and that's how he became a screenwriter."

Also, the Self-Defense Forces are presented as bumbling Keystone Cops, and are nothing more than a laughingstock in the movie.

"Well, I don't think of the SDF as particularly useful in any way. Yeah, we were making fun of them."

The human beings, while being killed as collateral damage in the fight between the monsters, can do nothing but gape on the sidelines.

"In effect, human beings are powerless."

His arm melted, one eye put out, pushed into a pit with sludge thrown in after him, Godzilla is covered with wounds as he valiantly continues to fight Hedorah.

"We made Hedorah so strong that we couldn't find a way to defeat him. I talked to science-fiction writer Masami Fukushima, who told me about how they were using electrodes to dry up rice paddies in Hokkaido."

During the climactic battle, Godzilla takes to the air, flying for the first time ever—a controversial move that reportedly shocked and horrified producer Tanaka.

"We got the idea from seahorses: blow air from the mouth, and move backwards."

After his maiden flight, Godzilla tears the dried-up remnants of Hedorah into little bits,

GIANT MONSTERS

as if to ensure that once and for all, the monster will never come back to life. As he does so, there is a palpable feeling of tremendous rage.

"It's not so much that Godzilla himself is angry—it's more like we had him act out the anger of human beings, or rather of us, the movie's creators."

After destroying the monster, Godzilla directs a fierce stare at the people around his feet, and then turns and strides off into the dawn. "Give Us Back the Sun!" comes onto the soundtrack, but it's a mournful version sung only by a male chorus. The visions of pollution shown during the movie now reappear in flashback, as if being remembered by the departing Godzilla.

"Godzilla!!"

The boy Ken calls him. Godzilla turns his head, and lets out a single roar.

But Godzilla never looks back again at the child's shouts, which carry the hopes of all powerless human beings. And then, a new Hedorah emerges from the mire....

Godzilla vs. the Smog Monster was the first Godzilla movie made after Osaka Expo '70, which glorified scientific progress, and after the death of Eiji Tsuburaya, the god of Japanese special-effects movies. Made in this mood of impending finality, this film pushed its vision of destruction—which, after all, is the essence of monster movies—to its furthest limits.

Looking back now, we can say this film is a product of its times, when people were gripped by a fear of something that could still be embodied—pollution, in this case. At the same time, the amorphous, self-replicating monster Hedorah made Banno's film a bridge to the next generation.

With global environmental issues dominating headlines in recent years, the works of Rachel Carson have been reissued and are being read again. What kind of work would be today's equivalent of *Godzilla vs. the Smog Monster*?

After the film's initial release, Banno was thinking of a plot in which a starfish living in the polluted seas metamorphoses into a monster, which ends up battling Godzilla. He also considered making another Hedorah film.

"But the only idea I had in that regard was that Hedorah appears in Africa. If those chaotic, dynamic countries developed a little further, it wouldn't be so implausible for Hedorah to show up there. And I was really into Jacopetti's and Prosperi's movie, *Africa Addio* [aka *Africa Blood and Guts*] at the time."

Banno also shot *Zankoku kiga tairiku* (Cruel Famine Continent), a 1973 documentary appealing for relief operations against drought in Africa. He also wrote the screenplay for 1974's *Nostradamus no dai yogen* (The Great Prophecies of Nostradamus, aka *The Last Days of Planet Earth*) which is steeped in a theme of environmental destruction caused by pollution. The film has numerous motifs in common with *Godzilla vs. the Smog Monster*: powerless hippies get high and dance feverishly, while one of the protagonists has hallucinations. Sections of this movie filmed on location in New Guinea were shot by Banno in his capacity as associate director.

"I did a lot of research to write that screenplay, so I was seeing data like, one out of every four babies born in the Niigata Prefecture at the time was deformed. When that's all you're reading every day, you really start to think the world is going down the tubes, that tomorrow it will all be over. But well, here we are. [laughs]" 東

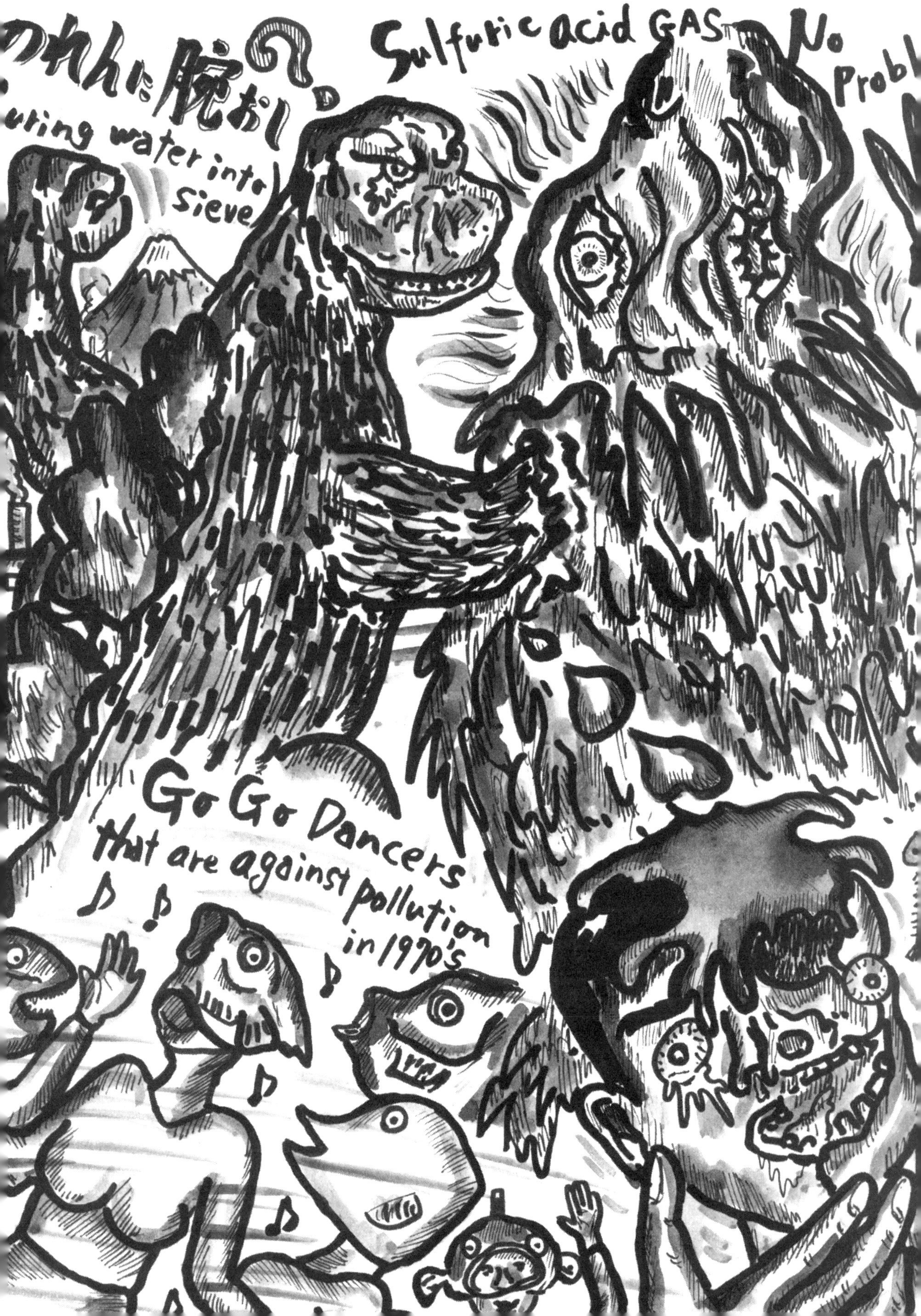
れんに腕おし
uring water into sieve
Sulfuric acid GAS
No Probl
Go Go Dancers
that are against pollution in 1970's

SONNY CHIBA
Sonny Chiba
CHAMPION

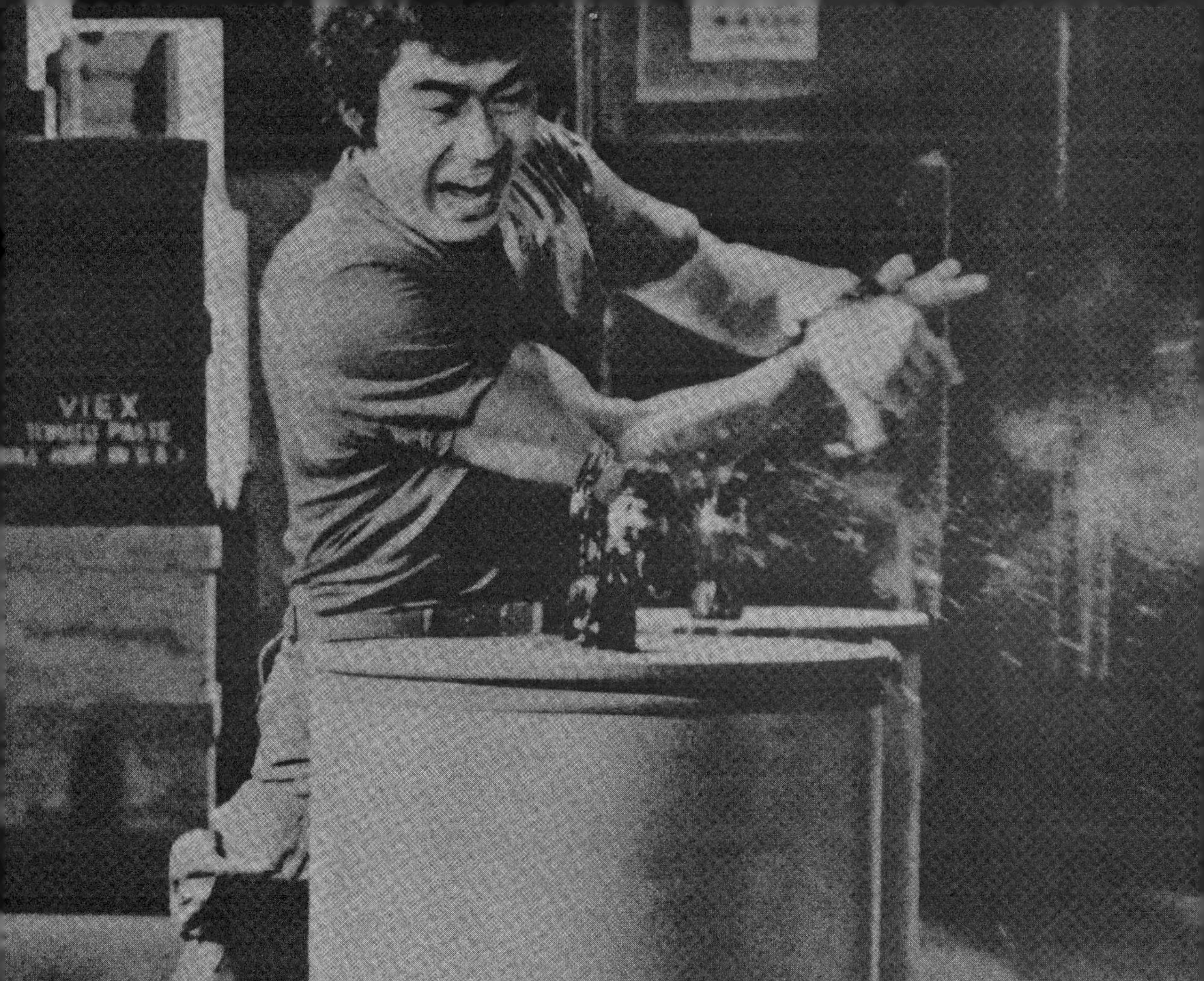

H OF DEATH"

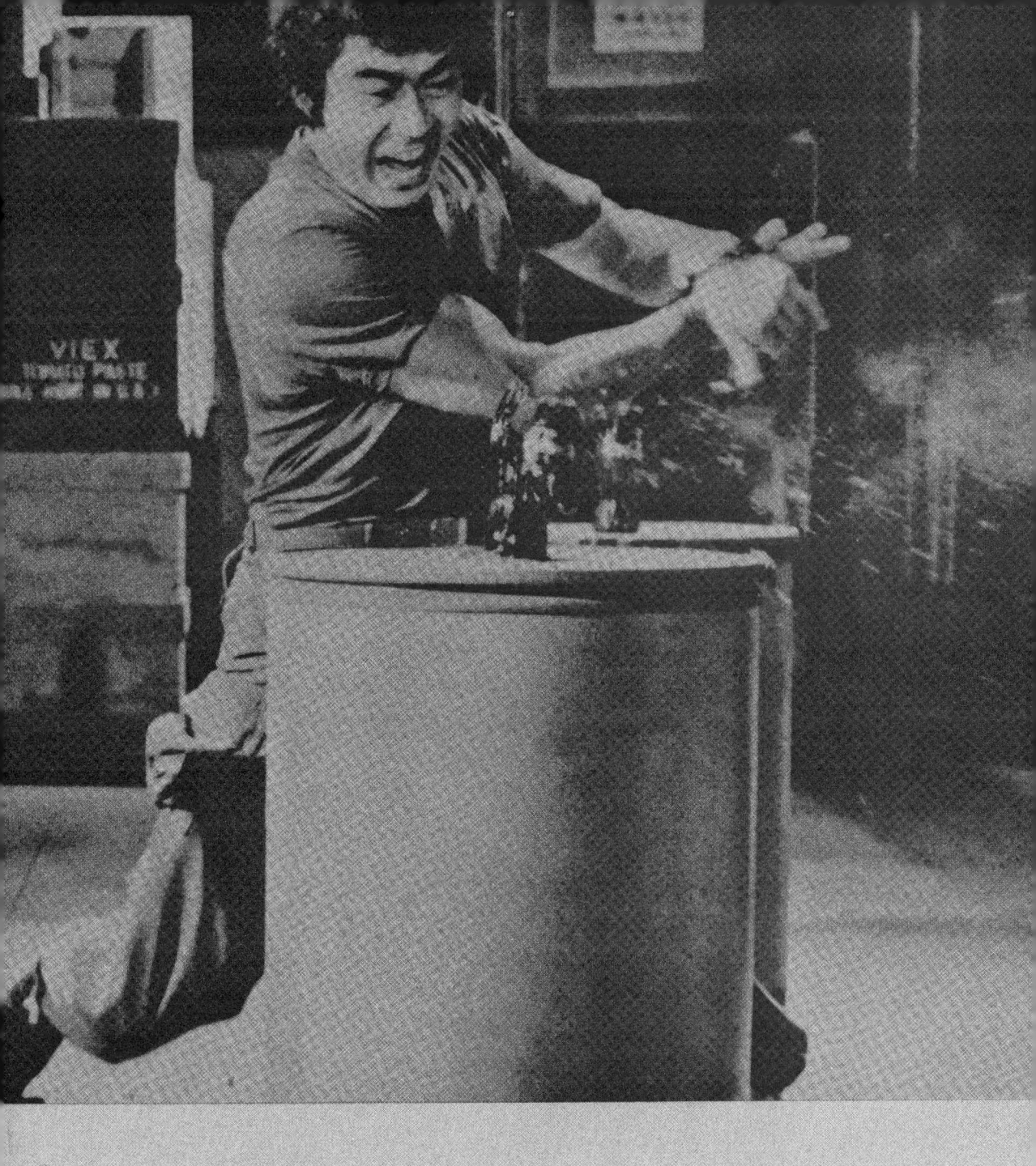

R United Artists

Sonny Chiba

SONNY CHIBA— KING OF PAIN

Sonny Chiba is The Street Fighter. The Killing Machine. The Champion of Death. Sonny Chiba is many things, but he is not a chump.

He is a Japanese cult film superstar, perhaps *the* quintessential Japanese cult film superstar who made a major contribution to cinema history by breaking bones and spilling blood for Toei Studios in the freaky deaky seventies. Modern audiences tend to either adore or misunderstand him. *The New York Post* paid Chiba a compliment (I think) by calling him "the ultimate movie badass," while detractors say he's nothing special when compared to Jackie Chan or Bruce Lee.

Neither a consummate master of the martial arts like Lee, nor a crowd-pleasing populist movie star like Chan, Sonny is in a class by himself. He crushes the competition as a groundbreaking practitioner of highly stylized, over-the-top, screen violence. Splatter and kung fu are two great tastes that taste great together, and Sonny is the Iron Chef.

His murderous fighting techniques and camera-mugging facial expressions are delirious exaggerations, even in a genre subsidized by delirious exaggeration.

This man is action incarnate. And when paired with the right director, particularly Teruo Ishii (*The Executioner*) or Shigehiro Ozawa (*The Street Fighter*), the mix of cheeky humor and physical violence makes for dynamite entertainment.

And yet there's much more to Sonny Chiba than just a bloodsoaked celluloid persona and the *Street Fighter* films. His life story reads like an atlas, mapping the highs and lows of the Japanese entertainment industry and ending on the right note of redemption.

He was born Sadao Maeda on January 23, 1939 in Fukuoka and was an aspiring Olympic gymnast until a back injury suffered on

INTRO

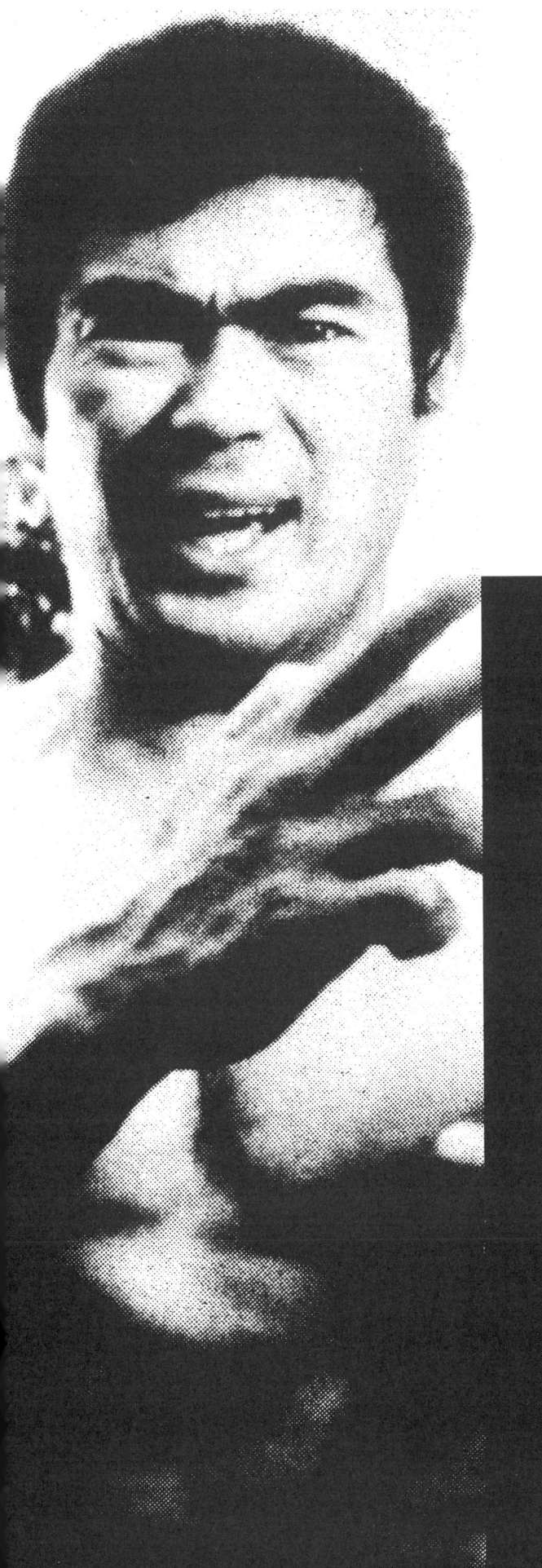

a construction job cut his athletic career short. Nevertheless, he physically recovered and began studying martial arts and racking up black belts, under the guidance of legendary Korean martial arts master Masutatsu Oyama.

In 1959, Chiba's luck took a turn when he won a Toei studios contract via their famed public audition known as the "New Face" contest. He spent the decade to come starring in television and films, and his karate-trained prowess found him taking on many action-oriented roles. In 1960, he donned turban and tights on the NET network for *Ala no shisha* (Messenger of Allah, a superhero show with characters' names taken from the snack foods belonging to the show's sponsor), while 1961's short film *Uchu*

Sonny Chiba

kaisokusen (Space Greyhound, shown in the US as *Invasion of the Neptune Men*) had him playing an intergalactic do-gooder with a nifty flying car. Slightly more dramatic turns were taken in both of director Kinji Fukasaku's *Furaibo tantei* (Drifting Detective) films (both 1961) and in Junya Sato's landmark yakuza film *Soshiki boryoku* (Organized Violence, 1967).

Sonny's first serious dalliance with major-league fame came when his action-packed TV series *Key Hunter*, which began airing in 1968, became a tremendous hit in Japan. In 1970, Chiba founded the Japan Action Club, a physical training school and employment agency that nurtured the careers of many actor-athletes, including Etsuko Shihomi (*Sister Streetfighter*) and Hiroyuki Sanada (*Roaring Fire*).

Chiba was an idol to millions of Japanese kids (they called him "Chiba-kun" affectionately), and was an ever present figure in ad campaigns for luxury items like cars and digital watches. His life story was even serialized in the pages of a girls' comic magazine. With Chiba taking over the Japanese airwaves, the time was ripe to take on the world.

Following *Enter the Dragon*, folks were hungry for the next level in Asian screen excitement. And in 1974's *Gekitotsu! Satsujin ken*, director Shigehiro Ozawa (previously a period yakuza film specialist) gave them just that. Sonny called attention to himself by ripping out still-throbbing larynxes or by philanthropically performing makeshift dental work with his fists.

Retitled *The Street Fighter* by New Line Cinema, the film became infamous in the US as the first movie ever to be given an X rating from the MPAA not for sexual content or naughty words but for gory brutality alone. New Line was forced to drastically reedit the film, but the victory was clear.

Sonny had found his true calling and spent the mid-seventies starring in numerous *Street Fighter* follow-ups and karate-oriented productions of wildly varying quality.

With his funky outfits and bushy hairstyle, Chiba came on like an old-school manga or anime antihero come to life. Fittingly, he played the title role in

THE FIRST FILM THAT FEATURES "SHOALIN" THE PUREST AND HIGHEST FORM OF THE MARTIAL ARTS

INTRO

SONNY "STREETFIGHTER" CHIBA IS THE KILLING MACHINE

numerous movies based on comic books. From the archetypal cold-blooded hitman Golgo 13 to the country bumpkin with a magnum pistol Detective Doberman to the lycanthropic Wolfguy.

In addition to battling bears and oxen in his martial arts films, Sonny wielded a mean samurai sword and utilized it in plenty of period films. His turn as the legendary one-eyed swordmaster Yagyu Jubei in Kinji Fukasaku's 1981 film *Makai tensho* (aka *Samurai Reincarnation*) is considered the definitive portrayal. As one of a handful of Japanese stars with a bankable reputation abroad, Chiba was also cast in mega-productions designed for international distribution, such as *Uchu kara no messeiji* (Message from Space, 1978) and *Fukkatsu no hi* (aka *Virus*, 1980).

Sonny Chiba

Yet Sonny the star wasn't above taking small parts in numerous Toei yakuza films and would always lend a cameo or his fight choreography skills to any project with strong Japan Action Club ties such as *Hoeru tekken* (aka *Roaring Fire*) and *Hissatsu onna kenshi* (aka *Dragon Princess*).

Unfortunately, the years to come would be less than stellar for the Street Fighter. He lost the Japan Action Club to a shady takeover and poured millions into a film flop that he also directed and produced (1990's *Remains utsukushiki yujo tachi*). Following several hit TV shows in Japan, Sonny made a full-scale assault on Hollywood in the nineties only to wind up playing second banana to Lou Gossett, Jr. in *Aces: Iron Eagle III* (1992), Brigitte Nielsen in *Body Count* (1996), and loudmouth wrestler "Rowdy" Roddy Piper in 1994's *Immortal Combat* (where Sonny can be seen still wearing his old *Street Fighter* wristbands).

In 1998, Sonny got his revenge by making his highest profile appearance in years, starring in Andrew Lau's glossy comic-book adaptation of Ma Wing-shing's *The Storm Riders*. Chiba stole the show from top-billed heartthrobs Aaron Kwok and Ekin Cheng with his fine Toshiro Mifune-esque turn as the scheming Lord Conquer for which he was nominated for a Golden Horse Award (Hong Kong's own Oscars) for Best Actor.

Now known as "J.J. Sonny Chiba," Our Man lives in Los Angeles and has lent prestige to an increasing number of Hong Kong productions. He also started a new Japanese acting school in the mold of the old JAC. "Japan Dream Movie" aims to teach English and acting chops to a new generation.

Meanwhile, Quentin Tarantino (who scripted a salute to the *Street Fighter* saga into *True Romance*) has announced Chiba will contribute to his next film, *Kill Bill*. It's the least he can do to pay back the grand old Street Fighter. After all, Samuel L. Jackson's famed reading of Ezekiel 25:17 in *Pulp Fiction* finds its origins not only in the Holy Bible, but also from the 1978 movie *The Bodyguard* starring you know who. 東

REVIEW

The Assassin
Yakuza deka—Marijuana mitsubai soshiki (Yakuza Detective—Marijuana Smuggling Operation)

1970, Toei
Director Yukio Noda
Cast Sonny Chiba, Jiro Chiba, Shohei "Giant" Baba

In 1976's *Doberman deka*, an adaptation of the manga of the same name directed by Kinji Fukasaku, Sonny Chiba takes long drags off a Cheech and Chong-sized joint and shows off his Magnum pistol to the local street punks.

But even at this point, Chiba was already well acquainted with cheeba, having first lit up in 1970's *The Assassin*—a movie so whacked out that Sonny admits at one point that "something's wrong with my ass" and is compelled to show off his beet-red cheeks to the camera.

He smokes like a steam engine too at a wild party loaded with kaleidoscopic color-gel effects. You'd half-expect a square like Sonny Bono to show up and spoil the fun with some kind of moralistic anti-drug message. Instead the film only descends further into a series of nutty events with huge sacks of weed motivating the nominal two-warring-gangs plot.

Early on, Sonny is about to exchange fisticuffs with a pack of snarling American soldiers in a bar when the late, great pro-wrestling sensation Shohei "Giant" Baba (all six feet, nine inches of him) shows up to act the impromptu bodyguard.

You can smell it a mile away: *The Assassin* is a film under the influence. Only about seventy percent of the film is even dubbed into English, and the rest—lengthy stretches of dialogue, a love song that Sonny croons—are still in Japanese. That must have been some killer stuff at the international office.

Director Yukio Noda (predictably, the credits get it wrong, listing "Tachiichi Takamori"—they probably mean Tatsuichi Takamori, who directed an earlier *Yakuza deka* movie but not this one) was a specialist in action comedy, honing it to a cacophonous racket in his contributions to the *Furyo bancho* (Delinquent Boss) series, which featured "King of Eros" Tatsuo Umemiya as a *Wild One*-esque bike-gang leader into heavy artillery and Nazi regalia. While Noda never really became a major Toei movie player (though he is fondly remembered for his 1974 Toei pinky violence title *Zero Woman—Red Handcuffs*), he would keep busy in the company's TV division directing episodes of Chiba's *Key Hunter* and the aptly titled *Mad Police*.

Copies of *The Assassin* can be found Stateside, but it has never been released on home video in Japan. So fittingly, Sonny's first tempestuous affair with Mary Jane will remain, like the real thing, hard to score in Japan.

Available dubbed on VHS from Arena Home Video

VIVA CHIBA!
SONNY CHIBA, HIRED TO KILL... IF HIS KICK DOESN'T GET YOU... HIS FATAL FIST WILL!
"THE STREETFIGHTER"
THE BODYGUARD
SONNY CHIBA

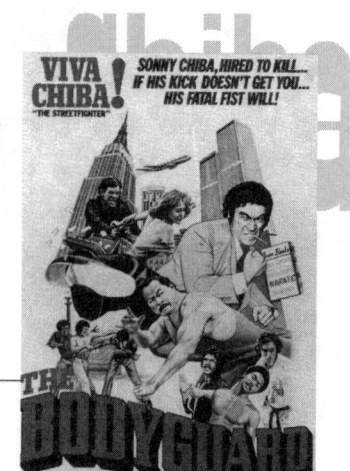

The Bodyguard

Bodyguard Kiba

1973, Toei
Director Tatsuichi Takamori
Cast Sonny Chiba, Eiji Go

A relic of seventies Chibamania, *The Bodyguard* opens with a dizzying, brain-damaging array of events that cry out to be catalogued.

After a quote from Ezekiel 25:17 (the exact same passage spoken by Samuel L. Jackson in *Pulp Fiction*, only substituting "Chiba, the Bodyguard" for "the Lord"), we are in New York City, where "Don Salvattore Rocco" is mowed down in front of a church Roaring Twenties-style by the Tommy-gun-packing "Yellow Mafia."

We cut next to a mass kung fu workout where guys break boards with their heads and chant the would-be catchphrase "Viva Chiba" like they're invoking Cthulhu or something.

Next, a disembodied camera drifts up from the subway and through filth-encrusted 42nd street, gliding up the stairs of The New York Karate Academy, which is located next door to a 25-cent Live Nude Girls storefront.

US Black Belt champion Bill Louie (sporting a snazzy jogging suit) beats the crap out of some anonymous dudes only to have "Mr. Karate USA" Aaron Banks tell him, "That's not the way Sonny Chiba did it." The duo then engage in a conversation that eerily mirrored hundreds like it in grindhouses around the world.

"Yeah, but Bruce had more speed and science."

Incredibly enough, Banks actually agrees with him, but still clings enough to ask, "By the way, where *is* Sonny Chiba?"

Well, right now Our Man is taking time out from his busy film career to wage a one-man war against drugs and the goons who sell them. So seriously does he take his mission that he even considers making some dough on the side by opening drug rehab clinics. (Can you even imagine what treatment would be like at the Sonny Chiba Clinic!??!)

Needless to say the American distributor, Aquarius Releasing (who also employed Louie and Banks in their incredible Bruce Lee neo-mockumentary *Fist of Fear, Touch of Death*), is responsible for most of this lunacy. In the Japanese version Sonny plays the Bodyguard *Kiba* (a character taken from a *gekiga* comic by Ikki Kajiwara), not *Chiba*.

While the rest of *The Bodyguard* doesn't really match the form and content mix of many of the post-*Street Fighter* triumphs, heroic doses of sex and gore still make it a fun ride. At one point, Sonny holds a severed arm and ponders it like Hamlet: "It sure was a bloody show, we should have sold tickets."

They still are. Takashi Miike directed a trio of *Bodyguard Kiba* movies sans Chiba for the direct-to-video market in the early nineties.

☞ **Available dubbed on DVD from Platinum Disc Corporation**

REVIEW

The Street Fighter
Gekitotsu! Satsujin ken (Sudden Impact! Killing Fist)

1974, Toei
Director Shigehiro Ozawa
Cast Sonny Chiba, Masashi Ishibashi, Goichi Yamada

The Street Fighter is truly essential viewing. A crucial Japanese cult film. The special blend of head-splitting comedy and (rip your) balls-out action makes it a masterpiece of content and form for both Sonny Chiba and his handlers at Toei Studios.

Sonny is Terry (Takuma in the Japanese version) Tsurugi, a baaaad motor-scooter who takes the anti-heroic aspects of James Bond and Clint Eastwood to monstrously transgressive extremes. Half-Chinese, half-Japanese, Terry is an Asian superman who's only in it for the money. Whatever redeeming qualities he has come almost by accident.

His foes, dogs dispatched by the Mafia and Hong Kong gangsters, are legion. His opposite number is Junjo (Masashi Ishibashi). While Sonny's mad-dog rage is widespread and unfocused, Junjo merely wants revenge, which is kind of understandable since Chiba has overseen the death of his kid brother and sold his sister (Etsuko Shihomi) into prostitution. If this had been a Hong Kong karate movie, Junjo would surely have been its protagonist.

But this is Toei's world and director Shigehiro Ozawa's 105th film. Logic is out the window. In lieu of a romantic interest, Sonny gets a mangy guy named Ratnose (Goichi Yamada) who nags, cooks, and tends to his wounds like a dutiful wife. Instead of humanizing Chiba, it just makes the film even nuttier.

Keeping this in mind, it might be best to consider *The Street Fighter* as an acid test of sorts. Grab the terrific uncut "collector's widescreen edition" widely available at video stores. If the lack of morality, Sonny's shameless mugging, and the action-first, plot-second mentality are a turn off, then perhaps it's time to count your losses and draw the line here. But if *The Street Fighter* strikes your pleasure centers with deadly precision (like Sonny's fist connecting to an X-ray of a skull, the film's most mind-blowing moment), you'll *need* to see the sequel, *Satsujin ken 2* (Return of the Street Fighter). Released in Japan a mere two months after the original, it might even be the slightly better film, save for an overdependence on stock footage.

Either way, the fringes of Japanese cult film are now yours to explore without fear. And with the ubiquitous Chiba at your side, you'll never walk alone.

Available dubbed on VHS from New Line Home Video and dubbed on DVD from Diamond Entertainment

Sonny Chiba

Direct Hit! Hell Fist—Big Reversal
Chokugeki! Jigoku ken—Dai gyakuten, aka *The Executioner 2*

1974, Toei
Director Teruo Ishii
Cast Sonny Chiba, Makoto Sato, Eiji Go

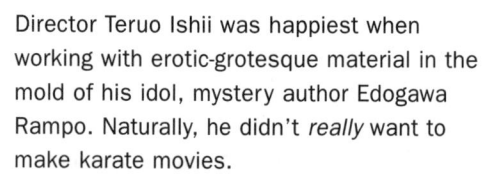

Director Teruo Ishii was happiest when working with erotic-grotesque material in the mold of his idol, mystery author Edogawa Rampo. Naturally, he didn't *really* want to make karate movies.

Too bad, because as a contract director at Toei, Ishii could not refuse the assignment to direct and script the 1974 post-*Street Fighter* Sonny Chiba outing *Chokugeki! Jigoku ken* (aka *The Executioner*).

In a risky bid to make Toei unhappy with the results, and thus lowering his chances of taking any further trips to the martial arts dojo, Ishii loaded *Jigoku ken* with comedy and a general air of anarchy, essentially turning it into a parody of Chiba's hit TV show *Key Hunter* (itself a Japanese take on *Mission: Impossible*).

The plan backfired. *Jigoku ken* did well enough for Toei to send Ishii back to the front with orders to deliver a sequel within three months.

The director rose to the occasion by hedging all bets and making the most mad mad mad, and certainly the funniest, Sonny Chiba movie ever made.

The raunch volume, already pronounced in the first film, is turned up to deafening volumes as modern-day ninja Chiba, professional killer Makoto Sato, and perpetually swollen sex addict Eiji Go (brother of *Branded to Kill*'s Jo Shishido) act like an unholy mix of the Three Stooges and Iggy and the Stooges.

Under orders from Ryo Ikebe, (warrior/scientist from numerous Toho sci-fi films) the gang attempts to rip off a diamond from a wheelchair-bound white woman deeply involved with the Mafia and Tetsuro Tanba (almost unrecognizable as a Col. Sanders-lookalike). As our "heroes" fail at every single task assigned them, countless lowbrow jokes and bodily functions (as his partner catches fire, Sonny urinates on Eiji minutes after farting in his face) take Japanese humor to somewhere just south of one million years BC.

You can feel Ishii's seething contempt and disregard for the material in every frame. The editing is haphazard throughout, and no attempt is made to hide the shadows of stunt cranes and helicopters during action sequences.

Again, his intentions made little difference. The sequel is beloved in Japan, even more so than the original, and sells out whenever it screens.

As recently as 2000, Chiba has suggested that he'd like to do another *Jigoku ken* sequel someday. Ishii, now an independent filmmaker, dares not dream of it. After all, it would probably be a blockbuster.

☞ **Import only**

REVIEW

Champion of Death
Kenka karate—Kyokushin ken (Karate Fight—Ultimate Truth Fist)

1975, Toei
Director Kazuhiko Yamaguchi
Cast Sonny Chiba, Mikio Narita, Yumi Takigawa

Korean-born Karate Grand Master Masutatsu Oyama (1923-1994) was known as the "God Hand" for a reason. He developed a fighting style known humbly as *Kyokushin* (Ultimate Truth) and would demonstrate its virtues by killing charging angry bulls with only his hands.

According to Oyama's current disciples, those who fraternized with "God Hand" over the years have included Sean Connery, Dolph Lundgren, Ronald Reagan (!), Nelson Mandela (?), and Sonny Chiba, who studied at Oyama's feet for a five-year stretch.

A manga based on Oyama's colorful life, *Karate baka ichidai* (The Fanatical First Generation of Karate) by famed sports comics writer Ikki Kajiwara, helped ignite a major martial arts boom in Japan during the early seventies. And in 1975, riding high on an international karate craze, Sonny played his teacher in a trilogy of films.

Kenka karate begins in 1949 as Oyama, a feral figure clad in a tattered *gi*, crashes the first postwar karate tournament. An entrepreneur (Mikio Narita) wants to groom the all-strength, no-style fighter, but Oyama is disgusted at the prospect of becoming a mere "karate dancer." While pulling rickshaws for money, he spies a girl (*School of the Holy Beast*'s Yumi Takigawa) who seems to be sleeping with American soldiers. After raping her in a desperate bid to rehabilitate the fallen woman it turns out she was: a) a virgin and b) merely an interpreter for the Occupation Forces. Oops!

Sneering MacArthur-lookalikes get revenge by forcing Oyama into a Coke-bottle-breaking contest. Soon after, a mad bull breaks loose and ol' "God Hand" beats it to death, becoming a media sensation in the process.

Act two is a doozy. Oyama's sole pupil (Jiro Chiba, Sonny's kid brother who came along for the ride on many films) rejects his master, Yumi rejects Oyama's offer of marriage, and Oyama himself renounces karate after killing a family guy in a drunken barroom brawl. After briefly pondering the morality of murder (of people, not bulls) he makes a stunning recovery by massacring Mikio plus all the members of the karate school who had been hounding him since reel one.

A pulpy, passionate, at times practically libelous elegy to self-discipline (scripted by Norifumi Suzuki), *Champion of Death* is frequently marred by flagrant abuse of hand-held camera during fight scenes. Unfortunately, the guilty party, cameraman Yoshio Nakajima (who also shot *The Bodyguard* and *Sister Street Fighter*), would return, as would director Yamaguchi and Chiba, for the following Oyama sequels: 1975's *Kenka karate kyokushin buraiken* (aka *Karate Bear Fighter*) and 1977's *Karate baka ichidai*.

☞ **Available dubbed on VHS/DVD from Gemstone Entertainment**

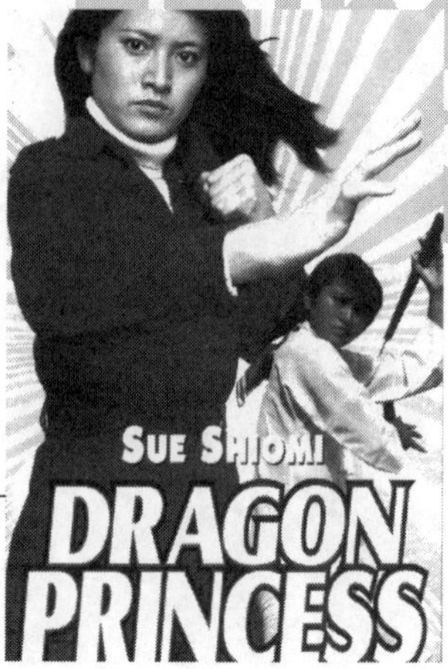
SUE SHIOMI
DRAGON PRINCESS

Dragon Princess

Hissatsu onna kenshi (Frenzied Woman Fist Fighter)

1976, Toei
Director Yutaka Kohira
Cast Etsuko Shihomi, Yasuaki Kurata, Sonny Chiba

Shown in US theaters as *Sonny Chiba's Dragon Princess* (ala *Don Kirshner's Rock Concert*), this is a very strong Etsuko Shihomi movie that probably deserves better than to be exiled to the shadows cast by that better known Shihomi movie, *Sister Street Fighter*.

Director Yutaka Kohira was the assistant director on Shunya Ito's first *Female Convict Scorpion* film and later directed two of the films in the series. While not nearly as pointed a treatise as *Scorpion*, Kohira gives *Dragon Princess* a strong female p.o.v. that uses its star to her full athletic potential while piling on just enough sleaze for good contrast.

Sonny (only in the film for the first reel) loses a key battle for control of the karate world. He moves, with daughter Shihomi in tow, to a grungy tenement in New York (complete with convincing English graffitti on the walls that says "Go Fuck!!"). While training his precious poppet in the deadly martial arts, he beats her fearfully with a rattan stick in a scene that can't help but make you wonder how Chiba taught pupils in his Japan Action Club.

Sonny exits this mortal coil a bitter, broken man and Etsuko goes back to Tokyo, dressed in a cape and bell bottoms, determined to get revenge on the karate instructor (Masashi Ishibashi) who wronged father and daughter. Now he's a big shot with political ties, scheming to win a big tournament and turn his karate students into voters.

The plot takes bizarre detours into topless dancing, Cuba, and Bolivia. The fights are great, especially the final showdown set in the tall grass where wildcard Yasuaki Kurata lends an arm and a leg and Shihomi is dressed like a monk, unbreakable virginal purity her greatest weapon.

Underlying it all is a punchy soundtrack by composer Shunsuke Kikuchi, whose heavy-on-the-brass-and-wah-wah-guitar scores have graced over 200 films and TV shows. His groovy tunes could liven up any party, let alone a flick about a frenzied woman fist fighter.

☞ **Available dubbed from Arena Home Video (VHS) and Platinum Disc Corporation (DVD)**

☞ **More: ETSUKO SHIHOMI p. 55**

REVIEW

Golgo 13: Assignment: Kowloon
Golgo 13—Kuron no kubi (Golgo 13—Necks of the Nine Dragons)

1977, Toei
Director Yukio Noda
Cast Sonny Chiba, Callan Leong, Koji Tsuruta

Assignment: Kowloon was the second live-action film based on Takao Saito's famed manga series about the world's top stone-faced assassin-for-hire. The first, from 1973, was directed by Junya Sato and starred superstar Ken Takakura in the title role (best scene: Golgo takes out a goomba with his sniper's rife, then blows away the dead man's pet parrot to make sure there are no witnesses. Those things talk, you know.)

For the 1977 Golgo follow-up, Sonny Chiba got an ultratight perm (okay, an afro really), a pinstripe suit, a plastic rifle, and a plane ticket to Hong Kong.

But despite the participation of fellow Toei stars Koji Tsuruta and Etsuko Shihomi, the result is very nearly an authentic chop-socky flick, filled with under-lit junkyard brawls, Black Belt Theater extras, and kicks in the head delivered via dirty white sneakers.

Sonny himself vanishes from the narrative for large chunks, leaving a dim-witted police inspector, played by Callan Leong (also featured in Ronnie Yu's *Jumping Ash*) to shadow a portly drug kingpin.

Golgo has been assigned to take this bad guy out, but when he finally gets him in the crosshairs of his trusty M16, a third party makes a hit on the intended target. Turns out that diplomat Jerry Ito (he played the unscrupulous producer of the "Secret Fairies Show" in 1961's *Mothra*—in *Golgo 13* he plays a "Mr. Polanski" who takes his prepubescent daughter to sleazy nightclubs) is behind it all, and Golgo and Callan team up to stop him.

Truth be told, Yukio Noda was never really one of Toei's top directorial talents and here he really drops the ball. *Golgo 13* has no momentum and the story just barely manages to unfold.

Nevertheless, the film certainly has its admirers. A scene where Sonny plans a surgical strike at a swimming pool race, synchronizing his shot to the sound of the starting pistol, reappears in barely concealed form in John Woo's gun-fu classic *The Killer*.

In an interview for the Criterion laserdisc of *The Killer*, Woo went public about how Teruo Ishii's 1964 film *Narazumono* (Scoundrel, starring Ken Takakura on location in Hong Kong and Macao) was the inspiration for *The Killer*'s love story.

Ever wonder where he got the "hitman who teams up with a cop" plot?

☞ **Available dubbed on VHS/DVD from Crash Cinema**

ROARING
FIRE

Roaring Fire

Hoeru tekken (Roaring Iron Fist)

1981, Toei
Director Norifumi Suzuki
Cast Hiroyuki Sanada, Etsuko Shihomi, Abdullah the Butcher, Mikio Narita

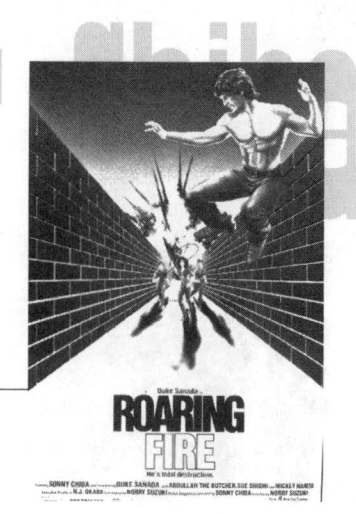

Talk about your tall tales. Hiroyuki Sanada (billed as "Henry Sanada" in the US version) is a Texas cowboy named Georgie who knows karate and, thanks to the local Indians, how to throw a mean tomahawk.

While out on the range one day, Georgie finds that father (Masashi Ishibashi) has gone ill. During a deathbed confession, dad lets spill that when Georgie was a toddler, he was kidnapped from his parents. Seems he has an identical twin bother, a sister, and a posh pad back in Japan.

With his fetching fringe vest and pet spider monkey in tow, Georgie heads for Dai Nippon. There he makes friends with pro wrestler Abdullah the Butcher and the locals at a bar called "Casablanca" run by a codger in a white tux named Bogey.

When Georgie meets his sister (Etsuko Shihomi), he finds she's as blind as a bat, though capable of swatting things out of the air with her martial arts abilities. The fine family fortune is now lorded over by their uncle (Mikio Narita), a Beethoven-loving sadist who likes to conduct business with a big portrait of Hitler in full view. Seems he had Georgie's parents killed in an unsuccessful bid to obtain the family jewels, which he intends to trade in for a bushel of heroin-flavored bananas. Georgie discovers as much when nightclub entertainer and ventriloquist Mr. Magic (a jaw-dropping cameo from Sonny Chiba) drops clues via his talking dummy. Multiple beatdowns and beat-ups ensue until the three-way finale: a concerto for helicopter, Humvee, and Sanada riding horseback.

Released in 1981, *Hoeru tekken* finds our beloved Toei studios in a demographics dilemma. On the one hand, they want to give youth audiences an idol film, but the transgressions that marked the sleaze-encrusted seventies have yet to be fully expunged. As it stands, director Suzuki is only too happy to veer crazily between his favored extremes: juvenile eye-rolling comedy and theologically loaded sex and sadism (seen here in the form of Nazi women whipping people). Suzuki would eventually get the hang of it and would score big with a series of highly successful action comedies, including 1983's *Iga no kabamaru* (also starring Sanada and Chiba) and 1986's *The Samurai*.

No Problem
なんのその
ブッチャー

☞ **Available dubbed on VHS from Torn/EMI Home Video**

☞ **More: HIROYUKI SANADA p. 54**

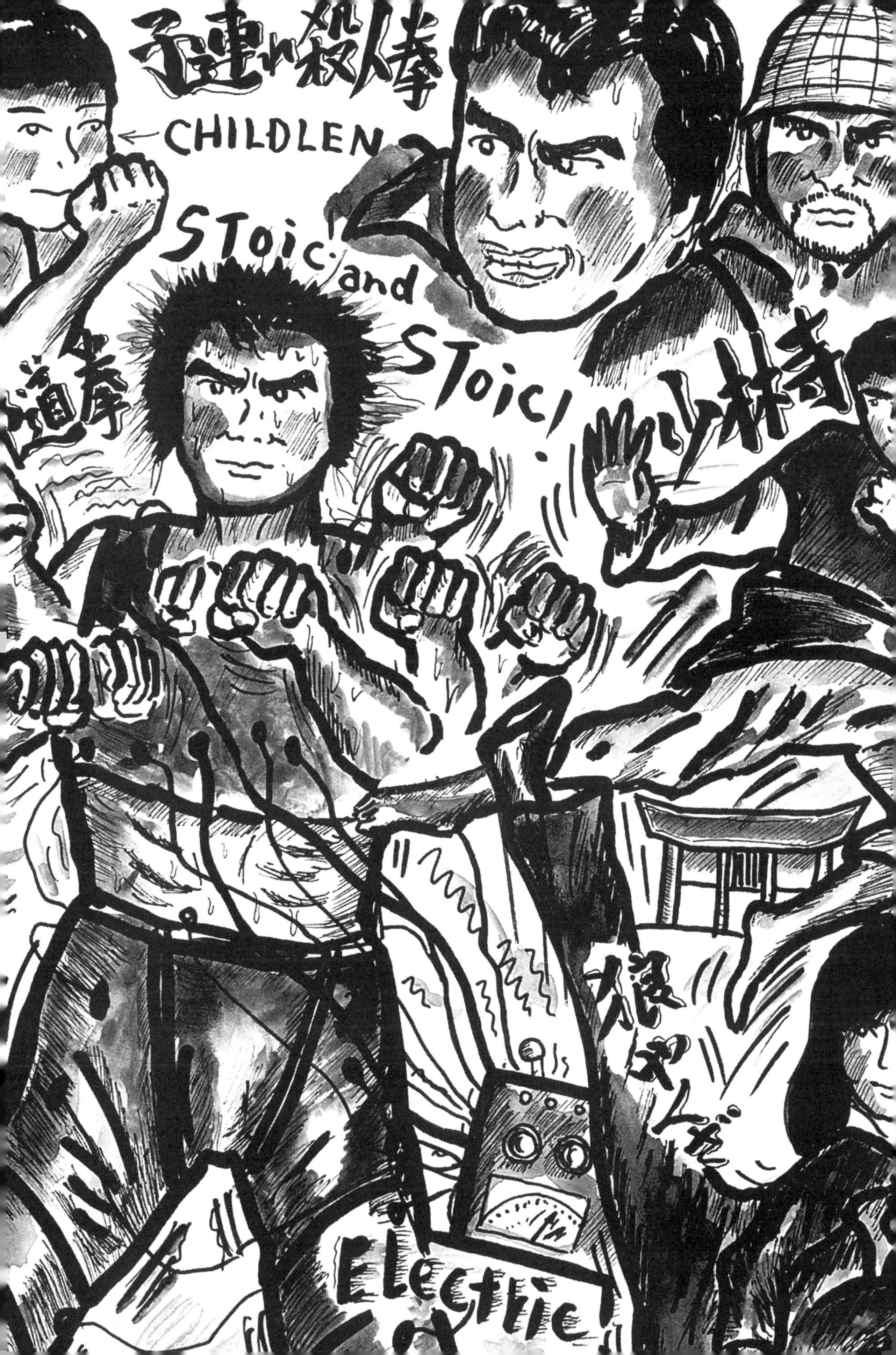
子連れ殺人拳
CHILDLEN
STOIC and STOIC!
少林寺
Electric!

Hiroyuki Sanada
Actor

You can take the actor out of Sonny Chiba's Japan Action Club, but you can't take the Japan Action Club out of the actor. Case in point: Hiroyuki Sanada's portrayal of The Fool in a London production of *King Lear* in 1999 was characterized by tumbling, somersaulting, and other acrobatic excesses in direct contrast to the more reserved performance given by costar Sir Nigel Hawthorne.

Sonny Chiba excepted, Hiroyuki Sanada is probably the JAC's most successful alumnus. The closest analogue to the stature of his fame in Japan would be Tom Cruise. But then again, Tom Cruise never jumped through a flaming windshield whilst providing the theme song to 1981's *Roaring Fire*. Sanada did, and that's why we love him more.

Born Hiroyuki Shimozawa in Tokyo in 1960, Sanada entered show biz at an early age, appearing on magazine covers at the age of four and making his film debut playing the son of a yakuza at five. At fourteen, he had a bit part in Teruo Ishii's *Chokugeki! Jigoku ken* (aka *The Executioner*) in the taxing role of "young Sonny Chiba in training."

After the requisite Japan Action Club education, Sanada appeared alongside mentor Chiba in a pair of Kinji Fukasaku's 1978 all-star vehicles: *The Yagyu Conspiracy* and *Message from Space*. Much ninjitsu and swordplay followed in films like *Samurai Reincarnation* (1981), *Shogun's Ninja* (1983), *Ninja Wars* (1982), and *Legend of the Eight Samurai* (1983).

1981's *Hoeru Tekken* (Roaring Iron Fist), directed by Toei's pinky violence specialist Norifumi Suzuki, was designed to be Sanada's modern-day martial arts blow out. When released in the US by New Line Cinema as *Roaring Fire*, Hiroyuki became "Henry Sanada" and possessed (according to the poster) "The Grace of Bruce Lee…The Speed of Sonny Chiba…The Force of Chuck Norris." (Thankfully, lacking the back hair of the latter.)

In the mid-eighties, Sanada branched out, singing and dancing in numerous JAC-affiliated stage shows, which helped lead to a long-lived singing career. Megacelebrity soon resulted and listkeeping of his various marriages, mistresses, and divorces has become a regular function of Japanese tabloids.

In recent years, Sanada played the part of long-suffering teacher Ryuji Takayama in the wildly popular horror films *Ring*, *Ring 2*, and *Spiral*. He's also been known to slum it up in stage versions of *Hamlet* and *King Lear* and can be seen in the Michelle Yeoh Hong Kong film *Royal Warriors*. 東

PROFILE

Etsuko Shihomi
Actress

志穂美悦子

Etsuko Shihomi is Japan's matriarch of the martial arts. Her only real contemporaries can be found in the Hong Kong cinema. Graceful, ferocious, beautiful, death-defiant, she is Sonny Chiba's Jungian anima made manifest: Sister Street Fighter.

Born in 1955 in Nishidaiji, Okayama in the Honshu prefecture, the teenage Shihomi was an ardent admirer of Sonny Chiba's screen exploits. After writing to him several times, she was invited to take the admission test to his elite Japan Action Club. Shihomi became one of the few women to enter the JAC's ranks and quickly became the best known.

Shihomi made her feature-film debut in 1973's *Bodyguard Kiba* (starring Sonny) and had a supporting role in 1974's *The Street Fighter*.

She took the lead for the 1974 *Street Fighter* spin-off *Onna hissatsu ken* (Lady Killing Fist, retitled *Sister Street Fighter* abroad) and kept the series alive for two sequels. Similar vehicles followed, including *Dragon Princess*, *The 13 Steps*, and *Great Chase*.

Throughout it all, Shihomi maintained an image of athletic health and purity, never once appearing less than virtuous. She was overwhelmingly popular among girls, who quickly turned their back on her husband, rock star Tsuyoshi Nagabuchi, when he was caught cheating on her.

In addition to being a martial artist and a gymnast, Shihomi was a fearless daredevil. Leaps from high places were a favorite pastime, and for the promotion of 1981's *Makai tensho* (aka *Samurai Reincarnation*), Shihomi jumped from the roof of a building in Shinjuku to the delight of hundreds of onlookers. She was also required to carry a tune, which led to a rash of LPs and 45 rpm releases.

As the kung fu craze wore off in the late seventies, Shihomi joined Chiba for increasingly more period films and did her share of dramatic TV work. Street Fighting aside, Shihomi *could* act and did a fine turn in Nobuhiko Obayashi's 1982 gender-swapping school drama *Tenkosei* (Exchange Student).

Sadly for us, Shihomi has been missing in action since a 1986 *Tora-san* movie. No one has since filled the void in Japanese action film that she's left behind. 東

Sister Street Fighter Sings!
45 rpm sleeve for the title theme from Etsuko's *The 13 Steps* (1975).

THE SONNY VIDEO ROUNDUP

In the aftermath of New Line Cinema's 1996 rerelease of Sonny Chiba's *Street Fighter* series, the enterprising folks at Xenon/Arena Home Video harvested a Chiba crop of their own. Some of their titles had been released before, but subsequently went out of print. Others had never before seen light of day in the US and remain unreleased on video even in Japan. But while any Chiba is good Chiba, Arena's less-than-pristine video quality and sometimes edited prints make their wares a patchy minefield of delights and peril. Here's a road map to what's what. Tread carefully.

KARATE WARRIORS is 1976's *Kozure satsujin ken* (Killing Fist with Child), directed by Kazuhiko Yamaguchi, who also helmed *Sister Street Fighter* and *Champion of Death*. It's a solid, if a wee bit pedestrian, Chiba film whose charms are marred by a crap video transfer. Sonny plays a cash-seeking professional killer (I know, a big stretch) who pits two brothers and their rival gangs against each other in the approved *Red Harvest/Yojimbo/Fistful of Dollars* manner. A traditional swordmaster and his little son lend the film an intentional *Lone Wolf and Cub* vibe. Funniest bit: narrator Peter Fernandez (best known as the voice of *Speed Racer*) refers to a "notorious gambling and porno shop" while a perfectly innocent pachinko parlor is shown on screen.

THE KILLING MACHINE is Norifumi Suzuki's *Shorinji kempo* (Shaolin Karate) from 1975. Suzuki was a top-notch sexploitation and action-comedy director. As if to show off his range, this is a tearjerking martial arts melodrama similar to *Champion of Death* (which was scripted by Suzuki). Here, Chiba plays real-life soldier-spy Doshin So who battled the black market and brought Chinese fighting techniques to Japan. Kinji Fukasaku never directed a Shaolin karate movie, but this is probably how he would have done it, with a mix of thug biography and bleak postwar setting. The cast includes Etsuko Shihomi, Makoto Sato, and Tetsuro Tanba. Unforgettable scene: Sonny snips a bad guy's dick off with a pair of scissors and feeds the offending article to a dog. Honest.

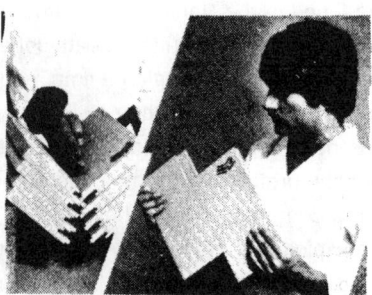

Break-up Boards
* You'll never have to pay for pine boards again!
* Same impact resistance as ¾" pine.

You can break it over and over again. Same impact resistance as ¾" pine. Patented breakable joint slides back together after each break. After 1000 test blows, no significant change in impact resistance. Made of rugged high-density polyethylene plastic compound.

Order No. 638

One board ......$19.95 ea.
Two boards.......18.95 ea.
Three or more 17.95 ea.

OPEN FINGER GLOVES

$12.50 pr.

Padding on back of gloves provides protection for the knuckles & bones. Finger tubes are cut so that fingers can project out. **Black or Red color.**

THE ASSASSIN is *Yakuza deka—Marijuana mitsubai soshiki* (Yakuza Detective—Marijuana Smuggling Operation) from 1970, directed by Yukio Noda. Ignore the cover art with the pic of Sonny the samurai holding a sword. *The Assassin* is a dazed and confused seventies time capsule where Chiba spends the entire film in appropriately funky fashions with a big floppy at least five sizes too big for his crown. Read the full-length review on page 45 for this, one of Sonny's biggest hits (in the Cheech and Chong sense).

G.I. SAMURAI is director Mitsumase Saito's *Sengoku jieitai* (Civil War Defense Force, aka *Time Slip*), a Kadokawa-Toei-Toho film from 1979. After a psychedelic light show, Self-Defense Forces lieutenant Chiba finds himself, his troops, and his tanks and helicopters transported back in time to Japan's feudal war-torn past. Chiba choreographed the spectacular large-scale action sequences, and it's great fun to see him work with both modern and period weaponry...sort of like what would happen if the cast of *Apocalypse Now* had a go at *Kagemusha*. The downside is that Arena's version is savagely cut down from 139 minutes to a little over 80 minutes, and the *only sometimes* letterboxed image looks like hell. The box art bizarrely has a picture of actor Masahiro Takashima from Kaizo Hayashi's completely unrelated 1990 film *Zipang* front and center. Maybe they thought it would boost sales. Or something.

THE SOUL OF CHIBA was released originally in the US under the gleefully misleading title *The Soul of Bruce Lee*. The film is actually Yukio Noda's *Gekisatsu! Jaro ken* (Violent Death! Way of the Evil Fist) from 1977. Set in Thailand with a cast that includes Bolo Yeung (*Enter the Dragon*) and Bronson Lee (aka Tadashi Yamashita, star of *American Ninja 5*), there's a major chopsocky vibe going on that's either bound to delight or anger viewers depending on their tolerance for this sort of thing. Sonny (who goes missing in action for long stretches) plays a Thai guy out to—wait for it—get revenge on the bastard who killed his teacher (pronounced "tee shirt"). Etsuko Shihomi shows up and plays a flute, and Sonny becomes addicted to stimulating himself with electricity and battles a quartet of men possessed by monkeys. The opening credits are in Italian. Frighteningly, this is one of the best-looking tapes from the Arena Chiba stable. Go figure. 東

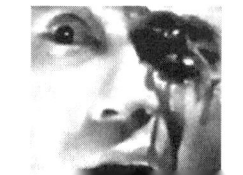

VIDEO

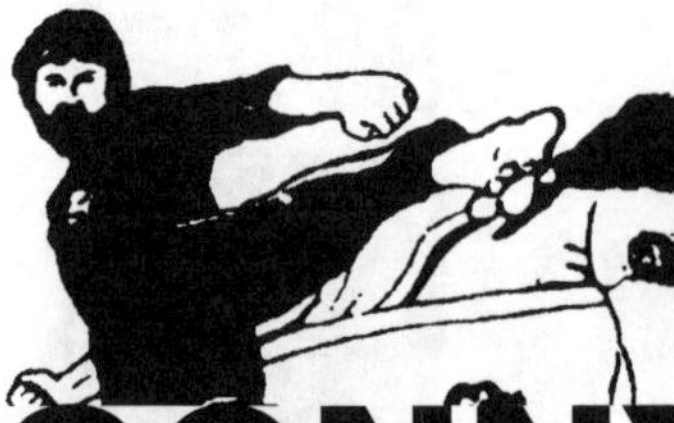

SONNY'S BEST SCREEN KILLS

When you want to watch a Sonny Chiba movie, the odds are you want to see him beat the crap out of jokers who may, or may not, deserve the very teeth in their skulls. For quick reference, here are some of the more memorable moments of crisis resolution from the esteemed Chiba filmography.

The Executioner (Chokugeki! Jigoku ken) While Willie Dorsey (the black guy whom Sonny seems to kill in every single movie) is makin' love to a lady friend, Sonny descends from the ceiling like a poisonous spider. After some sparring (including a brief pit stop on top of the surprised woman), Sonny pins Willie D. against the wall and unleashes a volley of rapid-fire punches like a speed-metal drummer being electrocuted.

Dragon Princess (Hissatsu onna kenshi) An old white-haired geezer in a buckskin fringe vest throws a silver dart into one of Sonny's eyes. As he lunges in for the kill, Sonny puts his beloved preteen daughter (the titular *Dragon Princess*) down long enough to poke out both of his opponent's peepers like Curly from the Three Stooges. Forget what they say about an eye for an eye. Sonny is all about plurals.

The Bodyguard (Bodyguard Kiba) At a Beatlemania-styled press conference, a reporter asks international film star and aspiring narcotics agent Sonny Chiba, "You killed five mobsters with your bare hands. That took great courage. Why did you do it?" The only answer: "Because I had to." Then someone brings him a bottle of Coke. Just like in *Champion of Death*, Sonny chops it in half with his bare hands (seems even caffeinated beverages cannot survive Sonny's war on drugs). Without missing a beat, he delivers the punchline: "This is what I intend to do to the head man of their organization."

Golgo 13: Assignment: Kowloon (Golgo 13—Kuron no kubi) Here's a new one: someone tries to *talk* Sonny Chiba to death. While mucking about in a junkyard, a mealymouthed white guy (think Shane McGowan from the Pogues only *with* a set of ill-fitting choppers) starts taunting one very unimpressed hitman. "I've been expecting you. You had it all figured out, didn't you? But you didn't plan on me waiting though, did ya? They didn't tell you about me, did they? So you're finished now, no problem." Sonny vanishes from view only to materialize seconds later on top of a crane, from which he tosses a massive pipe, penetrating his tormentor's solar plexus. Perhaps in hopes that language really is a virus (thus leaving Sonny with a head cold at the least), the jibberjabbering fool spends his last remaining moments muttering, "You're really good. Just like they said you'd be. But I nearly did get you though...." 東

KUNG FU PANTS

Black heavyweight material made of 50% polyester and 50% cotton. Will not shrink. **Send in your height and weight for correct size.**

RIBBED CUFFS DRAWSTRING WAIST — #KFP/DS
$13.95

(Shown in Photo)
RIBBED CUFFS — RIBBED WAISTBAND
#KFP/RW **$14.95**

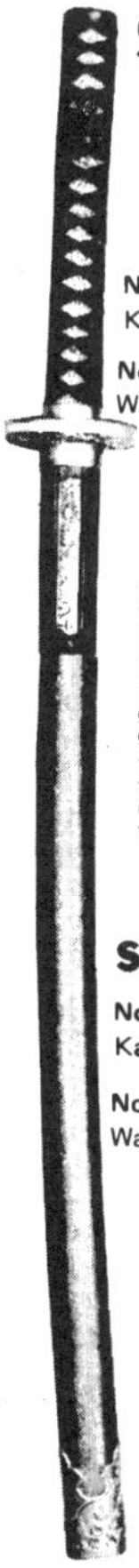

SAMURAI SWORDS
With Sharpened Steel Blades

No. 245 **$139.95**
Katana - 40" long sword

No. 246 **$114.95**
Wakizashi - 27" short sword

These, our finest swords, feature sharpened and tempered steel blades. Authentic detailing. Strong enough for almost any demo. Blades are polished steel. Handle has classic braiding with small Menuki (dragon figure) on each side. Scabbard includes a Kozuki knife near handle and is of wood covered in brown imit. leather. Fittings and guard are finished in antique gold. Guard & handle are carefully adjusted for tightness before leaving our shop. Shipped in extra thick card board tube to prevent damage.

Non-Steel Samurai Swords

No. 205 **$54.95**
Katana - 40" long sword

No. 206 **$42.95**
Wakizashi - 27" sh...

Authentic, highly detailed swords similar to steel models above. Suitable for display or light demo. Has unsharpened, non-steel blade. Scabbard is black laquered wood. Kozuki knife is not included. Gold finished metal fittings.

SWORD STAND Holds 2 swords horizontally on a table top. Black lacquered wood. No.207

VIDEO

59

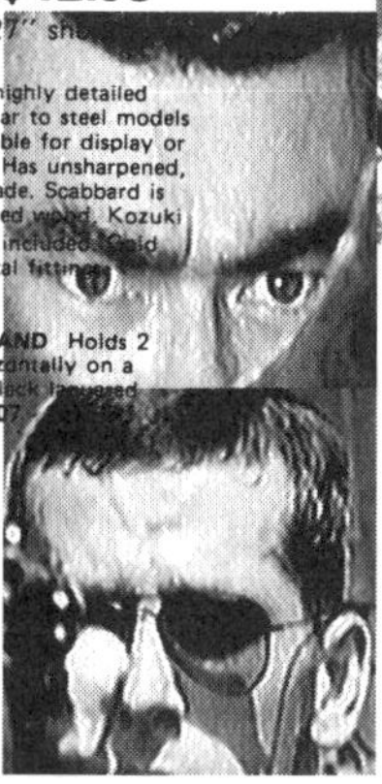

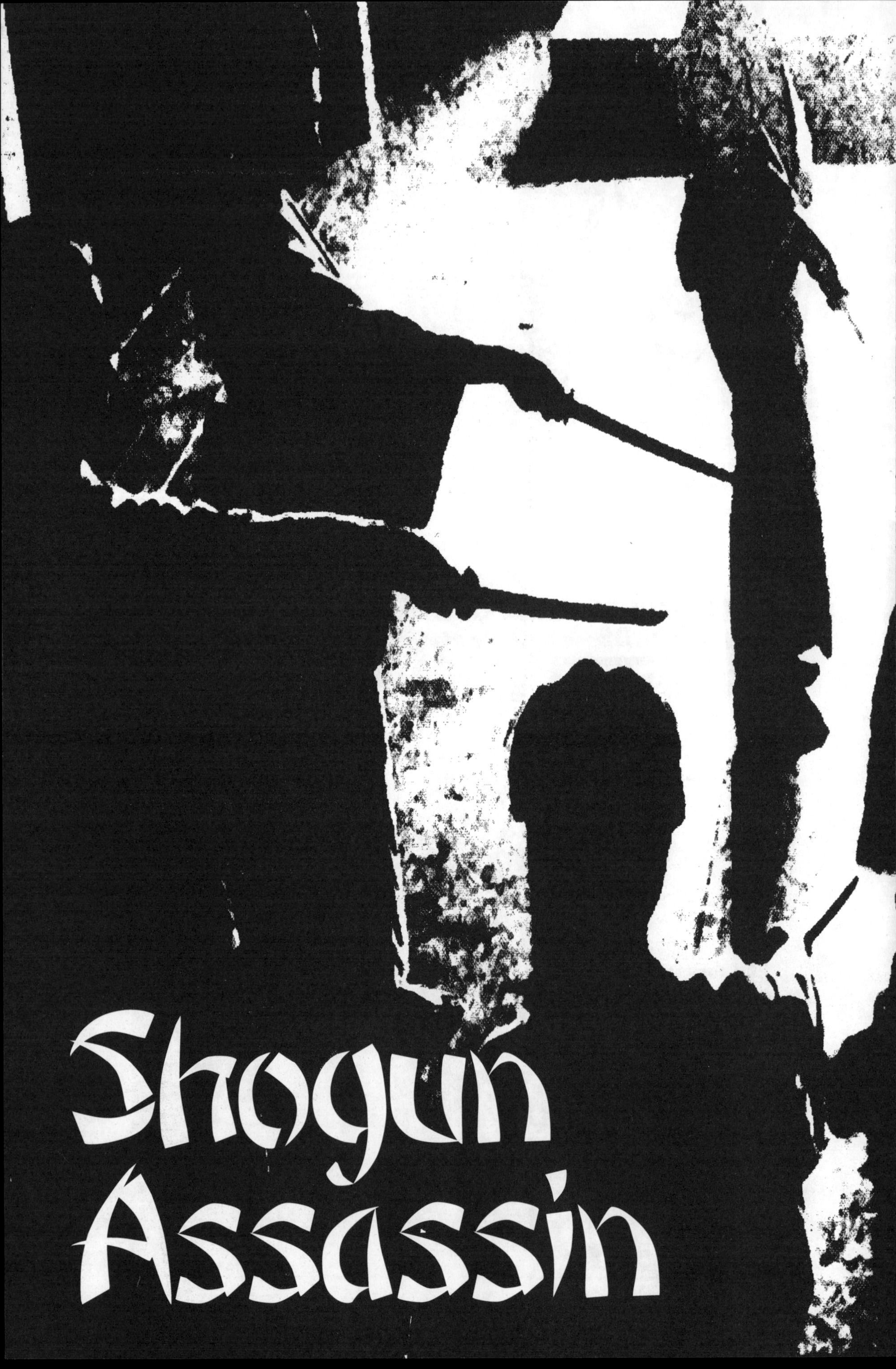
Shogun
Assassin

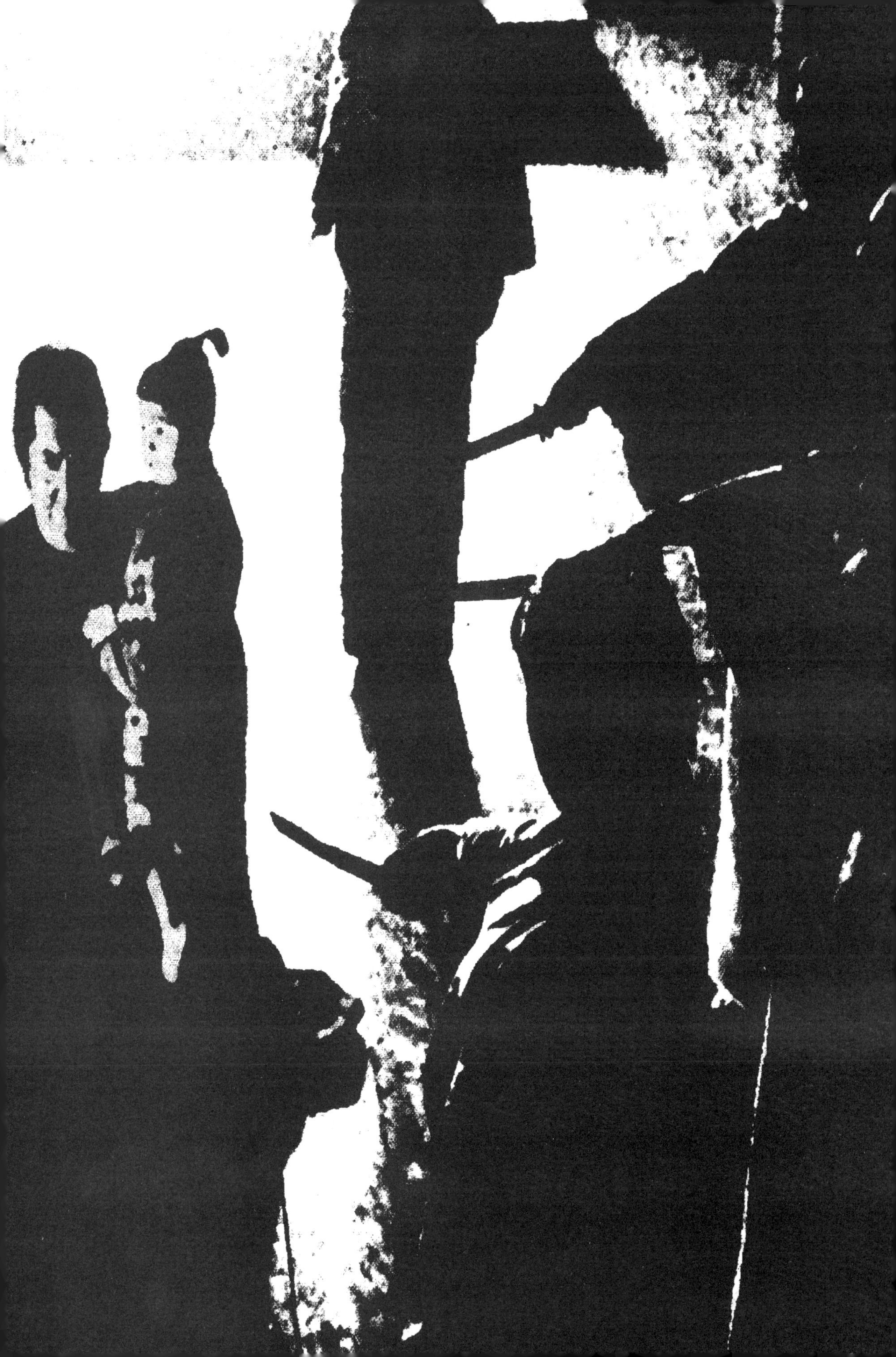

Shogun Assassin

A vengeful lone wolf. A talking baby. A faded rock star. Sandra Bernhard. Edie Sedgwick. The Spider Woman. The Wu-Tang Clan. Treachery. Greed. Roger Corman. The folly of exploitation film. An evergreen cult classic. "The greatest team in the history of mass slaughter." The making of Shogun Assassin!

September 1980. New World Pictures releases *Shogun Assassin,* a compilation film containing highlights from the first two *Lone Wolf and Cub* (aka *Baby Cart*) movies from Toho studios; i.e., it is an extensively rewritten, rescored, and dubbed-into-English version of *Kozure okami—Kowokashi udekashi tsukamatsuru* and *Kozure okami—Sanzu no kawa no ubaguruma* (both from 1972 and directed by Kenji Misumi). In a bold changeover from the original, Daigoro—the baby in the cart—performs a voiceover narration.

Shogun Assassin is something new, yet it retains the flavor of the original. The film becomes a cult classic and introduces the *Lone Wolf and Cub* characters to millions of viewers for the first time. Twenty years later, even though the original, unprocessed *Baby Cart* movies have become widely available with English subtitles, some folks still prefer to fire up *Shogun Assassin*. So how the hell did it all happen? We tracked down and talked to those who were there....

Robert Houston *(Shogun Assassin director/screenwriter)* I'd been going to a Japanese movie theater on Olympic Boulevard to watch samurai movies with my friend David Weisman. David had been to Japan, was teaching himself Japanese, only ate sushi, and, for a period of six to eight months, it was as if we were living a Japanese existence. *Shogun Assassin* was an outgrowth of this obsession.

David Weisman *(Shogun Assassin producer/screenwriter)* Bobby was right out of Harvard and, if I remember correctly, this was his first feature film venture. I had been struggling for five years with my film *Ciao! Manhattan* (1972) which was an adventure unto itself—if you can imagine five years with [Warhol superstar] Edie Sedgwick. The film broke the bank in Amsterdam, but, a couple slip-ups later, I found myself living like a beached whale out in California. I forgot all about the movie business for five years. But eventually, I wanted to get back in. I just wanted to get a ball rolling. When I moved to LA in 1973, there was the Toho La Brea. And I saw the *Baby Cart* films. I saw all of them. I mean, I'd been a Japanese culture freak since the sixties. I figured, I'd start shoving it down people's throats. But the big thing happened when James Clavell's *Shogun* became a bestseller. I knew they were making a mini-series out of it, so that really lit a fire under my ass. I raised some money from a bunch of wacky ex-hippie friends of mine, and we just sallied forth and did it. I dragged Bobby kicking and screaming into it, and I never could have done *Shogun Assassin* without him.

Jim Evans *(Shogun Assassin poster illustrator and logo designer)* It was chaotic in the beginning, but it was well organized in the sense that David was able to speak Japanese and get the rights to those films. He asked me one day what the coolest Japanese film I'd seen was, and I said there were these *Baby Cart* films that I had brought my kids to see in Little Tokyo. Of course, he knew what I was talking about, and he said, "I could probably get those things," and I said, "Well, why don't you?"

David Weisman In 1979, I approached the Toho-Towa office in Century City. Mr. Ueda, who was the Toho rep, was in a state of shock that someone actually wanted to buy something. It was a long, drawn-out negotiation. Very cautious. Very careful. It went back and forth for months and months, and it was the better part of a year before we settled on a licensing deal. $50,000 for the seven-year rights to part two of the *Baby Cart* series. The license also contained ten minutes of footage from the first film, which was the background story for the character of Ogami and Daigoro. We adapted the films as best we could and sold it to New World Pictures [Roger Corman's company] completely finished.

Robert Houston It was a horrible process. It was all the humiliation of post-production and none of the glory of production or pre-production. It was about six months in post-production. The whole thing was post. The most grueling part was working with the editor and cutting the material so we could lip-synch it phonetically. You couldn't come up with a worse job.

David Weisman We got some deaf-mutes in there for a couple of days on the editing machine, on the flatbed, and we showed them the film and asked them, "What do you think they could they be saying?" And they gave us suggestions and Bobby basically wrote from that. We took out all the material that had generically Japanese historical stuff that was incomprehensible to a Western mind and just pared it down to "Conan the Barbarian Walks the Earth."

Robert Houston Daigoro narrates *Shogun Assassin* because I felt that it was the only way to warm up and humanize this story for Americans. A friend of ours had a little son named Gibran who had this unreal, strange, captivating voice. So here was this little round-faced American kid and here was this little round-faced

Shogun Assassin

Japanese kid in the movie, and the two were just meant to be together.

Jim Evans I guess I was kind of a strange father, because I had a different take on violence. Gibran had probably seen those films before in Little Tokyo when he was about four years old. It was more like a poetic ballet of blood than anything else, so I really didn't mind him seeing it.

David Weisman I mean, this is not violence we're talking about, this is fucking fantasy! It takes a very, very well-tempered, pounded-60,000-times-over-ten-years samurai sword to cut someone's finger off! Where the fuck are you going to find that? You can't do it with a kitchen knife! You've got to chop it off!

Gibran Evans *(the voice of Daigoro)* I was seven at the time, living in the mountains in Malibu. We went to Little Tokyo a lot and collected tremendous amounts of Japanese robots and toys. We had one of the first VCRs out there, and I think I first saw one of the *Baby Cart* movies on tape. It was so different from anything I'd been exposed to. The most interesting thing to me was the baby cart itself, all the gadgets that the kid had at his disposal. It was really cool. They had this big Lay-Z-Boy chair in the studio, and they padded it with pillows under my legs and arms, so I couldn't make a move and make any noise that would affect the recording. They basically fed me the lines and I read them back. I was just a kid, so money wasn't the first thing on my mind. They told me I was going to get paid a dollar a minute, and it came out to about two hundred dollars. I was pretty happy. That was quite a lot for me back then. Plus I got all the Coca-Cola and Famous Amos cookies I could eat.

Robert Houston Sandra Bernhard dubbed numerous voices for the film and was the main female ninja. She was a struggling stand-up comedienne and a manicurist in Beverly Hills at the time. I thought she was just great. Sandra was willing to do it, but even then she knew she was headed for greater things. She said, "You've got to show up at the dubbing studio with $200 cash and you've got to put it in my back pocket without saying a word."

Jim Evans My wife and I had just split up and she was marrying her Aikido teacher, and he turned out to be a Kendo instructor as well. So I photographed his body holding two swords for the picture of Ogami as you see it on the poster. It's his body with Itto's head on it. This guy also did all the sound effects for the film. They recorded him cutting into watermelons and cantaloupes and things with David's own personal samurai sword.

Robert Houston Mark Lindsay [ex-lead singer of popular sixties rock and roll act Paul Revere and the Raiders] had a recording studio in his house and he had been dreaming of making a comeback for about ten years. So basically Michael Lewis, the composer, made nice with Mark long enough for us to spend eight weeks or so up there composing the music. They both had Ferraris. Lindsay and Lewis. That was their bond. So we would go up to the Ferrari parking lot and stay up all night doing this music. Six months after *Shogun Assassin* came out, I got a call from someone who said, "You better go to the Egyptian Theater and see this new movie." So I went to the film and New World had used our soundtrack from beginning to end on another picture. [The offending title was the 1981 T&A karate film *Firecracker*, aka *Naked Fist*.] We went to the New World business affairs guy and he said, "Yeah, okay, how much do you want?" They just did it as if it was a natural way to do business. They didn't even blink. They just started to negotiate like, "Okay, hey, we stole something so we'll pay for it."

David Weisman We had to get an R-rating. So we submitted the film to the MPAA and their carefully selected panel of housewives and Mormon businessmen saw it and said, "We can't give this film an R! My god, the children of America!" You know? So I asked, "What do I have to take out?" and they said, "Well, we're not a censorship board. You have to cut it and submit it to us." I starting wringing my hands saying, "Oh gee, gosh, what am I going to do?" So I came in a second time and they said, "It's still too violent. There's too many perforations, amputations, decapitations, too many dismemberments." So finally I went around the block two or three times. Each time, I'm doing cuts on a work print with a pre-mixed soundtrack and it's costing me money, so I said to them, "Look, you gotta give me a break somewhere, I can't afford to keep cutting the film and re-doing the soundtrack." So I started begging again, saying how much it was costing me. Now I had a theory that sound makes for sixty percent of your impression and the picture only makes for about forty percent. So I asked, "Can I show it to you without the soundtrack?" And they looked at each other and said, "Well, that's quite unusual, but we don't see anything in the rules that prohibits that. All right." So I showed it to them without the soundtrack, and they said, "That's better, but we'll have to see it one more time with the soundtrack." And I said, "So are these cuts approved?" And they said yes. So I put some footage back in and showed it to them again. Now here they are, taking notes, but at twenty-four frames per second. How fast can they write and still keep an eye on the ball? So it becomes a shell game. Back and forth. I kept slipping things back in. Finally I said, "Fuck 'em! We got the R rating certificate, who's gonna know? Put everything back in!"

Shogun Assassin

Robert Houston There was a big argument about the title. David had this Svengali figure around him named Nelson Lyon [director of the 1971 obscene phone caller comedy *The Telephone Book*]. Nelson insisted that the film had to have the word "assassin" in the title. David and I were much more enamored with title *Samurai and Son,* but at the end of the day we figured that it probably sounded too much like *Sanford and Son.*

David Weisman The convergence of the finished film, the distribution deal that I made with New World, all of these things converged with the forthcoming broadcast of the *Shogun* mini-series on TV. It was on the air virtually the same week that the film was released. There was no choice. We had to go with the word "shogun" in the title.

Robert Houston *The New York Times* said that we were not without talent, but that the film was a joke. The audiences went crazy. They fucking freaked. I mean, you're playing in grindhouses. You're on 42nd Street, you're on Hollywood Boulevard. People would leave the theater and get right back in line to see it again.

David Weisman I say probably one hundred prints were struck. Maybe it was two hundred. It could have been up to three to four hundred. I don't remember how much it ended up making. We wound up spending over $350,000. Most of it was spent on creating the soundtrack and doing it in Dolby. We could have done a lot better at the box office, but given the circumstances....

Robert Houston We had expectations of making a profit, but then again this is the film business, so we didn't see a dime beyond our advance from New World. Now, five years later, Roger Corman publishes a book called *How I Made a Hundred Movies in Hollywood and Never Lost a Dime* and Chapter Six begins, "And then I found a little gold mine called *Shogun Assassin.*" So it was a gold mine for Corman, but it was a no-profit, no-nothing for us. Not only did Corman steal the music, but he stole the profits as well.

David Weisman We considered doing another film from the *Baby Cart* series, but it never panned out. The second film is really the item, the most adaptable movie. The others get into this phantasmagoric, whacked-out, who-knows-what. You can't find a handle to put them together. It wasn't worth it to try.

Jim Evans In some ways, I sort of metaphorically saw myself as the character in the film. I'd broken up with my wife, and I had my two kids at the time, and I was raising them. I saw myself sort of like a lone samurai wandering through town, doing my illustrations, and taking the kids everywhere with me.

Gibran Evans It was something unique and pretty great. The experience rekindled in my memory when GZA/Genius from the Wu-Tang Clan sampled a lot of my voice for his *Liquid Swords* album.

Robert Houston I regret that I worked in exploitation film at all. It doesn't pay. There's just no respect. For every Sam Raimi, there are a thousand people who are talented who want to make exploitation pictures, and the only ones who get any notice are the guys who get made fun of in *American Movie*.

David Weisman Ask me what I think of it now, and I say, "Eh, it's okay. It's kind of primitive." I bought a house with it, so what can I regret? Without *Shogun Assassin,* I never would have made *The Kiss of the Spider Woman* [produced by Weisman, with a Best Actor Oscar for William Hurt]. *Ciao! Manhattan* and its aftermath was so devastating. I couldn't pull myself out of the gutter for five years. *Shogun Assassin* was how I finally did it. You know how in the movie, where Ogami Itto is lying half-dead, recovering from battle, and Daigoro brings him water? That's what *Shogun Assassin* was for me.

Robert Houston's film *Rocking the Boat* was released in 1999 to numerous festival awards and acclaim from *The New York Times.* He is currently producing documentaries.

David Weisman is developing *Girl on Fire,* a film about his experiences with Edie Sedgwick. Go to www.girlonfire.com for more information.

Jim Evans and **Gibran Evans** were recently the respective executive creative director and senior creative director of Atomicpop.com.

Mark Lindsay never got back to us to share his take on the film, but that shouldn't stop you from buying the Paul Revere & the Raiders CD re-issues from Sundazed Music (especially the 1967 pop-psych nugget *Revolution*). 東

Lone Wolf demonstrates his Roger Corman-inspired sword style.

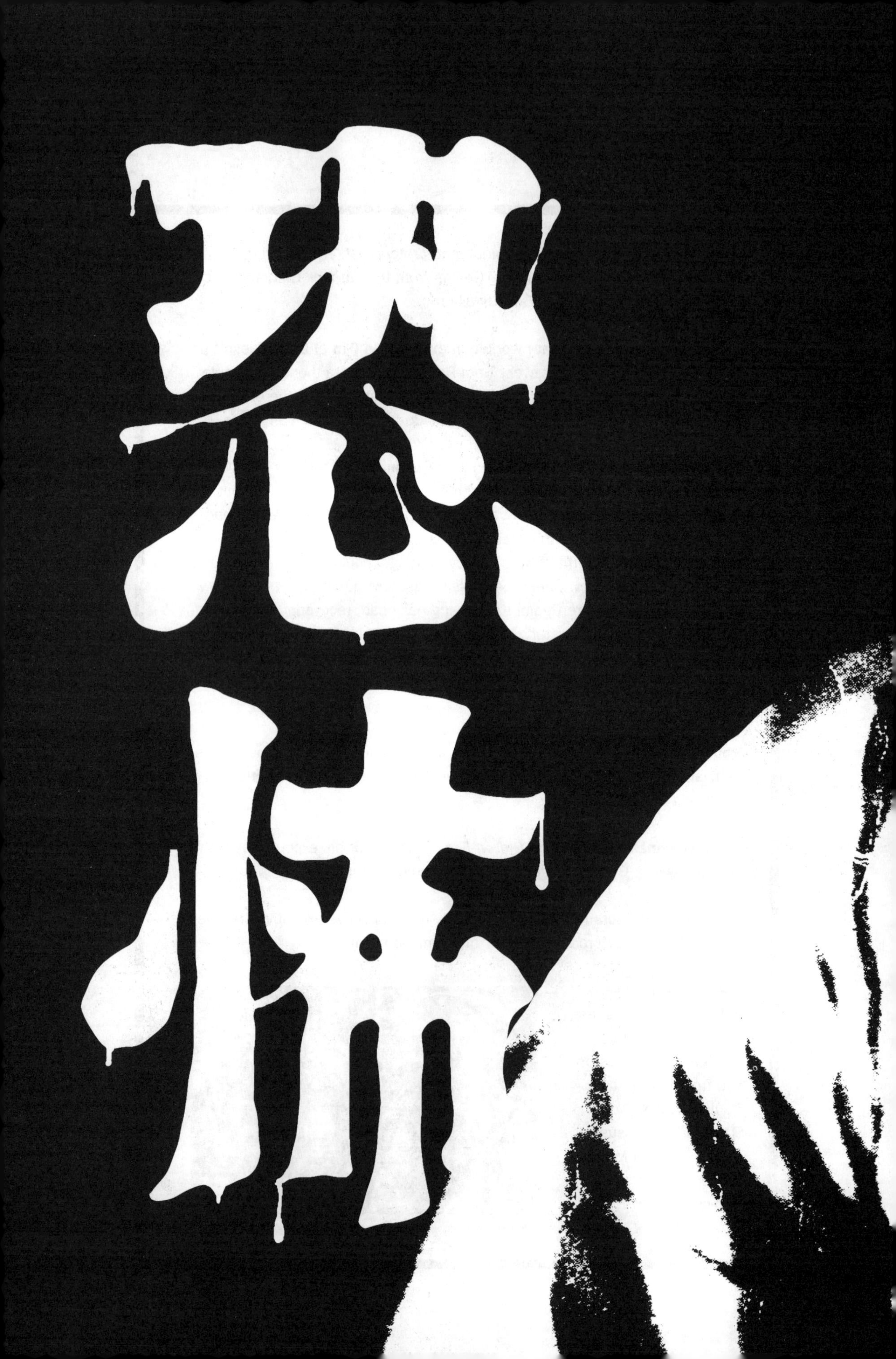
恐怖

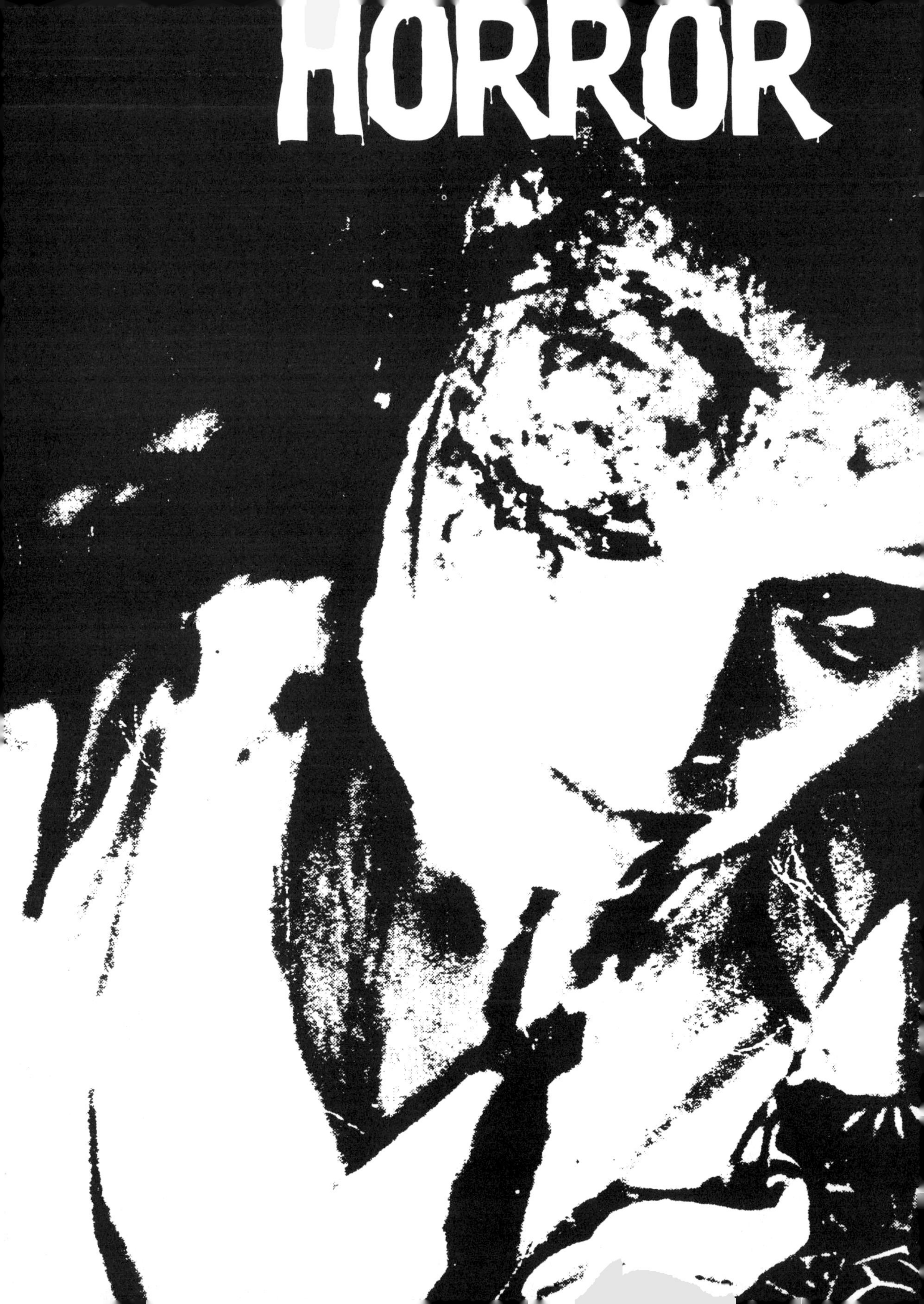
HORROR

HORROR

SO SHOCKING! MYSTERIOUS HORROR JAPAN!

According to animistic Shinto belief, everything (even old films, presumably) has a spirit. The ghosts and creatures who inhabit Japan's rich folklore continuously take on new forms. No surprise then: the versatility and sheer quantity of Japanese shockers are legion.

The scope is wide enough to embrace foreign devils like Frankenstein's Monster and Dracula and exclusive enough to keep homegrown horrors, like the water-demon Kappa and the one-eyed umbrella monster, steadily employed. (Both kinds of creatures, seen to good effect in Daiei's studios old *yokai* films, were recently revived in the 2000 period fantasy *Sakuya yokaiden*).

But if you desire a single figure that encapsulates the essence of Japanese horror, then turn to the most primal and recurrent: the vengeful woman. She is not always what she seems: sometimes, hidden behind her long, black hair, lies a pair of cat-like eyes or a terrible facial wound. From the ghost stories enacted on the Kabuki stage to the B-movies produced by the wily Mitsugu Okura in the fifties and sixties to the recent *Ring* virus currently infecting the world, this spectral female form represents the lifeblood of Japanese horror.

Yotsuya kaidan (Yotsuya Ghost Story) was first filmed in 1912 by Shozo Makino, one of the founding fathers of Japanese film. From this first glimpse of a masterless samurai named Ieumon who orchestrates the poisoning of his faithful wife Oiwa—only to receive first-rate vengeance from her disfigured spirit—sprang dozens of remakes and retellings. Director Nobuo Nakagawa delivered what is probably the definitive version in 1959 for Shin Toho. These films traditionally filled up theaters in the summertime, when audiences most welcomed the "chill" they provided. In 1998, *The Ring*, produced by Japan's current reigning house of horror, Omega Project, kicked off a new reign of terror for this evil feminine archetype via an angry spirit named Sadako.

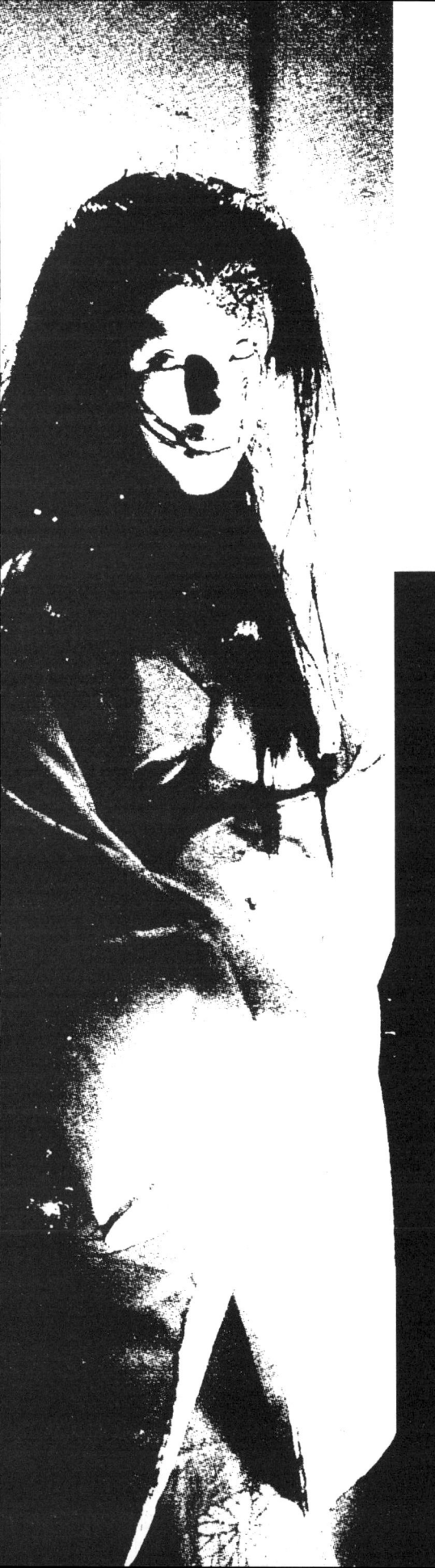

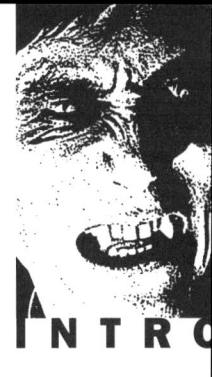

The ghost woman's male counterpart is more corporeal and less given over to karmic bonds. Sure, there's the phantom bald masseuse and monks that traditionally appear in the Yotsuya ghost story and the Shin Toho movies; yet, for the most part, the male figure of horror is very much a living being with bloodlust and depravity on the brain. He's the White-Haired Demon—as in Daiei's 1949 *Hakuhatsuki*, the first major horror film of the postwar era—or the Liquid Man menacing beautiful women—as in Toho's 1958 *The H-Man*—or he's the Body Snatcher from Hell. Gender roles in Japanese horror films play out a bit like Venus and

HORROR

Mars. Women are ghosts. Men are monsters.

Exceptions must now be made for mushroom people and mermaids who reside in manholes, whose anxieties are less about gender roles and more about loss of identity and bodily decay. Japanese horror goes beyond fear of death and grows concerned with the realities of biology, in all of its juicy infections and fetid mutations.

In 1979, Sakyo Komatsu, who authored the disaster novel *Nippon chinbotsu*, aka *Submersion of Japan*, wrote a nasty little short story called "The Savage Mouth" about a man who seeks to inspire madness in others by eating himself and replacing his missing body parts with mechanical bits. It anticipated the sci-fi Japanese splatterpunk films *Tetsuo: The Iron Man* and *Pinocchio 964*.

Flat-out mayhem and *Grotesque Perverse Slaughter* speak for themselves and rarely more eloquently than in the independently produced straight-to-video films that prospered in the late eighties and nineties. The faux snuff and low-budget ritual splatter of the *Guinea Pig* series allude to some traumatized spirit of the times that was briefly allowed an autonomous zone in Japanese pop culture. In truth, it was simply the emerging *otaku* culture, looking for new extremes to explore and hoard.

The gag reflex eventually burned itself out. In the wake of *The Ring*'s blockbuster success across Asia, the *shinrei mono*, or "spirit story," which first took over Japanese TV in the seventies when foreign films like *The Omen* and *The Exorcist* dominated the cinemas, returned in a big way. *Shinrei mono* is a more suggestion-based, mystery-based, sometimes even reality-based, form of Japanese horror whose shocks leave behind both lingering chills and enormous profits.

The attack plan has been expansive and multimedia. Corporations closely collaborate to make sure that new horror films arrive on the backs of novelizations, serialized TV dramas, and cell phone services that dispense scary stories for a price. But the disappointing returns that greeted Omega Project's 2000 film *Another Heaven* (conceived as a feature film, TV drama, video game, and amusement-park attraction) spelled, for some, the beginning of a decline.

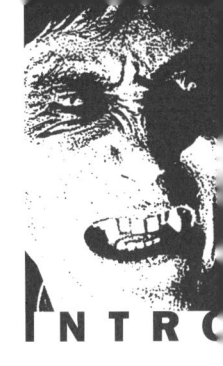

Fear has only now begun a retreat from the status of mass social activity, returning to the fringes of the girls' comic magazines, such as the phonebook-thick monthly *Kyofu no kaira* (The Joy of Horror), and the less costly straight-to-video market where post-*Ring* works like *Juon* can still find a captive audience.

Manga artist Junji Ito, whose manga *Tomie* and *Uzumaki* have both been adapted to the screen with success, believes that a horror boom grips Japan every ten years or so. He should know. Ito's titular character in Tomie is a young girl who is both an eternal predator and victim. And this beautiful creature, her steely eyes framed by long black tresses, simply cannot, will not, stay dead for long. 東

Claws of Iron
Tetsu no tsume

1951, Daiei
Director Nobuo Adachi
Cast Joji Oka, Maria Sono

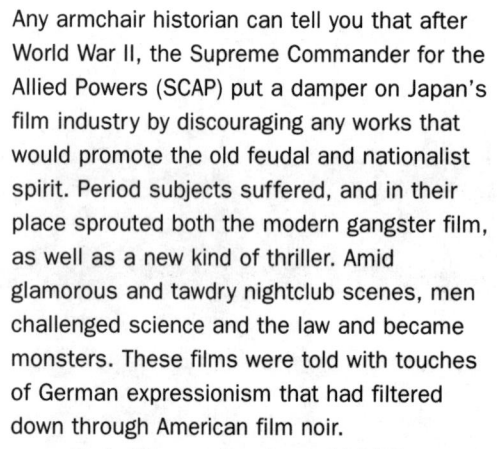

Any armchair historian can tell you that after World War II, the Supreme Commander for the Allied Powers (SCAP) put a damper on Japan's film industry by discouraging any works that would promote the old feudal and nationalist spirit. Period subjects suffered, and in their place sprouted both the modern gangster film, as well as a new kind of thriller. Amid glamorous and tawdry nightclub scenes, men challenged science and the law and became monsters. These films were told with touches of German expressionism that had filtered down through American film noir.

During the waning days of SCAP's influence, Daiei developed a cozy line of such shockers, among them *Hakuhatsuki* (White Haired Demon), *Niji otoko* (Rainbow Man), and *Toumei ningen arawaru* (The Invisible Man Appears), all of them from 1949. The trendsetting formula was a low-budget concoction of crime, women's kneecaps, and monster-on-the-loose mayhem. Toho would do slightly more upscale versions of these films in their "mutant" series including *The H-Man* and *The Human Vapor*, while Shin Toho would take the low road.

Directed by Nobuo Adachi (also in the chair for *The Invisible Man Appears*), *Claws of Iron* is charmingly little more than cabaret acts strung together by the memorable bits from *Jekyll and Hyde*, *Murders in the Rue Morgue*, and *King Kong*.

A series of gruesome murders leads a detective to the Melody nightclub and to vampish ingenue Yukie (Maria Sono). Many of her lovers are among the victims, and the chief suspect becomes ex-husband Tashiro (Joji Oka, who also wrote the film's scenario under a pseudonym). Seems while stationed in the South Pacific during the war, Tashiro was bitten by an unconvincing man in a gorilla suit. Since then, whenever he gets "strong stimulation," he transforms into a toothy, flat-nosed gorilla man, a fact which bodes ill for his new image as a man of the cloth.

After an overdose of "strong stimulation," Tashiro goes ape and grabs a showgirl. But a Konglike climb to the rooftops leads to his demise. His dead, double-exposed spirit walks across the sinful Ginza skyline to a church and a proper Christian burial. Amen!

Pulpy and permissive—at one point, the narrative stops so a scientist can make a woman's clothes disappear with the aid of an electrical machine—*Claws of Iron* proves that there was much more going on at Daiei than Kurosawa's *Rashomon*, which won accolades at the Venice Film Festival and the Academy Awards in 1951, the same year *Claws of Iron* struck.

☞ **Import only**

REVIEW

天然色
新東宝の怪談決定版
東海道四谷怪談

The Ghost of Yotsuya

Tokaido Yotsuya kaidan

1959, Shin Toho
Director Nobuo Nakagawa
Cast Shigeru Amachi, Kazuko Wakasugi, Syuntaro Emi

By the late fifties, there were already plenty of film versions of Nanboku Tsuruya's kabuki tale *Tokaido Yotsuya kaidan*. And there would be even more periodic retellings of this popular story in the decades to come.

And yet Nobuo Nagakawa's 1959 version has emerged from the pack, not only as the definitive film version of the story, but also as one of the greatest Japanese horror movies ever made.

The film begins in the guise of a stage play. A curtain is lifted, revealing a traditional seated storyteller. Her creepy incantation lays down the thematic foundation for what follows: "How can you kill one who is yours body and soul? O, the fury of a woman maddened is truly like unto the greatest horror there is."

As the tale proper kicks in, Nakagawa favors theatrical mannerisms not too far removed from the early silent films that he began his career with. Long takes and stagelike framing convey the story of masterless samurai Ieumon (played by Nakagawa's trademark actor Shigeru Amachi), who, egged on by his toady Naosuke, tries to murder his way to the top of the feudal-era social ladder. With a more prosperous bride waiting in the wings, Ieumon is even willing to orchestrate the poisoning and murder of his own dutiful wife-with-child Iwa.

However, once Iwa is both horribly deformed and killed, she returns in spectral form to vengefully haunt Ieumon from beyond the grave. The tempo of the film, the style, and the bloodshed begins to escalate in earnest.

By the end, as the tormented Ieumon begs for forgiveness, surreal imagery unbound by time and space invades the once formal constraints. A battered, bloody Iwa, her body dumped in a swamp, floats on the ceiling. The swamp at dusk appears impossibly inside an interior room. A moaning mosquito net descends on Ieumon like a monstrous womb out to reclaim him.

In effect, Nakagawa has taken the traditional *Yotsuya kaidan* and the Japanese horror film, with its origins in kabuki and silent film, into a new cinematic realm. From here on out, anything was possible and Nakagawa would prove it by descending into his next masterpiece, *Jigoku* (1960)—hell itself.

☞ **Available subbed on DVD from Beam Entertainment**

☞ **More: NOBUO NAKAGAWA p. 87**

Attack of the Mushroom People
Matango

1963, Toho
Director Ishiro Honda
Cast Akira Kubo, Kenji Sahara, Yoshio Tsuchiya, Kumi Mizuno

A lethal fungi pox on whomever it was at American International Pictures TV who retitled the elegant sounding *Matango* into *Attack of the Mushroom People*. This is probably the single best pure horror film to ever emerge from Toho studios, and its "hell is other people," drug-induced horror remains a trip even today. One might care to compare and contrast with *Attack of the Giant Leeches*, AIP's homegrown, from 1960.

Seven folks—five men and two women, one a virgin pure, the other a dishy nightclub chanteuse played by Kumi Mizuno—are stranded on a foggy island where humankind's innate nature to bitch, fight, and lust after each other takes over. Food is scarce, except for a surplus of "matango," a mind-altering psychedelic mushroom with a *very* bitter aftertaste. Observed from afar by strange creatures, the seven succumb one after the other to the great taste of the 'shroom while losing their humanity in the process…which, considering all the nastiness come before, maybe isn't such a bad thing after all.

Inspired by William Hope Hodgson's 1907 short story "A Voice in the Night," *Matango* has an ambitious yet taut screenplay by Takeshi Kimura (aka Kaoru Mabuchi), Toho's resident dour pessimist. There's a hell of a lot more here than merely "You are what you eat" or even "Just say no." Instead, like a very black episode of *Gilligan's Island*, *Matango* strips down the species to the ugly bits: reckless obsession, troubles with women, uncontrollable urges, temptation, and terrible existential isolation. Director Honda sets the whole film in a mossy, atmospheric dreamscape overdosed on EastmanColor.

Dope had been a fixture in Japanese fantasy films before. Daiei's *Niji otoko* (Rainbow Man), with effects by *Matango*'s Eiji Tsuburaya, from 1949 featured a killer who gave his victims a taste of mescaline. And even Honda's *King Kong vs. Godzilla* (also 1963) showed the great ape nodding out on a narcotic concoction. But *Matango* offers the cruelest fix of all. By all rights, nature's divine fruit should put its user in touch with the gods. Instead, the magik mushroom here only gives the user a tawdry kaleidoscopic trip (a tour of the Ginza complete with dancing girls) and corruption of the body.

Now that's really scary.

☞ **Available dubbed on video**

REVIEW

Goke, Body Snatcher from Hell
Kyuketsuki Gokemidoro (Vampire Gokemidoro), aka Body Snatcher from Hell

1968, Shochiku
Director Hajime Sato
Cast Teruo Yoshida, Hideo Ko, Cathy Horlan

1968: terrorism, political assassinations, and bird suicides are on the rise. Four of our feathered friends have just smashed themselves to death against the windows of a jet plane, a very bad omen for the already troubled passengers who soon endure, in fantastically short order, a bomb threat, a hijacking, a UFO sighting, and a plane crash in the middle of nowhere.

The survivors—among them shady politicians, greedy industrialists, mad bombers, psychiatrists, and weepy Vietnam war widows—hardly seem to deserve the life they cling to. They become easy pickings for a white-glove-wearing assassin (played by sickly looking chanson singer Hideo Ko), who soon has his head split open and penetrated by a sluglike alien. The alien proceeds not only to suck blood in the approved Dracula manner but also plans to use these turbulent times as a pretext to launch an invasion of our dumb planet.

With uncredited sci-fi inspiration from Robert Heinlein's novel *The Puppet Masters*, *Goke* nearly succumbs to conniption fits, flailing around screaming the sky is falling via anti-war speeches and stock-footage mushroom clouds. This earnestness constantly brings forth preposterous situations and frenzied performances made even more disturbing by director Sato's sickening color scheme and (depending on which *Goke* you grok) the bizzaro-world English dubbing.

Marginally successful as a real-world-relevant anti-everything tract, *Goke,* perhaps even more than the similarly themed *Matango,* nails down an amazing simulation of a headline-driven, anxiety-ridden bad dream, complete with no-exit ending.

Prior to *Goke*, director Sato was a veteran of numerous mystery-horror TV shows. His feature films, which benefit from lightning-fast pacing and a generous show-all sensibility, include a pair of pre-*Street Fighter* Sonny Chiba vehicles, 1966's *Ogon Bat* (Golden Bat), based on the old Japanese pulp character created by Takeo Nagamatsu, and *Kaitei dai senso* (aka *Terror beneath the Sea*, aka *Water Cyborg*, co-starring Peggy Neal, who was the spaced-out white chick in Shochiku's *X from Outer Space*).

The striking makeup and special effects were created in cooperation with P Productions of TV's *Space Giants* and *Spectreman* fame. Their realistic scene of a shampoolike substance oozing out of a human head is a testament to the talent at work. Co-screenwriter Kumi Kobayashi would later become an award-winning mystery novelist, and a cryptic anagram graces the movie's title. *Gokemidoro* is a composite of three words: *Go* for Golgotha (where Christ was crucified—course you *Golgo 13* fans knew that already), *kemi* for chemical, and *doro* for android. Proof that, like a certain soft drink that shall remain nameless, things go better with Goke!

☞ **Available dubbed on video**

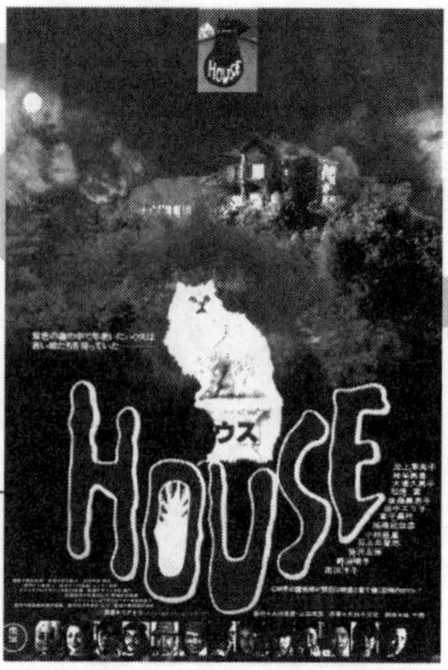
HOUSE

House
House

1977, Toho
Director Nobuhiko Obayashi
Cast Kimiko Ikegami, Ai Matsubara, Enko Tanaka

Nobuhiko Obayashi's *House* is one of the most brilliant, daring, irritating, and downright crazy Japanese horror films of all time. *House* is William Castle's *House on Haunted Hill* rebuilt as a lysergic-laced tempest of teen spirit. *House* is *Beetlejuice* made ten times better and many years earlier. *House* continues to fascinate because it contains multitudes.

Seven bubbly schoolgirls, led by Oshare (Kimiko Ikegami), who is mourning her mother's death and her father's remarriage, go to the countryside to visit an infirm aunt. While they spend the night at the creepy old woman's house, supernatural forces summarily begin to dispatch the girls one by one. Some are maniacally consumed by the house itself, while our heroine succumbs to possession by her dead mother's spirit.

It's a grim fairy tale of sexual awakening, fleshed out by horrors conceived by Obayashi's six-year-old daughter. A simple synopsis cannot begin to do justice. Wild visual imagination and a wicked sense of humor erupt from every frame, and Obayashi directs like a lunatic intoxicated with the possibilities of film, as *House* alternately veers from the look of a crass TV commercial to a slick Dario Argento movie.

Originally, all Toho Studios asked of the first-time feature-film director (who previously had helmed only commercials) was to deliver a youth film, preferably one with a hot cast and strong soundtrack possibilities. While Obayashi managed that, his ulterior motive was to make a movie that would make a new generation fall in love with Japanese film. Thus, *House* is filled with in-jokes and cameos alluding to the popular *Truck Yaro* and *Tora-san* series. The often slapdash special effects, overseen by the director, have an inspirational DIY quality.

The irrational kitchen-sink approach makes *House* both funny and scary, and there's also great deal of lyricism, some of it provided by the sugar-pop band Godiego.

Obayashi went on to become one of Japan's most prolific filmmakers, putting out titles like 1982's *Tenkosei*, 1987's Kazuo Umezu manga-inspired *Drifting Classroom*, 1989's *Beijing Watermelon*, and 1998's *Sada* (yet another version of the Sada Abe story, ala *In the Realm of the Senses*). To his credit, Obayashi's films remain, very much like his first one, a love-it or hate-it proposal. All the more reason to call *House* home.

☞ **Import only**

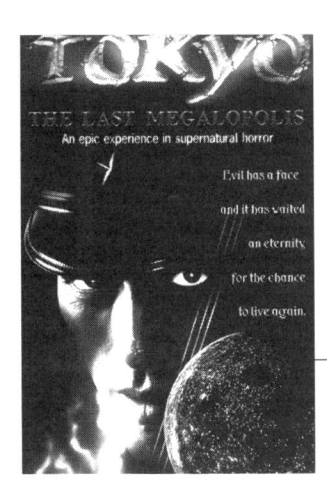

REVIEW

TOKYO
THE LAST MEGALOPOLIS
An epic experience in supernatural horror
Evil has a face
and it has waited
an eternity
for the chance
to live again.

Tokyo: The Last Megalopolis

Teito monogatari (Imperial Capital Saga)

1988, EXE Co./Toho
Director Akio Jissoji
Cast Kyusaku Shimada, Shintaro Katsu

The tail end of the bloated bubble-economy eighties got precisely the sort of scary movie it deserved in *Tokyo: The Last Megalopolis*, a big-budget, top-heavy mega-production that's more *nouveau riche* spectacle than honest horror film.

Beginning at the dawn of the 20th century, warring factions of religious leaders, psychics, and city planners (among them a cigar-smoking Shintaro Katsu, aka Zatoichi) struggle to guide the destiny of Tokyo to either modern utopia or mass graveyard. Dressed in an old-fashioned military uniform, black magician Kato (Kyusaku Shimada, also seen in the salaryman comedy *Made in Japan*) is the gargoyle-faced bogeyman, orchestrating events that lead to the great Kanto earthquake of 1922. The rush to modernization that follows is nearly an Occult Olympiad with events in *feng shui*, demonology, ancestor possession, robotics, and sociology.

Based on the Nihon SF Taisho Award-winning novel by Hiroshi Aramata, and later adapted into the anime *Doomed Megalopolis*, the screenplay of *Last Megalopolis* was written by Kaizo Hayashi, the director of *The Most Terrible Time in My Life*. Director Akio Jissoji was a star of the sixties avant-garde cinema who directed a number of films for the Art Theater Guild (ATG) as well as numerous superhero TV shows, including *Silver Mask* and *Ultraman*.

Even in the latter, Jissoji was an incredible stylist, favoring odd angles and expressionist lighting. Yet the ambitious *Megalopolis* has a visual sheen and a love affair with special effects that go against Jissoji's atmospheric strengths. There's so much going on visually: opticals, miniatures, stop-motion animation, hand puppets, even a non sequitur whatz-it designed by H.R. Giger (as in *Poltergeist II*). Perhaps partially because such excess fit the times, *Last Megalopolis* was an enormous hit and spawned two sequels.

Overcooked, but still far from a bust, *Last Megalopolis* is most fascinating when offering a subtext about the birth of modern Tokyo, and the latent psychic landscapes of cities. What lingers in the imagination afterwards is not so much the ghoulies and admittedly impressive FX, but rather the vision of Tokyo as a city of continual growth and destruction that feasts on the lives of its citizens.

☞ **Available subbed on VHS from ADV Films**

DOUBLE FEATURE
Mermaid in a Manhole
ANDROID OF NOTRE DAME

Mermaid in a Manhole

The Guinea Pig 4—Manhole no naka no ningyo

1991, JHV
Director Hideshi Hino
Cast Shigeru Saiki, Tsuyoshi Toshishige

Decay, disease, and death dominate the grotesque world of Hideshi Hino, the manga artist best known in the West for his comics *Panorama of Hell* and *Hell Baby* (both published in English by Blast Books). His considerable body of work, which has appeared in both underground publications like *Garo* and mainstream girl's manga, exhibits an obsession with psychosis, pestilence, and slow death. That Hino is able to bring a queasy poetry, and a cathartic power, to his vision is a testimony to his odd talents—talents that also include directing a couple of entries in the notorious straight-to-video *Guinea Pig* series.

The second film in the series, which credits no director, was mistaken for an actual filmed murder by gullible actor Charlie Sheen and made headlines when seized by customs in the UK. By contrast, *Guinea Pig 4—Mermaid in a Manhole* is no mock snuff film, rather it's a love story!

Morose painter Hayashi (Shigeru Saiki) is an artist who paints pictures of objects he finds in the sewer. One day, he stumbles upon a beautiful mermaid (Tsuyoshi Toshishige) with a nasty looking wound on her stomach. Hayashi takes her to his apartment and puts her in his bathtub, painting her portrait as she continues to fester. At one point, live worms erupt from her body, as do multicolored fluids, which she begs the terrified, but committed, Hayashi to use as paint. He does until the bitter end.

Mermaid in a Manhole's power comes from its depiction of the literal, painful decay of a relationship. This is a messy, emotional affair in all respects. Rather than an impressive manga come to life, Hino's shot-on-video methods are crude and most of the budget seems to have gone into creating the gourmet grue.

And the message? What truths can Hino hope to offer in his muck-encrusted metaphors? Perhaps sewers can inspire art, and great love can be a feast for a great number of worms.

☞ **Available on video from Tokyo Shock**

The Ring
The Ring

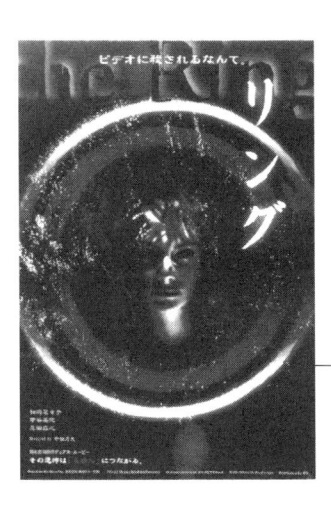

1998, Omega Project
Director Hideo Nakata
Cast Nanako Matsushima, Hiroyuki Sanada

For the entirety of its first half, *The Ring* is one of the greatest horror movies ever made, in the company of *The Exorcist, Rosemary's Baby, The Haunting*. A videotape is on the loose, its popularity slowly spreading throughout Japan. Whoever watches will mysteriously drop dead one week later. Quite a tasty concept from original *Ring* novelist Koji Suzuki, weaving together the creepy strands of snuff movie, urban myth, and Bloody Mary pajama-party game.

When intrepid TV reporter Reiko (TV drama idol Nanako Matsushima) and her ex-husband Ryuji (Hiroyuki "Duke" Sanada, man was he ever great in *Message from Space*) track down a copy, they sit down and make you watch it too. It's like that wonderful trick that Terence Fisher used in that old Hammer movie *The Devil Rides Out*. Whenever something horrible happens, Christopher Lee begs you not to look at what's happening on the screen: it'll be the death of you. But you can't help it.

Ring's haunted tape is a collection of disassociated visual clues and lost-and-found images. There's a water well somewhere. There's someone with a white cloth over their head. There are words that float by themselves on the surface of a newspaper. There's a woman looking in a mirror. Nothing so odd about these things in and of themselves, but the brain can't tie them together in any sort of coherent fashion. And of course it dearly wants to. And of course merely watching all of this will make you drop dead seven fateful days later.

Having both been cursed and now needing a cure, Duke and Reiko start to get down to the nitty-gritty. From there *Ring* becomes a mystery film, the protagonists trying to bring order to the unexplainable. They uncover the sad story of an angry girl named Sadako and her very bad father, a doctor named Ikuma. The possibilities, so endless and nameless when first introduced in the form of the video, begin to shrink.

Amazing, then, that interest isn't lost. The saga of Ryuji and Reiko, a divorced couple, has plenty of drama to run on, and the burgeoning Sadako mythology has its own rewards. It's fascinating to see the traditional ghost story retransmitted through video signals and television screens. But, to its detriment, the movie assumes a working knowledge of things that would only be apparent to someone who's read the novel.

But forget for a while the details. Relish *Ring*'s primal scene of terror, a point of no return, a lidless eye from where modern Japanese horror has sprung.

Available subbed on VHS and DVD from Tartan Video (UK)

Uzumaki
Uzumaki (Spiral)

2000, Omega Project
Director Higuchinsky
Cast Eriko Hatsune, Ren Osugi, Fhi Fan

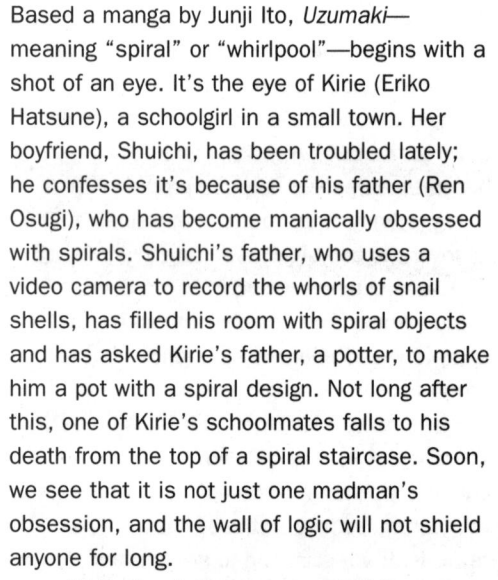

Based a manga by Junji Ito, *Uzumaki*—meaning "spiral" or "whirlpool"—begins with a shot of an eye. It's the eye of Kirie (Eriko Hatsune), a schoolgirl in a small town. Her boyfriend, Shuichi, has been troubled lately; he confesses it's because of his father (Ren Osugi), who has become maniacally obsessed with spirals. Shuichi's father, who uses a video camera to record the whorls of snail shells, has filled his room with spiral objects and has asked Kirie's father, a potter, to make him a pot with a spiral design. Not long after this, one of Kirie's schoolmates falls to his death from the top of a spiral staircase. Soon, we see that it is not just one madman's obsession, and the wall of logic will not shield anyone for long.

While the "when spirals attack" concept may sound fairly abstract, *Uzumaki* is actually one of the most dynamically rendered horror movies of recent years. Higuchinsky's directorial technique is self-consciously artistic; the film quickly creeps forward with disorienting transitions and camera movements, with gory shocks hammered home by freeze-frames, rewinds, and fast-forwards. Even computer graphics are used effectively to subtly disfigure the real world. Lurking in the corners of many shots, a spiraling shape observes the action like a dead eye.

The small town is a memorable environment, gloomy and melancholy, with gray and green tones dominating the twisting streets and pouring rain. The idea that there is a monstrous pattern to the world, that nature itself is evil, recalls works like H.P. Lovecraft's "The Colour Out of Space." For a horror film, a genre where most filmmakers rush to explain irrational surprises, this conceit makes for perfect cover.

Admittedly, *Uzumaki* is not a completely serious endeavor. The pseudo-comedic aspects aren't limited to the often exaggerated performances. Most of the spiral manifestations are effective, but some are laughably literal. Perhaps the film's best attribute is the ease with which it switches gears from whimsical "Did you see that?" moments to gory shocks such as a schoolmate's brains spattered and blood pumping onto the floor. Here, *Uzumaki* manages a graceful navigation, rather than a downward spiral. (Jason Thompson)

☞ **Available from Tidepoint Pictures/Viz Films**

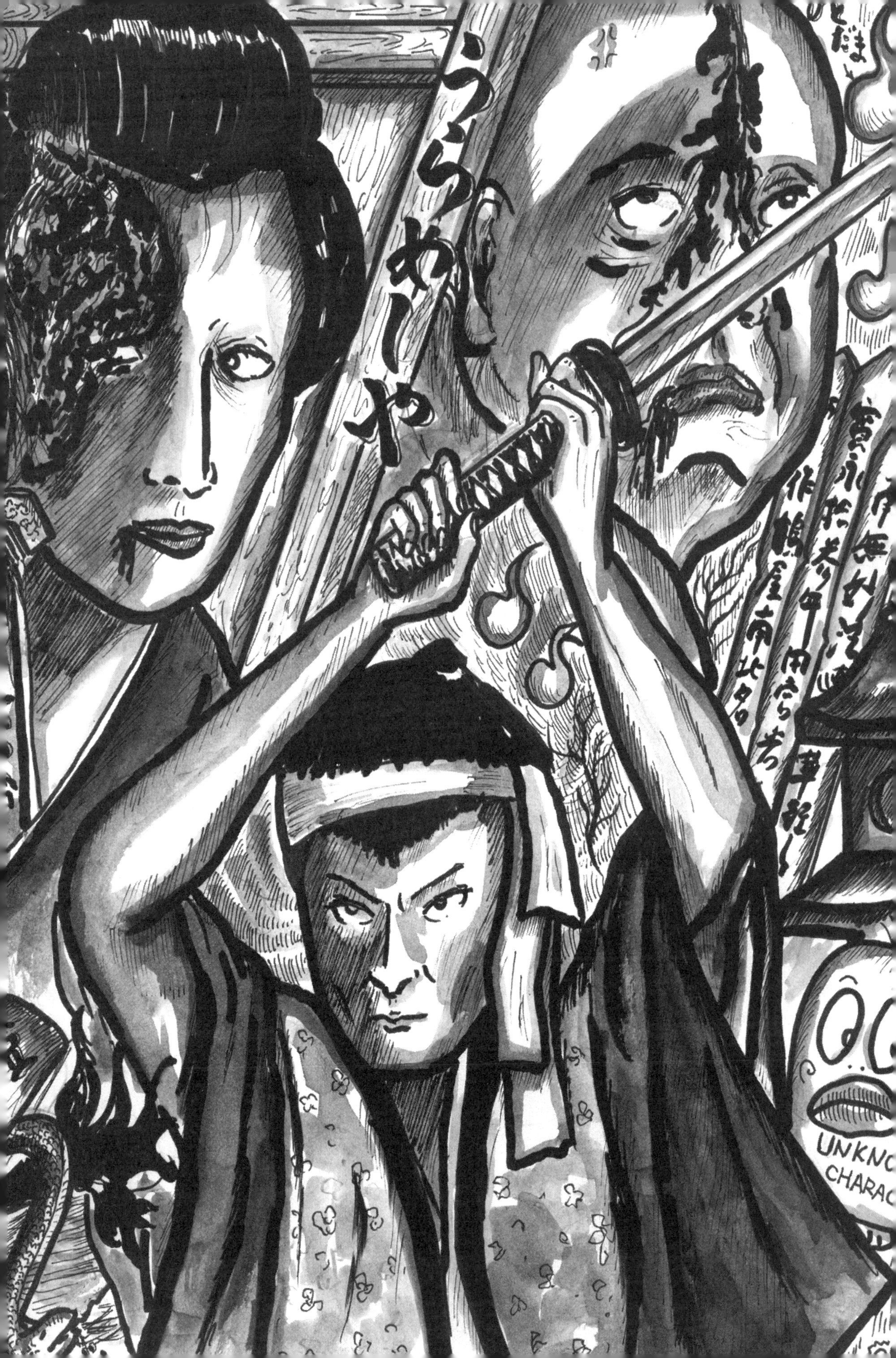
うらめしや

HORROR

Mitsugu Okura
Mogul

大蔵貢

Mitsugu Okura was the pioneer of the low-budget Japanese exploitation movie. In many ways, Okura's style of showmanship was kindred to that of savvy American filmmakers and producers like Herschell Gordon Lewis and David F. Friedman, who spent their careers in search of a fast buck via minimal investments and maximum returns. Also, like his contemporaries across the water, Okura productions were not limited to one genre. He would show anything that he could get away with: adults-only films, right-wing propaganda, "shocking" sex education movies, erotic thrillers, utilizing recycled footage at every opportunity. But at the end of the day, Okura's keepers were his horror films.

Okura's lowbrow mix of scares and sexploitation may have pushed the boundaries of what was acceptable, but at least two films he produced, 1959's *Tokaido Yotsuya kaidan* (Tokaido Yotsuya Ghost Story, aka *The Ghost of Yotsuya*) and 1960's *Jigoku* (Hell), have emerged as incontestable classics.

Okura kicked off his illustrious showbiz career as the ringmaster and operator of a traveling carnival. He also worked as a *benshi*, or silent film narrator, which gave him practical experience on how to work an audience. Following World War II, he began opening movie theaters in red light districts and other disreputable areas of town. (Our beloved Shinjuku Showakan was once an Okura-owned theater.) By the 1950s, the former carnival barker had his very own theater chain.

At first, Okura was hesitant to get involved in the high risk business of film production, but managing some 2,000 screens meant that he was constantly in need of more and more product.

Enter Shin Toho (New Toho), which was an independent studio formed by actors and directors who had left Toho studio in 1947 after a long, bitter struggle over union affiliations and labor policies. The new company had begun as a proud endeavor, employing top stars and leading directors. The problem was, none of their films had been commercial hits.

In 1956, Okura moved in and took control of the fledgling studio, leading Shin Toho to their first, and last, massive hit in 1957: *Meiji Tenno to nichiro dai senso* (The Meiji Emperor and the Russo-Japanese War). Okura milked postwar feelings of patriotism and the desire to see a strong military (not to mention a god-emperor) in action again.

More Emperor movies followed in a steady stream. But when a 1958 staging of the Sino-Japanese War failed to do the big business of its predecessors, Okura decided to switch exclusively to a no-fuss policy, stated as "fast, cheap, and exciting."

A year earlier in 1957, Okura had produced the pioneering erotic-grotesque film *Kenpei to barabara shi bijin* (The Military Policeman and the Dismembered Beauty), and it proved to be the model for the sex-and-spook films that followed.

Females swam amok in 1959's *Kaidan ama yurei* (Woman Diver Ghost Story) in which Kazuko Wakasugi, also featured in *Tokaido Yotsuya kaidan*, played an oyster-diving phantom who haunted the modern world.

Directed by Kyotaro Namiki, 1960's *Hanayome kyuketsuki* (Vampire Bride) was the sensational tale of a beautiful girl named Fujiko out to get revenge on the jealous women who pushed her off a cliff and disfigured her. After a mysterious rite involving vampire bats, overseen by her grandmother, Junko could transform into a wild, hairy beast hungry for the blood of revenge.

The apocryphal story goes that lead actress Junko Ikeuchi (later to costar with Toshiro Mifune in 1970's *Band of Assassins*) was so ashamed of her involvement with Okura and *Hanayome kyuketsuki* that when she finally became a major star, she bought up all the film prints she could find and had them destroyed. One has to wonder why Ikeuchi didn't also acquire the Superman-inspired *Super Giant* films, produced by Okura and directed by future Toei troublemaker Teruo Ishii, in which she also routinely appeared.

Perhaps even more important than the films was Shin Toho's function in breaking in new talent. Actors like Bunta Sugawara and Tetsuro Tanba got their first big breaks with Okura, as did director Teruo Ishii.

And while many of the Okura-produced Shin Toho films had a whiff of creative and fiscal impoverishment about them, the films of director Nobuo Nakagawa, such as *Borei kaibyo yashiki* (House of the Ghost Cat, 1958), and *Onna kyuketsuki* (Female Vampire, 1959) always seemed to have an extra touch of class to them. Cinematographer Tadashi Nishimoto, who would later lens the Bruce Lee film *Return of the Dragon*, worked closely with Nakagawa to create the ultimate Shin Toho achievements in terror: *Tokaido Yotsuya kaidan* and *Jigoku*.

Sadly, the elaborate *Jigoku* proved to be a costly box office failure for Shin Toho. This, coupled with a disastrous fire at the studio, proved to be devastating blows. Okura left the company to fend for itself in late 1960. The end of his tenure symbolized the end of an era in Japanese film. A new generation, split into TV and the Oshima-led New Wave, would soon sweep in. And by 1961, Shin Toho was exclusively producing pink films.

Meanwhile, Okura started a new film outfit of his own, humbly known as Okura Eiga (Okura Films), which would aggressively distribute foreign films as well as produce original titles.

Okura brought such treasures as Roger Corman's Edgar Allan Poe adaptations and Jess Franco's *Awful Dr. Orloff* (Okura's retitling: "The Man Who Peels the Skin Off of Beautiful Women") to Japan for the very first time. But he also had a penchant for drastically cutting his acquisitions, retitling them to play up an often nonexistent "sexy" angle, repackaging them into anthology formats (under his "World Ghost Story Collection" banner), and sometimes even misleadingly promoting a single feature as a double-feature!

Okura Eiga's in-house productions were a truly motley lot. Their first big release, yet another patriotic flagwaver, tanked at the box office, leaving the newly minted company

in debt almost as soon as it had begun. Minus the studio facilities and experienced staff that Shin Toho provided, Okura Eiga horror movies had the rough texture of porn movies (and they made those too, the first being 1963's *Sex Market*).

This feeling is compounded by the use of amateur nonactors which often included the womanizing Okura's latest mistress. Quality mattered little, and perhaps art was imitating life. Films like *Kaidan zankoku yurei* (Cruel Phantom Ghost Story), *Kaidan ijin yurei* (Foreign Phantom Ghost Story), and *Kaidan barabara yurei* (Dismembered Phantom Ghost Story) were as thoroughly cheap and disreputable as the Okura-owned theaters that they were made to screen in.

When Okura finally retired from the movie business in the mid-sixties, he did so as a wealthy man. The combined real estate value of Okura Eiga and his theater chain was enormous. Okura also owned Fuji Eiga, a distributor of hardcore foreign films, which was acquired by Shochiku.

While Okura himself passed on in 1978, Okura Eiga still exists as one of Japan's leading producers of adult videos. Shin Toho too, once a noble worker-owned studio until they crossed paths with Okura, still exists. *Train of Molesters* and *Fellatio Nurse* are the names of some recent straight-to-video releases.

Meanwhile, vintage Okura productions are finding a new home on DVD thanks to a handful of Japanese companies such as Eclipse Films and Super Premium Collection.

Although removed from the original sideshow atmosphere of the seedy grindhouse from which they sprang, Mitsugu Okura's "fast, cheap, and exciting" aesthetic now lives on in digital perpetuity. 東

1957's *Ghost Story—Seven Wonders of Honsho*, a 55-minute epic from Shin Toho.

SHINTOHO
怪談本所七不思議
血みどろの首が笑う
妖気に狂う七つの怪

Nobuo Nakagawa
Director

中川信夫

Director Nobuo Nakagawa's influence on the development of Japanese horror films is so enormous it's scary. With his pair of back-to-back masterworks *Tokaido Yotsuya kaidan* (1959) and *Jigoku* (1960), Nakagawa bridged the gap between the old fashioned ghost films of the past and a new age that warranted more graphic shocks. His feverish depictions of a universe strictly governed by vengeance and karmic bonds belied a quiet hardworking man who was seldom seen without a hiking hat and wooden *geta* shoes.

Nobuo Nakagawa was born in Kyoto on April 18th, 1905 and grew up interested in literature and cinema. In 1929, he joined Makino Studios as an assistant director. Nakagawa made his directorial debut in 1934 with the silent film *Yumiya hachimanken* (Bow and Arrow Yumiya Sword) for Utaemon Ichikawa Productions. Soon he moved to Toho where he directed numerous entries of the popular comedic *Enoken* series.

After serving in Shanghai at the tail end of World War II, Nakagawa found himself at then-prestigious Shin Toho studios, where among his peers were Akira Kurosawa and Kenji Mizoguchi. But beginning with the arrival of legendary exploitation mogul Mitsugu Okura in 1956, Shin Toho began the dubious production of thrillers, titillating fare, right-wing war films, and horror movies.

Even with the notoriously cheap Okura acting as producer, Nakagawa somehow during this period directed the supernatural titles he is best known for. These include 1957's *Kaidan kasanegafuchi* (later remade by Nakagawa as a 1971 TV movie), 1958's *Kenpei to yurei* (The Military Policeman and the Ghost), and 1959's *Onna kyuketsuki* (Vampire Woman).

Beginning with 1958's *Borei kaibyo yashiki* (Mansion of the Ghost Cat), a story about an ancient evil invading the modern world told in black and white with color temporal shifts, Nakagawa hit an artistic peak. And yet, in the rush to the pair that followed, *Tokaido Yotsuya kaidan* and *Jigoku*, it mustn't be forgotten that he didn't create his films alone. The contributions of director of photography Tadashi Nishimoto (who later moved to Hong Kong to influence a whole generation of cinematographers) on *Yotsuya kaidan* and art director Haruyasu Kurosawa on both *Yotsuya* and *Jigoku* were immense.

After leaving Shin Toho for Toei studios in 1962, Nakagawa began directing non-supernatural titles. He returned to horror for 1968's *Kaidan hebi onna* (Snake Woman Ghost Story) and spent the seventies directing for television, work which included episodes of the proto-*Charlie's Angels* show *Playgirl*, *Ultraman* shows, and numerous ghost story TV movies.

In 1982, Nakagawa delivered what would be his final film, *Kaidan—Ikiteiru Koheiji* (Ghost Story—Koheji Lives Again).

He died in 1984, having directed some 98 films. 東

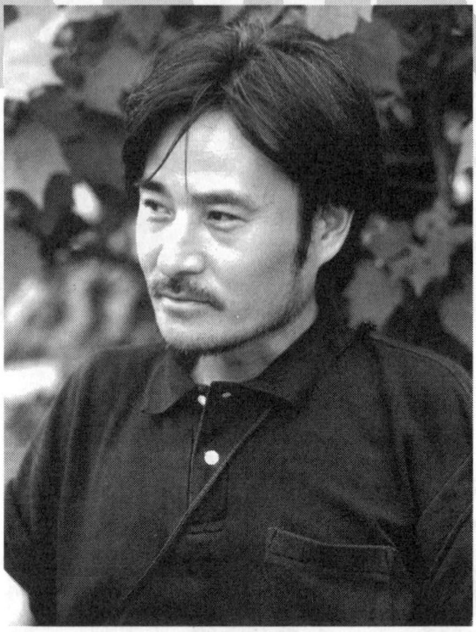

Kiyoshi Kurosawa
How to Scare the Shit Out of People

Kiyoshi Kurosawa may be an expert at spooking an audience, but it wouldn't be fair to simply label him a horror director. Instead, Kurosawa plays a mean shell game, making genre overtures with one hand and obscuring the familiar way out with the other. Still, his films do work as horror—amid their philosophy and bad trips, they also possess the raw power to make you cover your eyes in fright.

Born in Kobe in 1955, Kurosawa made his directorial debut in 1983 with *Kandagawa Wars*. In 1989, he helmed the big-budget *Sweet Home* (1989), a haunted-house story inspired by Tobe Hooper's *Poltergeist* which featured make-up effects by Dick Smith of *The Exorcist* fame.

Since then, murder and mystery have provided the foundation for several of Kurosawa's unique films, such as *Cure* (1997) and *The Serpent's Path* (1997), where a thick coat of existential dread invokes nightmarish texture and tension.

Kairo (Pulse, 2001), an internet-fueled encounter with the afterlife, is perhaps the closest Kurosawa has come to making a proper post-*Ring* horror film. That is, until an apocalyptic third act takes this genre in a radical new direction not too far from Kurosawa's much debated "art film" *Charisma* (1999).

While not exactly a horror director, Kurosawa could be considered a horror fan. He doesn't hesitate to heap praise on the director of *The Texas Chainsaw Massacre*—whom he happened to have dinner with the night before he was interviewed for this book.

"I like all of Tobe Hooper's films very much," he said, "but to name only two, the first would be *Spontaneous Combustion,* and the other would be *Lifeforce*. I've seen a lot of films, but these two should be considered masterpieces in the history of cinema."

From here, Kurosawa went on to reveal his secret recipe for directing scary scenes, the differences between Tobe Hooper and George Romero, and why ending the world is sometimes the most logical way to end a film.

Kurosawa on How to Direct Horror:

"Directing horror is difficult to explain. If I really knew how to put it into words, I'd write

INTERVIEW

a book like Hitchcock and explain away the technique. What I do know is that it tends to be about creating a feeling.

"There are many different ways to create frightening images, but with the actors and the cast, I basically tell them, 'Something scary's happening, and there's going to be an encounter of some kind. But I don't want you to act that frightened. You can't be more scared than the audience.' This technique also extends to the art direction, the sound design, the music, and other elements of the film.

"When filming a scary scene, I don't try to make it clear to the audience whether they should be scared or not. One thing I tell actors is that, 'If you act more frightened than the audience, it gives them a sign how to react. So, even though it's supposed to be a scary situation, they end up feeling comfortable.' I don't want my actors to signal what kind of scene it's going to be. You have to leave it ambiguous, whether it's supposed to be frightening or not. So while the actor acts, without indicating how the audience should feel, the viewer is stuck in the middle, unsure what's going to happen next. And that's how you make people feel truly unsettled."

Kurosawa on How to End the World:

"When working with an individual character, I start with his most essential relationship in his daily life.

"As the story progresses, his relationships expand to reveal things about his daily life, his relationship to society, and even wider to finally include the whole world.

"I find that as I develop the story, the protagonist inevitably comes into conflict with the world around him. And in that conflict, only three possible solutions come to mind: suicide, becoming a criminal, or going insane. For instance, in *Cure*, the protagonist becomes a criminal. But every once in a while I come across a character that I don't want to become a criminal, kill himself, or go insane. The only other option is to destroy the world. Essentially, at the end of my films, the character is forced to choose between destroying himself or destroying the world.

"This theme is similar to those of the films of George Romero, in which the heroes are working with a group of people that essentially have to make a decision: us or the world? What I like about Romero's films is that, while they're good horror films, they're not pure horror films. Maybe they're more 'panic films,' or 'invasion films,' or maybe, more accurately, they're 'survival films.' In any case, they seem to have very clear power relationships and a clear destination: 'If we can get through this, then we can achieve this.' I find that very refreshing.

"On the other hand, you have the type of film where you have no idea what you have to accomplish in order to get somewhere, and those are the kinds of films that Tobe Hooper makes." 東

"Help!" Poster art for Kiyoshi Kurosawa's *Pulse* (2001)

YUKIO "SCISSORS" ODA
WEST STUDIO NO. 5
BY J-TARO SUGISAKI
TRANSLATION BY YUJI ONIKI

Panel 1:
TSUNEHIKO AMAGUCHI—DIRECTOR EMPLOYED BY GOKUEI FILMS

WHAT!? ODA ONLY SPENT ¥2,000,000 ON HIS MOVIE!?

YEAH, THE ODA CREW CAME IN UNDER BUDGET, SO THE STAFF SPLURGED THE REST ON **MASSAGE PARLORS**!

WOW!

Panel 2:
WHEN IT CAME TO SHOOTING A MOVIE UNDER BUDGET, **NOBODY** COULD BEAT OUT YUKIO ODA OF GOKUEI'S KYOTO STUDIO.

KLOP KLOP

ODA WAS SO GOOD AT CUTTING COSTS, HE EARNED THE NICKNAME **"SCISSORS."**

FOR INSTANCE, ACTION SCENES ARE EXPENSIVE, BECAUSE THEY REQUIRE **ACTION CHOREOGRAPHY, STUNTMEN, AND LOTS OF EDITING.** HOWEVER...

BLAMM BLAMM

NAH, WE DON'T NEED TO SHOOT THAT.

ODA WOULD JUST SPLICE IN ACTION SCENES FROM **ANOTHER FILM!**

THEY NEVER LOOK AT THE FACES ANYWAY.

Oda's Film ← | Action Scene from Another Film

Panel 3:
ODA, I LOVE YA BABY! I'M THE LUCKIEST PRODUCER IN THE WHOLE WORLD!

GORO WAKATABE, PRODUCER OF GOKUEI FILMS

AHHH!

SAME WITH SEX SCENES

NAH, THAT'S FINE.

AS LONG AS WE GOT T&A, IT DOESN'T MATTER WHO'S IN IT.

OF COURSE, NOTHING EVER ENDED UP ON THE CUTTING ROOM FLOOR.

SORRY, I GOT MY LINES WRONG.

NAH, IT'S OKAY!

AND IF A HELICOPTER FLEW IN DURING A SHOOT...

KUMA! GET A SHOT OF THAT CHOPPER!

HUH?

I'M SURE WE CAN USE IT LATER. IT'S EXPENSIVE TO HIRE ONE OUT!

THAT'S HOW THINGS WORKED.

Panel 4:
ONE DAY ODA RECEIVED A SCRIPT.

GOKUEI Medical Suspense: Internal Organs Explosion

"MEDICAL SUSPENSE" MIGHT SOUND LEGIT, BUT IT WAS JUST A **SPLATTER MOVIE** THAT WOULD MAKE AN OPERATION LOOK REAL.

NO ONE WOULD TOUCH THAT PROJECT, BECAUSE THE PRODUCER'S BUDGET WAS SO LOW. SO IT GOT PASSED ON TO THE SCISSOR MAN.

PLEASE ODA!!

YOU'RE THE ONLY ONE WHO CAN DO THIS UNDER BUDGET!!

...

AWRIGHT, I'LL DO IT...

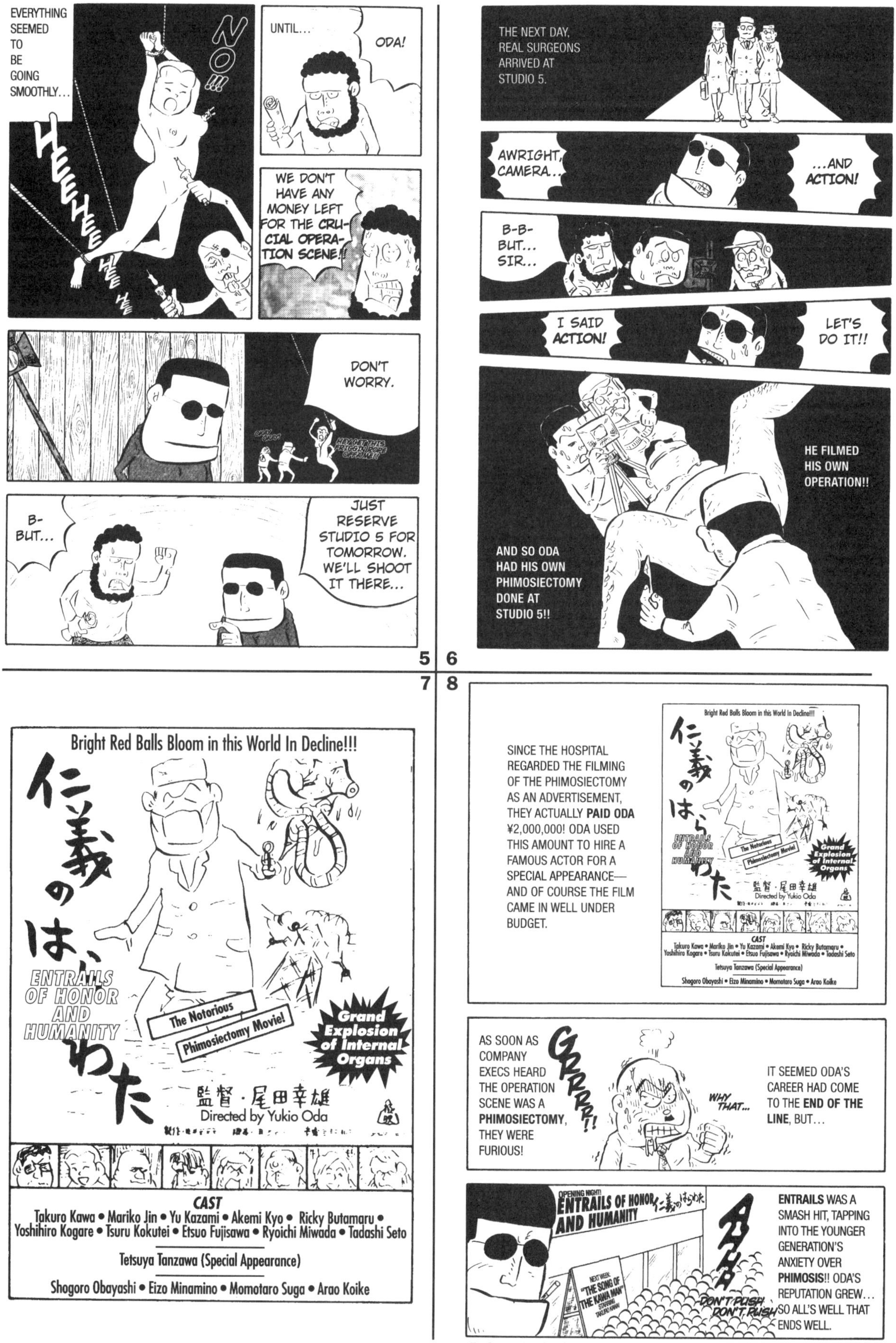

EVERYTHING SEEMED TO BE GOING SMOOTHLY…
NO!!!
HEEHEEHEEHEE
UNTIL…
ODA!
WE DON'T HAVE ANY MONEY LEFT FOR THE CRUCIAL OPERATION SCENE!!
DON'T WORRY.
B-BUT…
JUST RESERVE STUDIO 5 FOR TOMORROW. WE'LL SHOOT IT THERE…
5
6
THE NEXT DAY, REAL SURGEONS ARRIVED AT STUDIO 5.
AWRIGHT, CAMERA…
…AND ACTION!
B-B-BUT… SIR…
I SAID ACTION!
LET'S DO IT!!
HE FILMED HIS OWN OPERATION!!
AND SO ODA HAD HIS OWN PHIMOSIECTOMY DONE AT STUDIO 5!!
7
8
Bright Red Balls Bloom in this World In Decline!!!
仁義のはらわた
ENTRAILS OF HONOR AND HUMANITY
The Notorious Phimosiectomy Movie!
Grand Explosion of Internal Organs
監督・尾田幸雄
Directed by Yukio Oda
CAST
Takuro Kawa • Mariko Jin • Yu Kazami • Akemi Kyo • Ricky Butamaru • Yoshihiro Kogare • Tsuru Kokutei • Etsuo Fujisawa • Ryoichi Miwada • Tadashi Seto
Tetsuya Tanzawa (Special Appearance)
Shogoro Obayashi • Eizo Minamino • Momotaro Suga • Arao Koike
SINCE THE HOSPITAL REGARDED THE FILMING OF THE PHIMOSIECTOMY AS AN ADVERTISEMENT, THEY ACTUALLY PAID ODA ¥2,000,000! ODA USED THIS AMOUNT TO HIRE A FAMOUS ACTOR FOR A SPECIAL APPEARANCE—AND OF COURSE THE FILM CAME IN WELL UNDER BUDGET.
AS SOON AS COMPANY EXECS HEARD THE OPERATION SCENE WAS A PHIMOSIECTOMY, THEY WERE FURIOUS!
GRRRR!!
WHY THAT…
IT SEEMED ODA'S CAREER HAD COME TO THE END OF THE LINE, BUT…
OPENING NIGHT! ENTRAILS OF HONOR AND HUMANITY 仁義のはらわた
NEXT WEEK "THE SONG OF THE KAWA MAN" STARRING TAKURO KAWA
DON'T PUSH DON'T PUSH
ENTRAILS WAS A SMASH HIT, TAPPING INTO THE YOUNGER GENERATION'S ANXIETY OVER PHIMOSIS!! ODA'S REPUTATION GREW… SO ALL'S WELL THAT ENDS WELL.

THIS MANGA IS A COMPLETE WORK OF FICTION.

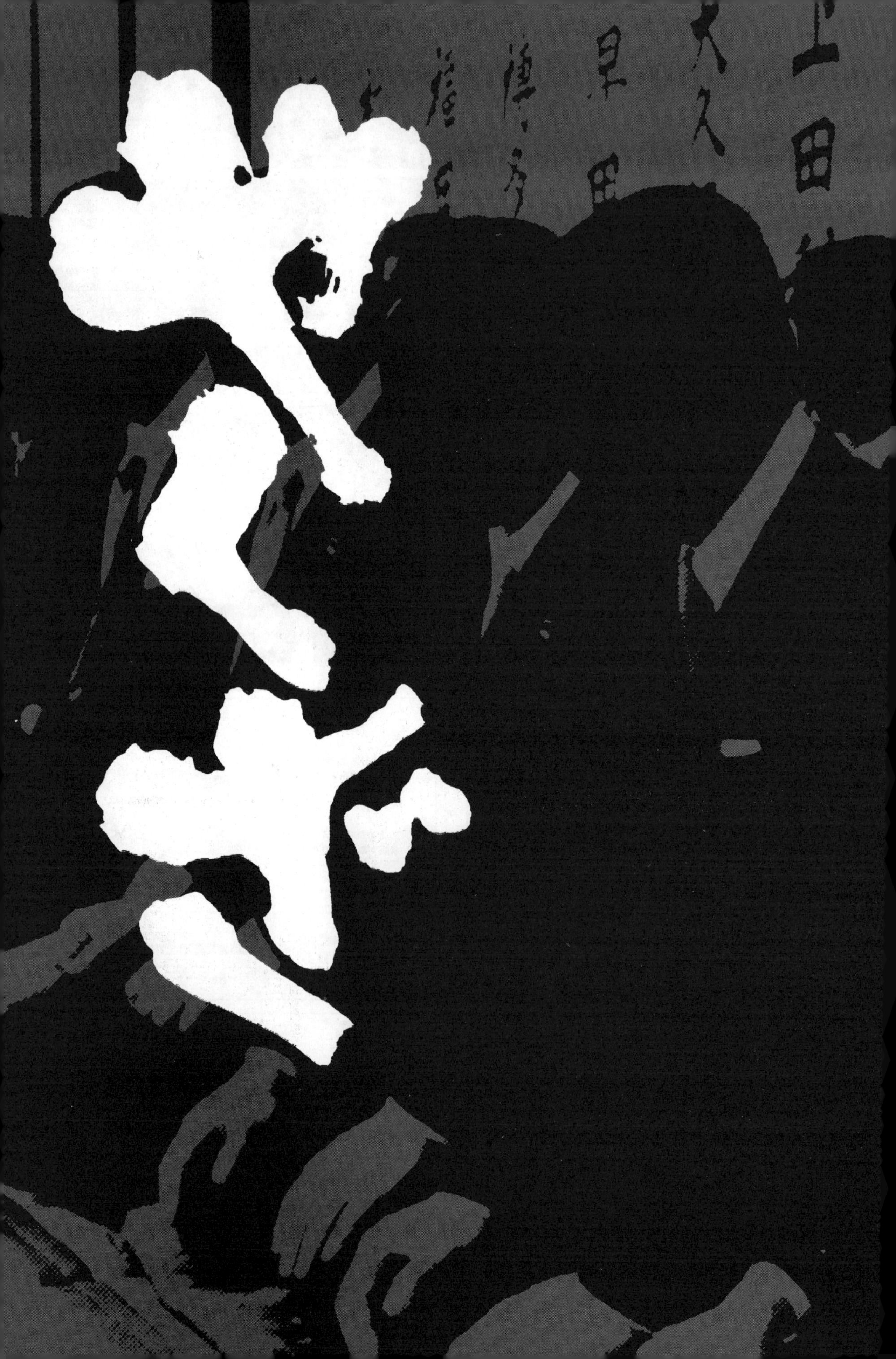

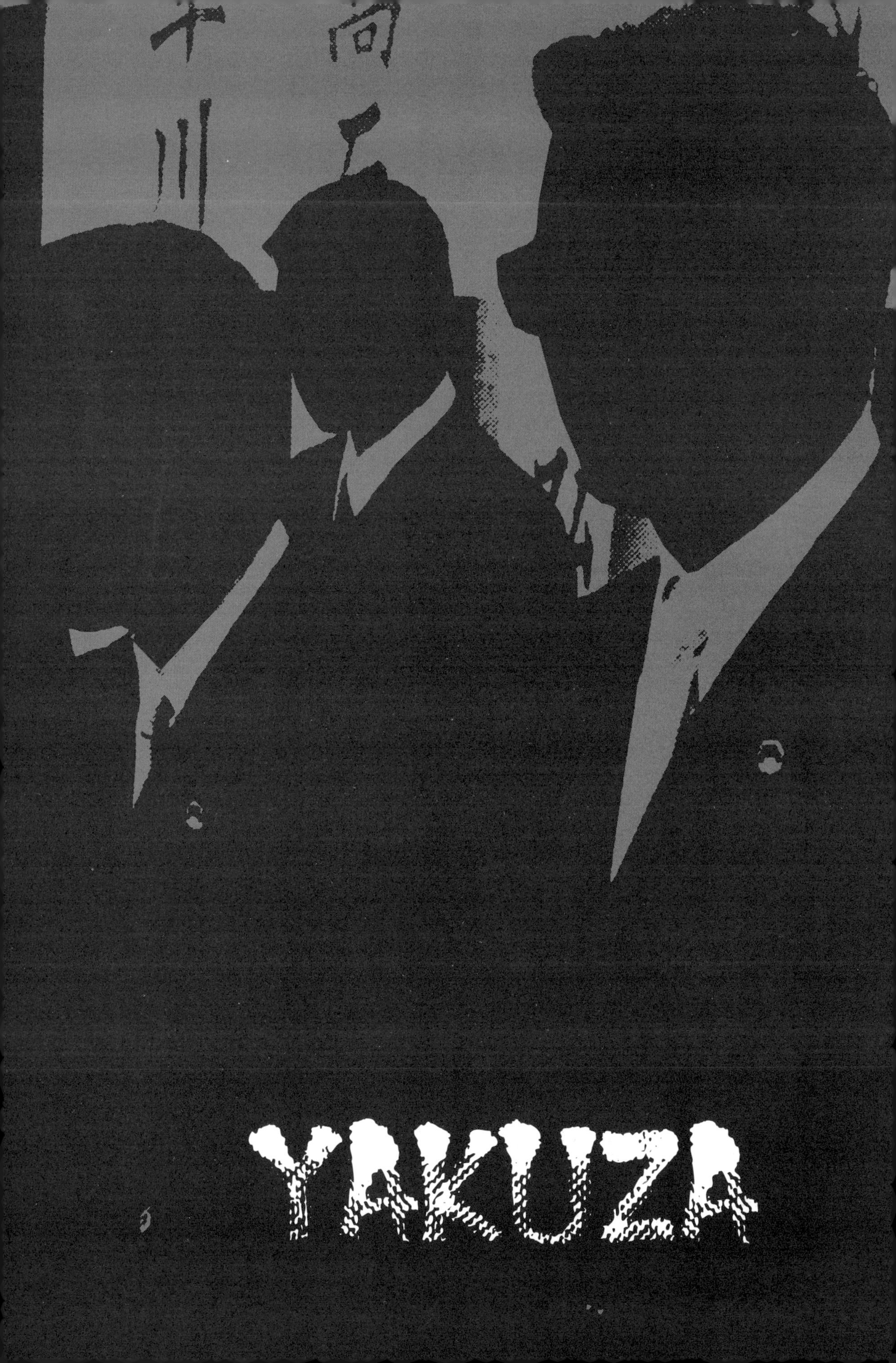

YAKUZA

WANTED
Ken Takakura born 1931, aka The Yakuza, symbolic leader of the syndicate.

YAKUZA

"YAKUZA EIGA"— GANGSTER MOVIES

It was a balmy, moist night near the Showakan Theater at Shinjuku Station's South Exit that I first saw—and knew I was looking at—a yakuza. He was a middle-aged man of moderate build and extreme dress sense. Bleached-blond dyed hair. Gold chain dangling around the neck. A shiny blue jogging suit. His only concession to traditional yakuza attire, the wooden *geta* shoes on his feet. In his hands, both of which still possessed a complete set of fingers, he carried...two crepes, banana and chocolate.

Real life offers us a wide variety of Japanese gangsters. There are those that enforce protection rackets and have restaurant owners carry their moist, hot towelettes. There are the sort who serve as muscle for loan companies that advertise in women's fashion magazines. Or perhaps you'd prefer the kind that kill people to collect their insurance money.

And some like to eat crepes.

But odds are, all of them like yakuza movies.

Why shouldn't they? Yakuza movies are the final word in Japanese cult film: full of lore, laws, history, and ritual, they are documents that catalog the dreams of society's outlaws, outcasts, and downright losers. And of all the genre films that screen regularly at our favorite theater, the Showakan, yakuza titles continue to this day to be the staple.

You already know about the full-body tattoos and the missing fingers that say "I'm sorry" more eloquently than a bouquet of flowers. Maybe you even saw Robert Mitchum mix it up with Ken Takakura in 1975's *The Yakuza* or Ann Jillian and Jennifer Jason Leigh shake it for the boys in the 1983 TV movie-of-the-week *Death Ride to Osaka*.

Half-baked Western knockoffs aside, Japanese yakuza-movie protagonists can be roughly divided into two basic types: in the world of movies, members of the underworld are either wandering, sentimental heroes who abide by strict moral codes, or they are violent thugs only in it for the money. But he

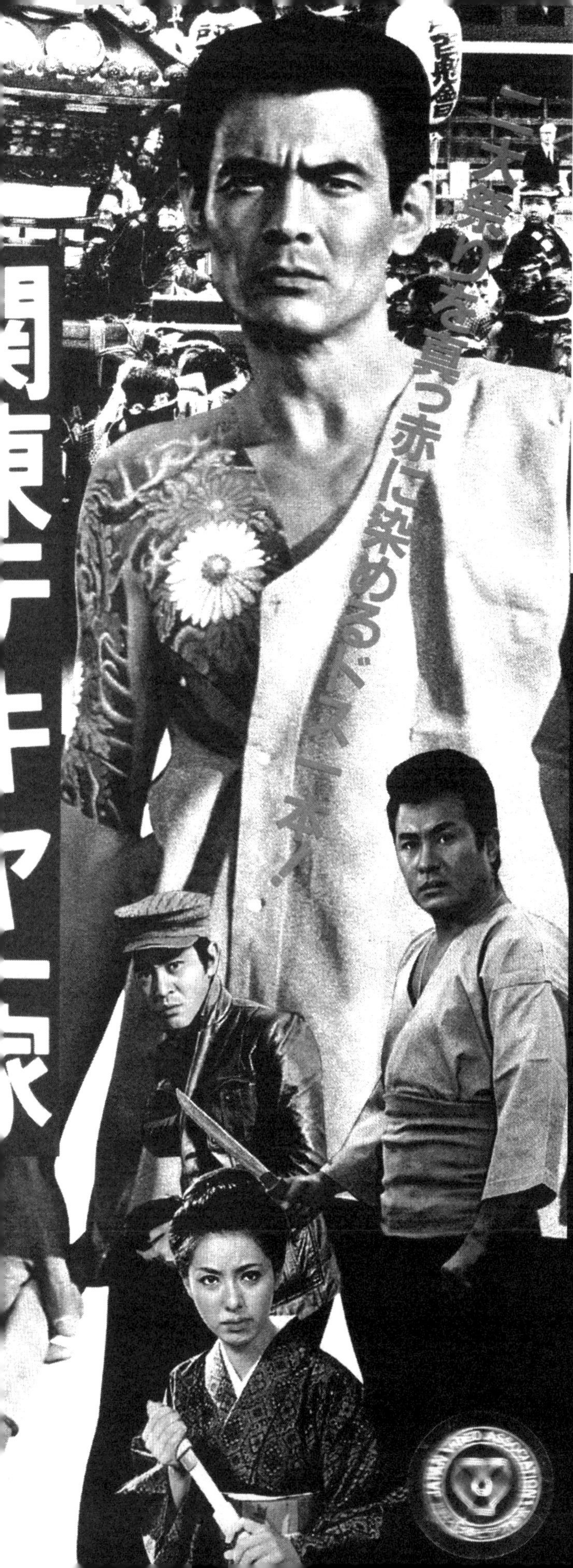
大祭りを真っ赤に染める

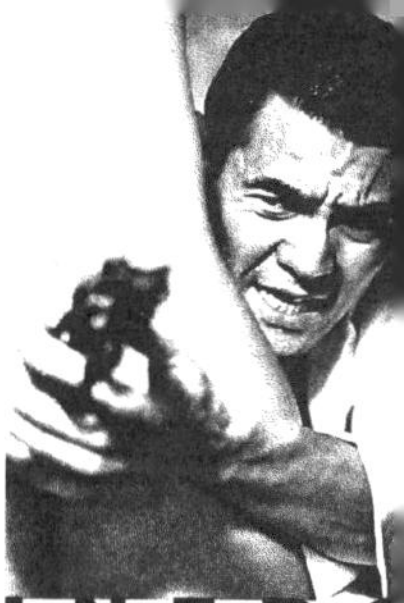

INTRO

they heroic or backstabbing, the operative word for both schools is "antisocial"; yakuza became folk heroes because their stories are the perfect outlet for nonconformist fantasies, rebellious dreams that bloom from the compost of reality and history.

Yakuza. Yakuza.

What's in a name? A crummy toss of the dice, that's what. 8-9-3. Rolling a *ya-ku-sa* in a gambling den means you just sank the eight ball, you loser.

Some say that the roots of Japanese organized crime can be found in classical Chinese history, as recorded in novels like *The Water Margin*. The yakuza code of honorable conduct, known as *jingi*, is itself made up of the first two of the five Confucian virtues, *jin* (humanity) and *gi* (honor). Historians will point to packs of

YAKUZA

WANTED. Mikio Narita, 1935-1990, leader of the Toei "Piranha Army." His face was painted silver for *Message from Space*.

gamblers, known as the *bakuto*, and racketeering salesmen, the *tekiya*, who wandered through the feudal countryside ("helping like…here and there as it might be," to quote Em from *Clockwork Orange*). The yakuza themselves will tell you tall tales about Robin Hood-like individuals who once valiantly protected villages from marauding samurai and corrupt government officials.

Out of the latter came the early legendary yakuza hero Chuji Kunisada, a Tokugawa-era tough guy who led his gang against a greedy, tax-crazy magistrate. His life story of heroism and hard suffering was passed down through oral tradition to become the basis for one of the first yakuza film epics, 1927's three-part *Chuji tabi nikki* (Chuji's Travel Diary), directed by Daisuke Ito. Chuji enjoyed status as *yakuza du jour* for a healthy run as other filmmakers retold the legend, each time laying down more ground rules for the genre to follow. The *matabi mono* (wandering gambler stories), popular during the turn of the century, were also mined for material, especially the works of author Shin Hasegawa, whose novels became the basis for numerous early yakuza films.

To the untrained eye, these primal gangster films differed little from the multitude of *chanbara eiga* (sword films) that fueled the first golden age of Japanese cinema. But whereas samurai movies usually delineated the duties of vassal to lord, early yakuza films were fueled by defiant antiauthoritarian conflicts. As Chuji sought to repel the taxman, other movie yakuza formed alliances, or, like *Nezumi Kozo*, the Rat Kid, committed crimes to keep encroaching hegemony at bay. It proved a powerful vision in a society that was still governed by feudal ideals and Emperor worship.

And then the yakuza were gone. Just like that. Owing to the Allied Forces' campaign to stomp out Japan's fighting spirit, *jidaigeki* (historical) subjects vanished from studio slates. Former period film stars who lived by the samurai sword found their careers in jeopardy.

Then, in the fall of 1951, immediately following the Japanese Peace Treaty conference in San Francisco, period subjects returned with a vengeance. But it was samurai films, rather than yakuza movies, that benefited from the massive boom in production and box-office take

INTRO

in this second golden age.

In part, the absence of yakuza movies during this period owed to the fact that real life *had become* a yakuza movie.

The postwar era saw the emergence of a violent new gangster class, the *gurentai* (hoodlums). Fierce territorial battles were fought between yakuza and *sangokujin*, liberated minorities of Chinese, Taiwanese, and Koreans. Most scandalous of all, gangs were president, boasted of a past as a former street punk. Toei's army of artisans and contract workers (the *shokunin*), with their traditional master-apprentice (*oyabun-kobun*) style of operation, were virtually inseparable from the yakuza. And many an underworld figure could be found holding court on location, negotiating with the locals and authorities on the behalf of filmmakers.

Crime movies during the fifties were more influenced by tattooed yakuza. Toho studios specialized in this new sub-genre with a whole slew of *ankoku gai* films beginning in 1956, the most accessible example to US viewers being the 1958 film *The H-Man* (*Bijyo to ekitai ningen*, "Beautiful Women and the Liquid People"), with its urbane villainous gangsters and swanky jazz-club settings.

At the dawn of the sixties, as Japan entered a new age of prosperity, the soul of

YAKUZA

WANTED
Tomisaburo Wakayama, 1929-92, aka Lone Wolf, aka Capone older brother to Shintaro Katsu.

favored period setting had shifted from the Tokugawa and Edo periods to the late Taisho and early Showa era, from the turn of the century to the mid-thirties, a period when Japan was marching towards modernization—not unlike the early sixties. *Ninkyo eiga* offered affirmation that the Soul of Japan had not yet been eclipsed by rapid social change, and were also blood rituals, bullfights, and chances for heroes and audiences to bask in the triumph and glory of a nihilistic death wish.

The classic *ninkyo* storyline went something like this: an honorable yakuza gets out of jail only to find his old team broken up or in bad shape and his old girlfriend either married or a whore. A greedy new gang, preferably one with a taste for Western dress and trappings, has taken over. They make life hard for the weak (widowers and people with tuberculosis preferred but not essential) or pit old friend against old friend, until the final reel, when our hero, carrying only a *dosu* knife, marches into the enemy stronghold (usually accompanied by a song about blood and loyalty), wherein he kills everybody before wandering off wounded into the horizon, presumably to die, full of holes, soaked in blood.

Living links to the past were placed behind the cameras. For instance, Masahiro Makino (1908-1993), who directed many films in Toei's *Nihon kyokaku den* (Chivalrous Story of Japan) series, could trace his career all the way back to the first era of yakuza film, which gave his *ninkyo* titles a core authenticity. Also, Toei director Tai Kato had learned filmmaking while working as an assistant director for Daisuke Ito, a major director of the silent era (the historic three-part 1927 *Chuji* film was his work).

Kato (1916-1985) directed perhaps the definitive *ninkyo eiga* with his 1965 title *Meiji kyokyaku den—Sandaime shumie*, which starred Koji Tsuruta in the lead role. With a script co-written by future *School of the Holy Beast* director Norifumi Suzuki, Kato's film (also known as *Blood of Revenge*) enacts exactly the *ninkyo* scenario as described above. A thematic similarity to the American Western is apparent, with weary, hardened Koji as a kind of Gary Cooper. Tai Kato's movies for Toei were often formal and dazzlingly beautiful, despite their low budgets and rushed production schedules. While some of his films, such as 1963's *Sanada*

The real violence organization is disclosed!

INTRO

funroku, mixed genres and modern techniques in a kaleidoscopic fusion, the director remains best known by yakuza enthusiasts for his *Hitoban bakuto* (aka *Red Peony Gambler*) series, starring Junko Fuji as an alternately comely and fierce lady *bakuto* (imagine Audrey Hepburn with a dagger and a pack of *hanafuda* cards), and for his definitive takes on oft-told tales.

Gradually, though, *ninkyo eiga*'s highly wrought

Action films, with their fast-moving plots and light flavor, were the alternative. While *ninkyo* films, indeed many Toei films, were for blue-collar types who wanted their old values confirmed, Nikkatsu Action films, such as director Yasuharu Hasebe's 1966 *Ore ni sawaru to abunaize* (available on DVD as *Black Tight Killers*), courted a younger, urban crowd in search of pop thrills. Mid-sixties glamour was supplied in bulk

perfected during the samurai boom, meant directors now had to grind out double features, both A- and B-movies alike, on small budgets and rushed production schedules. If Ken Takakura proved popular in 1964's *Nihon kyokaku den* (Chivalrous Story Japan), then there would be not only eleven *Nihon kyokaku den* films by 1971, but similarly titled *Meiji kyokaku den* movies as well. And if Ken also struck big in October 1965, with his *Showa*

WANTED
Shintaro Katsu
(1931-97) aka Zatoichi, aka Heitai Yakuza. Actor. Director. Producer. Party animal.

YAKUZA

codes of *jingi* to prop them up. Formed in postwar Kobe, the Yamaguchi-gumi (who would eventually authorize Toei to make a handful of films about their organization) best embodied the new breed. During the sixties, they began violently taking over smaller gangs and eliminating *gurentai* organizations in a bid to form a single national syndicate. While their public face was that of a real estate company, their fearsome Korean fighters buried rival gang members up to their necks and drove cars around them until either conversion to the syndicate or violent death resulted.

The era of the ultraviolent yakuza movie was nigh. Old myths and archetypes, having served their purpose, were going to die hard, and this time they were denied the honorable protagonists. Director Junya Sato's 1967 film *Soshiki boryoku* (Organized Violence) starring Tetsuro Tanba and Sonny Chiba, was a breakthrough in yakuza cinema, depicting in a realistic and unflattering light cutthroat modern mobsters at war with each other and the police. In 1969, the *Gendai yakuza* (Modern Yakuza) series, a showcase for the ex-Shin Toho idol Bunta Sugawara, also exhibited a shift to increasingly jaded notions of yakuza law and disorder. The final entry in the *Gendai yakuza* series, 1972's *Hitokiri yota*, descended the furthest by depicting, with pseudo-documentary trappings, the sordid life and times of a postwar ramen-tossing punk who turns against his own gang. The film marked the first collaboration between actor Sugawara and director Kinji Fukasaku.

1973 then saw the release of Fukasaku's epochal *Jingi naki tatakai* (Fight without Honor and Humanity), with Bunta in the lead role. Closely based on the machinations of the Hiroshima-based Minno gang, *Jingi naki* created both a box-office sensation and a new style of yakuza film: the *jitsuroku* eiga (true story films), tales torn from recent history and headlines. The superviolent yakuza films and based-on-a-true-story *jitsuroku eiga* that followed in the wake of *Jingi naki tatakai* were full of former *ninkyo* stars, such as Hiroki Matsukata and Tatsuo Umemiya, who took a blow torch to their previous screen images as good guys. A stable of supporting players, known as the *Piranha gundan* (Piranha

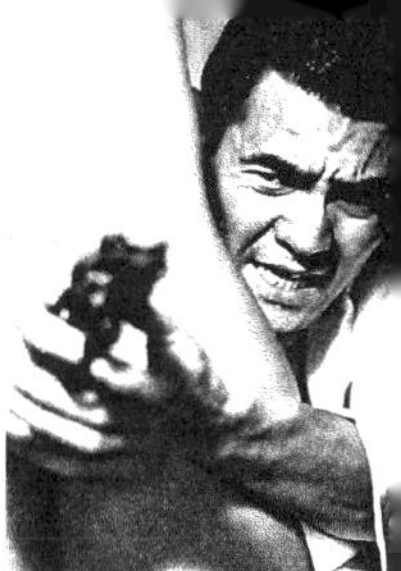

INTRO

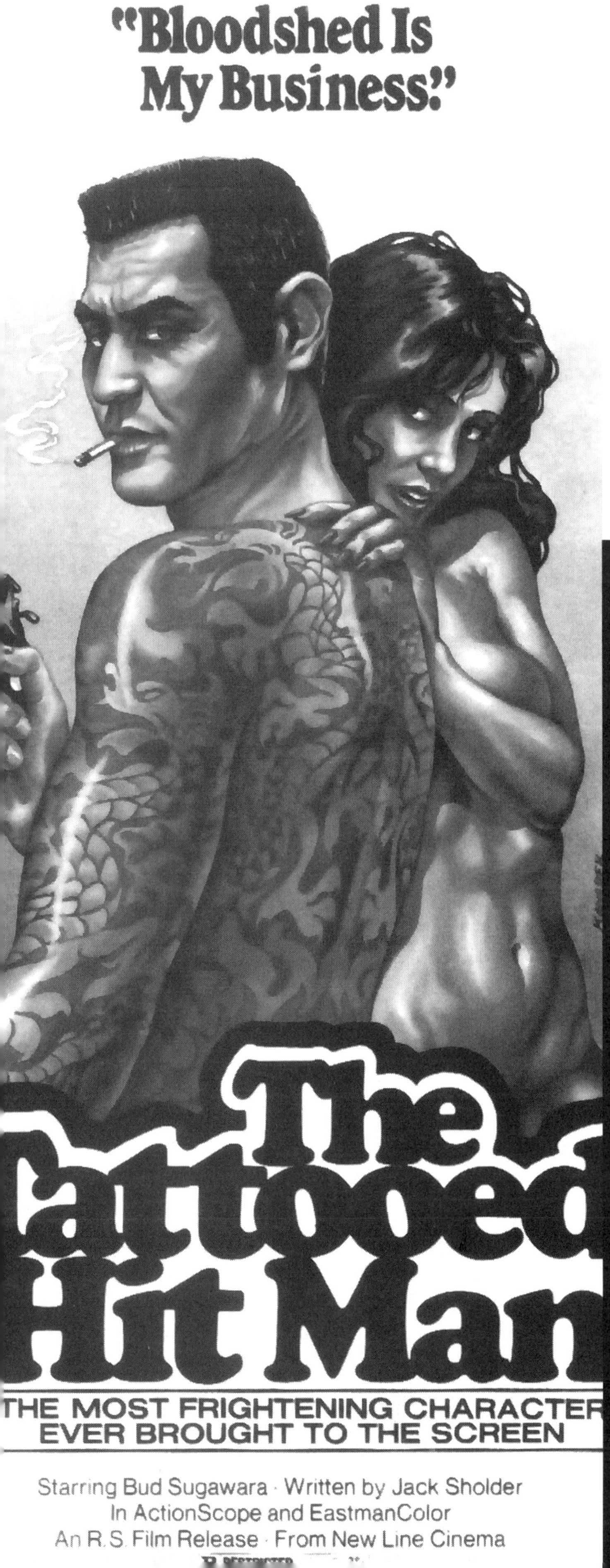
"Bloodshed Is My Business!"
The Tattooed Hit Man
THE MOST FRIGHTENING CHARACTER EVER BROUGHT TO THE SCREEN
Starring Bud Sugawara · Written by Jack Sholder
In ActionScope and EastmanColor
An R.S. Film Release · From New Line Cinema

every Toei yakuza film during the seventies, only to get nastily rubbed out every time.

Even more striking than the novelty of seeing previously heroic gangsters, or even real gangsters like Noboru Ando (who previously commanded a Shibuya-based gang before becoming a movie star by essentially playing himself) strut across the screen was the newfound ferocity of the violence. Previous yakuza films had taken a highly staged approach to duels and raids. Now yakuza cinema, fueled by Suntory whiskey and cigarettes and New Wave film technique, spontaneously combusted into pure chaos, illuminated by the red-pink flash of Toei's fake gunfire and rinsed out with downpours of blood.

Predictably, there were accusations from polite society that Toei was further glorifying crime by wallowing in its worst elements.

WANTED
Kunie Tanaka (born 1932) aka The Snake, former comic relief in Toho's Young Guy movies turned slimeball under its *jitsuroku* regime.

YAKUZA

The new style was sensational, for sure. But at its very best *jitsuroku eiga* provided the rarest of mixtures: action films with an agenda. Fukasaku's *Jingi naki tatakai* series depicted not only the violence of gang war, but also provided a postwar history lesson, showing how Japan's economic miracle was built on the backs of nihilist gangsters.

Toei's new-breed *yakuza eiga* created such a clamor that they brought people back backdrops populated by mad dogs were immensely popular, as were invasion narratives, such as Kansai gangs versus Kyoto gangs, which were a reflection of the Yamaguchi-gumi's devastating bid for a unified underworld. In these films, the yakuza were extreme salarymen, appearing in rival territory with sharklike fleets of Mercedes Benzes to conduct business with literally cutthroat tactics.

Moving into the late were shifting away from program pictures and double features, and moving more towards single pictures in the Hollywood mode. Yakuza movies seemingly could not thrive under these modes of production. Periodic attempts at reviving the genre, such as Hideo Gosha's big-budget 1991 film *Kagero*, bombed.

It was not the best time for domestically produced action movies and other macho entertainments. During the

INTRO

films, 1986-99).

Eventually, though, the bubble would burst and there would be hell to pay. Morale, money, and fighting spirit were low. And thus, like a host of tarnished fallen angels in aviator sunglasses, the yakuza reincarnated into a host of straight-to-video "V-cinema" features. Actors like Show Aikawa and Riki Takeuchi invoked the fighting spirit of old, while their economically motivated dreams and schemes mirrored those of a grim new economy where one's life, along with drugs, women, and whale meat, were the only solid commodities.

The old-guard actors like Bunta Sugawara and Hiroki Matsukata regularly appeared in V-cinema productions, providing flesh-and-blood continuity to previous epochs. Even Noboru Ando got another chance to tell true tales of postwar struggle in the guise of his *Kizu* (Scar) V-cinema series. Kanto versus Kansai conflicts have now taken a back seat to more international battlegrounds. One of the most popular themes in V-cinema has been "Chinese triads versus yakuza." This comes not out of mistrust of foreigners, but seemingly from a genuine admiration for the Chinese gangsters who seem to be acting with a truth and passion that the yakuza might have misplaced along the way.

Today's underworld movies, often produced by independent companies, reflect a more diverse underworld than ever before. Every criminal or anti-authoritarian pastime gets its own row of V-cinema boxes in the video store. The *pachipuro* movies (always next to the mah-jong movies, it seems) are about career pachinko players, clear descendants of the old *bakuto* gamblers. Loan-company movies (known as *sarakin*), like Riki Takeuchi's *Minami no teio* series, are almost educational films, illustrating the intricacies of shady personal finance. Movies about pachinko hackers depict them as outlaw heroes, liberating information from The Man. The *sagi* films, about career playboys and conmen who get rich by bilking wealthy women or people in power are often based on real people and events, and sometimes even star the perpetrators themselves.

It's enough to make you think that everyone around you is a yakuza of some sort. And some nights, around Shinjuku, around South Exit, you'd be right.

WANTED

Hiroki Matsukata (born 1942) Former *ninkyo* star. Multiple roles in *Jingi naki tatakai*. Currently still active in V-cinema.

やくざ刑罰史
菅原文太
吉田輝雄
大木 実
大友柳太朗
TOEI VIDEO
監督・石井輝男

Yakuza Punishment History—Lynch

Yakuza keibatsu shi—Rinchi, aka Yakuza's Law

1969, Toei
Director Teruo Ishii
Cast Bunta Sugawara, Teruo Yoshita, Ryutaro Otomo

A nauseating theremin soundtrack screeches and wails like fingernails on a chalkboard. Between credits for cast and crew, a yakuza has his eyes cooked in his head by a magnifying glass. Another is buried alive like a pig on a spit. Here's a poor fellow with a red hot branding iron pressed on his forehead. Here's a close-up of a bit drill burrowing though a hand, the blood spraying everywhere.

The message is clear: break the iron-clad yakuza commandments at your own risk!

Made up of three self-contained stories, *Lynch* is simultaneously an outrageous splatter movie and an encyclopedia of yakuza film themes. Although clearly inspired by Tadashi Imai's *Bushido zankyoku monogatari* (Cruel Story of Bushido, 1963), which similarly dismembered myths of the samurai, such a nasty little variant could have only sprung from a team-up between director Teruo Ishii and Toei's reigning exploitation producer Kanji Amao.

The first story, set in the Edo period, features Bunta Sugawara trying to help a woman and her kid escape the yakuza world with a short-tempered *oyabun* (boss) standing in the way. Bunta breaks the underworld law regarding fooling around with married women and gets an eye and an ear hacked off. Instead of protesting, he says, "I have lived by the rules all my life. I must be judged by those rules." His mutilated body provides a living text of hard-line yakuza law.

Episode three, set in the *really* amoral modern age, makes for one hell of a climax. Here Ishii plugs back into the *film noir* world of his late fifties films and foreshadows the manic energy of his Sonny Chiba movies. After someone steals a suitcase full of gold from a yakuza faction, the gang goes nuts trying to flush out the suspected rat on the inside. Gun battles, femme fatales, betrayals, blackmail, and exploding oil refineries ensue, as do the mounting tortures. Faces are set alight with Zippo lighters, people are turned into concrete blocks or reduced to Spam in a junkyard car crusher—acts overseen by the yo-yo wielding Hideo Ko (*Goke*).

One would think, or perhaps even hope, that this messy atrocity exhibition would spell the very end of the Toei yakuza movie. Surely such excess signaled the end of the line.

Instead, it was only the beginning of a bold new era of screen violence and yakuza behaving badly.

☞ **Available subbed on VHS from Japan Shock Video**

REVIEW

The Violent Street
Boriyoku gai

1974, Toei
Director Hideo Gosha
Cast Noboru Ando, Bunta Sugawara, Tetsuro Tanba, Akira Kobayashi

In the wonderful world of yakuza film, the right casting and the right director are often everything.

The Violent Street could have easily been yet another Kanto versus Kansai (east Japan vs. southwest Japan) yarn. Instead, it rockets to the crucial list owing to the posturing of its quartet of top yakuza actors (sold as "The Big Four") and the eccentric talents of director Hideo Gosha.

Noboru Ando has abandoned gang life and now runs a swanky Ginza nightclub that specializes in flamenco acts. His old buddy Akira Kobayashi shows up out of the blue to try to buy Ando out. Their old gang now fancy themselves as a legit company and want to divorce themselves completely from their unsavory past. Yet conflict continues to plague them. A pop singer, under contract to the company's talent agency, is kidnapped and held for ransom by invading Kansai gangsters. After Kobayashi drops off the ransom dough, which is picked up by a bagman disguised as Frankenstein's monster, he finds that she's been murdered (by the gorilla-masked kid brother of Ando's barmaid girlfriend no less, in a botched rape attempt).

Kobayashi cries for an all-out war and tries to woo Ando back into the fold, but the boss, fearing for his reputation, tells both to cool it. Meanwhile, another Kansai faction has sent over a highly unusual hit team: a transvestite and a guy with a pet parrot, to rub out the rogue Kansai faction.

Meanwhile, Ando decides he wants to wreak revenge on his old boss, who is now married to his old girlfriend. He enlists the headphone-wearing, Coca-Cola swilling Bunta Sugawara to ride and fire a shotgun when Ando drives his car through a wall and into a sleazy company party to shoot the place up.

Kobayashi is ordered to kill his old buddy—by which point everyone has a secret motive and an axe to grind. It even turns out that the entire Kansai invasion was faked by a rebellious faction inside the company, who merely wanted a good war to fight like in the old days.

But where's that goddamn money? And what does lurker on the threshold Tetsuro Tanba have up his sleeve?

Director Gosha continually mines dark nuggets of surrealism from the proceedings. Strange settings, like a mannequin-strewn junkyard and Ando's Spanish-themed cabaret, keeps things continually off-kilter. Every scene seems to end with a bottle being broken over someone's head. Gosha, who passed on in 1992, is best known for his *Goyokin* and *The Wolves*, but *The Violent Street* perhaps best illustrates the underworld milieu and eternal mystery of yakuza cinema.

☞ **Import only**

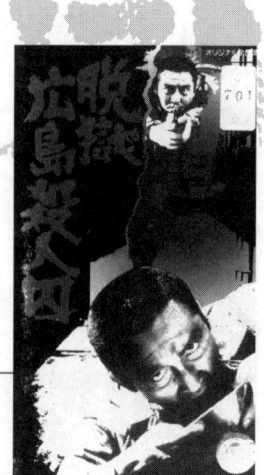

WANTED
Tetsuya Watari (born 1941) aka the Tokyo Drifter, good boy gone bad in *Jingi no hakaba* and *Yakuza no hakaba*.

Escaped Murderer from Hiroshima Prison
Datsugoku Hiroshima satsujin shiyu

1974, Toei
Director Sadao Nakajima
Cast Hiroki Matsukata, Tatsuo Umemiya, Tomisaburo Wakayama

As the dumb, rowdy punks featured in the *Mamushi no kyodai* (Mamushi Brothers) movies proved, director Sadao Nakajima (born in Chiba Prefecture, 1934) seemed to have a soft spot for the lowest guys on the totem pole. And while Nakajima would eventually create the lofty *Nihon no don* trilogy (Don of Japan, 1977-78), one of the few yakuza epics to rival *Jingi naki tatakai* in terms of ambition and scale, the sympathetic, rebellious, and relentless *Escaped Murderer* is perhaps his single finest yakuza picture.

A small-timer named Ueda (Hiroki Matsukata) kills two people over some black market goods and is duly sentenced to twenty years in Hiroshima prison.

He quickly sneaks out of solitary confinement through the sewage system, but is soon nabbed outside of a movie theater (playing a yakuza movie, naturally) and is dragged back to the slammer.

Undaunted, he teams up with a murderer (Tatsuo Umemiya) and an elderly rapist to plan another break. His old buddy on the outside sneaks him a razor in a tempura lunch during a visit and the trio escapes.

Ueda goes to his sister in countryside, where he finds her at the mercy of local butchers running an illegal, lucrative beef trade. He soon takes over the gang and enjoys a brief period of prosperity before being arrested yet again during a fight in a brothel.

Now facing forty years in the joint, he plans a third escape with his old buddy Umemiya, but an attack by a jailed gang puts Umemiya in the infirmary and Ueda on the offensive, leading Ueda to kill both the gang boss and his henchman.

While going to trial on a new set of charges, Ueda jumps out of the courthouse window, leading to a massive manhunt. His weary sister aids him one last time, but finds herself in handcuffs after helping her criminal brother escape arrest.

The last we see of this jailhouse escape artist (who can forge weapons out of tin food dishes with his hands tied behind his back), he's wandering down some railroad tracks, munching on a radish, trying to light a cigarette butt on the tracks.

Nakajima is really exploring how people choose to live their lives: either as conformists or fugitives from society. Hiroki Matsukata (who previously worked with Nakajima in 1966's *893 gurentai*) gives a fantastic performance as the impossible-to-keep-incarcerated hood. His voiceover narration never offers a single moment of soul-searching introspection, only single-minded defiance. Presumably, wondering why his antisocial behavior keeps landing him in jail would only distract him from planning yet another escape.

☞ **Import only**

REVIEW

Yokohama Underworld—Machine Gun Dragon
Yokohama ankoku gai—Machine Gun no ryu

1976, Toei
Director Akihisa Okamoto
Cast Bunta Sugawara, Yutaka Nakajima, Kunie Tanaka, Sonny Chiba

You know this one is going to be a wild ride. Act one, scene one: Bunta Sugawara strolls into the center of the frame, dressed to the nines in hat, gloves, and trenchcoat, flower in lapel. In his paws he grips an M3A1 grease gun. He points it at the camera, pulls the trigger, and blows you away.

A tale of a mother-fixated dandy with a chrysanthemum tattoo on his back, *Machine Gun Dragon* isn't your typical yakuza movie. Released in Japan on the heels of *Godfather II* and *Chinatown*, director Akihisa Okamoto (who also helmed the straight-to-video *Lady Battlecop* in 1991) tosses down retro movie imagery with playful postmodern abandon. The result is something like a Nikkatsu Action film, only now supercharged with superaction, superviolence, funky seventies soundtrack, and inexplicable Oedipal hijinx borrowed from that eternal ode to the mother-loving gangster, *White Heat*.

Wearing rubber monster masks, Bunta and his doting old mother steal a suitcase full of dope from a yakuza gang on the Yokohama docks, leaving a trail of bodies behind them. By day, mom runs a café while Bunta, clad like a 1930s big shot, runs with a motorcycle gang of mohawked punks. Mom and son love each other dearly, into the realms of the unhealthy. While inspecting his unwashed underwear, mom is furious to discover that her little boy has picked up a new lady friend (Yutaka Nakajima).

Meanwhile, the ripped-off gang calls in two wily, kind-of-English-speaking members of the New York Mafia, who massacre Bunta's boys by throwing them off a skyscraper. Soon, mother and son are backed into a corner. Bunta gets himself arrested while mom undergoes police interrogation as to the whereabouts of the dope. After dodging a series of jailhouse assassination attempts, Bunta is heartbroken to discover that mom has died during her epic grilling. He escapes with the aid of fellow inmate Kunie Tanaka.

A karate-kicking passport forger (Sonny Chiba!) fingers Tanaka as a traitor, and he's quickly killed in gruesome fashion, as is the cop responsible for mom's death. Bunta and his best gal head north to take a boat out of the country. But at the shipyard, the yakuza and Mafia lie in wait, forcing Bunta to cut loose with his magnificent machine gun once and for all.

The last image is a doozy: a badly wounded Bunta limps off into a wave-swept horizon, Yutaka's body slung over his shoulder, a slave to maternal figures to the very end.

Flash, furious, and owing absolutely nothing to reality, *Machine Gun Dragon* is a yakuza wet dream. What will mom think when she washes the sheets?

☞ **Import only**

WANTED
Tsunehiko Watase (1944), aka Kid Brother, Watari Tetsuya's sibling always ready for street action.

Noboru Ando's Chronicle of Fugitive Days and Sex

Ando Noboru no waga tobo to Sex no kiroku

TOEI VIDEO
安藤昇の
NTSC Japan

1976, Toei
Director Noboru Tanaka
Cast Noboru Ando, Renji Ishibashi, Maya Hiromi

Imagine if convicted mobster John Gotti got financing from a major studio to make a movie about his sex life and spliced in between the couplings was a filth-encrusted critique of the American Dream. No way. Couldn't happen, right?

Well, this seemingly impossible scenario was actually played out in *Noboru Ando's Chronicle of Fugitive Days and Sex.* Directed by famed Nikkatsu *roman porno* chieftain Noboru Tanaka (*A Woman Called Sada Abe*), this "true story" penetrates the viewer's mind on multiple levels: as filthy movie, as social commentary, as a continuation of the "outlaw on the run" myth fundamental to yakuza film since the silent era.

It is 1958. Ando's pack of seven hoods are blamed for the shooting of company boss Hideki Yokoi. The cops call for a nationwide dragnet on the gang and their leader. While Ando's tubercular dum dum boys are roped in one by one (or die horrible deaths), Ando aims to make it out of Japan alone.

Slowing him down considerably are seven different women whom he willingly beds (copulation in this film consists of a naked woman writhing either below or on top of a completely poker-faced Ando) and whom all beg him to stay afterwards.

Despite the stressful Casanova existence, Ando finds just enough time to rail against a hypocritical society that condemns honest criminals like himself who have done the dirty work necessary to create Japan's economic miracle. Ando reasons, if he's going to be called a social disease, then he'll pledge to become the worst infection he possibly can, hoping to permanently cripple his host.

Thwarted in her attempts to keep Ando to herself, one girl (Maya Hiromi, who performs an explosive striptease with an uncooked hot dog in her mouth) tips off the cops, who finally slap the cuffs on Ando mid-coitus. "Wait until I'm finished!" he demands, but he's quickly tossed into the back of a police car.

In transit and in cuffs, Ando begins to jerk off, explaining to the mortified cops that "It's your fault. You didn't let me finish back there." Now a prisoner, Ando is in fact more triumphant than ever. "I feel like the Emperor!" are the final words of the film, followed by actual archival footage of Ando's real-life arrest.

Made during the decline of Toei's *jitsuroku* cycle, *Chronicle of Fugitive Days and Sex* is Ando's most corrosive shot in a lifelong battle against The Man, one that's sticky and hard to rub off.

☞ **Import only**

☞ **More: NOBORU ANDO p. 114**

Yakuza Cruel Secrets—Arm Dismemberment
Yakuza zankoku hiroku—Kataude setsudan

1976, Ando Planning/Toei
Director Noboru Ando
Cast Gangsters, Whores, Junkies, Good People

A punk in shades howls straight into the grimy lens of a shaky handheld 16mm camera, "Hey! What do you think you're doing? Stop filming!" before briefly assaulting the beholder.

This jolt of in-your-face footage, shot in grainy black and white, kicks off *Yakuza Cruel Secrets*, Noboru Ando's first and only session in the director's chair. His 65-minute production, filmed mostly around Shinjuku and Shibuya, penetrates the squalor of the Japanese underworld with an arsenal of hidden microphones and cameras in fine mondo movie fashion.

After interviews with middle-aged gangsters, who speak glowingly of brotherhood and loyalty, the film cuts to faceless men passing around a needle and shooting up speed. Two scenes, tracking the elaborate ceremony of the heads of two gangs meeting in time-honored ritual, are capped by dubious-looking stomach stabbings and titular arm hackings. Shocking!

The film's *tour de force* is a shot-in-color pinkie chopping, complete with hammer and chisel. As if to ask menacingly, "Does this look fake to you?" the camera zooms in on the severed digit.

The quest for truth cannot turn a blind eye, not even from human garbage and jizz-stained tiles. A gang of youth openly sniff great, big plastic bags full of paint thinner in the Shinjuku streets. The camera peeps through the window of a Turkish bathhouse where a voyeuristic sex scene is cut short, forcing Ando, doing double duty as narrator, to apologize, "This is all the censors will let us show."

Whatever myths still remain must be debunked even further. The traditional yakuza classes of *bakuto* (gambler) and *tekiya* (traveling salesman and racketeers) have respectively turned into addicts who compulsively bet on horses and old men who push plastic Ultraman masks and robot toys at outdoor festivals. Scandalous!

And just to show that the yakuza world is all about equal opportunity, there's a color segment on yakuza mistresses, which features fair maidens getting gorgeous full-back tattoos. We then get to admire the finished work as they take a bath.

As you'll discover in his interview, Ando's whole film career has been a tightrope walk between fact and fiction. Sold as a documentary, it's awfully hard to tell how much of his directorial handiwork is real and how much is staged. And after viewing the finished product, which feels like it was burnt into tinfoil and edited with a white-flecked razor blade, you'll probably agree that it's simply better not to ask.

☞ **Import only**

WANTED
Tatsuo Umemiya (born 1938), aka King of Eros, father to dishy Anna Umemiya. Currently playing host on cooking and comedy TV shows

the tattooed hit man
In the violent underworld of the Japanese mafia, there is only one rule... kill or be killed.

The Tattooed Hit Man

Yamaguchi-gumi gaiden—Kyushu shinko sakusen (Yamaguchi Gang Side-Story—Operation Kyushu Siege)

1974, Toei/1976, New Line Cinema
Director Kosaku Yamashita (Japan), Jack Sholder (US version)
Cast Bunta Sugawara, Tatsuo Umemiya, Tsunehiko Watase

After releasing Sonny Chiba's first two *Street Fighter* films in the US, New Line Cinema decided to capitalize on Sidney Pollack's *The Yakuza* and ignite what was certain to be the next big craze after karate movies: yakuza flicks! Sadly, *The Tattooed Hit Man* failed to take America by storm...or even make a minor cult star out of Bunta Sugawara—imaginatively billed by New Line as "Bud Sugawara."

Even so, *Hit Man* was the only *jitsuroku eiga* ever dubbed into English and remains the only legitimate place to see "Bud" and the whole sick crew on US home video.

The original Japanese film, an authorized account of the Yamaguchi gang's invasion of Kyushu in the early sixties, was an average-to-good Toei yakuza movie, much influenced by the previous year's trio of *Jingi naki tatakai* titles. Director Yamashita, who also helmed a previous film about the Yamaguchi-gumi in 1973 starring Bunta and Ken Takakura, would much improve in time with his ferocious *Nihon boryoku reto—Keihan shinko roshi no gundan* (Japan's Violent Islands—Kyoto-Osaka Killer Gangs), about Korean front-line hoodlums, in 1975.

The task of domesticating *Yamaguchi-gumi gaiden* fell to Jack Sholder (later to direct both *Nightmare on Elm Street 2* and *The Hidden* for New Line), who rewrote the script and did some trimming, including axing the entire last reel containing the climactic Kyushu invasion and the fate of numerous characters. Dubbed by Peter Fernandez and the *Speed Racer* pit crew (here's your chance to hear Speed say, "Hey asshole, you're in my way!"), the compromised quality of the new film is apparent when swarthy Hiroki Matsukata shows up and announces himself, as "Big Sonny of the Bobcat gang," which makes him sound about as menacing as an elementary school kid.

Yet, despite the numerous changes, Bunta's clap-ridden *gurentai* still gets to makes *the* classic yakuza movie speech, the message undiluted by translation: "I won't spend my life sitting around an office. We used to have guts. Not anymore. Now we hide behind the syndicate."

Perhaps the reason *Hit Man* failed to capture the imagination of a wider audience is because it isn't about a hood trying to shoot his way to the top ala *Scarface*, a smash-and-grab American dream. Instead, mad dog Bunta wantonly blows off any hope of success in favor of an inevitable downfall, winning via losing, a very yakuza gambit.

☞ **Available on VHS from New Line Home Video**
☞ **More: BUNTA SUGAWARA p. 112**

Tattooed Hit Man

He'll slay for pay, slash for cash, and kill for the thrill! The most deadly and charismatic Yakuza killer in underworld history - the TATTOOED HIT MAN! His name is Ginji! His body is illustrated! His every move is lethal!

A rival gang wounds his best friend. Ginji exacts revenge, eliminating one of their leaders. Escaping to Osaka, he forms another fighting force and extorts money from heroin smugglers. His friend becomes captain of the Kobe underworld. Gang war erupts! With mechanical efficiency, Ginji wipes the enemy off the map!

Feared by friend and foe alike Ginji stand alone - a human killing machine dealing death with bullets, blades, and bare hands! His heart is black -the color that's said to suit him best. No one can face him without facing oblivion!

Ginji runs wild! He blackmails Mr. Big, silences the silencers, wrecks the wrecking crew, and lays them low on murderers' row!

A raging rampage in a gambling house may cost him his last chance. Has his luck run out? Can he hit the hit men? Will Ginji plunge into the biggest bloodbath in Yakuza history? The TATTOOED HIT MAN has all the answers!

Running Time: 88 Min.

WANTED
Sonny Chiba, aka The Street Fighter, king of all street punks. A major player in the Okinawa Ten-Year War.

YAKUZA

Bunta Sugawara
Superstar

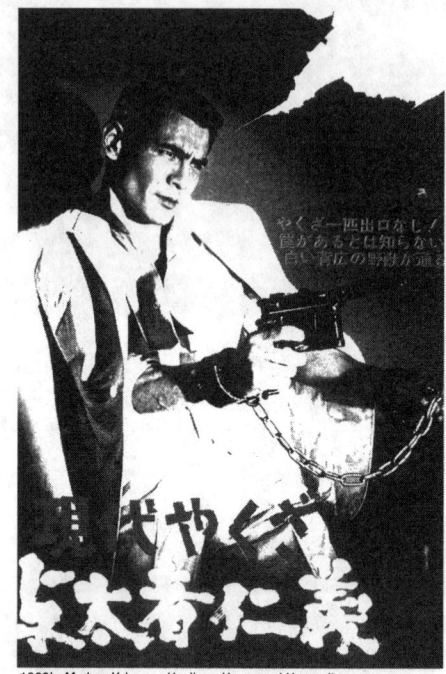

菅原文太

1969's Modern Yakuza—Hooligan Honor and Humanity.

If anyone is the burning soul of seventies yakuza film incarnate, it's Bunta.

Whether Bunta is essaying the role of yet another rubber-faced thug named Goro in the *Gendai yakuza* series, or burning cool in the role that rocketed him to fame, as Shozo Hirono, the last decent gangster in Japan, in the *Jingi naki tatakai* series, the odds are, if he's scowling and howling on the poster or video box, it's going to be worth a look.

In his numerous yakuza roles, Bunta (or "Bud," if you prefer his US *Tattooed Hit Man* billing) was like a *bento* box combination of James Cagney and Kirk Douglas, alternating between spastic street punks and authority figures. No one was badder at the game. No one was better.

Born in 1933 in the Miyazaki prefecture of Kyushu, Bunta dropped out of prestigious Waseda University to work as a fashion model. He made his first screen appearance in the 1956 Toho film *In the Town of Pathos, the Fog Falls*. Sighted by director Teruo Ishii, Bunta was cast in the lead for Ishii's 1958 Shin Toho mystery film *Hakusen himistu chitai* (White Line—Secret Zone).

Bunta soon became a fixture in many of the exploitation-minded studio's war films, horror flicks, and action movies. His tall size and good looks found him billed as one of the studio's "Handsome Towers." (The other two were Teruo Yoshida and Shigeru Amachi.)

After Shin Toho started to sink in 1961, Bunta moved to Shochiku for a host of period film roles and made it over to Toei just in time to take supporting roles in various *ninkyo* (chivalrous) yakuza films, work which included the five-film *Kanto tekiya ika* series and playing a blind whip-master in Tomisaburo Wakayama's *Wicked Priest* (*Gokuaku bozu*) series.

After his early seventies yakuza revisionist collaborations with Kinji Fukasaku, the new anti-heroic, Hiroshima-dialect-speaking

PROFILE

Bunta was a major star, racking up best actor awards for his performances in the *Jingi naki tatakai* films.

The decade also saw him packing houses as Momojiro Hoshi, the star-branded big-rig driver in Norifumi Suzuki's comedic *Truck yaro* series (Truck Rascals, ten films 1975-79) which had him driving across Japan with his buddy Kinya Aikawa, like wandering travelers of old.

As the ultraviolent yakuza era wrapped up, Bunta took up one of his best non-mobster roles, that of police inspector Yamashita in 1979's *The Man Who Stole the Sun,* co-scripted by Leonard Schrader.

Bunta's output slowed down slightly in the eighties while he devoted time to raising his son, whom he took out of public school to educate himself. (A testimony to a job well done, his son recently graduated with top honors from law school.)

Bunta has joined the ranks of Japan's most venerable actors, appearing in Kon Ichikawa's *Dora Heita,* and lending prestige to anime productions like *Tekken* with his distinctive voice. He also still takes the occasional role in action-oriented V-cinema productions, work which includes the 1992 shot-in-the-USA *Distant Justice* starring George Kennedy and David Carradine.

Bunta has long since refused to play the role of celebrity as agreeably as his peers, by either authoring cookbooks (like Jo Shishido) or playing game-show contestant (like Tatsuo Umemiya) to keep himself in the public eye. In fact, Bunta has actively chosen to separate himself from his past, refusing interviews and downplaying his old hell-raising days as king of modern yakuza.

All of which only makes him even cooler. 東

東映
なぜ吠える
なぜ暴れるか
野良犬文太！
現代やくざ
カラー作品
監督・深作欣二

"Why do you bark? Why do you behave wildly? You stray dog Bunta!" 1972's *Modern Yakuza–Outlaw Killer.*

WANTED
Tetsuro Tanba (born 1922) aka Tiger, aka Nostradamus. An ever-present shadowy figure alluding to deeper conspiracies

Noboru Ando: From Gangster To Gang Star

By TDC Fujiki

This article first appeared in Japanese in *Eiga Hi-Ho* magazine. Translation by Akemi Wegmuller.

Noboru Ando stars in 1967's *Imprisoned for 18 Years—Parole*.

Parco, Loft, Tokyu Hands, HMV...some of the coolest and most fashionable stores in Japan line the streets of Udagawa-cho, the most hopping quarter in Tokyo's trendy Shibuya district. It's the kind of place that goes with the sounds of Japanese R&B, where schoolgirls in mini-skirted uniforms stroll around licking ice cream cones and boys in hip-hop gear sprint through the streets, cell phones in hand. A youth-culture mecca, a symbol of peace and prosperity and the focus of worldwide fascination...

And yet, only fifty years ago, this very same Udagawa-cho was known as "a place that will silence a crying child"—a realm of blood-soaked, bullet-strewn violence!

Its maze of little alleys, which today bear stylish names like Spain-zaka, Organ-zaka, and Penguin-dori, was back then the "Casbah of Tokyo," crowded with shady bars and cabarets into which hostesses in garish makeup would beckon passing men.

Hoods and G.I.s walked the streets like they owned the place, while in back of the bars, drunken customers were being punched, kicked, and worked over by gangs of hooligans.... Oh yes, Udagawa-cho in the days following the end of the Pacific War was a terrifying Den of Iniquity!!

In this era of anarchy was a man who, barely in his twenties, attained the pinnacle of the quarter's pyramid of violence.

Noboru Ando: leader of the Ando-gumi yakuza organization, whose name reverberated throughout Tokyo's postwar underworld. Born in 1925 in Shinjuku, Ando had made a name for himself among local delinquents by his mid-teens. Returning to Tokyo after spending the war training in the Navy's "suicide attack" forces, he plunged into the bloody gang warfare of Shinjuku and Shibuya while enrolled at Hosei University, becoming a prototype "student yakuza" who swaggered around with an entourage of several dozen followers. The Ando-gumi (formal name: Higashi Kogyo), which he formed at the age of 26, had over 500 members at its zenith, and before long Ando was inspiring terror as the young hellraiser of

INTERVIEW

the postwar yakuza world, setting his sights on domination of the entire metropolitan area.

In 1958, however, Ando was sentenced to six years in prison for his role in the shooting of Hideki Yokoi, a young industrialist known as "The Takeover Kid," who had taken the business world by storm. (Yokoi himself was later arrested in connection with a fatal fire at the Hotel New Japan, which he owned.) Following his release, Ando dissolved the Ando-gumi and, turning himself into a movie star, burst into the world of the silver screen!!

His debut feature, Shochiku's *Chi to okite* (Blood and the Code), was a major hit, unleashing a steady stream of Ando vehicles, most of which were "true story" yakuza flicks portraying the life and times of Ando himself in his bad old days. In other words, Noboru Ando the actor was playing none other than the young, real-life yakuza and Ando-gumi boss, Noboru Ando!!

The head of a criminal gang, arrested as the prime culprit in a sensational incident, enjoys a successful career as a movie star after his release from jail, primarily by reenacting his own violent past! Search the world over, and you probably won't find a story like it. Even Ice-T, Ice Cube, the late Tupac Shakur, and other black West Coast gangsta rappers in the US who achieved Hollywood stardom in the nineties never actually acted out their own youthful transgressions on screen.

From this fact alone, you get an idea of what an extraordinary life Ando has led. Today as the president of the film production company Ando Kikaku (and naturally making guest appearances as an actor, with his own large photo featured as prominently as the stars' in all the posters!!), Noboru Ando looks back on his youth as follows:

Ando: "Back then, fighting was like playing around. You go out, play around, fight people, make a name for yourself. Fighting was a good way to make pals, too. That's what made it fun.

"The time I slashed that college student, Akimoto, I used one of those cheap razors like they sell at public baths. You break off the handle, and...at the time, the fashion for students was to wear a buckle with their school crest on it, and that's where you hid it. You pull it out real fast and cut the other guy. It doesn't go very deep—you just sort of graze him with it. But all this blood spurts out, right? And on top of that, the other guy can't believe this high school kid just slashed him. For me, it was here. I'm facing off against someone older and way bigger than me, and I know if I fight him fair and square, I lose. So I'm desperate, right?

"After that first time, I used the razor a lot, slashed a lot of guys. I wasn't afraid of anybody. I didn't care if they were older or what, I'd cut them with the razor, and then make sure they knew who I was. I'd say, 'You're looking at Ando of Shinjuku!!'

"And that's how your name gets around. But I slashed so many people in the face, later I got it here (indicating left cheek) myself. Well, you reap what you sow.... But everything changed after the war. Those days were...how do I put it...that time had a special mood of its own." Ando spent the war in the Mie prefecture, training with the Navy's aircraft division. Having closed the door on delinquency and violence, the 17-year-old Ando endured the brutal preparatory training for a year and a half, and in June 1945, was assigned to a kamikaze base in Yokosuka. Any day now, he would be climbing into a plane and diving down from the sky into an enemy ship...*banzai!* But the order that came instead was to undergo the hellish

WANTED
Koji Tsuruta (1924-1987) former *ninkyo* star turned leader of Japan's Violent Gangs and the Foreign Gambler's Corps.

YAKUZA

training for the special diving unit, the *Fukuryutai* (Crouching Dragon Unit).

Crouching dragon—an apt name indeed. In this unit, marines wearing thick rubber suits with shoes of lead were trained to dive and cling to the underside of enemy vessels carrying explosives in their arms, to bomb them from below. You could call it a training camp for killer robots of the depths.

But on August 15, 1945, before the order had been given for this unit to begin operations, Japan acknowledged it had lost the war.

Suddenly released from a fate of sure death, Noboru Ando came back from the war unexpectedly alive, filled with a nihilism and confusion that derived from this experience.

Ando: "Suddenly one day, they tell you we lost the war, so you're demobilized…and Uncle Sam rules the world, right? Everything you believed in until that point is, poof, gone. And on top of that, America—your enemy until the day before—is now the good guy.…

"That's when I thought, 'Might is right.' From now on, if you're strong enough, you can get away with anything. So that's what I did! That's what that time—the period after the war—was like."

Carrying a big hollow space in his soul, Noboru Ando took to prowling the black markets of Shinjuku.

In the black markets, people from former colonies liberated by Japan's defeat—Chinese, Taiwanese, Koreans—lorded it over the locals.

Ando teamed up with some rough buddies from the old days to begin selling foodstuffs to black marketeers, earning some income in the process. With money in his pocket, he naturally started making more friends. Using a coffee shop in Shimokitazawa as his hangout, Ando began to form a group. Its main members were Ando and his childhood pal, Mitsugu Kano.

Kano raised hell in postwar Shinjuku together with Ando, and when Ando later moved into Shibuya, became the leader of all the hooligans (*gurentai*) in the entire Shinjuku area. These two young toughs—who called each other by their childhood nicknames of "Anchan" and "Mitchan"—were the strongest tag team in Shinjuku.

With the money brought in by their food supply business, Ando and his cronies bought made-to-order suits and shoes. The suits were wide in the shoulder and narrow at the waist in accordance with the latest style, while the shoes were US Army surplus, shiny and brand-new.

Dressed to the nines in this movie-star attire, Ando and his followers swaggered around the postwar hot spots like they owned them, immediately attracting the envy of all the young toughs around. The youths who swarmed around Ando were all fearsome, dreaded fighters—members of the Hosei University karate team, Nippon University boxing team, Meiji University cheering squad, Kokushikan judo team and so on—what you might call "fight professionals."

The battle royale of Ando's Shimokitazawa period was with the Sanda-gumi, a local gang of racketeers (*tekiya*). The Sanda-gumi boss, feeling his authority questioned by these greenhorn students insolently strutting around his hard-earned black market territory, sent a sword-wielding assassin into the Ando group's hangout.

Ando was just twenty years old at the time.

Ando's feud with the Sanda-gumi ended in a truce the following spring of 1946, with the intercession of Toichi Bannen, a Shinjuku big gun. Bannen had made his name in the prewar era, and as the original "lone wolf" *gurentai* who never belonged to any yakuza gang, was highly respected by Ando, Kano, and other young toughs. Ando and Kano began to associate more closely with Bannen following his mediation of the Sanda-gumi conflict, and later came to be known as "the dragon and tiger of the Bannen set."

Noboru Ando's left cheek bears a long, thin scar stretching from the edge of his mouth to his ear.

Also in April 1946, Ando enrolled in Hosei University's preparatory course (at the time, universities had six-year programs consisting of three years of prep and three years of specialized study), becoming a "student yakuza" in both name and fact.

Hosei's prep classes at the time were taught in Musashi-Kosugi on the Tokyu Toyoko train line, so Ando was forced to pass through Shibuya, the Toyoko line's terminus. The black market in front of Shibuya station was a student hangout.

A recent film depicting this era in Ando's life is *Jitsuroku—Juku no tsura dai ichibu* (True Story—Master of Shinjuku, Part One), a 1997 release from Toei. (However, the protagonist is Koji Matoba's Mitsugu Kano. Ando is a supporting character played by Toshiro Yanagiba and Toichi Bannen is played by Tatsuo Umemiya. It's a pity that the movie in general is pretty sentimental, but you can more or less catch the mood of the stylish hoods in their coffee shop hangout waiting for their enemies to show up.)

But the most important movie in this regard is definitely Toei's 1973 *Yakuza to koso—Jitsuroku Ando-gumi* (Yakuza Warfare—The True Story of the Ando Gang). Based on *Yakuza to koso*, Ando's classic memoir, this was the first in a series that make up the "Ando-gumi Saga," followed, in order of release, by *Jitsuroku Ando-gumi—Shugekihen* (True Story of the Ando Gang—The Attacks, 1973, director Junya Sato), *Ando-gumi gaiden—Hitokiri shatei* (Ando Gang Side Story—The Killer Swordsman Follower, 1974, director Sadao Nakajima), and *Ando Noboru no waga tobo to Sex no kiroku* (Noboru Ando's Chronicle of Fugitive Days and Sex). (Chronologically, the events in *Hitokiri shatei* take place before those in *Shugekihen*).

Jitsuroku Ando-gumi starts out with Noboru Ando forming a fast friendship with Kano following a knock-down, all-out fight. It then moves from Ando getting his face slashed in 1949 to the formation of the Ando-gumi. The first half of the film, with its scenes of Ando brawling in his student uniform, were played by Noboru Ando at the age of 48!!

Above all, the main impact of this film lies in some of the most brutal scenes ever depicted in Toei's "true story" yakuza movies. The savage lynch scenes include:

• Facial branding with a red-hot iron rod (Aaargh!)
• A chisel stabbed straight in the eyeball!! (Gyaaargh!)
• Ears being sliced off (Awwwoo!)
• Face pressed onto a hot stove (OUCH)
• Scissors chopping off private parts!! (....!!)
• Arms hacked in two with a broadaxe!! (Stop already!!)

I thought I'd better ask the man himself if such tortures had in fact been inflicted by the Ando gang.

Ando *(laughing)*: "We never went that far. The director was probably copying Spaghetti Westerns or something."

So much for that.

WANTED. Akira Kobayashi (born 1937) former Nikkatsu youth idol and singing cowpoke turned denizen of the Violent Street.

YAKUZA

Noboru Ando's left cheek bears a long, thin scar stretching from the edge of his mouth to his ear. Without it, this handsome actor would remind you of a pedigreed hunting dog. But it's there, proof of the wild, hungry wolf he actually once was—the alpha male among the hooligans who controlled Shibuya in the days after WWII.

Ando: "...yeah, my scar...If I didn't have this, I might have ended up in an ordinary line of work....Might have, who knows...nah, I don't think so *[laughs]*. I never was cut out to work in some 9-to-5 job. But I'd never had a care in my life, and that scar gave me something to worry about. I mean, at first it was like this huge centipede on my face. You get a scar like that, you're never going to make it in the straight world. Yeah, I'd have to say it was a real blow."

Yakuza, yakuza...I might as well face it, that's what I am.

1949. Noboru Ando was sailing along full mast with his black-market and legit businesses, when he was assaulted by the flash of a sharp blade.

Dressed in a freshly tailored expensive suit of fine English wool, and sporting a flashy red tie with a flower print, Ando was strolling though Ginza, attracting the admiring glances of passing women. An acquaintance called his name.

"Hey, Ando-san!!"

Turning towards the voice, he saw Sai, a notorious hooligan with the Korean mob that was running wild in the black markets.

"Ando-san! I greet you, so why you ignore me?!"

He was clearly itching for a fight.

Fwip! Something skimmed his cheek. And then a hot, heavy jolt assaulted Ando's head.

"Uh! What the hell...?"

An enormous wound gaped open on the left side of Noboru Ando's face, and bright red blood was gushing out like spring water. The left half of his new suit was soon soaked black with blood.

Staggering, Ando chased after Sai, who was fleeing with the glinting knife in his hand.

"I'll kill you, dammit, I'll kill you, I'll kill you...!"

Now I'm a yakuza for life! I can rub it and wash it all I want, this centipede-like scar on my face ain't going away. Yakuza, yakuza...I might as well face it, that's what I am. Submit to it, Noboru! (quote from Ando's book, *Yakuza to koso*)

It was at this juncture that Ando made the decision to shift his life's course from that of "black marketeer" to "yakuza." A month later, he had one of his underlings stab the Korean, Sai, to death.

This incident, the turning point in the life of Noboru Ando, is depicted in the opening scenes of Toei's 1973 movie, *Yakuza to koso—Jitsuroku Ando-gumi*. But there, the man who slashes Ando has been changed from a Korean to the Japanese Ginza boss, Dosu "Dagger" Ken played by Rin-ichi Yamamoto. This change may have been made for political considerations, by either Toei management or the director, Junya Sato. However, the fact that it was a Korean who gave Ando his scar has not been entirely obliterated from the Ando-gumi saga. In 1974's *Ando-gumi gaiden—Hitokiri shatei*, there's a scene in which a young member of the Ando-gumi (Tsunehiko Watase) boasts of his boss' exploits to a prostitute. He says, "That Korean who slashed his face, I heard he turned him into hash!"

Looking at all these acts of violence, you

INTERVIEW

might get the impression that the 24-year-old Noboru Ando was an extremely brutal outsider, but he was also following the code of yakuza society, which stresses respect, courtesy, and conformity within its own rules. Or you might say he was a resourceful, strategic leader of young hooligans, a youthful elite yakuza.

Kei Hanagata. The man who stood at the very vertex of Tokyo's student hooligans. Tall and powerful, with a body hardened by boxing and rugby, Hanagata had never once been beaten in a bare-knuckle fight and barehanded was the only way he fought. Known as the "Ogre of Greater Edo," he always dressed like a dandy, the way a Shibuya gangster should: rimless spectacles, white felt hat, white suit, with a white trenchcoat slung over his shoulder.

Ando and Hanagata first met in 1950.

While Ando was in prison, Kei Hanagata took over as interim Ando-gumi leader in 1961 (Hanagata himself was in jail from 1958 to 1960), but was stabbed to death with a sashimi knife in 1963, by a young member of the Machii-gumi. He was 33.

The life of Kei Hanagata was depicted in such movies as *Ando-gumi gaiden—Hitokiri shatei* and *Kizu* (Scar), a 1988 Toei film directed by Shunichi Kajima. In *Hitokiri shatei*, he was a character named Ken played by Bunta Sugawara like a rabid dog. In *Kizu*, Takanori Jinnai portrays him in a lighter vein. There's another movie, *Shuraba no ningengaku* (Anthropology of a Fight Scene, 1993, Toei, directed by Shunichi Kajima), in which Kei Hanagata appears as a major character. Here he's played by Shinji Yamashita. Although violent scenes are few in this film, Yamashita's performance gives you a glimpse of the volcanic fury and sadness lurking below the surface. Noboru Ando also praises Yamashita's portrayal highly, saying "Shinji Yamashita's Kei Hanagata is the closest to the real thing."

In 1952, the offices of Higashi Kogyo—commonly known as the Ando-gumi—opened in Shibuya's Udagawa-cho. With regard to hanging out this shingle, Noboru Ando has written:

Although our group had pulled together tighter than ever before, as a "new emerging force" of the postwar era, we got a lot of pressure put on us from the outside. They do you, you do them back—if you didn't follow this hard and fast rule, no matter what, you would never be able to come out on top. (from *Yakuza to koso*)

Ando made his top lieutenants and other ranking members wear grey suits as a uniform to let others know they belonged to the Ando-gumi. It wasn't only their style that made the Ando-gumi different. "Ando-gumi" was only the commonly used name for the organization, which was formally called "Higashi Kogyo"—also the name of a registered joint-stock corporation. Its operations were centered around real estate and entertainment, as well as bills of exchange and loans. The bills of exchange were handled by Hiroshi Shimada, who was well versed in the requisite laws. The Ando-gumi, in other words, was a forerunner of what would later be known as "economic yakuza."

On the night of June 11, 1958, as the rain poured down in Ginza, the sound of a gunshot rang out.

What had happened a few minutes earlier in that building—the Dai-ni Sennari Building in Ginza 8-chome?

At 7:20, a waxen-faced man entered the reception area to the president's office of the Toyo Shipping Company, located on the eighth floor of the building.

The man, pale and thin like an angel of

WANTED
Junko Fuji (born 1945) The Red Peony Gambler. Back in action after long retirement.

YAKUZA

death, slipped through the door and into the president's office, without making a sound.

"You Yokoi?"

Without waiting for an answer, he pulled out a Browning .32 from inside his jacket, and pointed it at the man in the bow tie.

"Gyaaaah!"

By the time the receptionist's scream echoed through the building, the specter was gone.

The Hideki Yokoi shooting incident, a decisive chapter in the life of Noboru Ando, has been depicted in numerous movies such as *Chi to okite* (1965, Shochiku/Dai-nana Group, director Namio Yuasa) and *Jitsuroku Ando-gumi—Shugekihen* (1973, Toei).

To trace the cause of the incident, we have to go back one week before, when Tomio Motoyama, a debt collector with an office in Hibiya, paid Ando a visit.

Hideki Yokoi had suddenly skyrocketed to prominence in financial circles in the early 1950s and was a major celebrity. He had first attracted widespread media coverage with his bid to take over the venerable Shirakiya department store. By his early forties, Yokoi had acquired a controlling interest in numerous companies.

Motoyama was asking Ando for his help in recovering 20 million yen of the Mitsuzuka family's money from Yokoi who had only paid back 10 milllion of the original 30 million loan.

Ando thus paid a visit with Motoyama to Hideki Yokoi's sanctuary, the president's office of Toyo Shipping.

But Yokoi only called in his counsel in charge of the lawsuit (brought by the widow Mitsuzuka, which was found in Yokoi's favor because the only assets in his name were ¥30,000 in a post office account) and had him lazily explain the trial proceedings and the legitimacy of the verdict.

The fury I had been suppressing exploded at Yokoi's next words.

"If you'd like, I can teach you fellows how to borrow money and never have to pay it back, ha ha!"

I leaned forward: "You sonofabitch, you call yourself a human being? Yokoi, you'll pay for this...." (quoted from the book *Gekido—Chi nurareta hansei*, "Upheaval—Half a Lifetime Covered in Blood")

With this parting threat, Ando and Motoyama left the office. Following this meeting, Ando embarked recklessly on a plan to shoot Yokoi like a man possessed.

And so, at the age of 32, Noboru Ando went on the lam. His sex-filled days as a fugitive had begun.

Kazuhiro Chiba, who had worked in a gun shop in Marunouchi and was an experienced marksman, was chosen to do the deed.

Chiba was already infected with tuberculosis. Looking back later, Noboru Ando speculated that, with his weak constitution, Chiba didn't expect to live much longer and wanted to go out with a bang.

In *Ando Noboru no waga tobo to Sex no kiroku* (1976, Toei, director Noboru Tanaka), the scene in Higashi Kogyo's Akasaka branch office has actor Renji Ishibashi's Hiroshi Shimada coughing non-stop while Keizo Kanie's Kazuhiro Chiba spews blood all over the place, giving the scene a gloomy beauty typical of Noboru Tanaka, who started out making Nikkatsu *roman porno* flicks. I initially found the robust, virile characterizations of Ando-gumi members in 1973's *Jitsuroku Ando-gumi—Shugekihen* (the consumptive Shiga and Chiba portrayed by the suntanned Tatsuo Umemiya and Eiji Go, and

INTERVIEW

Rikiya Yasuoka as the character apparently based on Hiroshi Yasuda) to be more believable, and considered Tanaka's direction to be a little overdone. Doing research for this series of articles, however, I was astonished to realize that *Waga tobo...* is actually closer to reality. The Ando-gumi may have been stylish, but it was also a surprisingly unhealthy band of men.

The night of June 11, 1958.

Ando-gumi member Kazuhiro Chiba, under the order of Noboru Ando, sped through Ginza in the pouring rain, clutching a Browning .32 under his coat and feeling an oppressive pain in his chest, perhaps due to the changing weather of the rainy season. He raced up the stairs to the building's eighth floor, and slipped into the president's office.

Bang!

The bullet pierced Hideki Yokoi's arm.

But (contrary to Ando's order) it was not his right arm. Kazuhiro Chiba had shot Yokoi in the left arm, where it passed through into Yokoi's torso, making a goulash of his internal organs before coming to rest in his abdominal region. Although hemorrhaging heavily, in critical condition, and unconscious, Yokoi survived.

June 12. The Tsukiji station of the Metropolitan Police determines, from the business cards found in Yokoi's office, that the crime was carried out by the Ando-gumi.

June 13. A warrant is issued for the arrest of Noboru Ando, along with an unrelated charge of extortion. The police announce that, if Ando is not arrested that day, they will send out an all points bulletin.

And so, at the age of 32, Noboru Ando went on the lam. His sex-filled days as a fugitive had begun.

Having spent the first day after the shooting in Atami with a woman whose bar he'd wandered into the night before, Ando parted with her that evening and took a taxi with Shiga to Hakone, where there was an inn he frequented. A maid, who already knew about the situation, led them to a back room where they wouldn't run into other guests. There, finally freed of their tension, they slept like the dead.

Day 2 (June 13): Ando and Shiga leave Hakone around noon, taking the Odakyu line into Tokyo to deal with the uproar. At this juncture, Ando's intention was to spend the night with his lover in Harajuku, and then turn himself in the next day. But after reading in the paper about the additional extortion charge, a trumped-up one at that, he changed his mind.

Now that I'm in it this far, I might as well offer up Yokoi's boss Keita Itsushima, aka "Plundering Keita," as a sacrifice.... The thought crossed my mind. From now on, it was clear that no matter how this thing played out, I'd have political pressure put on me by Itsushima's forces. This was the almighty "Plundering Keita," after all. Take him on, and forget about coming up short—I'd be getting too much in change. The decision was made to attack Keita Itsushima. (quoted from *Gekido*)

Day 3: Ando was still at his lover's place in Harajuku. He actually had several women, but this one was his newest, and the police didn't know about her. Appearing as "Yasuko" in Ando's memoirs, she was still in her late teens. We know this much about her from *Gekido*:

Yasuko was 19, and a New Face actress at Toei studios. Crowned as Miss Nagoya, and then an actress, she had always been envied by those of her own sex as she followed a path of glory. She would stroll around Ginza dressed in the height of fashion....

So who was this "Yasuko"? Noboru Ando himself gave me the answer.

Ando: "Yasuko was Yoko Yamaguchi.

WANTED
Tora-san (born 1969) violent criminal mastermind of the *tekiya* rackets. May have faked his own death to elude capture. Shoot to kill!!

YAKUZA

You didn't know that? It's famous. She was hired with Yoshiko Sakuma and others in Toei's fourth round of 'New Face' hirings."

Yoko Yamaguchi. The glamorous mama-san of Hime (Princess), an exclusive Ginza nightclub, and a talented lyricist to boot. Yamaguchi wrote the lyrics for Hiroshi Itsuki's "Yokohama Tasogare" and "Yozora" (which won a Record of the Year award), Kiyoshi Nakajo's "Uso," Yujiro Ishihara's "Brandy Glass," and many other major hits. In 1980 she published her first novel, and in 1985 won the Naoki Prize, a prestigious literary award.

Might Yoko Yamaguchi have written about her relationship with Ando in her novels? It turns out she has. The story *"Jofu—Onna—"* (Whore—Woman—) in her short story collection *Bad Boy* is about a woman, Matsu Yamazaki, whose lover, Kirishima, stays with her while on the run. Although the names have been changed, the story contains vivid descriptions that could only be based on real-life experience. For example:

I (Matsu Yamazaki) repeatedly boiled water in a small kettle, and filled two buckets with it. Kirishima removed his clothing, and completely naked, stood with one foot in each bucket. His dark-skinned body was magnificent.... "Wash me like this." I wrung a towel and, starting at his shoulders, began to swab him carefully. As I descended to his chest, then his stomach and further down, Kirishima watched me teasingly, as if to say, "Don't skip anything, be thorough now." Kirishima's manhood lay asleep, surrounded by thick grass.... I poured warm water over it, over and over. The surrounding grass grew damp, and the sleeping animal began to rouse itself, gathering strength. When it was standing straight up, Kirishima pressed it against my ear...." "No..." It tickled. As I pulled away,

giggling, he grabbed me by the hair and rubbed it against my eyes and then my entire face, finally bringing it to my lips. "Purse your lips, like you're whistling. Now roll your tongue around, mmm, that's good. Not just the tip, take it deeper into your throat.... Yeah, like that, now hold still—stop!" Kirishima suddenly tensed his thighs and ceased moving. Some green-tasting sap pooled by the side of my tongue, but Kirishima had apparently restrained himself from coming.

Ando, the dandified hero of street toughs everywhere, appearing buck naked in a porno movie...!

Ando stayed with Yamaguchi until the 18th, the seventh day after the incident. Why did he leave the safety of this hiding place, which was unknown to the police?

Even with a new lover, I couldn't spend more than a week holed up nose-to-nose. That's just the way I was back then. (quoted from an article in the March 29, 1965 issue of *Shukan Bunshun* magazine)

The movie depicting this period in Noboru Ando's life is director Noboru Tanaka's *Ando Noboru no waga tobo to Sex no kiroku*. This film is virtually a faithful adaptation of the section in Ando's memoir, *Yakuza to koso*, recounting the period after the Hideki Yokoi incident (parts of the story overlap with *Gekido*). But the sex scenes, which were pretty terse in the book, were greatly expanded in number, drawing disbelief at the time of the film's release. "Noboru Ando's starring in a porno flick?!" The actresses playing his lovers were Moeko Esawa as the bar proprietress in Atami, Mayumi Ogino as Yoko Yamaguchi, Aoi Nakajima as K.H. (great performance!), and Maya Hiromi as T.H. As for

INTERVIEW

the twelve days that Ando spent in the Tamura residence of which almost nothing is known, perhaps former stripper Maya Hiromi was used because T.H. started out as a *nichigeki* dancer (though that's a very different kind of dancing), but there are erotic scenes such as T.H. doing a private striptease for Ando, which may derive from new information provided by Ando when the screenplay was being written. By the way, Ando and Hiromi perform two sex scenes in this movie.

Waga tobo... was the final film in which Noboru Ando played the leading role. It ends with Ando's arrest, and the incredible sight of the former gang boss masturbating in a police car! Ando, the dandified hero of street toughs everywhere, appearing buck naked in a porno movie, which ends with him jacking off onscreen.... I believed for a long time that Ando had quit the movie industry due to dissatisfaction with this humiliating last scene and shame in general at the way the film was directed. At our April 1999 interview, I asked him straight out if this was the case, and received the following answer.

Ando: "Doing that movie was fun because all you had to do was get it on with the girls *[laughs]*. You sit there in the dressing room in a bathrobe, throw it off when they call you, and go at it. It was great, having these actresses rubbing their pussies against me. I'd do it again today, but my body isn't up to it *[laughs]*. Would be nice if it wasn't just a movie and you could actually do the deed *[laughs]*."

But didn't the jack-off scene piss him off?

Ando: "Well, that didn't actually happen in real life, but what can you do, it's a movie. But that was a fun experience."

On July 4, Ando's 23rd day as a fugitive, the situation took a new turn.

That morning the Prime Minister, Shinsuke Kishi, called in the head of the Metropolitan Police for a tête-à-tête meeting. "The suspect in the Yokoi case has not been arrested yet," he said, adding a rare request, "Put greater effort into arresting the suspect and cracking down on gang activity in the streets." The order went out to all police stations to put the entire police force on the job of arresting Ando and his men.

At the same time, this signaled the start of a "hooligan roundup" (*gurentai-gari*) campaign by all the police in the metropolitan area.

The night of July 5th through the wee hours of the 6th, some 260 uniformed and plainclothes officers were dispatched to the nightspots of Shinjuku. They took into custody 136 gang members, street punks, and prostitutes. Ando-gumi leader Kei Hanagata was also arrested that day, in Jingu Gaien park.

That morning, Noboru Ando stole away from the Tamura residence in Shibuya and, disguised in a Pan Am pilot's uniform, slipped through the roadblocks set up on the main arteries to arrive at a villa in Hayama, near Zushi, which he had rented through a man called Hirose, who ran an entertainment firm in Kawasaki.

Ando was finally traced because, the morning he left the Tamura residence, he had dropped T.H. off at her parents' house.

Day 35. July 15, 1:30 p.m.

Twenty policemen in riot gear, from the Kanagawa Prefectural Police and the local Hayama station, surrounded the white villa.

"You... you Noboru Ando?!"

With a glance at the countless guns surrounding him, the man in the long cotton drawers quietly said, "Yeah, that's right."

Noboru Ando, leader of the Ando-gumi wanted for attempted murder, was arrested

123

YAKUZA

together with key member Hiroshi Shimada.

Even after Noboru Ando's arrest, the security forces continued to crack down mercilessly on the metropolitan area's hoods. Most of those arrested were in their teens and twenties.

Noboru Ando, leader of the Ando-gumi wanted for attempted murder, was arrested.

While holed up in Hayama, Ando claims to have written the following letter to the *Mainichi Shimbun* and *Yomiuri Shimbun* newspapers:

This policy of the government is a hoax.... Have they ever, even a little, tried to empathize with the hopelessness, the pain of today's youth? I assert that the anger I feel is not restricted to those of us you refer to as gangsters, but smolders in the hearts of all the young people in Japan.

This text has been used as a voice-over in practically every movie starring Noboru Ando that dealt with the Hideki Yokoi incident. You might call it the message that Noboru Ando has tried to convey throughout his life.

But there were reasons why the security forces had to crack down on hoodlums such as Ando.

In the early fifties, business interests, no longer able to tolerate the frequent mass demonstrations being organized by socialist union activists, got the right-wing bigwig, Yoshio Kodama, to act as the mastermind in forming an anti-communist paramilitary force comprising *bakuto* and *tekiya* (gamblers and peddlers, two traditional types of yakuza) from all over the country. But the *gurentai*, the hooligans who emerged from the hurlyburly world of the black markets in the immediate postwar era, were antiestablishment at heart, and were viewed by both the business world and the traditional yakuza as a dangerous element that must be eliminated or brought into the fold.

In later years, Ando made the following statement:

At first, I had no intention of shooting Yokoi. Yokoi was a villain, but he wasn't the biggest villain in Japan at that time. I planned to punish the top ten villains in Japan, and had even made a list. Among politicians, it included the LDP's Ichiro Kono, among business interests there was Keita Itsushima, head of the Tokyu Concern who was known as "Plundering Keita," and among fixers there was Yoshio Kodama, the right-wing big wheel. These were the Top Three. Teach them a lesson, and the world would be a better place. (from an article in the February 1999 issue of *Gendai* magazine, by Eiji Oshima)

December 25. The court's decision in the first hearing handed Noboru Ando a fine Christmas present: an eight-year prison sentence.

On September 15, 1964, Noboru Ando was released on parole after serving six years. He was 38. His return immediately brought new life back to the Ando-gumi, but circumstances surrounding these ex-*gurentai* yakuza had undergone a major change. A new era of gang warfare had begun.

On November 7, less than two months after Ando's release, Kengo Nishihara, a young Ando-gumi member, was shot dead in an Aoyama restaurant by a member of the Kinsei-kai, later the Inagawa-kai.

This endless spiral of blood washed away with more blood...I had spent several years fighting to survive in this life, and for what? An indescribable sense of isolation pressed down on my soul. I decided to dissolve the Ando-

INTERVIEW

gumi. (from *Gekido*)

On December 9, 1964, a poster was put up in front of the entrance to the Sendagaya Public Auditorium. In clear brushstrokes, it read, "Ando-gumi Dissolution Ceremony Venue."

Having performed the last rites for his own organization, Ando planned to leave Japan and move to Southeast Asia. Countries such as Thailand and Laos were eager to have Japanese industries open local plants, and Ando dreamed of clearing the jungle to build factories and leisure facilities. However, although he received a visa to make a preliminary inspection tour of the region, he was denied one for a second visit and was unable to leave the country. Just when his dream of launching a business career in Southeast Asia went up in smoke, a movie director showed up at his door.

His name was Namio Yuasa. Yuasa was an up-and-coming director with Dai-nana Group, an independent production company specializing in porn, who was making a name for himself with sex films such as *Yoru no masho* (Temptress of the Night), *Kinjirareta toi michi* (The Forbidden Distant Road), *Seien* (Sex Banquet), and *Mesubachi* (Queen Bee). He had read Noboru Ando's story in an autobiographical article published in a weekly magazine and wanted to turn it into a movie. The rest, as they say, is history. Let's hear it from the man himself.

Ando: "I didn't mind if they made a movie out of it, but I said I had to okay the screenplay. Because I didn't want it to be just some shoot-'em-up gangster flick.... If even one gangster who saw the movie decided to get out of the life, that would make a difference. So I helped them write the script. Looking back now, I was really raw, but I put everything I had into it. Then they come and say they want me to act in it.... So what could I do, I became an actor. And what do you know? The movie was a big hit. They pulled a Frank Sinatra movie from the theaters to give it a longer run."

This was *Chi to okite* (1965), Noboru Ando's first starring feature. Although it was produced by Dai-nana Group, the distributor was Shochiku.

Ando: "Shochiku made a lot of money out of that movie. It was produced for 8 million yen, and Shochiku bought it for 10 million. They ended up making hundreds of millions of yen from it, so it was a real bonanza. So then they came and said, make another one. I hadn't given up on my Southeast Asian business plans yet, so I said I'd only do it if they paid me 20 million yen. Fat chance they'd cough that up is what I thought, but they did *[laughs]*. They brought it in cash to a fancy restaurant, all wrapped up in a purple *furoshiki* (wrapping cloth). On top of that, I got paid 5 million for acting in it."

Ironically enough, one of Shochiku's top shareholders at the time was Hideki Yokoi.

Ando: "There was even one time we had to do an interview together, for a magazine. But by that time, neither of us held a grudge anymore. After a year acting for Shochiku I moved to Toei, and Toei was originally established by Keita Itsushima. Things like hate and bitterness, I guess they get washed away with time."

According to Ando, actors and yakuza have a lot in common. Looks and show are crucial. They like the ladies. And above all, he says, "They're both pretty frivolous professions." Just change the ending of *yakuza*, and you get *yakusha* (actor).

Ando: "I feel like I've lived my life three times. I guess you could say I've enjoyed life three times more than most people." 東

The Boss of the biggest YAKUZA organization told about his story
山口組三代目
YAMAGUCHIGUMI SANDAIME
実録安藤組
I act Ando (me) in my true gang story, right after world war II in Sibuya
true Yakuza boss changed to an actor
天照皇大
大神
Jitsuroku
1973 実録路線スタート
True Stories of YAKUZA Series were started!
THE First movie is 仁義なき戦い series
like movie "Valachi"
東映
Private GINZA Police
安藤昇のわが逃亡とSEXの記録
Noboru Ando my chase and sex journal
Kobe international Gang
神戸国際ギャング
Briefly
about
YAKUZA
CHIRO 51
仁義なき戦い
JINGI NAKI TATAKAI
(The fight without Honor) series
agreement "We are brothers"
兄弟の契り
Stage is HIROSHIMA right after WWII
Nonfiction! written by real YAKUZA Boss
廣島
ホルモン
a dog was eaten
SHOWA ZANKYOUDEN series
昭和残侠伝
池部
RYO IKEBE
Koji Tsuruta
鶴田浩二
博徒
BAKUTO series
花札
Hanafuda gambler
博奕打ち
BAKUCHI-UCHI series
極道
GOKUDO series

やくざ映画の人生
YAKUZA MOVIE HISTORY
Before Ninkyo movies line (1963~1972)
- Historical (140 years ago) old style YAKUZA
- Movies mainly were presented
國定忠次
KUNISADA CHUUJI
I'm no connection with YAKUZA
TOEI 東映 (MOVIE Campany) established YAKUZA Movies as 任侠映画路線 (Ninkyo movie line)
鶴田浩二
Koji Tsuruta
昭和38年
START!
1963
東映
TOEI
次郎長
Jirocho
For example, Movies of Shimizu-no-jirocho or Kunisada-Chuuji (dramatized nonfiction)
1969
男はつらいよ
OTOKO WA TSURAIYO
The hero (Tora) is a kind of Yakuza
managing free market
Tekiya
人生劇場
飛車角
HISHAKAKU
JUNKO FUJI
STORY OF WOMAN YAKUZA WHO has tattoo FLOWER
TETSURO TANBA
丹波哲郎
渡哲也
TETSUYA WATARI
We have been producing many YAKUZA MOVIES in TOEI
Producer
Director
KOJI SHUNDO
俊藤浩滋
He is JUNKO FUJI's father
マキノ正博
MASAHIRO MAKINO
無頼
Burai series
まむしの兄弟
MAMUSHI Brothers series
likes Blues Brothers
NIKKATSU CO. presented YAKUZA movie line too from 1968

TOEI CO., LTD HYPERBOLE DPT.

From the early sixties into the seventies, Toei released hundreds of yakuza movies. We've tried to run longer pieces on the really exceptional and remarkable ones, but to give one a fuller appreciation of the primo years of the yakuza eiga here are some tasty tidbits culled from movie posters, promotional materials, and video boxes:

Narazumono (Scoundrel, 1964): "Ken Takakura and director Teruo Ishii create the spectacle of the gang world in Hong Kong and Macao. A man who was betrayed by his gang arrives in Hong Kong to get revenge. Many obstacles get in his way. He tries hard to locate the gang, but he only knows the route of their drugs. The story moves at a fast speed with thrills and suspense. Astonishing gunplay in the outlaw town! Also starring Tetsuro Tanba and Mariko Kaga." (Note: John Woo has acknowledged this film, with its tragic ending, as a major influence on *The Killer*.)

Nihon kyokaku den—Ketto kanda matsuri (Chivalrous Story of Japan—Bloody Kanda Festival, 1966): "Number four in the *Nihon kyokaku den* series from Toei's *ninkyo* line. Masahiro Makino directs the famous duo of Ken Takakura and Koji Tsuruta. Set in Kanda during the Edo times, Ken is a fireman who leads a gang of firefighters against the yakuza who try to take over the oldest kimono store in the neighborhood. This movie shows the passion of Edo firemen with their katana swords. Makino's style shows the *ninkyo* way of living against the nostalgic backdrop of the Kanda Meijin festival." (Note: Makino was one of the yakuza film's most prolific directors, having made his debut in 1926. Gangs comprised of firemen were common in the Edo period.)

Gendai yakuza—Shinjuku no yotamono (Modern Yakuza—Hooligan of Shinjuku, 1970): "Bunta screams, 'My knife cuts once, twice, I've got to avenge my brothers!' His red muffler flows like blood!! He is Goro, a man who walks sideways down a shadowy path, stealing, threatening with his buddy Kitami. Eventually, Kitami discovers that yakuza have been controlling their every action, but gets killed trying to get to the bottom of the conspiracy. Goro turns into a beast hungry for blood, ready to open his knife and target the bastards!" (Note: this film is number three in the *Gendai yakuza* series.)

Choueki taro—Mamushi no kyodai (Prison Guys—Mamushi Brothers, 1971): "No regard for honor or loyalty! Hated by the world like a couple of roaches! Stealing, extortion, going beyond the law, and going wild! Bunta Sugawara and Tamio Kawachi combined to star in this first entry in the Mamushi Brothers series, set in the harbor town of Kobe. The visuals are replete with the fast feeling of director Sadao Nakajima. The screen is full of hardboiled tough outlaws!!!!" (Note: the *Mamushi Brothers* series lasted eight films until 1975.)

VIDEO

Jitsuroku Ando-gumi—Shugekihen (True Story of the Ando Gang—The Attacks, 1973): "June. 1958. 11 p.m. Noboru Ando gives the order to shoot. 'Don't kill them, just wound them,' says Ando. A violent document! The true story of Ando's gang in Kanto!" Starring Tetsuro Tanba, Tatsuo Umemiya. Directed by Junya Sato. (Note: Ando sings the film's theme song "Blood and Soul," available on Canyon Records.)

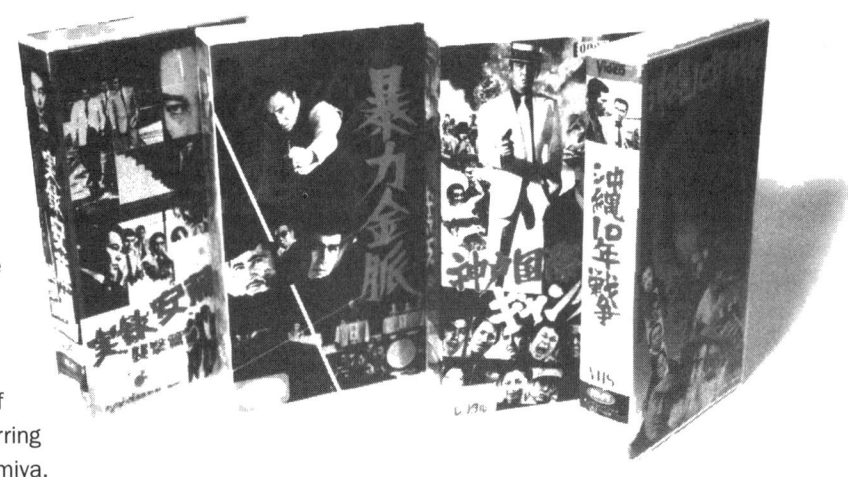

Boryoku kinmyaku (Violent Cash Connection, 1975): "This is the story of four roaches feeding off the wealthy with their sleazy money-making schemes. These hoodlums intimidate, blackmail, and make trouble. The truth about the shame of today's society: the *sokaiya*. They strike a gold mine, but what is the main target? Company violence! A hard battle struggle!" Starring Hiroki Matsukata, Tatsuo Umemiya, Tetsuro Tanba. Directed by Sadao Nakajima. (Note: *sokaiya* are financial racketeers.)

Kobe kokusai Gang (Kobe International Gang, 1975): "Jazz, gunfire, G.I.s, whores. Kobe is an amoral town controlled by racketeers, killings, and take-overs. Angry gangs appear like weeds. Explosive sounds of machine guns and carbines! Ken Takakura vs. Bunta Sugawara! They light the fires of gang war dressed as dandies! A battle of destiny! Bazooka Ken is the dandy in the white suit. Machine gun Bunta is the white wolf that burns cool. Violent gang series with dynamic action!" Directed by Noboru Tanaka.

Okinawa junen senso (Okinawa Ten Year War, 1978): "Guns, death, and violence! The battling children of Okinawa! Sonny Chiba and Hiroki Matsukata star in this passionate and powerful violent action film depicting the ten-year history of blood, guns, bullets, and killing. Violent gangs come together to form the Okinawa syndicate and prepare for the invasion of Japan. But from the beginning of the consolidation, divisions within the ranks pile up and the group splits into two factions. Against the background of the ocean, the Hondo gang aspires for possession of Okinawa and merges with a minority faction. The climax is a fierce three-way battle as the Okinawa police call out the previously unheard of 'assassination order'!!!" Directed by Akinori Matsuo. 東

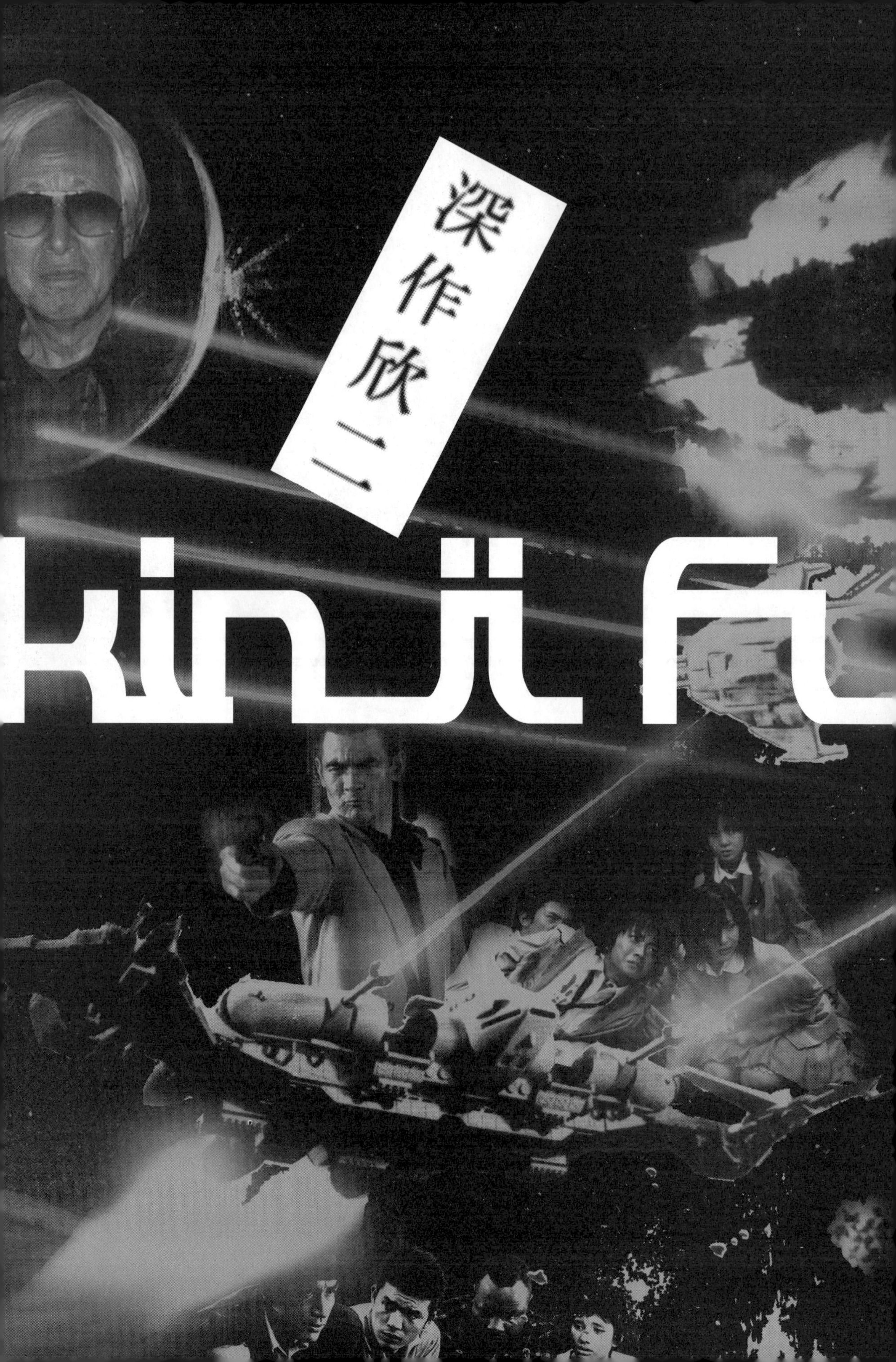

深作欣二
kinji

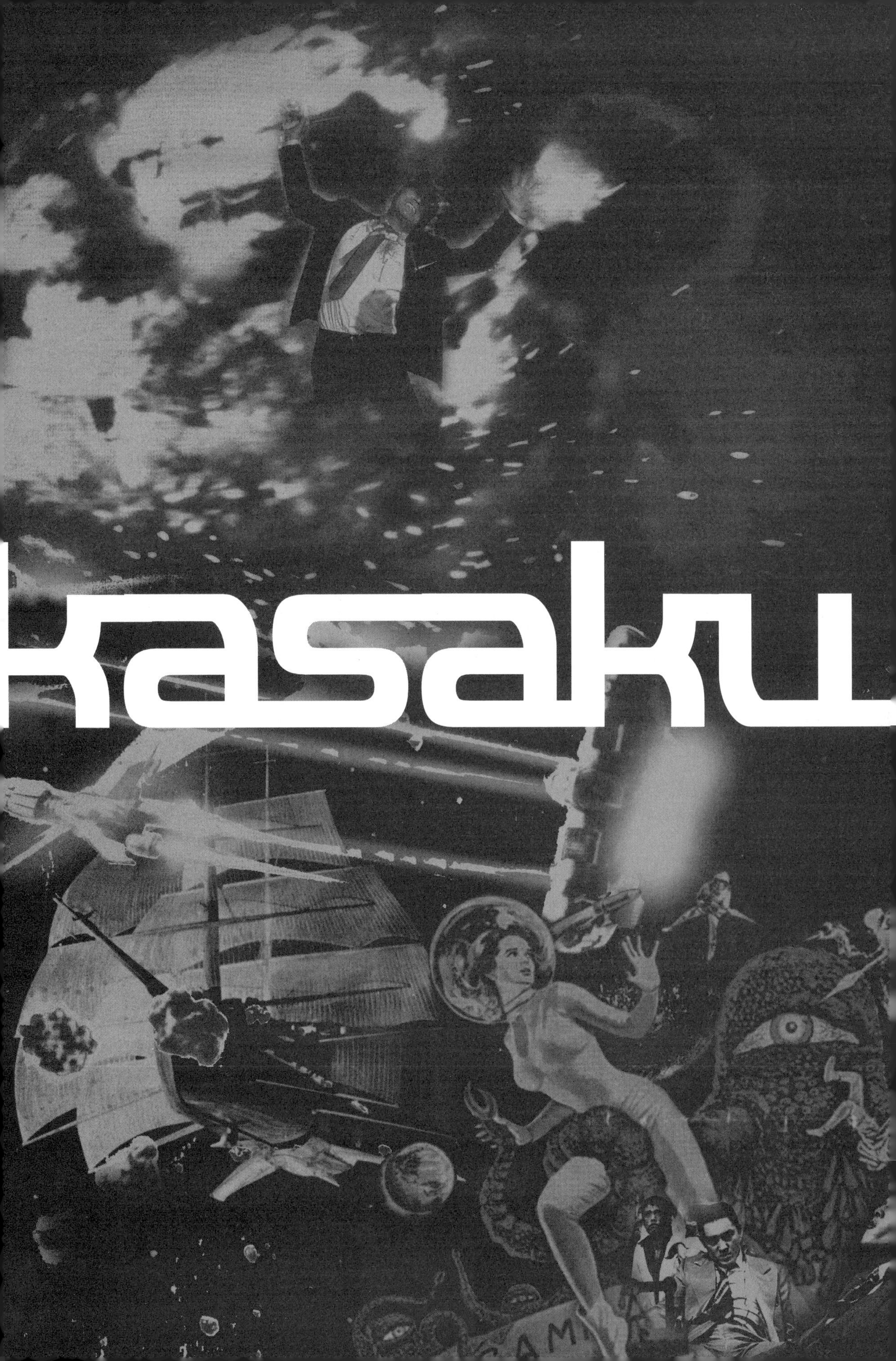
kasaku

kinji Fukasaku

THE FILMS OF KINJI FUKASAKU

Who is Kinji Fukasaku? A Japanese Sam Peckinpah—a masterful purveyor of chaotic screen violence and macho aesthetic. Or: a politically radical film craftsman, whose keen-eyed observations engage the moral complexities of postwar history. Outside of Japan, Fukasaku's name is connected, if at all, to four wildly anomalous films that saw light of day in the international marketplace: the late-night TV fave *The Green Slime* (1968), the 1968 pop-art picture-show *Black Lizard* (which Western viewers seem to love even as Fukasaku seems to cringe whenever it's mentioned), the warped-speed *Star Wars* rip *Message from Space* (1978), and the Japanese portions of *Tora! Tora! Tora!* (1970). Imagine if all Peckinpah were known for internationally were *Convoy* and that Julian Lennon video.

In Fukasaku's early-to-mid seventies prime, Japanese audiences were polarized by his no-blink brutality. It wasn't until his later years, when he doled out big-budget, all-star, period spectaculars, that he was fully embraced by mass audiences. In the meantime, hardcore film fans and esteemed critics like Sadao Yamane considered the five films that make up the core of his *Jingi naki tatakai* series (Fight without Honor and Humanity, 1973-1974) to be among the greatest Japanese movies ever made.

If all this sounds contradictory, that's because Fukasaku seems to court extremes. Case in point: Fukasaku's 61st film, *Battle Royale*, was greeted with controversy, condemnation, and derision from film critics, politicians, the Japanese PTA, and the film ratings board. But *Battle* also surprisingly cleaned up

HELP US
MESSAGE FROM SPACE
where fantasies are real & reality is FANTASTIC
MESSAGE FROM SPACE Starring VIC MORROW • with PHILIP CASNOFF
PEGGY LEE BRENNAN • and SONNY CHIBA • Music Performed by COLUMBIA SYMPHONY ORCHESTRA
IN COLOR • With a SPECIAL EFFECTS and SPACE FLYING OBJECTS TECHNICAL UNIT
Recorded in SUPER-SPACE SOUND © Copyright 1978 Toei Company, LTD All Rights Reserved.
A Joint Production of Toei Company, LTD. & Tohokushinsa Company, LTD.
PG PARENTAL GUIDANCE SUGGESTED
SOME MATERIAL MAY NOT BE SUITABLE FOR CHILDREN
Distributed by
United Artists
A Transamerica Company
THEATRE

2 Cols. x 125 Lines—250 Lines (18 Inches) Mat 205

INTRO

at the box office among youth audiences, garnering the 70-year-old filmmaker a whole new generation of fans.

You might have already pegged him as some kind of New Wave rebel instigator, but in fact Fukasaku has been throughout his long career the consummate company director, toiling (apart from the odd independent production) primarily for Toei Studios, whose ranks he first joined as an assistant director at the age of 23. With Fukasaku firmly seated in the director's chair, you get a steady mix of cynicism and passion, lightning pace, restless energy, and a general attack plan of all-killer, no-filler. And no wonder. At his peak, he was

kinji Fukasaku

whipping out a film, from pre-production to finished product, in little over a month. Signature trademarks: the crazed handheld camera work that documents the violence, the freeze-frame punctuation marks that strike like breaks on a roller coaster.

Born on July 3, 1930 in Mito City, Fukasaku came of age during the Allied Forces' occupation of Japan. He still wrestles with the

anything could happen. When foreign film once again flooded Japan after the war in 1946, Fukasaku found kindred spirits via Italian neorealism, particularly *Paisan* and *The Bicycle Thief*. The style became a lasting influence.

Following a quartet of short subjects for Toei studios starring Sonny Chiba, Fukasaku's first feature-length films were Westernized heist capers

disastrous fallout is a mixed-race mute girl, her innocent face by the end transformed into an expression of horror and rage.

Fukasaku spent the rest of the decade cranking out modern crime and gang films. *Nihon boryokudan kumicho* (Japanese Organized Crime Boss, 1969), starring Koji Tsuruta and Tomisaburo Wakayama, is a clear illustration of Fukasaku and the yakuza

MIND-BOGGLING "THEME FROM THE GREEN SLIME"

The "THEME FROM THE GREEN SLIME", recorded by the nation's leading Baroque-rock group, THE GREEN SLIMES, is a neo-psychedelic, mind-boggling R&R "trip" guaranteed to take-off on top 40 charts across the country. MGM/Verve Records will release this smash recording to coincide with national openings of GREEN SLIME, and key national distributors and dealers have been alerted to cooperate with theatres in setting up window displays and imaginative record promotions. Additional information can be obtained from . . .

SOL HANDWERGER
MGM/VERVE RECORDS

1350 Avenue of the Americas, N.Y., N.Y. 10019

TEEN QUEENS ARE GOING GREEN!

Don't fight it! The "GREEN SLIME" ARE COMING!, and you might as well join them with the Super!, Ultra-Chic! "GREEN SLIME Gook Look!" Note Teen queens are definitely going GREEN in '69, so bedeck a bevy of your burg's best beauties and promote the "GOING GREEN IS MY SCENE!" look. Tie-in with leading beauty salons, and saturate your community with the following garish goop: Green Cologne, Green Pour Le Bain, Green Face Powder, Ghastly Green Blush-On, Gasping Green Lipstick, Ghostly Green Eye-Liner and Shadow, and (HORROR OF HORRORS!) Ghoulish GREEN SLIME Hair Coloring (Substitute A Sickening Puce For Those Unfortunates Who Are Naturally Green). Get your gals glowing like a traffic signal!

DO THE GROOVY "GREEN SLIME"

Promote a groovy, intergalactic dance contest with your leading sub-teen, gum-chomping top 40 R&R radio station to find the young couple exhibiting the most mind-expanding rendition of the GREEN SLIME TWO-STEP, [known in leading interplanetary circles as the "GASHTLY, INTER-GALACTIC GREEN SLIME GIG"]. Danced to the scintillating strains of "THE THEME FROM THE GREEN SLIME", the undulating and rhythmic version of the GREEN SLIME TWO-STEP will take your teen community by storm. Everybody, BUT EVERYBODY, is doing it!

INTRO

"Eventually, I wanted to replace the old style of yakuza movie with a new kind of film where I could overlay my own experiences of postwar Japan. From growing up in that era, I was attracted to characters who had nothing but their strength, and violence, to believe in."

In the films that immediately followed *Nihon boryokudan*, like *Bakuto—Gaijin butai* (Gambler—Foreign Force, 1971) and *Gendai yakuza—Hitokiri yota* (Modern Yakuza—Outlaw Killer, 1972), Fukasaku made the material fully his own. The breakthrough was 1973's *Jingi naki tatakai*, a film based on the confessions of a jailed Hiroshima gang boss. It was an alternate version of Japanese postwar history,

kinji Fukasaku

one that probed into that glossed-over territory where few films had before. Fukasaku had pioneered the *jitsuroku eiga* (true story films): neo-realism from a yakuza point of view. He questioned old yakuza codes of honor while searching for emotional truth and catharsis where only hypocrisy had prevailed.

The new style became a sensation. Imitators and cash-ins grew legion. For a while, seemingly every gang (the Ando gang, the Yamaguchi gang, the Okinawa Ten-Year Gang War) got its own lurid true-crime tribute film. In the end, it was Fukasaku who shut down the cycle with the nihilistic *Jingi no hakaba* (Graveyard of Honor, 1976) and *Yakuza no hakuba* (Graveyard of Yakuza, also 1976), both starring former Nikkatsu youth idol Tetsuya Watari, now recast, respectively, as a transgressive mad dog and a Bad Lieutenant.

From these heights Fukasaku went on to follow Japanese film trends—diversifying his product line, as it were. Lush period spectaculars (1981's *Makai tensho*, aka *Samurai Reincarnation*, and 1983's *Satomi hakkenden*, aka *Legend of the Eight Samurai)* and sometimes cumbersome international co-productions (1980's *Fukkatsu no hi*, aka *Virus)* followed. While the genres and working methods changed, Fukasaku's fundamental stance did not, viewing these international films as an opportunity to better understand foreigners (specifically Americans) by working with them.

Recent years have seen Fukasaku crusading for the rights of his peers as the president of the Japanese Director's Guild. His recent titles have included *Itsuka giragira suru hi* (Double Cross, 1992), *Chushingura gaiden Yotsuya kaidan* (a mix of the classic stories of *Chushingura* and *Yotsuya Ghost Story*), and *Omocha* (aka *The Geisha House*, 1999). Decent enough films all, but 2000's *Battle Royale* truly returns Fukasaku to form. Criticizing contemporary Japanese society via violence and passion, mixing up smooth professionalism with hellraising, and taking no prisoners in between, Fukasaku remains postwar Japan's prime filmic force. 東

REVIEW

Greed in Broad Daylight
Hakuchu no buraikan

1961, New Toei
Director Kinji Fukasaku
Cast Tetsuro Tanba, Isaac Sackson, Hitomi Nakahara, Robert Dunham

1961 was a busy year for the then 31-year-old Kinji Fukasaku. In addition to debuting as a director with a quartet of action shorts starring Sonny Chiba, Fukasaku also made his first feature length title: a fast-moving heist film which unfolds to the syncopated beat of a furious jazz soundtrack. It was produced for the short-lived "New Toei" label, Toei's Tokyo branch created especially to compete with Nikkatsu's popular and ultramodern "Nikkatsu Action" line.

Criminal mastermind Miyahara (Tanba) plans to rip off half a million dollars from a US army payroll truck using a Wile E. Coyote-like combination of detour signs and dynamite. To aid him in the task, he enlists a cross-section of minorities: a half-breed girl, a pair of Americans (one of them *Godzilla vs. Megalon's* Robert Dunham, the other a black G.I.), a Korean, and a sneering knife-wielding street punk. At first, it seems like the disenfranchised bunch are going to cooperate and strike it rich, but their own individual avarice eventually brings the house of cards down fast and hard. By the end, a shantytown slum is covered in dead bodies, and the only survivor, the once-innocent half-breed Hanako, stares vacant with shock and rage into the sun. It matters little that she has all the loot.

Greed in Broad Daylight makes it clear that the main themes of Fukasaku's oeuvre announced themselves from the very beginning. Miyahara's right-hand man is a clear antecedent of Bunta Sugawara's violent modern yakuza characters. Deadly back-stabbing and double-dealing would serve *Jingi naki tatakai* well, and the bilingual cast prefigures any number of future Fukasaku international co-productions. The scenario may owe much to Stanley Kubrick and Jim Thompson's *The Killing* (1956), but Fukasaku's treatment of his crooks adds layers of significance. Miyahara considers the diverse members of his gang not as comrades, but as highly disposable tools to use. Even the rip-off reflects the dog-eat-dog reality of postwar Japan as it groped towards economic supremacy.

Still, the film is no masterpiece. Stagey, overchoreographed fight scenes show how far Fukasaku had to go before maximizing his action scenes, and the multiracial types fall too easily into crude stereotypes.

Here then is a pulp novel that would eventually evolve into a genuine treatise.

☞ **Import only**

The Green Slime are coming!
The Green Slime
Invaders From Beyond the Stars!

The Green Slime

Gamma dai sango—Uchu dai sakusen (Gamma III—Operation Outer Space)

1968, Toei/RAM films
Director Kinji Fukasaku
Cast Robert Horton, Richard Jaeckel, Lucianna Paluzzi

Kinji Fukasaku's *Gamma dai sango* was conceived as a noble symbol of international goodwill and brotherhood. It was a collaboration between East and West, RAM films, MGM, and Toei studios. Working from a story idea by comic-book and pulp writer Bill Finger (an uncredited co-creator of *Batman*), Italian-backed American producers Walter Manley and Ivan Reiner (who had previously made the swinging pop-art pic *Wild Wild Planet* in 1965) poured their greenbacks into a script called *Battle beyond the Stars* that was destined to be known as *The Green Slime*.

It begins as a tale of brave astronauts who are sent to blow up a big rock before it hits the earth (Finger should sue the *Armageddon* guys), only to be contaminated by a mysterious green substance. Taking it unawares back to the orbiting Gamma III space station, the innocuous Green Slime grows into an army of murderous electric half-pint ghoulies. It could mean the end of civilization as we know it. Or, at worst, the whirlwind of events will finally bring closure to a love triangle between the dueling heterosexual principal characters.

Down at Toei studios, director Kinji Fukasaku held court on the set. It wasn't an easy shoot. Amateur actors flubbed lines, children were imprisoned inside Green Slime costumes, and the foreign producers were demanding everything on time and on budget.

The ever visionary Fukasaku may have dreamed of handling the material as a depiction of, as he's been quoted as saying, "the American stereotyped notion of communism," but the grim reality of directing a movie about Green Slime for penny-pinching movie moguls forced him to hold back on the subtext. The result is some uncharacteristically wooden direction from the man who later would redefine widescreen mayhem. But given the right state of mind (or a six-pack of Burgie! on an empty stomach), one can still see traces of what Fukasaku intended: a Vietnam parable set in space decades before James Cameron made *Aliens*.

Baloney? Maybe. Maybe not. To quote a couplet from *The Green Slime*'s acid-rock theme song (written by Charles Fox of *Barbarella* and *Happy Days* fame), "Is it just something in your head? Well, you'll believe it when you're dead!"

☞ **Available dubbed on VHS from MGM Home Entertainment**

REVIEW

Gambler—Foreign Force
Bakuto—Gaijin butai, aka Sympathy for the Underdog

1971, Toei
Director Kinji Fukasaku
Cast Koji Tsuruta, Noboru Ando, Tomisaburo Wakayama

Okinawa: that great political football at the southern end of the Japanese islands. Previously a battleground for the some of the bloodiest fighting of the Pacific War, Okinawa remains torn between a strong US military presence and its own unique identity, long suppressed by the Japanese government. It's an outsider's paradise, and thus the perfect setting for many a yakuza movie.

Deadpanning old-timer Koji Tsuruta (in permanent shades, a look favored by director Fukasaku himself) gets out of jail and finds his old gang, who once controlled the docks, reduced to a mere handful of loyal losers. Since their old turf has been taken over by a rival gang, Koji and crew (along with wildcard Noboru Ando) head to sunny Okinawa for a fresh bid for underworld prosperity. There they collide with the locals, including a crooked *gaijin*, a Flamin' Groovies-style boogie band, and one-armed, one-eyebrowed giant Tomisaburo Wakayama (*Lone Wolf and Cub*) wearing a pair of pants held up with hand grenades. After some sacrifices and hard knocks, the gang finally strikes it big and winds up in a lovely mansion by the sea where they can read magazines, play cards, practice golf, and yawn their way to total inertia. Meanwhile, the rival gang that originally drove Koji and crew out of town arrives en masse in Okinawa....

Released a year before the US occupation of Okinawa officially ended, Fukasaku's you-are-there location footage captures a fascinating time and place (off-duty G.I.s flash peace signs to the camera). The poster may have screamed "Blood! The wolves are calling! Men in suits cross the sea!", but the film itself is far more relaxed and humorous than you might expect.

It plays like a charming instructional film on how to take over rival turf in three E-Z steps, and what to do once ennui sets in. It becomes downright boozy and sentimental as the conclusion nears—a tone appropriate to the "battle for the whiskey racket" subplot. After a night of carousing, an old woman sings the Okinawa migrant workers' song, about men who have left home for work abroad, never to return. It's then that you realize that Koji and company have taken on one of the tougher tasks imaginable, making daily bread with knives and revolvers. Wouldn't it be easier to just knuckle down and get a real job? Perhaps it would, but Fukasaku's sympathy is solely reserved for underdogs.

☞ **Import only**

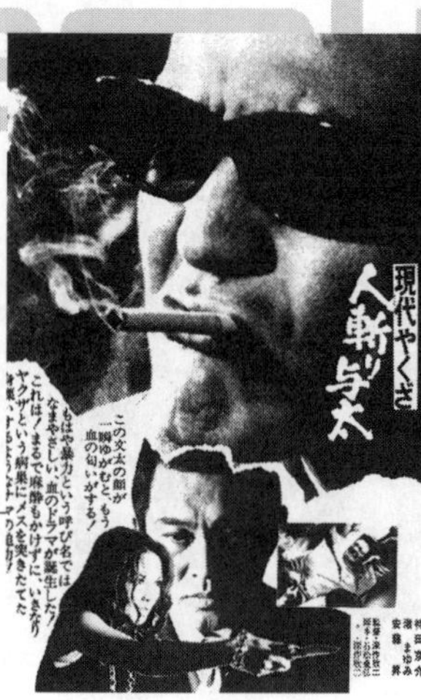

Kinji Fukasaku

Modern Yakuza—Outlaw Killer
Gendai yakuza—Hitokiri yota, aka Street Mobster

1972, Toei
Director Kinji Fukasaku
Cast Bunta Sugawara, Mayumi Nagisa, Noboru Ando

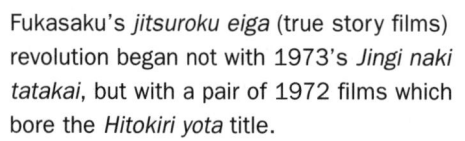

Fukasaku's *jitsuroku eiga* (true story films) revolution began not with 1973's *Jingi naki tatakai*, but with a pair of 1972 films which bore the *Hitokiri yota* title.

The first, *Gendai yakuza*, broke new ground by retelling an old yakuza movie chestnut, the one about the guy who gets out of jail, only to find that things have drastically changed—with a difference. Fukasaku's screenplay (co-written by Yoshihiro Ishimatsu) told the story from the point of view of the plankton of the underworld: the *gurentai*, young street thugs eager to ingratiate themselves into a "real" gang.

And while Bunta Sugawara would play the reluctant sole man of honor in *Jingi*, *Gendai yakuza* (his first leading role in a Fukasaku film) finds him as a ferocious anti-everything antihero with a fascinating range of camera-mugging facial tics and body contortions.

Goro (Bunta) narrates his own hard luck story, how he was born on August 15th, 1945 (the date of Japan's surrender), had a crummy childhood as a postwar waif, and put together a gang of fellow toughs in reform school. Goro ran afoul of the local yakuza and had a stint in the joint after assassinating one of them. Back out on the streets, he quickly cultivates a core group of fellow punks. They manage to ingratiate themselves into the established Yato gang. When a larger Osaka-based gang moves into the area, a mutually beneficial merger is planned, but rising hood Goro spoils it with his explosive temper and violence. The elder Yato (Ando) keeps preaching the virtues of compromise, but the words fall on deaf ears. Pretty soon, Goro has started a gang war, and has pissed off everyone. He's down to his last pinky, up against the wall, and abandoned by everyone except his whore girlfriend Kumiyo (Mayumi Nagisa) who stands by her man even when the final cache of guns and knives is unleashed.

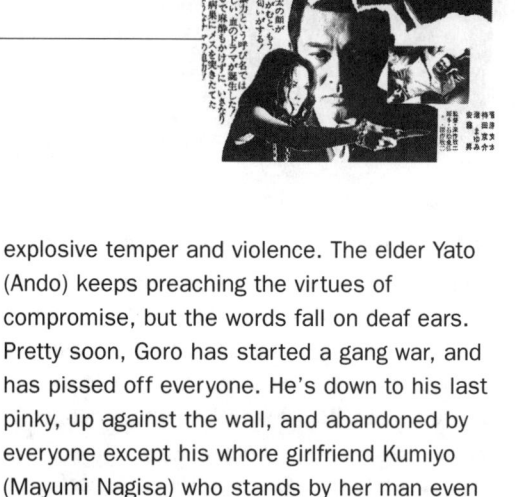

The combination of Bunta's fiery performance, alternating between playful punk and terrifying monster in an heartbeat, and Fukasaku's newfound command of technique makes *Gendai yakuza* a work pulsating with vitality and defiance.

The truth is, Fukasaku's yakuza films are less about tough guys answering the siren's call of the death wish and more about simply trying to survive. Hence the moral of *Gendai yakuza*, uttered from the knowing lips of lowdown street punks, "Don't dare depend on gangsters. Get what you want with your own hands."

☞ **Import only**

REVIEW

Fight without Honor and Humanity
Jingi naki tatakai

1973-1974, Toei
Director Kinji Fukasaku
Cast Bunta Sugawara, Tatsuo Umemiya, Hiroki Matsukata, Sonny Chiba

Jingi is a hard-to-translate Japanese word for which there is no real English counterpart. Composed of the *kanji* characters for "humanity" and "honor," the code of *jingi* is the glue that holds the yakuza world together.

A lack of *jingi* among a gang can invite hypocrisy, chaos, and violence.

All the proof you'd ever need can be found in Kinji Fukasaku's five-film 1973-1974 *Jingi naki tatakai* (Fight without Honor and Humanity) series.

Tracing the rise and fall of the Hiroshima-based Yamamori-gumi (Yamamori Gang) from the postwar ruin of 1947 to practically right outside the theater doors in 1970, the proud history of a nation is exposed for what it really is: a sordid account of its underworld.

Based on a serialized two-volume novel by journalist Koichi Iiboshi, who interviewed the imprisoned former head boss of the Mino gang Kozo Mino, the first *Jingi naki tatakai* film was Fukasaku's breakout title as a director. While his two previous *Hitokiri yota* films (both 1972) had already pioneered a violent new cinematic world populated by yakuza living beyond the traditional codes of decorum, *Jingi* was painted on a much larger canvas and was summarily greeted as a box-office and critical success.

Told in tough-sounding Hiroshima dialect, backed by Toshiaki Tsushima's unforgettable musical theme (punk band Guitar Wolf use it as their intro music), the first *Jingi naki tatakai* film begins at ground zero with a tinted still of a towering mushroom cloud. It ends as the very concept of *jingi* is shot full of holes by disillusioned main character Shozo Hirono (Bunta Sugawara, formerly Fukasaku's titular *Gendai yakuza*). It's very nearly a post-apocalyptic world reduced to rubble inhabited by monstrous mutant yakuza.

The venerable rituals of yakuza life are systematically undermined and stripped away of artifice. Two future gangsters (Sugawara and Tatsuo Umemiya, who had previously starred together in Yukio Noda's comedic *Delinquent Boss* series) become blood brothers makeshift-style in a prison cell with none of the usual ceremonial pomp and circumstance. The classic chopping off of the pinkie to atone for one's sins scene is turned into a comedic farce (complete with a chicken plucking away at the severed appendage) that jolted audiences weaned on more traditional yakuza fare.

With something like 48 speaking parts, the original *Jingi naki tatakai* rips by at warp speed not unlike Fukasaku's later *Battle Royale*. The intricacies of the conflict between the dueling Doi and the Yamamori gangs can be nearly impossible to get a handle on at times, which is fitting, since even the protagonists themselves seem to be in need of a scorecard.

Over the course of the saga, Hirono tries to stay as neutral as possible, no easy task amidst a *jingi*-less maelstrom of shifting

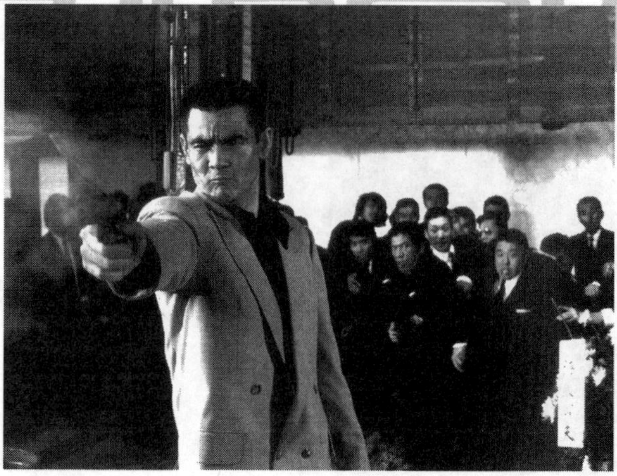

loyalties and back-stabbing betrayals, many of them set in motion by his own bosses. For the most part, he's merely a helpless witness to the grim machinations of the new yakuza, among them Hiroki Matsukata, an economic animal who'd like to see the yakuza reap in cash like a "real" company.

No-respect thugs led by super *chimpira* Sonny Chiba (who arrives in episode two) and anti-gang task forces formed by outraged citizens and the police (who make a big stink in parts four and five) only serve to pour gas on the fires of an internal brother-versus-brother gang war.

By the end of the fifth film, *Jingi naki tatakai—Kanketsu hen* (Fight without Honor and Humanity—The Final Episode), the Yamamori gang, Honzo included, have gone corporate and have played a key role in making Japan's economic miracle a reality, but fraternity among its now anachronistic members means nothing. The old yakuza ways have been reduced to Machiavellian tools used for power games of divide and conquer. But at what cost?

Fukasaku concludes nearly every film in the series with a shot of Hiroshima's Genbaku Dome monument, a symbol that suggests far more than the war ended in the flash of the atomic bomb.

The series, all save the fifth scripted by Kazuo Kasahara (who also penned Fukasaku's gang pics *Kenkei tai soshiki boryoku* and *Yakuza no hakaba*, as well as co-scripting the 1983 anime film *Final Yamato*), revitalized the yakuza genre which was beginning to collapse under the weight of so many chivalrous and honorable Ken Takakura movies. Post-*Jingi* yakuza films would portray conflicts often based on real gang struggles and events, a phenomenon known as *jitsuroku eiga* (true story films).

But the brand name *Jingi naki tatakai* would be the one to beat.

Fukasaku himself would deliver three films in *Shin jingi naki tatakai* (New Fight without Honor and Humanity) series (1974-1976), a trio of unrelated tales set in Hiroshima, Kyushu, and Osaka with no continuity to the previous *Jingi* series save for returning cast members, such as Bunta and Hiroki, in new roles.

In 1979 came director Eiichi Kudo's *Sonogo no jingi naki tatakai* (After Fight without Honor and Humanity), which depicted an even more unrelated internal struggle among the young and badly dressed members of an Osaka gang.

And in 2000, Toei and director Junji Sakamoto (*Face*) revived the *Shin jingi naki tatakai* name for a tale of Korean-versus-Kansai gang war set in the present day and featuring rock star Tomoyasu Hotei and trendy drama wooden man Etsuji Toyokawa.

☞ **Import only**

REVIEW

Graveyard of Honor and Humanity
Jingi no hakaba

1976, Toei
Director Kinji Fukasaku
Cast Tetsuya Watari, Tatsuo Umemiya, Yumi Takigawa, Noboru Ando

Something was up. The previews promised "Super Violence Action Cinema!" and this wasn't the sort of hype you'd normally expect to find heralding a new Tetsuya Watari movie. After all, in the sixties, Watari was best known as Nikkatsu Studio's preeminent shining youth idol. And despite the weirdness that surrounded him in Seijun Suzuki's tripped-out *Tokyo nagaremono* (Tokyo Drifter, 1966), audiences had reason to believe that Watari was still a stand-up guy.

But in 1976's *Jingi no hakaba*, he took on the role of notorious real-life gangster Rikio Ishikawa, one of the most violent outlaws of the immediate postwar era. And under Kinji Fukasaku's damning direction, the boyish Watari (who was suffering from a lung ailment during the filming) became a permanently hunched over, nihilistic, smack-addled demon.

Every since he was a kid, Rikio Ishikawa (born in Mito, just like Kinji) said he wanted to be a gangster. Even as an adult, he still clings to the idea that a yakuza should be a death-dealing, self-destructive time bomb.

Unfortunately, the real underworld operates in carefully orchestrated alliances and business moves. Ishikawa can't help but set the delicate gang relations that surround him ablaze, burning down aspiring politico Noboru Ando's shot at the big time in the process. Rikio has confused going up with going down, and his complete lack of decorum is equal only to his roachlike ability to survive epic beatings and bloody assassination attempts.

Even as his oddly loyal girlfriend Yumi Takigawa goes tubercular and Rikio starts to assemble his own grave (mysteriously inscribing the word *jingi* on it), Fukasaku refuses to judge or take sides. Despite the sensational elements of the story, no moment is more powerful or shocking than when Rikio slowly sifts through his girl's cremated bones and ashes (just prior to eating them in an demonic extortion bid).

Fukasaku has said that making this film forced him to ask "What is life? What do we leave behind when we die?" Perhaps only by freefalling into the void, can an urn full of answers can be found before slamming head first into the pavement.

☞ **Import only**

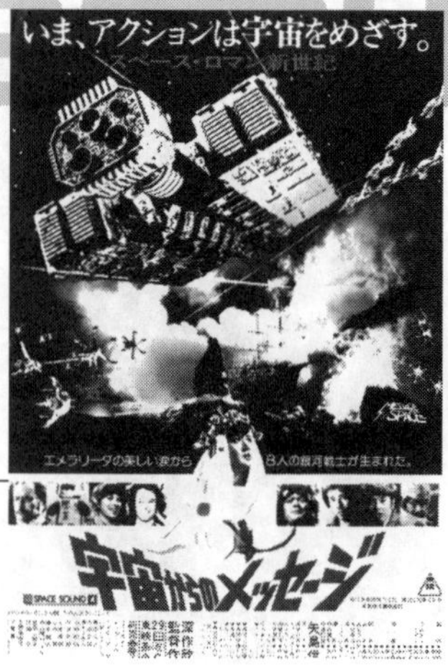
いま、アクションは宇宙をめざす。
スペース・ロマン新世紀
エメラリーダの美しい涙から 8人の銀河戦士が生まれた。
宇宙からのメッセージ
SPACE SOUND

Message from Space

Uchu kara no messeji

1978, Toei
Director Kinji Fukasaku
Cast Vic Morrow, Sonny Chiba, Mikio Narita, Peggy Lee Brennan

Long since written off by others as a shameless *Star Wars* rip off with few redeeming features, *Message from Space*—I'm willing to go to the mat in saying—is one of Kinji Fukasaku's most underrated films. While far from one of the best by a long stretch (who can forgive midgets in robot suits, faux cantina scenes, and space dogfights?), stylistically it is the Encyclopedia Fukasaku bolstered by one of the juiciest casts in Japanese cult film history.

The planet Jilucia is on the verge of death. Evil invaders led by mother and son team Eisei Amamoto and Mikio Nartia (the former in drag and both with their mugs painted silver) have taken over and turned it into a wasteland. The elderly leader of the peaceful fig-leaf-crowned Jilucian populace releases eight glowing seeds into the cosmos with the knowledge that these nuts will summon eight brave heroes to the planet's rescue.

And what heroes they are! Sonny Chiba, Makoto Sato (both of them reunited from Teruo Ishii's *Jigoku ken* films), and Hiroyuki "*Roaring Fire*" Sanada are joined by stray *gaijin* Vic Morrow (both the late actor and his character intoxicated during much of the film), Peggy Lee Brennan, and Philip Casanov (who?). Filling out the canvas are supporting players including Etsuko Shihomi and the ever-present Tetsuro Tanba as, basically, the king of the world.

Influenced as much by George Lucas as the oft-filmed Japanese legend *Satomi hakkenden* (aka *Legend of the Eight Samurai*), *Message*'s only constant is a wild state of flux amid optically printed laser fire and fiery plumes of conflagration. At any point it can shift gears, foreshadowing Fukasaku's epic sword films to come (he would later re-make *Satomi hakkenden* sans the sci-fi trappings), along with the teetering chaos and seediness of his yakuza pictures, to large-scale military spectacle ala *Tora! Tora! Tora!* This could have been a no-nonsense, no-fun space-opera (see Toho's *War in Space* to compare, contrast, and get a good night's sleep). Instead, the manic creativity and garish pop-art playfulness recalls Fukasaku's much-loved *Black Lizard*.

Okay, so maybe I'm a bit biased. Seeing *Message from Space* as a kid on the big screen (on a double-bill with Luigi Cozzi's *Star Crash*) was a life-changing experience. And if I could take only one Japanese cult movie with me to show to aliens on a distant planet, you can bet your medals and your loyal robot buddies that this would be it. As Vic Morrow puts it ambiguously, fittingly, "There are more beautiful dreams in space."

☞ **Dubbed version released to theaters by United Artists, video import only**

REVIEW

Battle Royale
Battle Royale

2000, Toei
Director Kinji Fukasaku
Cast Takeshi Kitano, Tatsuya Fujiwara, Aki Maeda, Masanobu Ando, Ko Shibasaki

"This is a fairytale. This is a fable," assures Kinji Fukasaku in an interview in this book.

But Fukasaku's 61st film, set on an island where 42 junior high school students are ordered to kill each other until the last boy or girl is left standing, must be swallowed without the reassuring "once upon a time" preamble.

As *Battle Royale* kicks off to the bombastic strains of the kind of music commonly played over Japanese school PA systems, we find that the economy has gone sour. Adults are powerless. The kids have blown off school and have long since lost themselves in solitary pastimes. Despite what you may have heard, this backdrop is not some dystopian near-future. This is Japan at ground zero, right now.

In Koushun Takami's original novel, the titular game of death was conceived in a nameless totalitarian nation. The premise was a parody of the classic "we love teacher" TV drama *Kempachi sensei* by way of the Bachman Books. Good old "individual versus the state" provided conflict, with Bruce Springsteen's "Born to Run" for a theme song.

Battle Royale: The Movie boldly does away with all disguises and pretense. The island is now explicitly Japan in miniature, the perfect setting for Fukasaku's ongoing evocations of war trauma and contemplation of postwar society, its conflicts and struggles, internal and external.

Working from Fukasaku's son Kenta's screenplay (he was also one of the film's producers), *Battle Royale* becomes a parable for a set of generations at war, brought together at a single moment where understanding or even revolution could be possible, if not for the exigencies of survival.

"Today, I'd like you guys to kill each other," teacher Takeshi Kitano says to a captive room full of students, announcing the film's nasty premise early on. Both Fukasaku and Kitano are hoping to awaken everyone out of their stupor: the class, themselves, society, film critics.

From this point on, an immaculately staged audio-visual assault follows, hurtling out unrelenting violence until the end credits spit you back out into your theater seat. Taken as a purely visceral experience, it's a hell of a ride.

The only possible point of comparison, in method of attack, would be the films of Paul Verhoeven, another filmmaker who often alludes to his traumatic World War II adolescence when asked why his films are so…oh…irresponsible?

Just as *Beverly Hills 90210* alumni had to battle giant killer bugs in *Starship Troopers*, so must doe-eyed teen idols blow each other away in *Battle Royale*. That both ideas are totally nuts is a given. The difference is that Verhoeven offers deviously little guidance through his sick jokes and moral minefields (at what point exactly does Kevin Bacon cease to be "the hero" of *Hollow Man*?).

kinji fukasaku

As the hostile reaction that greeted *Battle Royale* proved, the film apparently *can* be read as a simple joyride into body-count nihilism. Then again, so could the battle of Okinawa, when the Japanese government actually gave innocent children weapons and strict orders to die.

At any point, *Battle Royale* can be terrifying, tender, hopeful, cynical, mechanical, compassionate, you name it. The only constant is Fukasaku's unmistakable mix of hard-boiled hope distilled somehow from flat-out rage.

As our protagonist Shuya (Tatsuya Fujiwara) flashes back to his defeated father dead from suicide hanging from the ceiling with words of encouragement left behind scribbled on toilet paper, it's hard not to think of the father and son relationship on the other side of the camera. And as Takeshi plays out his own psychodrama with his 42 little action figures, there's a 70-year-director collaborating with children who have never known war. Make no mistake. This is a very personal film made with passion and real-life experience.

At first look, it hardly even looks like a Kinji Fukasaku film. Gone are the trademark freeze frames, the shifting film stocks, the wild handheld camera. But structurally, it's not so different from one of his vintage yakuza films, the likes of which film critic Edward E. Crouse described as "epics that would introduce twenty-plus characters in rapid freeze-frame only to have them sliced out by paintball gunfire a few seconds later."

With Fukasaku's thumbnail-sketch style of characterization, *Battle* lacks three-dimensional portraits. The types and performances are memorable enough, but only readers of the novel will be able to adequately fill in the blanks. (Fukasaku and Toei have since prepped a *BR* "special edition" containing eight minutes of additional footage and characterizations.)

Velocity and trajectory have always been given priority over motivation and depth in Fukasaku's oeuvre. And when *Battle Royale* charges forward on all cylinders, watch out. As the kids race across the island's coastline armed with TV-comedy paper fans and Uzi 9mms, the familiar-looking waves are crashing on familiar-looking rocks on a sunny beautiful day. You might find yourself wondering if every Fukasaku film graced with the trademark Toei logo has been a Battle Royale of sorts. A race for survival on a dangerous island. A fable. A fairytale. And if that's the case, why was everyone so worked up into a lather about just this one?

☞ **Import only**

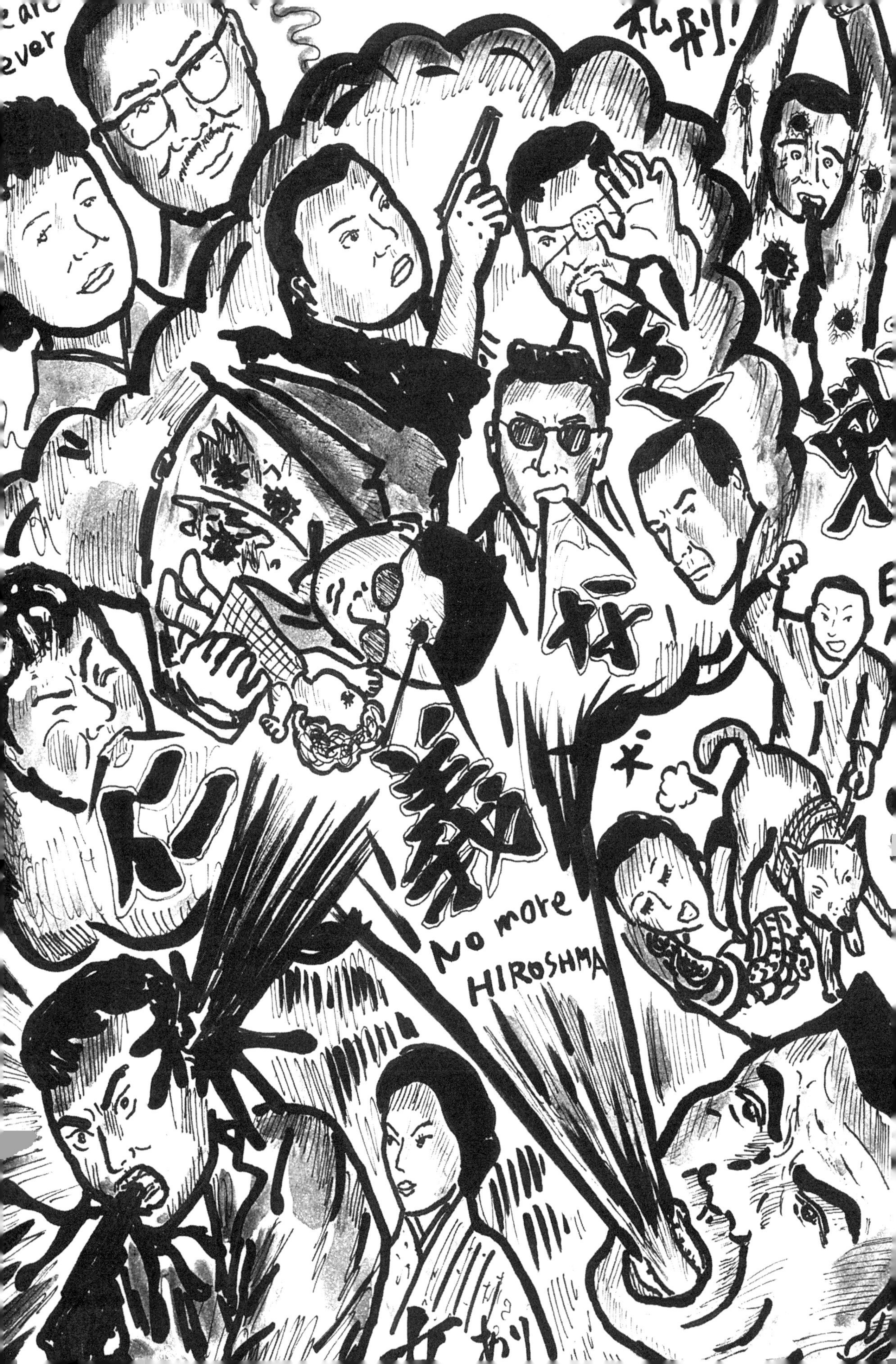
私刑!
No more
HIROSHMA

FILMS
Kinji Fukasaku
Complete Director's Filmography

1961.........Furaibo tantei—Akai tani no sangeki (Drifting Detective–Tragedy of the Red Valley, New Toei)

1961.........Furaibo tantei—Misaki wo wataru kuroi kaze (Drifting Detective–Black Wind Passing through the Peninsula, New Toei)

1961.........Fuanki hatto no kaidanji (Good Guy in the Funky Hat, New Toei)

1961.........Fuanki hatto no kaidanji—Nisenman en no ude (Good Guy in the Funky Hat–The 20,000,000 Yen Arm, New Toei)

1961.........Hakuchu no buraikan (Greed in Broad Daylight, New Toei)

1961.........Hokori takaki chosen (The Proud Challenge, Toei)

1962.........Gyangu tai G-men (Gangs vs. G-men, Toei)

1962.........Gyangu domei (Gang Alliance, Toei)

1964.........Jakoman to tetsu (Jakoman and Iron, Toei)

1964.........Okami to buta to ningen (The Wolf, the Pig, and the Man, Toei)

1965.........Odoshi (Threat, Toei)

1965.........Kamikaze yaro—Mahiru no ketto (Kamikaze Rascal–Duel in Mid-afternoon, Ninjin Pro.)

1965.........Hokkaido no abare-ryu (Violent Dragon of Hokkaido, Toei)

1967.........Kaisanshiki (The Breakup Ceremony, Toei)

1968.........Bakuto kaisanshiki (Gambler's Breakup, Toei,)

1968.........Kurotokage (Black Lizard, Shochiku)

1968.........Kyokatsu koso ga waga jinsei (Blackmail Is My Life, Shochiku)

1968.........Gamma dai sango—Uchu dai sakusen (Gamma III–Operation Outer Space, aka The Green Slime, Toei and RAM)

1969.........Kuro bara no yakata (Mansion of the Black Rose, Shochiku)

1969.........Nihon boryokudan–Kumicho (Japan Organized Crime–Boss, Toei)

1970.........Chizome no daimon (Blood Stained Crest, Toei)

1970.........Kimi ga wakamono nara (If You Were Young, Rage, independent, dist. by Shochiku)

1971.........Tora! Tora! Tora! (co-director)

1971.........Bakuto–Gaijin butai (Gambler–Foreign Force, Toei)

1972.........Gunki hatameku moto ni (Under the Flag of the Rising Sun, independent, dist. by Shochiku)

1972.........Gendai yakuza—Hitokiri yota (Modern Yakuza–Outlaw Killer, Toei)

1972.........Hitokiri yota—Kyoken san kyodai (Outlaw Killer–Three Rabid Brothers, Toei)

1973.........Jingi naki tatakai (Fight without Honor and Humanity, Toei)

1973.........Jingi naki tatakai—Hiroshima shito hen (Fight without Honor and Humanity–Deadly Fight in Hiroshima, Toei)

1973.........Jingi naki tatakai—Dairi senso (Fight without Honor and Humanity–Proxy War, Toei)

1974.........Jingi naki tatakai—Chojo sakusen (Fight without Honor and Humanity–High Tactics, Toei)

1974.........Jingi naki tatakai—Kanketsu hen (Fight without Honor and Humanity–The Final Episode, Toei)

1974.........Shin jingi naki tatakai (New Fight without Honor and Humanity, Toei)

1975.........Jingi no hakaba (Graveyard of Honor and Humanity, Toei)

1975.........Kenkei tai soshiki boryoku (Cops vs. Organized Crime, Toei)

1975.........Shikingen godatsu (Robbery–Source of Capital, Toei)

1975.........Shin jingi naki tatakai—Kumicho no kubi (New Fight without Honor and Humanity–The Boss's Neck, Toei)

1976.........Boso Panic—Dai gekitotsu (Speed Tribe Panic–Big Collision, Toei)

1976.........Shin jingi naki tatakai—Kumicho saigo no hi (New Fight without Honor and Humanity–Last Day of the Boss, Toei)

1976.........Yakuza no hakaba—Kuchinashi no hana (Graveyard of Yakuza–Flowers of Jasmine, Toei)

1977.........Hokuriku dairi senso (Hokuriku Proxy War, Toei)

1977.........Doberman deka (Detective Doberman, Toei)

1978.........Yagyu ichizoku no inbo (Conspiracy of the Yagyu Clan, aka Shogun's Samurai, Toei)

1978.........Uchu kara no messeiji (Message from Space, Toei)

1978.........Ako jo danzetsu (The Fall of Ako Castle, Toei)

1980.........Fukkatsu no hi (Resurrection Day, aka Virus, TBS/Kadokawa, dist. by Toho)

1981.........Seishun no mon (Gate of Youth, co-director, Toei)

1981.........Makai Tensho (Darkside Return, aka Samurai Reincarnation, Toei)

1982.........Dotonbori gawa (Dotonbori River, Shochiku)

1982.........Kamata koshin kyoku (The March of Kamata, aka Fall Guy, Shochiku)

1983.........Jinsei gekijo (The Human Theater, co-director, Toei)

1983 ....Satomi hakkenden (Legend of the Eight Dog Soldiers, aka Legend of the Eight Samurai, Kadokawa, dist. by Toei)

1984.........Shanghai bansukingu (The People of Shanghai, Shochiku/Asahi TV)

1986.........Kataku no hito (House on Fire, Toei)

1987.........Hissatsu IV—Urami harashimasu (Professional Killers–Will Take Care of Your Grudges, Shochiku/Asahi, dist. Toei)

1988.........Hana no ran (Flowers of Rage, aka The Rage of Love, Toei)

1990.........Remains utsukushiki yuja tachi (Remains Beautiful Heroes, supervising director, Sonny Chiba Enterprises, dist. Shochiku)

1992.........Itsu ka giragira suru hi (Someday We Will Shine, aka Triple Cross, Nippon TV/Bandai/Shochiku)

1994.........Chushingura gaiden—Yotsuya kaidan (47 Loyal Retainers Side Story–Yotsuya Ghost Story, aka Crest of Betrayal, Shochiku)

1999.........Omocha (Toy, aka The Geisha House, Toei)

2000.........Battle Royale (Battle Royale Production Committee, dist. Toei)

2001.........Gokudo no tumatati—Kumicho no borei (The Wives of the Yakuza–The Ghost of the Don)

THE MOST DANGEROUS MOVIE EVER MADE!
Behind the *Battle Royale* controversy in Japan

By Tomo Machiyama

"If you try to escape or take off the necklace you're wearing, the necklace will explode, like, WWHHAAAAMMMMM!!!"

Yuko Miyamura—the cute and popular voice actress known primarily for playing *Evangelion's* Asuka—appears early on in *Battle Royale.* In a parodic video shot in the style of a Japanese educational program, Miyamura cheerfully instructs our bewildered students how to kill—or else be killed. She was totally hilarious, but I was the only one who was laughing.

Why?

Because, except for me, the entire audience at the screening I attended were either politicians or else members of the PTA. This preview, which took place on November 28, 2000, was held solely for the sake of those who wanted to ban the film *Battle Royale*.

This wasn't the first obstacle *Battle Royale* had ever faced. Controversy began back in 1998, when the novel *Battle Royale,* written by Koushun Takami, was nominated for the Kadokawa Horror Novel Prize Contest. Even though *Battle Royale* had made it past the five preliminary judging rounds, writer Mariko Hayashi, a member of the judging committee, came out strongly against the book, killing its chances for the prize.

She said, "I was really offended by this disgusting thing" and "I hate not only this story, but also the guy who wrote it." I have absolutely no fucking clue why Mariko Hayashi was chosen for a horror novel prize contest. Just for your information, besides declaring open hatred for the films of David Lynch, she is the worst snob in the history of Japanese literature. She *is* a firm believer, though, in the Japanese emperor system, Gucci bags, and the plastic surgery she got, but, frankly, the surgeons failed, despite their best efforts.

The news that the book was shot down by Hayashi stirred up a storm of

Kinji Fukasaku

speculation: like, what kind of novel is too wild for a horror novel prize? Then, Yuichi Akata, an editor at Ota Publishing, got interested and found himself a manuscript of *Battle Royale*. Before he finished it, he was shocked, but made up his mind to publish it. The book came out in 1999. According to the publisher, it's so far sold more than 800,000 copies.

In 2000, Kinji Fukasaku started work on a film adaptation, but ran into trouble right away. Eirin, Japan's equivalent of the MPAA, checked out the script Fukasaku turned in and slapped a R-15 rating (no one under 15 allowed) on it right away.

Japanese juvenile delinquency has gotten more extreme and ghastly, especially recently. In May of 1999, a 17-year-old boy killed a housewife with a knife. A few days later, a boy the same age hijacked a bus and stabbed a woman to death. In August, a 15-year-old boy massacred a whole family in his neighborhood. In December, a 17-year-old boy tried to blow up a video shop with a bomb. Their motivations were far beyond our understanding. The bomber said that he just wanted to destroy humans. The housewife killer said, "It didn't matter who she was, because I needed to know how it felt to kill people." The busjacker said that he wanted to follow the housewife killer. Adults thought these kids might be confused and couldn't tell the real world from virtual realities, like movies and video games. That's why Eiirin thought the script of *Battle Royale* wasn't appropriate for young people.

Fukasaku, meanwhile, had the reverse idea. He thought today's teenagers needed to know the difference between real killing and DOOM. In order to do that, violence in *Battle Royale* should look as disgusting as possible. Fukasaku, the director who's said, "I'm not interested in 'action entertainment' at all. What I want to make is a film about what violence *is*," started to shoot the film without any self-restrictions or compromise. He cheered up his special-effects guy by saying, "Splatter more blood—generously!" In October, the film was completed. Eirin checked the rough cut and pointed out some scenes which they felt should be removed:

• *The scene where the teacher (Takeshi Kitano) throws a knife into a whispering female student's forehead*

• *The scene where a band around a male student's neck explodes* (actually, the gushing blood was added with CGI after shooting).

• *The scene where blood gushes out of a female student's throat cut by a scythe*

• *The scene where a dying female student is torn apart by a full-automatic machine gun's bullets*

• *The scene where a male student's decapitated head with a grenade in its mouth is used as a weapon*

Fukasaku refused to cut any of them: "Getting the go-ahead from Eirin means that the movie is wholesome, harmless, and boring. I'd rather accept a bloody R-15." The problem is, the movie was made for kids under 15. To resolve this contradiction, the 70-year-old director declared, "Kids, don't worry about the R-15. Just rush into the theater! I made this just for you, kids! I hope you guys have enough guts and wits to make it in!"

Unfortunately, his agitation might have gotten on the nerves of some parents and moral crusaders. On November 17th, *Battle Royale* became the subject of discussion in the National Diet, Japan's parliament. Koki Ishii, a representative of the Japanese Liberal Democratic Party, questioned the Minister of Education about it.

"Do you know this book?" Ishii asked, showing a copy of the *Battle Royale* novel.

"The story is about how the government forces 42 junior high school students to kill one another. Some girl gets her throat cut, and some boy gets his eyeball ripped out. To make matters worse, this story is being made into a movie. This kind of entertainment causes juvenile crime." Furthermore, he started to blame the rating system. *"Battle Royale* is rated R-15, but this rating is useless, because it's easy for kids to outwit ushers to get into a theater. If a kid gets caught, there's no law to punish him. The government needs to control and censor movies by law."

The answer of the minister and bureaucrats was, "So far, we can't say anything, because we haven't seen the movie yet."

"Me, neither," Ishii said. "Why don't we see it together?"

Thus Ishii ordered Toei, the distributor of the movie, to set up a preview for politicians, teachers, and parents on November 28.

I sneaked into the preview at the Ginza Toei theater, which was full of conservatively dressed old guys and women. Nobody came there to enjoy the movie. The crowd was waiting to see a witch get burned at the stake. Before the movie, Ishii, the inquisitor, stood on stage and appealed to the crowd, "Things harmful to young people should be banned." Next, Fukasaku, the scapegoat, appeared before the bloodthirsty mob. He had a slight, mysterious smile on his face and said, "I hope you enjoy my film."

"In the beginning of the new century, the country fell apart." The film begins with that subtitle, and the set up continues, "The Japanese economy collapsed, the unemployment rate skyrocketed, and all grownups lost their confidence. Therefore, the children came to feel contempt for parents, teachers, and authorities. Disorder in classrooms, stabbing of teachers, and boycotting of school became a widespread epidemic."

This was not fiction, but a real situation Japan had been undergoing ever since its bubble economy burst. Now the tables were turned. The audience was being blamed by the movie. I realized what Fukasaku's mysterious smile meant.

As a solution, the government creates a death game, called Battle

kinji Fukasaku

Royale. Teacher Kitano (played by Takeshi Kitano) forces his students to kill each other, but in the end he wants to die with the one student he really loves. That is his way to take responsibility for failing to bring up his students decently. Maybe he is wrong, but he's better than the audience, who avoided their responsibilities and laid the blame on the media.

Nobody kicked their seat or walked out in a rage during the screening. Some of the audience might have been ashamed of themselves. They might have thought *Battle Royale* was just another trashy exploitation movie cashing in on graphic violence, but in fact the film presented a very serious and strong political message to them. When the movie ended, unexpectedly, some of the audience applauded. After the movie, there was a discussion between politicians and the director.

Hiroshi Kawaguchi, a 39-year-old representative from the Liberal Democratic Party, confessed he was deeply touched by the movie. "Even though I've seen a lot of body-count movies, like *A Better Tomorrow* and *Natural Born Killers,*" he said, *"Battle Royale* is different from them, I think. It gives serious and earnest commentary about family, friendship, education, parenthood, and love. I was really impressed. I think it should be shown to junior high school students."

Maybe he knows more about the meaning of the name of his party than Ishii. Ishii continued his stringent attack on Fukasaku, "Your movie was just a parade of offensive, brutal, bloody violence. I couldn't keep my eyes open. I wonder, is such violence necessary? Couldn't you take a more decent route to tell the same story? I am really sorry that this kind of movie is going to open the gate of the new millennium." He seemed not to understand any of the messages in the movie.

Fukasaku calmly—but it was easy to hear the deep anger in his voice—answered Ishii, "Do you really want the government to control movies? Do you really want to get back to the time of World War II, when the government really made children kill people?"

There wasn't any room for compromise. The argument ended. After the preview, the Minister of Education summoned people from the film industry and Eirin and complained about recent movies being inappropriate for young people.

In spite of these political pressures, Toei went on to release *Battle Royale* on December 16. It became a box-office phenomenon. Though Toei ordered theaters to check the ID of young ticket buyers, they couldn't manage—because theaters were full of kids who looked 15 or 16 years old. It was impossible to keep track of the crowds that rushed in.

Takeshi Kitano joked, "Ishii was probably bribed by Toei to help hype the film." Maybe he was right. If not, I am really sorry that such stupidity represents the people of Japan. 東

INTERVIEW

Conversations with Kinji Fukasaku

What follows is a composite of three separate interviews with Kinji Fukasaku, conducted over the phone (1999), in Rotterdam (1999), and inside the Egyptian Theater in Hollywood (2001). Thanks to Toshiko Adilman who acted as translator during all sessions.

So what were your feelings about yakuza films before you began making your own?

Toei Studios was created after the war, so they didn't really have a very long history as a film company. They only cared about working hard to make films that would appeal to audiences. They didn't have a sense of tradition, but that was a good thing, inasmuch as they were keen to make good use of young filmmakers and their energy. That kind of studio with that sort of attitude was very beneficial to me.

That doesn't mean that there were no problems. One problem I had was the fact that the movies Toei made before were mostly just period pieces and costume plays. They had reached a dead end and people wanted to see something new. That's how the yakuza films originally came to be made.

But Toei was still making them in the style of the old period pieces. The stars were still carrying on the image of the stereotypical Japanese hero from before the war. Even if they were yakuza, they were never bad guys and there was no concept at all of the antihero. I wanted to make yakuza movies that had a sense of reality. I wanted to make them youthful and violent, but this was in direct conflict with the old methods. I wanted to replace the old techniques with a new kind of film, where I could overlay my own experiences of living in postwar Japan.

I grew up surrounded by the ruins of war. Life was extremely difficult. It was like living in a constant state of violence. Another thing was that we were living under the US Occupation. We had no food and such, and without the help of Americans, we could not get on with our lives. This was a great humiliation. We had been fighting the USA one day, and the next they were giving us food and clothing. As a boy aged 14 or 15, this had a tremendous impact on me. I was very upset about it.

From growing up in the postwar era, I was attracted to characters who had only violence and strength to believe in and depend on. I was hoping to meet actors who had the same kind of feeling, and that was when I encountered Bunta Sugawara. I was delighted to find that we shared the same kinds of ideas. That's how we came to make *Gendai yakuza—Hitokiri yota* (Modern Yakuza—Outlaw Killer) which is one of my favorite films. I don't

kinji Fukasaku

think I would have realized how much fun it could be making a film without Sugawara.

Now, in those days when you went to the cinema, say from the end of the sixties to the early seventies, they used to show newsreels. Many of them showed images from the student movement, such as the students and the farmers fighting the police. That's when I was inspired to begin using hand-held camera. I believe I first came to use it on *Hitokiri yota*. I myself took the camera in hand and ran into the crowds of actors and extras.

At the peak of the seventies yakuza boom, what was the average amount of time it took to produce a single title?

Once a project was in production, it took about a month to forty days. That included production, editing, and post-production. A lot depended on how long it took to write the screenplays. Some took a long time, while others came in very quickly, like ten days.

What sort of reaction did your films get from the actual yakuza?

After I made *Jingi no hakaba*, I started doing research for the follow-up *Yakuza no hakaba* (Graveyard of Yakuza). I went to a quarter of Osaka called Kamagasaki where many poor people and criminals live. I put on some shabby clothes and went to look for script ideas. All of a sudden, I was surrounded by two or three guys. I thought for sure I was going to be mugged, so I started to brace myself when all of a sudden, they said "Oh! You are that director! We just saw *Jingi no hakaba* and out of all your movies that is your masterpiece!"

I was absolutely delighted to hear these compliments. At the time, I was sort of depressed, because film critics, who I suppose could be called intellectuals, had harshly criticized my filmmaking. But here I was getting compliments from people whose own lives were deeply rooted in their environment. It provided great stimulation for me.

Why do you think that audiences are once again interested in your yakuza films?

In the seventies, my films were probably seen by society as being too brutal. I felt rejected by mass audiences. I don't know how it was in the States, but wasn't it in the sixties that American films started to deal with the Vietnam War?

There were a few, but it wasn't really until the seventies and eighties that American films really started to tackle Vietnam.

It's almost the same thing in Japan. There was a time lag before audiences were ready to confront the postwar environment. Although it was made in 1973, a film like *Jingi naki tatakai* (Fight without Honor and Humanity) is really about the time period immediately following the war. *Jingi naki tatakai* and other films like it couldn't have been made until a time lag of sorts had occurred.

As the president of the Japanese Director Guild, what does your work entail exactly?

The key issue right now relates to directors' rights. In Japan in the late forties there was an agreement made between the politicians and influential studio producers that was entered into the legal system. It basically said that film directors don't own the copyrights to their

INTERVIEW

work. They had *moral rights* [moral rights concern the right to have your name attributed to your work, the right not to have your name falsely attributed to someone else's work, and the right to protect the integrity of your work], but no copyrights. However, these moral rights now give the same kind of protection to directors as copyrights do. That was something that the director's guild fought for many years to accomplish.

Also, since I became the president, there have been more opportunities to show my films abroad. Because of this, I became shockingly aware of the poor state of prints in circulation. Each studio seems to have destroyed film prints after only four or five years following release. This was abominable. Also, you haven't really seen any enthusiasm on the part of the studios to introduce Japanese film abroad at all. A few names like Ozu, Kurosawa, Mizoguchi are known, but even then only at a minimum level, and mostly that is due to the efforts of Daiei Studios, who worked really hard to show their films abroad. Little has been known about films made after those directors. I would like to introduce more films by colleagues of mine to show internationally. Just to show Ozu, Kurosawa, and Mizoguchi won't do anymore.

Regarding Battle Royale, I noticed the style seemed very different from your older films. I'm curious how your style evolved to make Battle Royale.

What were the differences you noticed?

I noticed there wasn't as much hand-held camera during violent scenes. The camera was more locked down. And no freeze frames. Text became a more essential part of the film.

You know, I had to direct 42 youths inexperienced in this kind of genre. Hand-held camera requires a high level of professionalism, in order to create good communication among the cameraman, director, and actors, in order to create quality images. With these kids, many were first-timers. We did have two cameras, but instead of moving shots, we created detailed scenes through editing, through cuts and inserts. That was the effect I went for in this film.

Can you explain the context for the controversy around this film? I'm afraid Americans aren't aware of the significance of the image of stabbing the teacher in the classroom.

What do you mean, it's not familiar? It's not familiar to American students to see teachers stabbed?

With American students, it's more that they kill each other in the classroom.

They kill each other, but don't hurt the teacher?

They don't focus their anger toward the teacher.

Why?

Because teachers are powerless in America. They're not respected. They have no authority.

If there's no authority, they don't bother. Is that it? So, in other words, they don't bother with the teacher, so it doesn't matter.

kinji Fukasaku

That is my opinion.

What are the teachers doing in school?

Just doing their job.

And they're oblivious to what's going on with the students?

They're just afraid that something bad will happen. They're afraid of that relationship. They're not the target, but you know.

Well, that I can understand.

Maybe we can just talk about the general controversy. My question, then, is, what is it in the film that caused it? Because maybe to, say, an uninformed audience the movie might just seem to be about a bunch of people fighting. So what is it in the film that caused such a political outcry?

In the film, the kids are all gathered onto the island and forced to kill each other. And it's clear that this was a measure that was decided by politicians, but no politicians show up in the film. This makes politicians who see the film very uneasy, because they don't have the floor to say anything in it. And the adults, the people who are close to the politicians, they don't show up in the film, either. And that makes them nervous, too.

Adults think they have a lot to say, even though they've already actually given up on life. In reality, they haven't bothered with their children for a long time, but all of a sudden they feel they have to impose their opinion. And they don't have that opportunity in the film. Faced with the situation in the film, kids immediately realize it's a kind of game. But adults, maybe because their kids seem kind of eerie and distant to them, have been nervous about letting young people see this film. And that was the start of the controversy. The point of the controversy shifted to whether or not to show this film to young people or not.

This reaction was exactly what I had in mind when we depicted this kind of confrontation between adults and young people—without adults actually appearing in the film. And the politicians, officials, and PTA all just got themselves caught in the snare.

I don't understand what the fuss is about. This is a fairytale, a fable. The politicians get very nervous, because they might be afraid that it's exposing the fact that they've been doing nothing. At the same time, they're trying to regulate and control media, saying it's harmful to young people. In the name of what's good and educational for kids, they are trying to control the media. This was already happening in Japan at the time *Battle Royale* came out. Let me reiterate, just to make it clear: politicians believe it is necessary to control the media, but they only think the need is there because they're looking forward to elections. The politicians have been targeting recent crimes by minors, hyping it as an issue. And it is true that youth crimes have been happening, but the number of such incidents hasn't changed much over the years. It's just that they've been sort of intensified.

Do you think it's an optimistic or hopeful film?

I think it's full of messages. First of all, I don't think a lot of kids today believe in, or don't know, the pleasure of movies. They are just so immersed in games, they're not aware of the pleasure that films can give, because the movies are very open and embracing. I really

INTERVIEW

want to see as many people as possible become fond of movies—even just one more person would make me happy. And the construction of this movie, the music in it and the way it was shot—that was why we didn't use the hand-held camera to produce violent effects—was directed toward that goal. I thought this film would move the audience, through a repetition and demonstration of this world, to appreciate the qualities of film.

There's a history in your films of very violent antiheroes who refuse to take either side. It's usually almost a celebration of that kind of character. In Battle Royale, this character would be Kiriyama, the transfer student. Has your approach to that type of violence and character changed?

It's not that my approach has changed. I think the society that used to see my films where violence was the fundamental element has changed. The stories in *Fight without Honor and Humanity* start from the end of the Second World War. At that time, a large portion of the population of Japan had experienced war. Very few now. I was 15 when the war ended. I was 40 when I made *Fight*. I'm 70 now. That means the majority of the population don't know the war now. The kids in this movie, and even their parents, don't know the war. Only their grandparents do.

At the time *Fight* came out, the audience knew the war and the confusion and turmoil afterwards. I think this explains the differences you might observe in this film. There may have been some big changes within myself as well, but I'm not aware exactly what those changes are. In making this film, I tried to put myself at the level of these kids who were 15 years of age. I was 15 in 1945. That was still before the end of the war, and then the war ended and Japan collapsed. During the making of *Battle Royale,* I was seeing myself as a 15-year-old. I continued to talk to those 15-year-olds, telling them that the war is different from this kind of game. I talked to those kids who were interested in hearing me relate my experiences and also when I felt this kind of explanation would be useful in my direction. I related my experiences to facilitate communication between myself and these young actors.

You mean looking at all those dead bodies and being attacked during aerial bombardments? The war is different from this game?

Well, it's true that this is not the kind of game where you manipulate machines, have all sorts of choices, and hit the "reset" button to start all over. No, this is the kind of game where you have to act yourself in the game, you have to live through this game. It was in that context that I talked about my war experience. 東

Kinji Fukasaku at the Egyptian Theater in Hollywood, January 20, 2001.

157

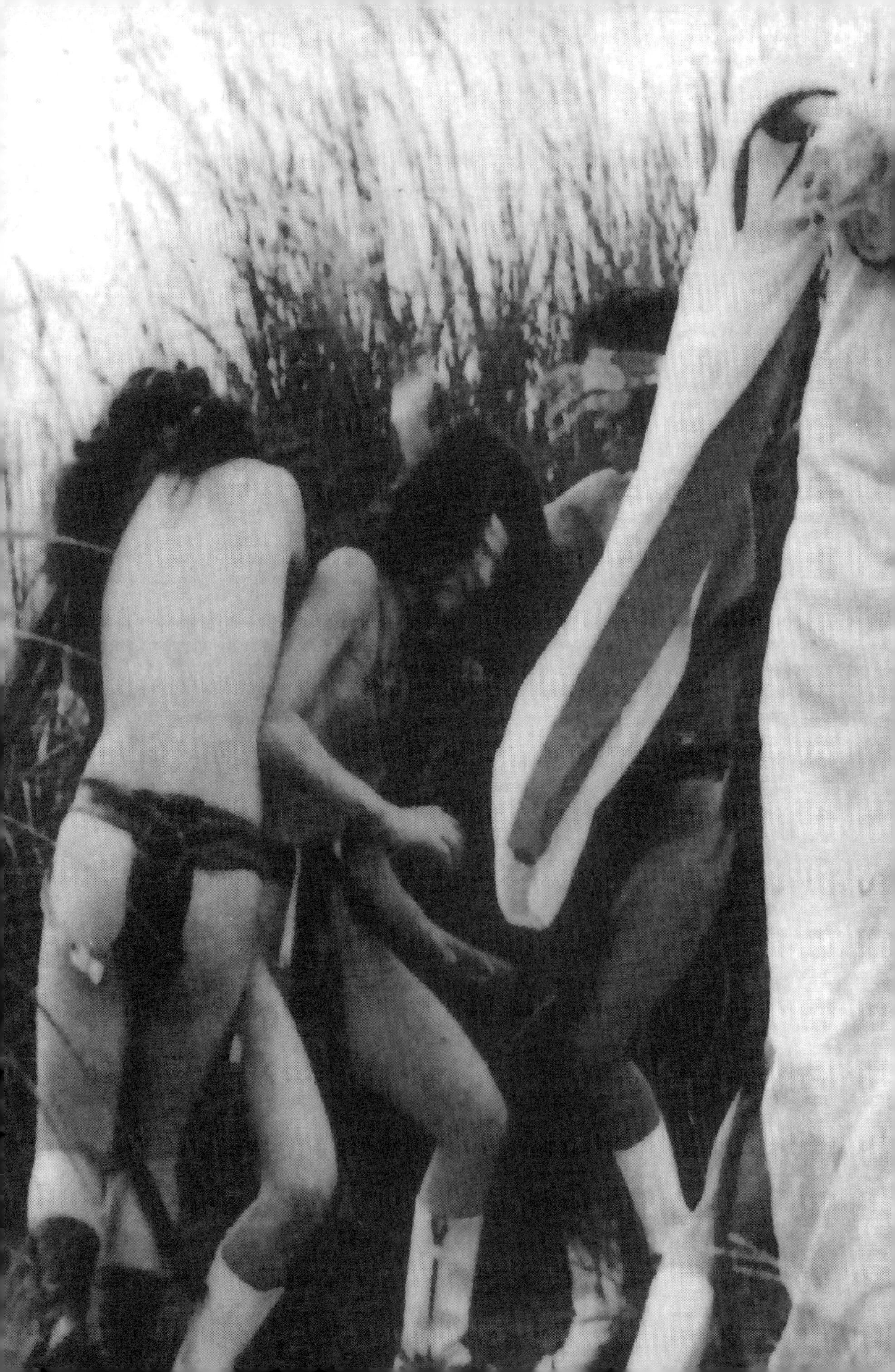

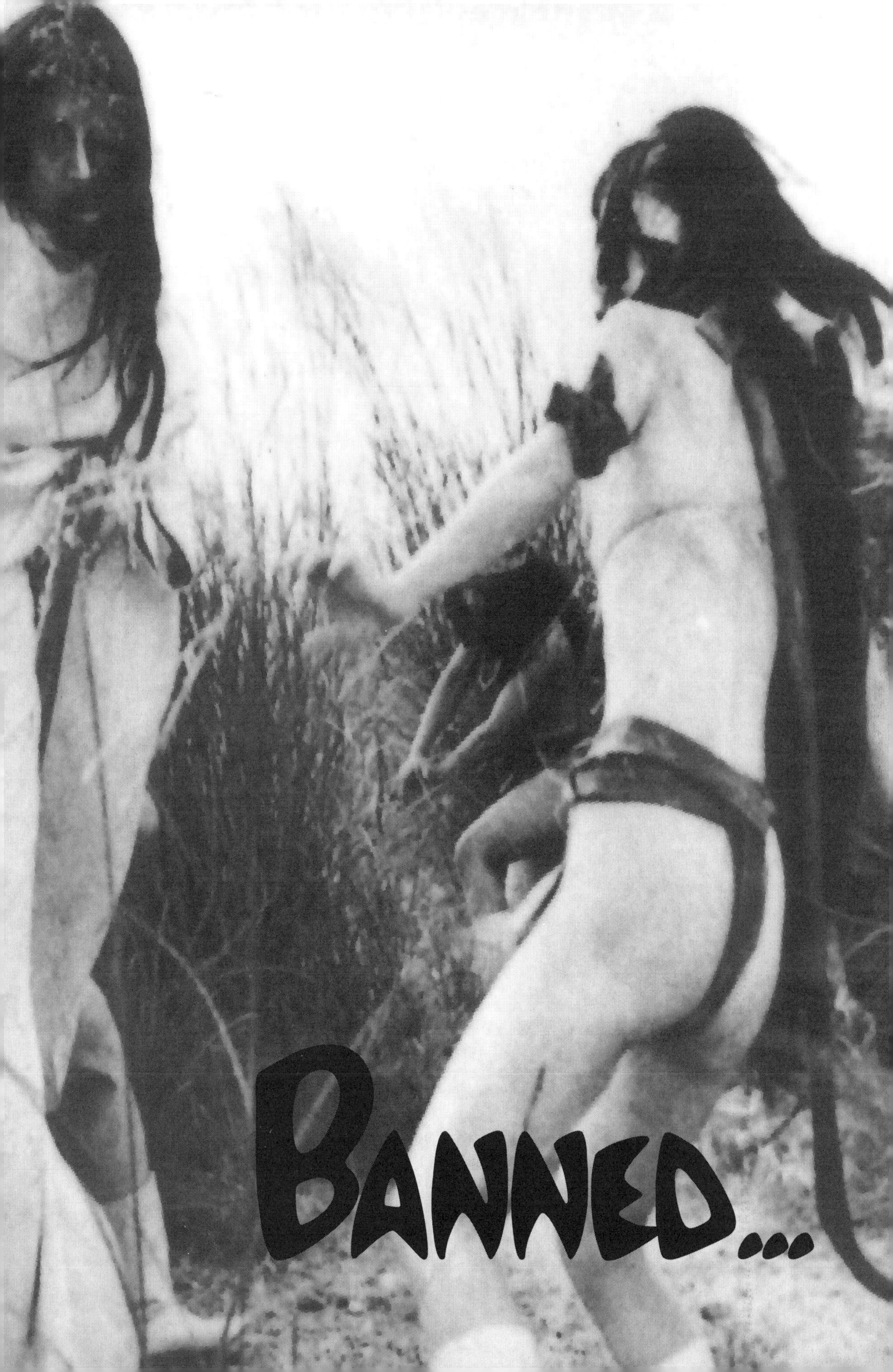
BANNED...

BANNED...

FIVE FORBIDDEN FILMS

Here's a pair of sweeping generalizations for you: Japan is a place where reality is carefully regulated and imagination is allowed to run crazy and screaming in the streets. In America, the situation is reversed: the fact that practically anyone can own a gun is neatly balanced by a cultural war on media and fantasy. Meanwhile, over in Dai Nippon, the odds are no one will ever shoot you, even if you are reading *Rapeman* manga on the train.

Or something like that.

Or maybe not.

In truth, morality and conformity are closely allied in Japan. In such a socially conservative climate, one of the worst things you can do is to call attention to yourself by offending someone else. The fear of stigmatization can play a major factor in what's permitted in the movies and what isn't.

Which brings us to our Five Forbidden Films: *Kyujukyuhonme no kimusume* (The 99th Virgin), *Kaijin yuki otoko* (aka *Half-Human*), *Edogawa Ranpo zenshu—Kyofu kikei ningen* (Collected Works of Edogawa Rampo— Horrible Malformed Men), *Keido zero dai sakusen* (aka *Latitude Zero*), and *Nostradamus no dai yogen* (aka *The Last Days of Planet Earth*).

All of them as *verboten* and delicious as whale meat, the Fatal Five have been deemed unfit by the very studios that produced them. While the members of this club have not been "banned" in the legal sense, they have been effectively banished from the realm. Outside of very occasional, once-in-a-blue-moon screenings (usually held at midnight or during other circumstances far from the gaze of civilized folk), finding these films in Japan is difficult. Especially when all five are currently considered unsuitable for home viewing and television broadcast. Consigned to the vaults or wiped from "official" studio history, each picture has its own story to tell.

The Japanese film industry not only polices itself through the studios, but through the Eirin ratings board. This self-regulation has, for the most part, kept government suits out of the screening room. And as the recent controversy over Kinji Fukasaku's *Battle Royale* showed, it's not a pretty sight when politicians try to step

INTRO

in. Take for instance the *taiyozoku* (sun tribes) films that appeared in the wake of Shintaro Ishihara's 1955 novel *Taiyo no kisetsu* (Season of the Sun). When these violent and sexual forerunners of the pink movie (many of which starred the author's younger brother Yujiro Ishihara) inspired an unfortunate rash of copycat crimes, the Japanese government responded by forbidding the use of the word *taiyozoku*. Yet the genre survived, sex and violence and all, with nary a change, except for the new moniker of *yajuzoko* (beast tribes).

So what would make a studio recall its own product and knowingly lose out on all that box-office dough and ancillary profit? The overriding reason, for all of these films, is "sensitivity"—political correctness Japanese-style, sometimes minus the politics. Often it's simply better simply not to take any chances, lest someone complain and invoke the scalding shame of embarrassment.

For Toho's *Keido Zero dai sakusen* (Latitude Zero), a hazy copyright situation keeps the US-Japan co-produced film out of circulation, in case it should ever prove to be a liability.

The remaining quartet of titles are lost in a formidable fog of taboo topics: atomic radiation, physical disabilities, and the legacy of those who have been branded social outsiders.

Toho learned the hard way when their big-budget 1974 film *Nostradamus no dai yogen* ran into trouble with a no-nukes activist who saw the film and ignited a national scandal. To this day, books that dare to show photos of the film's shocking post-nuke mutants can be yanked from the shelves.

The legacy of the *hibakusha* (victims of the atomic bomb) runs deep in Japan. It has also created problems for Tsuburaya Productions, who now refuse to acknowledge the existence of episode 12 of their late-sixties *Ultraseven* superhero TV show. It depicted space vampires in search of fresh blood to cure their radiation sickness.

Offensive or not, it should now be noted that the people who complained about episode 12 of *Ultraseven*, as well as *Nostradamus no dai yogen*, were merely acting on behalf of the *hibakusha* and were not themselves victims of the atomic bombings.

Then you have the *burakumin*, Japan's outcast class, who have suffered institutionalized prejudice

161

BANNED...

dating back thousands of years. Once legally considered unmentionable, unemployable, or unmarriageable for transgressing the religious taboo of killing animals, the *burakumin* (which only literally means "hamlet people"—all the same don't go yelling it around Shinjuku) issue is so sensitive that Toho's *Kaijin yuki otoko* (1955) and Shin Toho's *Kyujukyuhonme no kimusume* (1959) have been pulled simply for depicting people who live in hamlets who *might* be considered *burakumin*.

A curious double standard is evident in Toei's handling of Teruo Ishii's *Kyofu kikei ningen* (Horrible Malformed Men). Even though the disabled people in the film are nothing more than a troupe of costumed butoh dancers, the film remains a pariah. Meanwhile, Tod Browning's 1932 *Freaks*, which features very real physically challenged performers, can be had on tape, shown on TV, and screened without a hassle—the difference being that *Freaks* is a "foreign film" and thus permissible.

Since the full weight of Japan's native taboos doesn't apply outside of the island nation, English-language versions of Toho's *Nostradamus no dai yogen* and *Kaijin yuki otoko* have long been available in the West as *The Last Days of Planet Earth* and *Half-Human* respectively.

But for Japanese fans who have long dreamt of experiencing these monster and special-effects-heavy films, the parent studio, Toho, has tried to strike a compromise by releasing expensive, elaborate box sets for these two films containing reproductions of posters, lobby cards, reams of data, everything but the film itself which is represented solely by a CD containing the entire soundtrack of the film—dialogue, sound effects, and all.

Still, it seems a shame that the entire set of five seems destined to be seen only in badly edited versions, English-dubbed "international versions," or by hordes of bootlegging video collectors. These films never intentionally set out to upset anyone.

Okay, the jury is still out on *Horrible Malformed Men*.

Perhaps, in the end, it is best not to think of the Forbidden Five as actually offensive, be it deliberate or otherwise, but rather to consider them as yet another extraordinary exotic phenomenon of the inscrutable Orient.

Did I say something wrong? 東

Half-Human
Kaijin yuki otoko (Monster Snow Man)

1955, Toho
Director Ishiro Honda
Cast Akemi Negishi, Akira Takarata, Nobuo Nakamura

Director Ishiro Honda's first fantasy film following his epochal 1954 *Gojira* (Godzilla) was an atmospheric black and white abominable snowman tale meant to give a *kaiju*-crazed public a new Japanese monster (albeit one that owed something to King Kong). Yet following its initial theatrical run, Toho opted to slap a self-imposed ban on the film, where it has dwelt in darkness ever since.

While combing the Japanese Alps in search of a missing mountain climber, a rescue party stumbles across an isolated community of natives who worship an apelike creature as a god. The climax of the film is a pitched battle between the enraged beast, whose only begotten son (the last of its kind) has been killed by bad guys out to make a quick buck, and Chika, a fiery village girl (a striking fur-clad figure played by Akemi Negishi, "discovered" by Josef von Sternberg and seen in his 1953 film *Anatahan*).

While the superstitious, monster-worshipping villagers are not *explicitly* portrayed as Japan's discriminated social class, the *burakumin*, they were apparently close enough for Toho to put the film on quarantine.

Complicating matters is a troubling hint of interspecies sex between the half-human creature, who only wants to perpetuate his dying breed, and the animalistic Chika, who at one point almost seems willing to oblige him.

Following *Kaijin yuki otoko*, Toho retreated back to more typical monster-on-the-loose formulas for 1956's *Rodan* and 1958's *Dai kaiju Baran* (Giant Monster Baran, aka *Varan the Unbelievable*), which would run into problems thanks to some discriminatory language pointed at the folks inhabiting the Tohoku region where the film is set. So it goes.

As *Kaijin yuki otoko* has been rarely seen since its original 1955 engagements, video copies of the American version of the film, re-titled *Half-Human* ("Half-Man, Half-Beast but ALL MONSTER!") fetch high prices in Japanese collectors circles. Unfortunately, this alternate version is slashed down to nearly a third of the original running time and comes minus Masaru Sato's (*Yojimbo, Son of Godzilla*) score. In its place is unimaginative library music and some new footage featuring Dr. John Carradine, M.D., who pontificates (somewhat rather unconvincingly it should be noted) over the body of a dead snowman.

☞ **Taboos: discrimination and bestiality overtones**

☞ **Currently under self-imposed studio ban. Japanese video release and television broadcast not possible. Edited version available on US home video.**

The 99th Virgin
Kyujukyuhonme no kimusume

Shin Toho, 1959
Director Morihei Magatani
Cast Bunta Sugawara, Yoko Mihara, Yoichi Numata

Produced by exploitation king Mitsugu Okura, in a year when he managed to crank out nearly forty films, this trashy black and white adaptation of Tsunehei Ogouchi's pulp novel, *The 99th Bewitched Sword*, paints yet another unflattering picture of Japanese country folk. Owing to increased sensitivity of *burakumin* discrimination, *The 99th Virgin* was withdrawn from a home video release in the mid-eighties and cannot be shown on Japanese television.

Way out in the backwaters of rural Japan, near the mouth of the Kitakami River in the Iwate Prefecture (near where Toho's monster *Varan the Unbelievable* resides) a strange "fire-making festival" is held once every ten years. During this ancient rite, a legendary sword must be cleansed with the blood of a living virgin, instead of the usual splash of water.

The superstitious villagers, spearheaded by an old crone and the wild-eyed village leader, kidnap a modern girl from Tokyo (who unfortunately happens to be the daughter of police chief Bunta Sugawara) to be the 99th sacrifice, but they are enraged to discover that she's anything but a virgin.

The film stars future Kinji Fukasaku collaborator and *Gendai yakuza* Bunta Sugawara (who was then billed as one of Shin Toho's "Handsome Towers") and reigning busty sex bomb Yoko Mihara. The meaty Mihara rocketed to fame for her fleshed-out figure, something few women in the immediate postwar era could boast of. The Sugawara-Mihara combo would be revived for Yoshiki Onoda's 1960 *Female Slave Ship*, another spectacular Shin Toho film almost certain to still offend someone out there.

- **Taboo: buraku-sploitation**
- **Unavailable on Japanese home video—television broadcast not possible. Unavailable in international markets.**

REVIEW

Latitude Zero
Keido zero dai sakusen (Operation Latitude Zero)

1969, Toho/Don Sharp Productions
Director Ishiro Honda
Cast Joseph Cotton, Akira Takarada, Cesar Romero

Latitude Zero, based on a 1941 American radio serial, was originally budgeted at a whopping one million dollars. But as members of the international cast arrived in Japan, they discovered that the American half of the deal had fallen apart, leaving Toho to pick up the tab for a physically ill *Citizen Kane* alumnus (Joseph Cotton), a former Miss Miami (Linda Haynes, who would go on to star in *Coffy* and *Rolling Thunder*), a *Green Slime* star (Richard Jaeckel), and a Joker (Cesar Romero).

The resulting film, a wild Jules-Verne-by-way-of-James-Bond tale cloaked in groovy gold lame, is about a pair of scientists (Cotton and Romero) dueling it out with their submarines, the Alpha and the Black Shark, for control of a hidden undersea utopia. While the monsters who populate the picture, such as giant rats, bat men, and a winged lion, aren't up to the usual Toho high standards (blame it on the budget drop), the plentiful submarine battles are fantastic. Either way, *Latitude Zero* was the last major science-fiction film from the dream team of director Ishiro Honda, special-effects guru Eiji Tsuburaya, and screenwriter Shinichi Sekizawa. And it pains hardcore Japanese fans of the genre greatly to know that the film might never again be seen as intended.

Ted Sherdeman, who also created the original *Latitude Zero* radio show, wrote the original screenplay (before Sekizawa adapted it into Japanese) and also penned the sci-fi classic *Them!* (1954) and *My Side of the Mountain* (1969). Owing to the complicated nature of the failed US-Japan deal, as well as the uncertain status of Ted Sherdeman's intellectual property, Toho, fearing that they might have a potential liability on their hands, has opted simply to shelve the film.

☞ **Problem: copyright-mares**

☞ **Currently under a self-imposed studio ban. Video release and television broadcast in Japan unlikely. Unavailable on US home video, but has been screened on television.**

Collected Works of Edogawa Rampo—Horrible Malformed Men
Edogawa Ranpo zenshu—Kyofu kikei ningen

1969, Toei
Director Teruo Ishii
Cast Teruo Yoshida, Tatsumi Hijikata, Asao Koike

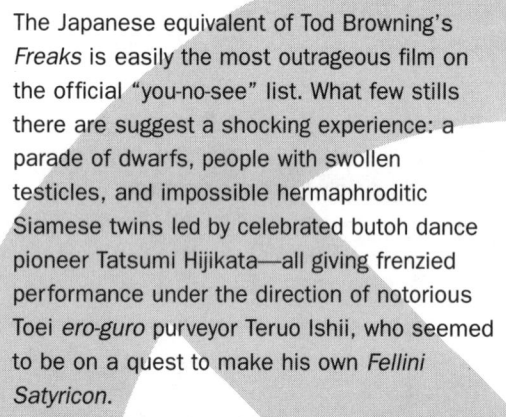

The Japanese equivalent of Tod Browning's *Freaks* is easily the most outrageous film on the official "you-no-see" list. What few stills there are suggest a shocking experience: a parade of dwarfs, people with swollen testicles, and impossible hermaphroditic Siamese twins led by celebrated butoh dance pioneer Tatsumi Hijikata—all giving frenzied performance under the direction of notorious Toei *ero-guro* purveyor Teruo Ishii, who seemed to be on a quest to make his own *Fellini Satyricon*.

A hodgepodge of *Panoramato kidan* (The Strange Story of Panorama Island) and several other tales by mystery author Edogawa Rampo (*Moju, aka Blind Beast*), the gruesome scenario concerns a capitalist (Hijikata) born with webbed fingers and toes. To improve his self-esteem, he takes to abducting normal folks and surgically remaking them into monsters, whom he then lords over on an island retreat. Eventually, one of his employees betrays him, tipping off the legendary detective Kogoro Akechi (a character featured in Kinji Fukasaku's 1968 Rampo adaptation *Black Lizard*), who soon pays the dangerous isle a visit.

Reasoning that Ishii's film wasn't all that different from an innocuous carnival sideshow, the film initially passed the studio and ratings boards without a blip. After all, the titular "Malformed Men" were played by members of a butoh troupe and were not the genuine article. The march of time saw Toei eventually taking it out of circulation themselves, for fear that, sooner or later, someone would be mightily offended.

Forget about the movie. Even the title *Kikei ningen* (meaning literally "Deformed Man") is a howler, sounding like some kind of messed-up superhero. If this wasn't enough already, one of the very first lines of dialogue is *"kichigai,"* a now *verboten* phrase which means "lunatic," only very unflatteringly so.

Rare one-night-only screenings are now the only way to see this mythical work of mad art which preserves a major performance by the late (and ironically now culturally revered) Hijikata, who said of the film, "Being drawn to the erotic and grotesque is an essential part of human nature. Teruo Ishii is great in pursuing this path undaunted by criticism. Sugar-coated love stories are all fake."

☞ **Taboos: physical deformities, loaded language**

☞ **Currently under a self-imposed studio ban. Video release, TV broadcast not possible. Unavailable in foreign markets.**

☞ **More: TERUO ISHII p. 169**

The Last Days of Planet Earth
Nostradamus no dai yogen—Catastrophe 1999
(The Great Prophecies of Nostradamus)

1974, Toho
Director Toshio Matsuda
Cast Tetsuro Tanba, Toshio Kurosawa, Kaoru Yumi

Nostradamus no daiyogen is such an amazing piece of work that we are going to cover it again later in the "Panic & Disaster" chapter, but for now here's the tale of how this movie about a 16th-century French astrologer became a Japanese cult film outcast.

When a book on the prophecies of Nostradamus by journalist Ben Goto grew into a best-selling phenomenon in Japan, Toho producer Tomoyuki Tanaka decided to mount a massive big-budget adaptation.

However, one week after *Nostradamus no dai yogen* hit theaters, a self-righteous member of a "No Nukes" group caught the film in a Kansai-area theater and quickly lodged complaints to Eirin, Japan's film ratings and censor board. Although the movie contains plenty of material that could be considered tasteless and exploitive, the viewer was offended by only two sequences: one showing a pack of radioactive aborigines on the attack in New Guinea, and the other featuring two mutant children fighting over a snake in the aftermath of a nuclear holocaust—scenes they believed treated survivors of atomic catastrophe as monsters.

Toho scrambled to dub in the line, "Don't shoot! They are human beings!" to the New Guinea sequence and ordered projectionists to snip offending frames (amounting to about 1 minute and 45 seconds of footage) from release prints, and even made a public apology through print ads in major newspapers (on Christmas Day no less).

But the PR damage was done. Following a television broadcast of the complete unedited film on Japanese television in 1980, Toho consigned the film to the vaults.

Currently the only "official" way to experience the film in Japan is through a "drama CD" containing the complete soundtrack. But bootleg video copies can be found in Tokyo *otaku* hotbeds like Akihabara and Nakano. In such places, the American laserdisc *The Last Days of Planet Earth*, which is English-dubbed and drastically cut—yet contains the forbidden frames originally cut from Japanese prints—goes for about 300 bucks.

☞ **Taboo: radioactive bad taste**

☞ **Currently under self-imposed studio ban. Japanese video release and television broacast not possible. Edited version available on US home video and television.**

☞ **More: The Last Days of Planet Earth p. 205**

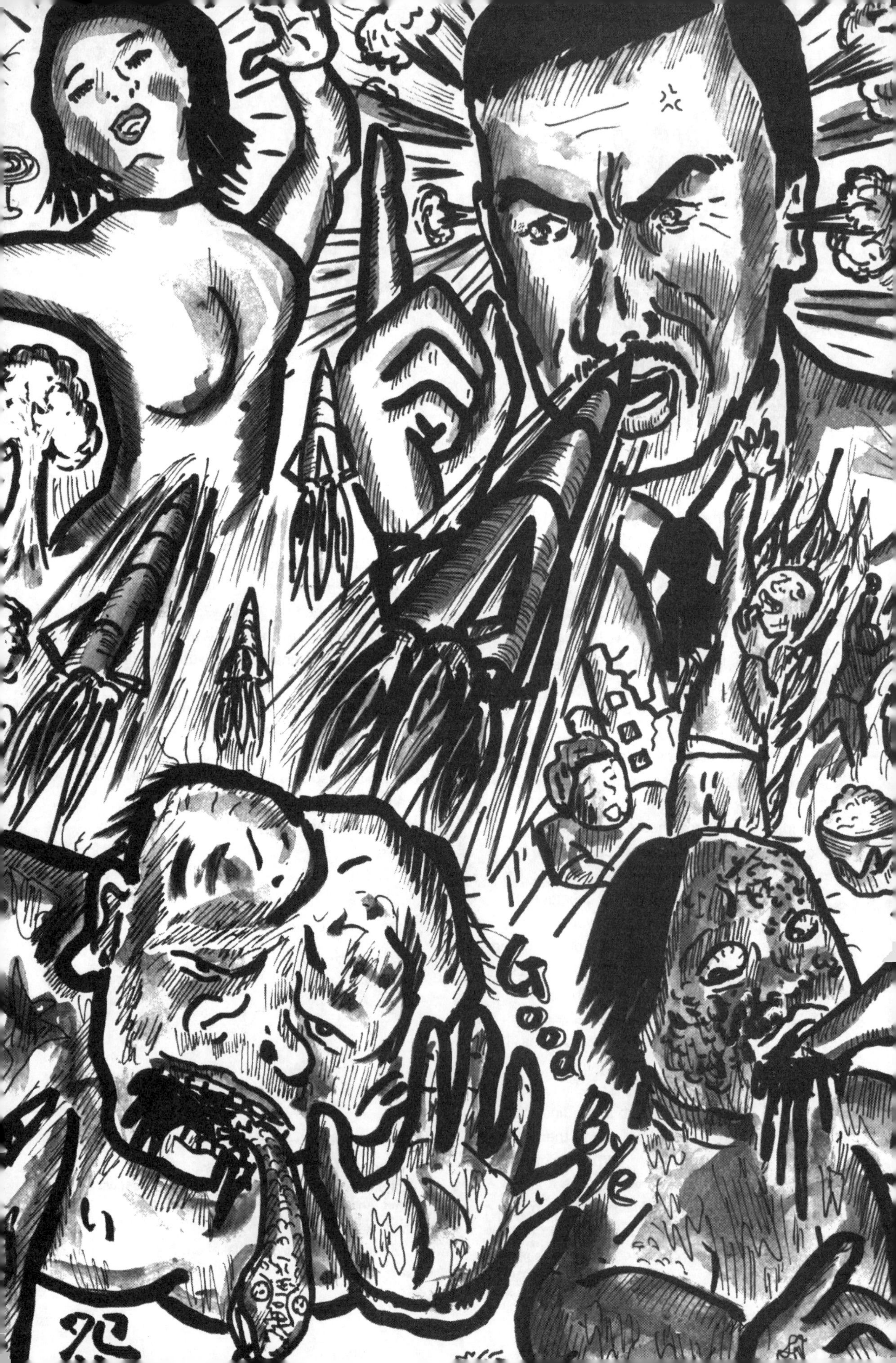
Good Bye

石井輝男

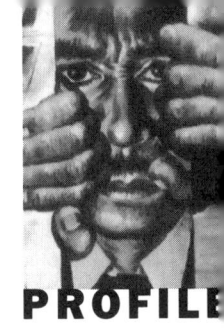

Teruo Ishii
Director

PROFILE

Out of all Toei studio's contract-bound directors, Teruo Ishii (born in Tokyo, 1924) perhaps sailed the furthest out on the high seas of exploitation. Exemplified in 1968's notorious (and eventually pulled from circulation) film *Collected Works of Edogawa Rampo—Horrible Malformed Men*, Ishii's excesses continually set the standard for how far (or how low) his peers could push filmic taboos and celebrate freakishness.

Ishii grew up heavily influenced by writer Edogawa Rampo, and the author's distinctive sense of the erotic-grotesque has served Ishii well as an ideal to aim for. The young artistically minded Ishii dropped out of high school to become an assistant cameraman at Toho. After the formation of splinter studio Shin Toho in 1947, Ishii moved there to work as an assistant director before making his directorial debut with 1957's boxing film *King of the Ring—World of Glory*. Ishii next toiled on six installments of producer Mitsugu Okura's nine-film *Super Giant* series, featuring future big-name star Ken Utsui as a cut-rate Japanese Superman.

Ishii next refined a slightly more personal style with tales of spicy mystery in the modern underworld. His *Chitai* (Zone, aka *Line*) films (*Black Line*, *Yellow Line*, *Fire Line*, *Sexy Line*, 1958-1961) were popular hits and brought the writer-director his first taste of success.

Ishii moved to Toei in 1961 just in time to be swept up by the studio's need for mass-production directors. Ishii's additional skills as a screenwriter kept him busy with numerous gang and period yakuza films before he struck gold and helped create a major Japanese star in Ken Takakura, with 1965's *Abashiri bangaichi* (Abashiri Prison). But success condemned Ishii to grinding out sequels. Within two years, he had directed and scripted *ten* separate *Abashiri Prison* films.

As Toei's audience began to wane in the late sixties, the studio quickly tried to lure viewers back with an unprecedented attack plan of sex and violence. In this permissive environment, Ishii came fully into his own as a new master of erotic-grotesque nonsense, leading to a triple crescendo with 1969's *Horrible Malformed Men*, 1973's *Porno jidaigeki—Bohachi bushido* (Porno Period Film—Way of the Outlaw Samurai), and 1973's *Yasagure anegoden—Sokatsu Lynch* (Wild Woman Boss Story—Total Lynch).

In the mid-seventies, new studio trends steered Ishii towards action films. Unhappy with making karate movies with Sonny Chiba, Ishii was soon making biker-gang *bosozoku* titles. Following 1979's *Boryoku senshi* (Violent Warriors), the frustrated director took a long sabbatical from filmmaking.

Freed from studio obligations, Ishii staged a comeback in the nineties as a fully independent filmmaker. His recent work includes 1998's *Neji-shiki* (Screw Style), an adaptation of the celebrated avant-garde manga by Yoshiharu Tsuge, and 1999's *Jigoku—The Sinners of Hell*, a hallucinatory partial remake of Nobuo Nakagawa's classic Shin Toho chiller of the same name.

The passing of strange eons has not diluted Teruo Ishii's original inspiration one bit. His latest production is *Moju tai issunboshi* (Blind Beast vs. Midget). Like *Horrible Malformed Men* before it, the film is a greatest-hits tribute to, you guessed it, Edogawa Rampo. 東

Pink & Violent

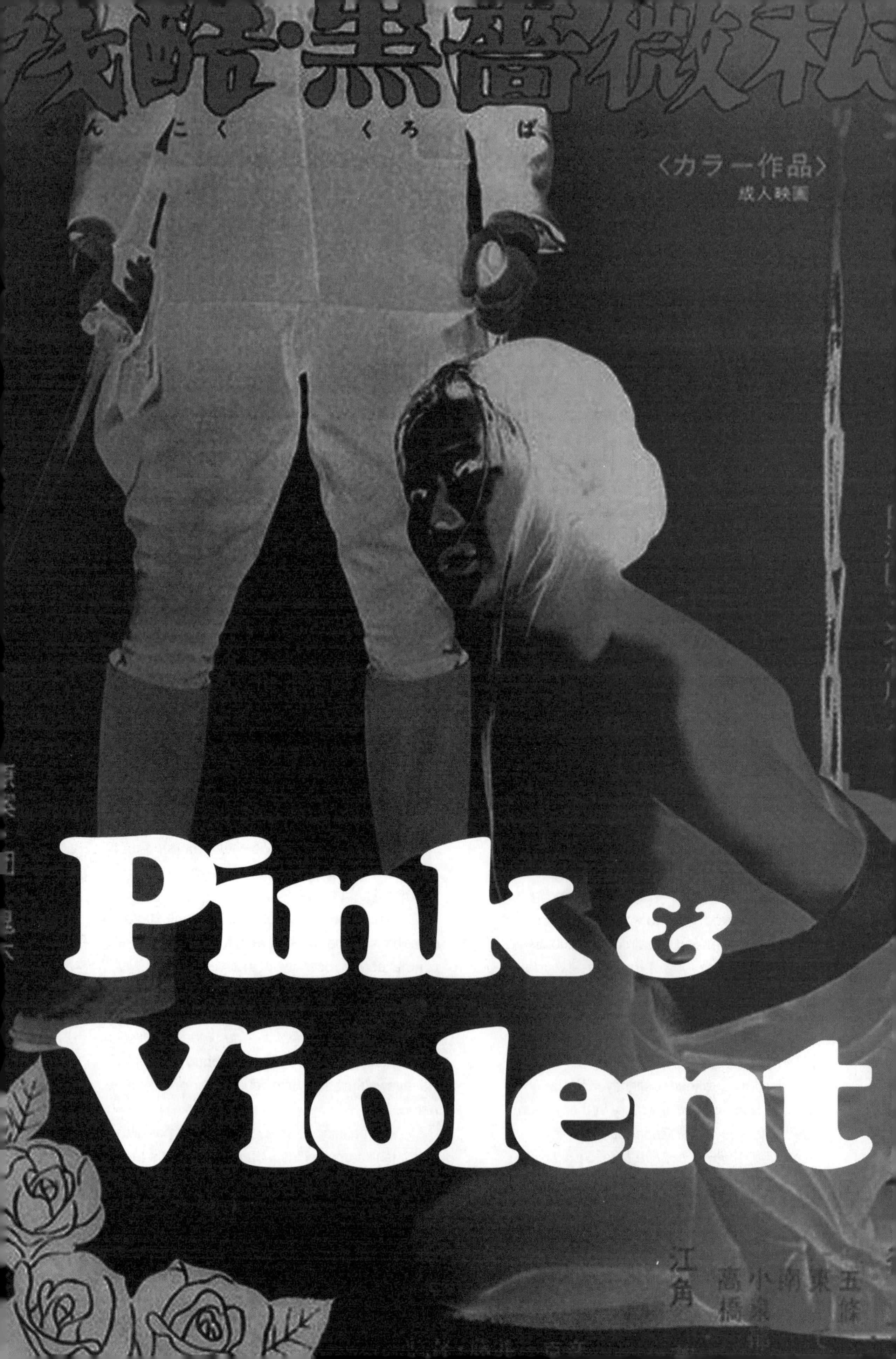

残酷・黒薔薇私刑
ざんこく・くろばらリンチ

〈カラー作品〉
成人映画

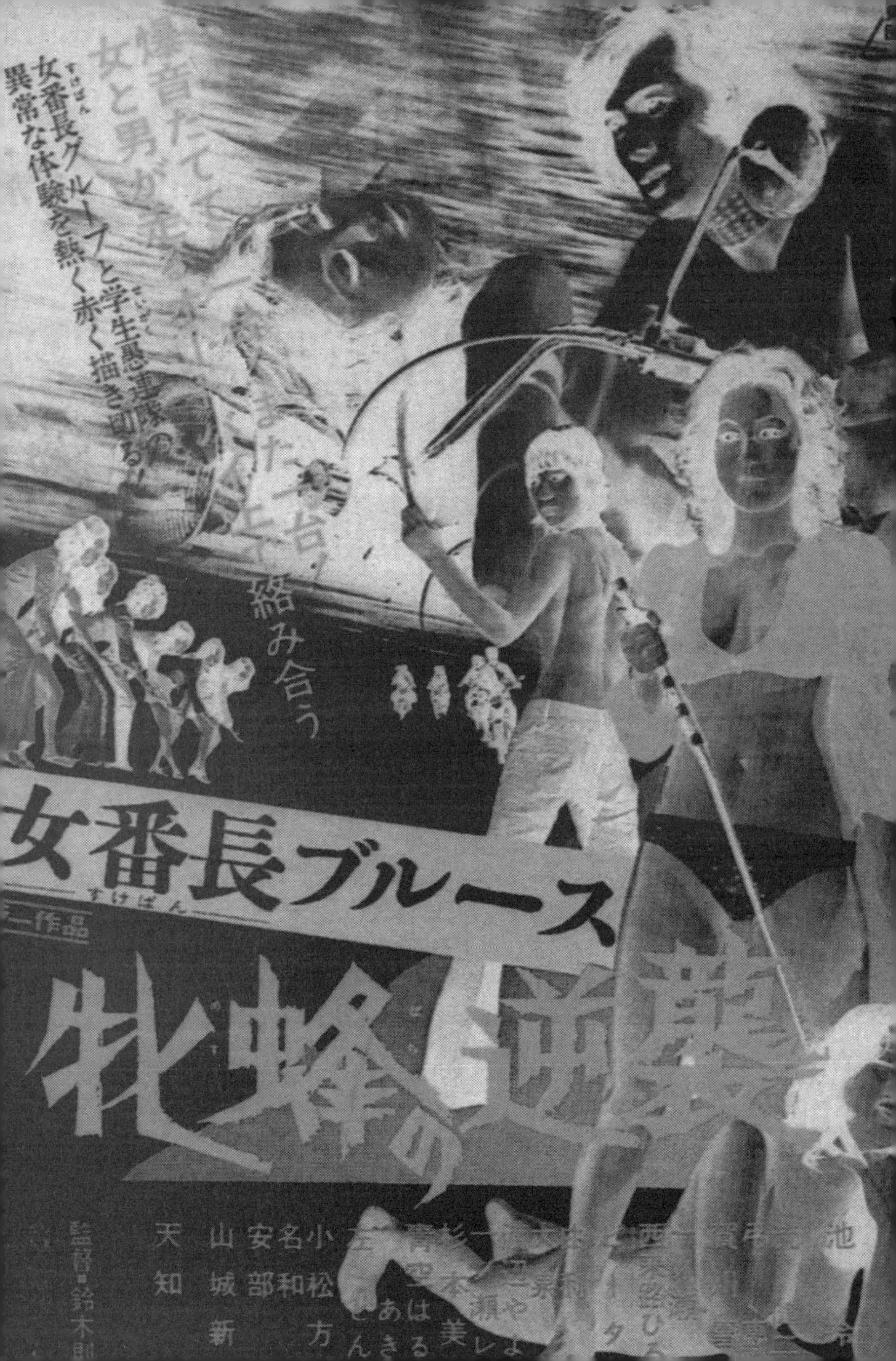

女番長グループと学生愚連隊の
異常な体験を熱く赤く描き切る!
絡み合う
女番長ブルース
牝蜂の逆襲
天知
山城新
安部
名和
小松方
監督・鈴木

Pink & Violent

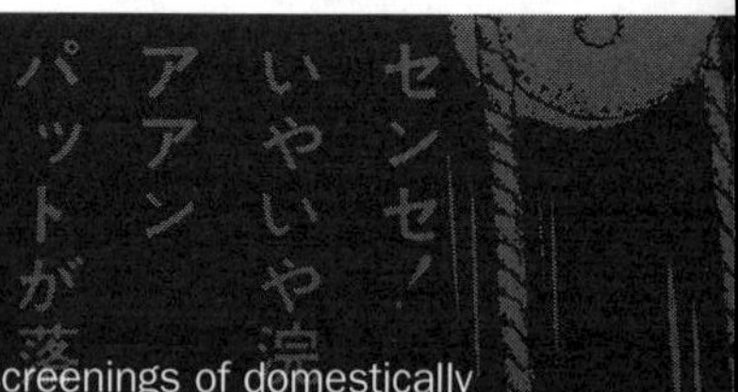

センセ
いやいや
アアン
パットが

The Shinjuku Showakan actually has two screens, one of them devoted to showing dirty movies. The Shinjuku Showakan Chika Gekijyou (Shinjuku Showa-Era Hall Underground Theater) is owned and operated by the same management that runs the Showakan's main theater.

PINK & VIOLENT

The Chika Gekijyou requires a separate admission fee, and a separate entrance, to get in.

Local legend says that the place is a gay pick-up joint. But in truth, it's frequented almost exclusively by old men who, according to the theater staff (who are only slightly kidding), either wouldn't dare watch sex videos in a crowded home or simply don't know how to operate a VCR.

It makes for a good fit. Holdovers from another era gather to watch holdovers from another era. Just as the Showakan screens old films primarily from the Showa era (1926-1989), the cozy Chika Gekijyou features celluloid relics of Japan's independent pink and studio-sponsored adult film past—as it was before the home video revolution made sex tapes omnipresent and sex *films* an endangered species.

Before World War II, the only way to see intimate relations of any kind on screen was to visit the big city and find an *erotogoshi* (aka "smut peddler"), who might have some black-market *burumubi* (blue movies) for sale. There were also underground screenings of domestically produced stag films, which were common around tourist spots like hot springs, hotels, and wherever men gathered in packs away from the watchful eyes of wives and girlfriends. The money earned by these two methods of distribution would inevitably find its way back to the source of production—organized crime.

In an era when the Japanese government was playing an active role in film censorship, these hardcore films, which showed everything and censored nothing, were highly illegal. Major studios had yet to even consider making sex films.

During the postwar American occupation, film content was controlled by the Allied Forces under the Civil Information and Education Section. In 1949, Eirin (the

Top: Who could resist this tantalizing triple feature?

Bottom: Not him! A gentleman proudly purchases a ticket at the Chika Gekijyou. Porno in broad daylight!

INTRO

Motion Pictures Ethics Regulation and Control Committee), was formed by the Japanese film industry as a self-regulating organization, something like the American MPAA. Since then, Eirin has kept tabs on moral standards not only for adult films, but all films produced in Japan or imported from outside. Few are the theaters that would dare screen a movie without Eirin's seal of approval, since doing so can result in arrest and legal prosecution.

The big problem with Eirin is that they have only vague guidelines, not writ-in-stone rules, for what is explicitly taboo. This can lead to a film running into problems for reasons that can seem arbitrary and subjective (as was the case with Takashi Miike's *Fudoh*, which was attacked by Eirin in 1996 for a general aura of obscenity, rather than for specific shots that could be trimmed).

But when it comes to skin flicks, three categories have long been considered instant trouble: pubic hair, genitals, and, most definitely, penetration shots. Thus, no matter how carnal or perverse the proceedings become in a film like, say, *Tokugawa Sex Prohibition—Lustful Lord*, sequences that would almost certainly go hardcore in another country never venture beyond softcore in Japan.

So instead of fetishizing up-close copulation and gynecological-styled exams, Japanese adult films have adopted a polymorphous perversity—the erotic is found in pretty much anything and everything. And yet from fifties-era fully clothed female shellfish divers to state-of-the-art strap-on-wielding dominatrixes, an aura of deep frustration eternally hovers around Japanese adult films.

It's not easy being denied the knockout punches of XXX porn, and sometimes lack of fulfillment leads to wires getting crossed. Sex and sadism start to mingle in uniquely Japanese fashion. The embryo goes hunting. Pink goes violent.

Back in the fifties, exploitation movie mogul and Shin Toho president Mitsugu Okura was among the first to tiptoe around Eirin's boundaries. The Okura-produced *Ama* (female diver) films, inspired by earthy Italian neorealist films like 1948's *Riso amaro* (Bitter Rice), tempted folks into theaters with the promise they would show everything. But no actual nudity was on display:

Pink & Violent

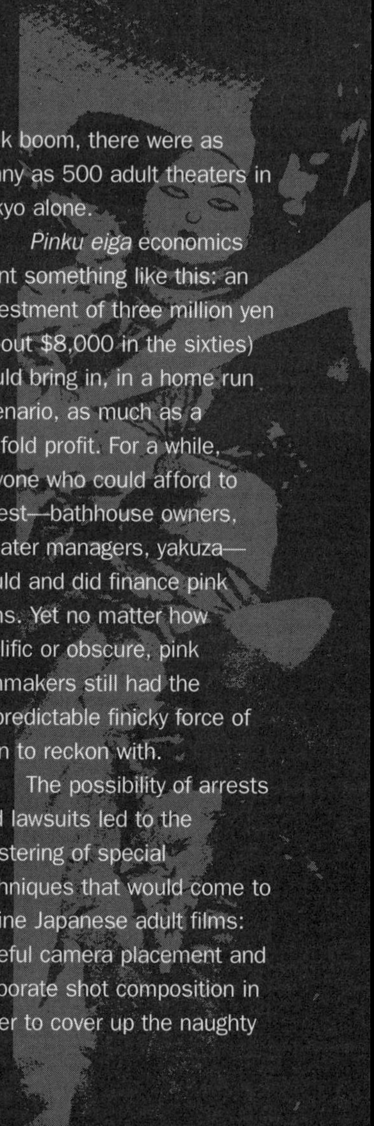

audiences had to be content with the decidedly mixed message about the dignity of hardworking Japanese women and the wet actresses in white formfitting outfits.

Meanwhile, in 1955, author Shintaro Ishihara (brother of Nikkatsu's famed youth idol Yujiro Ishihara—currently Shintaro is the mayor of Tokyo) wrote a bestselling book called *Taiyo no kisetsu* (Season of the Sun), which spawned a whole cycle of controversial *taiyozoku* (sun tribe) films, depicting the roughhouse sex habits of angry young men whose ennui sometimes led them to assault and rape.

Sweeping anti-prostitution laws passed in April of 1958 punched the red lights out for real sex-for-profit (at least for a while), but opened a new market for erotic films: the blue movie underground, the take-your-money and tease of the *Ama* series, and the sexual violence of the *taiyozoku*. These provided the foundation for the *pinku eiga* (pink movie), which would spread like an unchecked STD in the sixties.

According to some counts, from 1965 to 1973 pink movies amounted to as much as half of Japan's total domestic film product. The sheer abundance of pink films owed in part to the fact that they were produced, and more often than not distributed, outside of the monolithic studio system of the Big Five (Toho, Toei, Daiei, Nikkatsu, Shochiku). In the late sixties, theaters that had been dumped by downsizing majors were taken over wholesale by pink films. At the peak of the pink boom, there were as many as 500 adult theaters in Tokyo alone.

Pinku eiga economics went something like this: an investment of three million yen (about $8,000 in the sixties) could bring in, in a home run scenario, as much as a tenfold profit. For a while, anyone who could afford to invest—bathhouse owners, theater managers, yakuza—could and did finance pink films. Yet no matter how prolific or obscure, pink filmmakers still had the unpredictable finicky force of Eirin to reckon with.

The possibility of arrests and lawsuits led to the mastering of special techniques that would come to define Japanese adult films: careful camera placement and elaborate shot composition in order to cover up the naughty

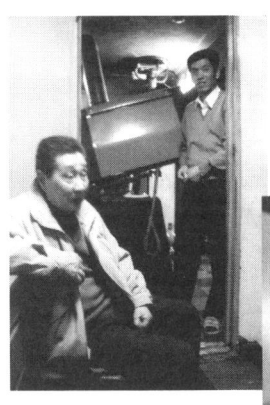

Left: Hard work, but someone has to do it. The tech staff of the Chika Gekijyou.

Bottom: What the projectionist saw!

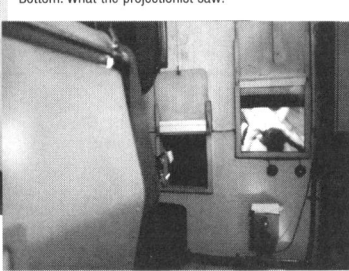

INTRO

bits, or optically "fogging" selected portions of the screen in post-production (sometimes known as the "mosaic" in its digitally blocky home video incarnation).

The pink era could be seen as a something of a creative boom as well. Aspiring directors, who had previously been denied entry into the notoriously closed world of the "real" film industry, could finally get a taste of life behind the camera.

The typical pink title was designed to play on a triple-feature bill. Individual features ran little over an hour, were shot in anamorphic 16mm for widescreen engagements, and, save for a color sex sequence, were cheap black and white affairs.

Sadly, a great deal of works from this golden age of Japanese DIY moviemaking have been lost to the ravages of time. For many, garish posters are the only remaining evidence of their existence. These posters catalog the legions of small companies with big names (Million Film, Nihon Cinema, Gold Promotion) and the dubious aspect ratios (UltraScope, UniScope, CentralScope) unique only to the pink film.

During the mid sixties, the popularity of Hollywood films and television started to cut deeply into cinema profits. Smaller studios began downsizing, reorganizing, and became more interested in distribution rather than production. Going pink, with all the profit to be made from a tiny investment, started to look very tempting indeed. In this climate, Shochiku and Nikkatsu studios quietly began distributing independently produced pink films.

But they quickly discovered that *pinku eiga* could lead to problems as well as profit. Shochiku had a national scandal on their hands when they released Tetsuji Takechi's film *Hakujitsumu* (Daydream), a mix of dental anesthetic and sexual molestation, against the background of the 1964 Tokyo Olympics. Takechi, who was a Liberal Democratic Party member who had been disowned for blowing his campaign finances on hard partying, followed up *Hakujitsumu* a year later with the explicitly perverse and politically charged *Kuroi yuki* (Black Snow), which would have him arrested on obscenity charges leading to a high profile trial.

Meanwhile, over at

175

Pink & Violent

Nikkatsu in 1965, a film by a former construction worker named Koji Wakamatsu, *Kaba no naka no hibegoto* (Secret Acts within Four Walls) caused headaches when the studio submitted it, perhaps somewhat unwisely, to the Berlin International Film Festival.

By the late sixties, mavericks like Wakamatsu and Takechi had left the studio system and gone fully underground in search of a true cinematic sexual revolution, pursuing their mixes of transgression and politics in a manner not entirely dissimilar to, or removed from, their more internationally acclaimed peers in the Japanese New Wave.

Nikkatsu, having purged all free radicals (including the visionary director Seijun Suzuki), began cultivating a slick new house blend in 1972, the *roman porno* (a hopeful abbreviation of "romantic porno"), just in time to help bail them out of near bankruptcy. Toei, in turn, created their *shigeki rosen*, the "sensational line."

Years later, some of the groping, poking, and prodding looks like trash. Some of it like art.

By the early eighties, Nikkatsu, Shin Toho, and Okura Eiga had emerged as the main producers of adult movies in Japan. Even as the home entertainment revolution went big bang, creating a multitude of new production outfits, the core trio still tried to hang on to theatrical markets by continuing to make new movies, made cheaper than ever before, thanks to a shot-on-video methodology.

But by the middle of the decade, adult theaters began shutting down en masse. Everyone converted to AV, adult videos, which meant niche marketing like never before. Here were tapes for guys strictly into hips. Legs. Breasts. Hidden cameras. Enemas. Amateurs. Professionals. Old pink film stock characters like nurses, teachers, and office gals easily made the transition to video, but now, if a filmmaker did fill time with drama and narrative, viewers could zip by with the flick of the fast forward button.

Nevertheless, pink film staged an artistic comeback in the nineties.

A quartet of directors (referred to by the *Mainichi Daily News* as "the so-called kings of dirty movies"), Kazuhiro Sano, Takahisa (Keikyu) Zeze, Toshiki Sato

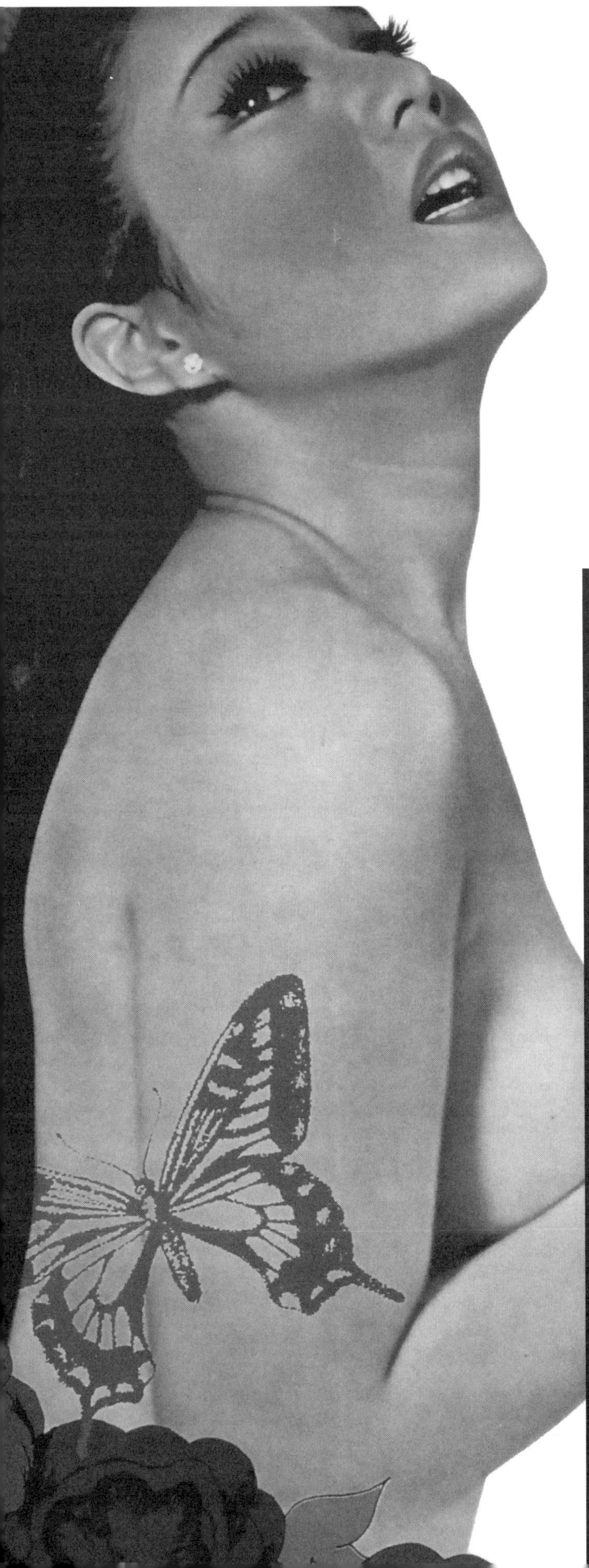

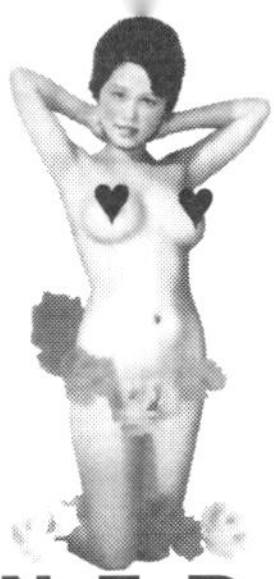

INTRO

and Hisayasu Sato, mixed up sex, violence, and radical politics to a frenzied punk rock soundtrack. While they were following in the tradition of *pinku eiga* pioneers Wakamatsu and Takechi, they also took a good deal of inspiration from the "transgressive" films of Richard Kern and Nick Zedd.

Currently, the count of adult theaters in Tokyo amounts to about 150, but the passing of every year seems to bring about more and more closures.

The AV market remains as healthy as ever. Yet their text-intensive, market-segment-driven mentality seems uncomfortably close to the hordes of cooking shows that clog up Japanese airwaves.

But you can still find the real thing, the thrill of sex laced with low drama, as always, underground. 東

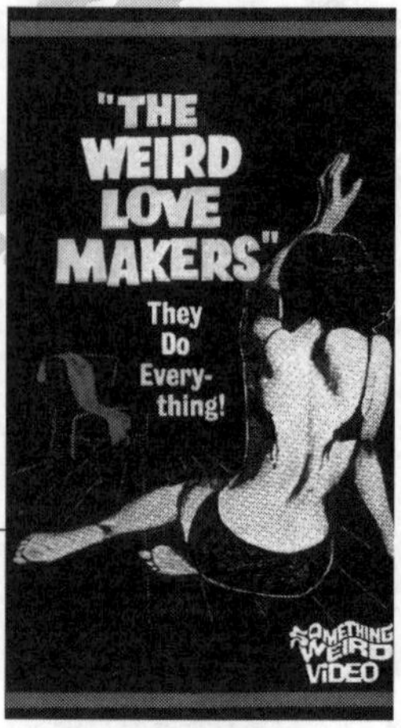
"THE WEIRD LOVE MAKERS"
They Do Every-thing!
SOMETHING WEIRD VIDEO

The Weird Love Makers

Kyonetsu no kisetsu (Season of Crazy Heat), aka The Warped Ones

1960, Nikkatsu
Director Koreyoshi Kurahara
Cast Kawaji Tamio, Chiyo Yuko, Noriko Matsumoto

Youth rebellion, contemporary urban settings, American pop culture references, and a zippy visual style characterized the new "modern" cinema of mid-fifties Japan. Nikkatsu led the way with its *taiyozoku* (sun tribe) films, beginning with the 1956 adaptation of Shintaro Ishihara's best-selling novel of sexually unleashed youth, *Season of the Sun*. A spate of sun tribe films followed, including Ko Nakahira's *Crazed Fruit* (1956) and Nagisa Oshima's *The Sun's Burial* (1960). Many of these films might be regarded as little more than youth exploitation, but the best of them (say, those of Nakahira, Oshima, and Yasuzo Masumura) were important forerunners of the more radical disruptions of the New Wave.

On the other hand, sun tribe films were great just as exploitation, too, and as much as they anticipated the New Wave, their liberatory outlook served as forerunners to pink films as well. Thus *The Weird Love Makers* perhaps better epitomizes the genre than the early films of Oshima. Strangely, it was picked up for distribution and shown in the US—to whom?—in 1963, and the energetically dubbed print is still readily available on video.

Al is just out of reform school and immediately goes on the rampage. He and his buddy steal an American car and pick up a cheerfully blasé hooker named Yuki. The trio cruise around until they target a random couple strolling in a parking lot. Al runs over the male half of the couple and the trio kidnap the girl, leaving her boyfriend pulling himself off the pavement in the rearview mirror. They head to the beach, Al casually rapes their kidnapee, and "Fran," who it later turns out is some kind of artist, is destroyed by the experience, especially after she finds out she's pregnant. Time passes. While the psychologically fragile Fran wallows in her victimhood, Al responds to her fragile entreaties with astonishing callousness. Along the way, he trashes her hypocritical views and her circle of effete Bohemian phonies, basically making life miserable for everyone.

By 1960, the conventions of the sun tribe—sweating bodies writhing in heat, the ever present threat of kicks erupting into sexual violence—were well known, and *Weird Love Makers* runs with them. Crazy angles, drive-by camerawork, shock-cut freeze frames (all propelled by a stunning original bebop score performed by the "Nikkatsu Jazz Group"), and relentless mugging by "hero" Al—who spends most of the movie shirtless—lends this out-of-control vehicle an insane, amoral energy. Kicks, man, kicks: Tamio's performance as Al is ferocious, the very incarnation of the kind of social chaos that could be engendered by too much exposure to jazz, Coke, and hot dogs. (Alvin Lu)

☞ **Available dubbed from Something Weird Video**

REVIEW

Female Slave Ship
Onna doreisen

1960, Shin Toho
Director Yoshiki Onoda
Cast Bunta Sugawara, Tetsuro Tanba, Yoko Mihara

A pulp story (by author Jun Funazaki) come to life in vivid pastel colors, coated in tropical perspiration, *Female Slave Ship* is an adventurous relic from the golden era of Shin Toho sex and sadism. A classically Mitsugu Okura production, it mixes up *Captain Blood*-style naval battles and patriotic war movie sentiments along with a pioneering sense of female (maybe) empowerment that would pepper international exploitation films to come.

At the tail end of WWII, young army lieutenant Bunta Sugawara is ordered to sneak top secret information from the South Pacific back to the high command in Tokyo. Unfortunately, his model airplane is shot out of the sky and crash lands in what looks like the studio bathtub.

Bunta's bad luck turns out to be merely mixed when he awakens to finds himself on board a ship whose hold carries twelve scantily clad young women destined to be sold as sex slaves by the tempestuous Queen (Yoko Mihara). In time the ship and crew are overtaken by chantey-singing pirates (some of them wearing eye patches for authenticity) led by that terror of the high seas: the open-shirted, monkey-fondling Tetsuro Tanba!

The treacherous Queen snuggles up to the bad guys in a bid to save her own hide. Bunta is thrown under lock and key while the women are taken to be auctioned off on Pirate Island. But even now with Japan's war effort deeply endangered, Bunta swears to rescue the helpless girls from falling prey to money-waving foreigners. Time-killing cycles of escape, capture, and flagellation set in, until an explosive chicks-with-guns climax erupts, foreshadowing *The Big Bird Cage* and other tropical women in prison movies by many years.

While the sight of a very young Bunta Sugawara and Tetsuro Tanba (in one of the few films he made while under contract at Shin Toho) beating the crap out of each other in the low tide makes for fine entertainment, the movie clearly belongs to Yoko Mihara. Known as the "Monroe of Japan," the buxom starlet wowed hungry postwar audiences with her fleshed out pinup figure and peekaboo getups. She appeared in numerous Shin Toho films, including Teruo Ishii's *Sexy Zone* and *Queen Bee*. After numerous indie pink films, she moved to Toei in the late sixties to play matronly roles in their adult titles (she pops up in the first *Female Convict Scorpion* film and in *Tokugawa Sex Prohibition*). *Slave Ship* captures the tumultuous Mihara at the peak of her powers, stomping around like Tura Satana (*Faster Pussycat! Kill! Kill!*) and pausing long enough to perform a blistering belly dance.

☞ Available subbed on Import DVD

American Cinematheque
PRESENTS
ECSTASY of the Angels
A Film by
Koji Wakamatsu

Ecstasy of the Angels

Tenchi no kokotsu

1972, Wakamatsu Productions
Director Koji Wakamatsu
Cast Ken Yoshizawa, Rie Yokoyama, Masao Adachi

Koji Wakamatsu was, for the heady period of 1965-73 or so, the King of the Underground. Working entirely within the decidedly marginal pink movie circuit, Wakamatsu might have just ended up a footnote to cinematic history when his 1965 film *Secret Acts within Four Walls* was inexplicably submitted by producer Nikkatsu studios to the Berlin Film Festival, generating what some deemed "a national disgrace." Instead, Wakamatsu quit Nikkatsu, went indie, and went on to create some of the most singular films ever made, eventually gaining the attention of "overground" avant-gardists like Nagisa Oshima and Western structuralist film theorists.

No one had up to that point, or since, filmed porn with as overtly politically radical and aesthetically avant-garde an agenda as Wakamatsu had. Works like *Violated Women in White* (1967) and *Go, Go Second Time Virgin* (1969, also available on DVD from Image) combined, in still unique manner, disjunctive New Wave style, existentialist dread, sex, sadism, and gore, all on a ridiculously shoestring budget. Much of this can be attributed to Wakamatsu's collaborator Masao Adachi, an experimental filmmaker who came to prominence with his student films like *The Sealed Vagina* and became Wakamatsu's "aesthetic/political" advisor.

Ecstasy of the Angels, shot in alternating stark black and white and supersaturated color, is a remarkable document from late in the cycle. More politically involved than *Violated Women* or *Go, Go*, it is also something of a forerunner to landmark anime works like *Akira* and *Jin-Roh,* relating the details of an urban guerrilla war fought with time bombs, told from the point of view of the fraying psyches of the terrorists.

Wakamatsu's depiction of paranoid, faction-ridden life inside the spare apartment hideouts of these urban guerrillas feels privileged (in real life, Adachi was just about to disappear into the Middle East with his Red Army connections), while his numerous softcore digressions keep it all off-key, bleakly humorous, and grounded—in a kind of testament to Wakamatsu's professionalism, *Ecstasy* rests firmly within pink movie conventions. Still, the climactic montage of a nightclub singer orgasmically setting off bombs in her taffeta dress, to the strains of blaring free jazz, are the Revolution come as advertised, as well as some kind of ode to the undying desire for human liberation. Concluding with a stunning crawl through the streets of Shinjuku with the blind and probably insane protagonist, *Ecstasy* attains an ideal: if you had heard of, but never seen, a politically radical underground film of the sixties, this is probably what you would think it would look like. (Alvin Lu)

☞ **Available subbed on DVD from Image Entertainment**

REVIEW

Tokugawa Sex Prohibition—Lustful Lord
Tokugawa Sex kinshirei—Shikijo daimyo

1972, Toei
Director Norifumi Suzuki
Cast Miki Sugimoto, Hiroshi Nawa, Sandra Julien

Utilizing scenic locations, sets, costumes, and props on hand from countless Toei period pieces, Norifumi Suzuki's *Tokugawa Sex Prohibition* manages to juggle ribald humor, history, and sexy wayward foreigners with more than a little cunning political commentary.

The 11th Shogun Ienari Tokugawa (1773-1841) is a proud figure of vitality, with 21 mistresses and 54 children. His youngest daughter, Princess Kiyo (voluptuous Miki Sugimoto of Suzuki's *Sukeban* series), has reached marrying age but is having a hard time finding a groom. An arduous search is conducted, and a 34-year-old bachelor, Tadateru Ogura (Hiroshi Nawa), seems to be the best candidate. The trouble is that Tadateru is a country feudal lord who lives only for the samurai code of chivalry and has no patience for women. He doesn't really want to get married, but because the order comes from the shogun, he gladly accepts.

Tadateru doesn't know the first thing about sexually satisfying the poor princess. Tadateru's chief vassals decide to set him up with lots of sexy girls in the hope that he'll eventually get the hang of it.

A French girl (Sandra Julien, essentially playing herself) is shipped over from Europe in a crate and presented to Tadateru. Her incredible beauty and expert technique at last succeeds in getting him interested in sex big time. But his nonstop rutting about with Sandra further complicates his already strained relationship with Kiyo.

One day, Tadateru sees that the common folk are also enjoying sex amongst themselves, which makes him angry and jealous. He decides to make a new law essentially forbidding anyone but himself from enjoying the pleasures of the flesh. Social and political chaos ensues, with the villagers trying to break the walls of the palace down with penis-shaped battering rams.

While a bizarrely anachronistic Burt Bacharach-like soundtrack plays, sadism flows freely. Good Catholic girl Sandra is crucified upside down in the rising tide, and there's a bloodsoaked, eroticized *harakiri* scene that confuses cries of agony with moans of pleasure. But for every contradiction that Suzuki preys on (East/West, pain/pleasure), there is an equal amount of absurdity and truth. What better way for a ruler to control his subjects than by managing their sex drives? And what better reason for them to rise up? Literally.

☞ **Import only**

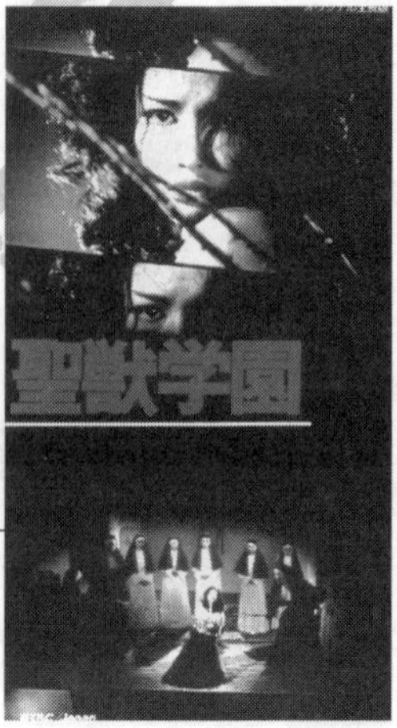
聖獣学園

School of the Holy Beast

Seiju gakuen

1974, Toei
Director Norifumi Suzuki
Cast Yumi Takigawa, Fumio Watanabe, Emiko Yamauchi

Since his 1965 debut film *Osaka do konjo monogatari—Doerai yatsu* (Osaka Courage Story—Big Shot) Tokyo University-educated director Norifumi Suzuki (b. 1933) has been Toei's resident comedic anarchist, famed for hits like the *Truck yaro* (Truck Guys) series and 1986's *The Samurai*. But Suzuki's grandest statements are to be found among his erotic titles, among them *School of the Holy Beast*, a *gekiga* comic adaptation and a blasphemous sermon of high camp and knowing literary intelligence.

When beautiful young *mo-gal* ("modern girl") Mayumi (Yumi Takigawa) hears about her mother's suicide, she decides to take up the habit and go undercover at the convent where she was last heard from. There, Mayumi discovers a veritable hellhole of sin run by a dictatorial Mother Superior and a perverted hairy priest. Alternating acts of vice and punishment occur, as Mayumi discovers the truth, not only about her mother, but about her father as well, amidst a neverending parade of murderous ritual.

While *School of the Holy Beast* is best known in Japan as a chance to ogle well-known actress Takigawa in her only nude screen scenes, the film is sure to please even the most hardcore fans of that venerable exploitation sub-genre known as "Nunsploitation." The film tries to cram every anticlerical taboo it possibly can into its running time of 91 minutes. As Suzuki admitted once in an interview, the only real taboo that existed in Japan at the time was the Emperor. Everything else, foreign religions included, was grist for the mill. Queasy-comedic episodes of lesbianism, cross-dressing, and incest all take place mere inches away from Madonna statues and rosary beads, with the most spectacular transgression being a fatal pissing on a crucifix while a hopeful "hallelujah" chorus plays.

Trashy as it may sound, Suzuki's film is absolutely gorgeous to gaze upon (an arts center projectionist once swore to me that it was the most beautiful looking film he's ever shown), many of its shots carefully framed and lit for maximum fearful symmetry. And as Mayumi receives a bloody flagellation via roses and thorns, the mix of cruelty and beauty expands into genuinely spiritual dimensions. As in Suzuki's later *Star of David* (yet another naughty comic adaptation), sexploitation proves to be an unlikely yet perfect arena for a cockeyed contemplation of God and his creations.

☞ **Import only**

REVIEW

Flower and Snake
Hana to hebi

1974, Nikkatsu
Director Masaru Konuma
Cast Naomi Tani

Dan Oniroku (b. 1931) is Japan's best-known author of erotic S&M fiction. Over the years, many films have been touted as being "based on a story by Dan Oniroku." Adapted from one of his very best works, Nikkatsu's film version of *Flower and Snake* was also one of the first true Japanese S&M films.

A big shot company president wants his prize wife Shizuka (played by Nikkatsu bondage queen Naomi Tani) to totally submit to him. But since the classy aristocratic Shizuka was lured into the marriage by his money, she only wants a divorce. One day Makoto, a company salaryman (and also the son of an adult toy store owner and porno filmmaker), is ordered by the president to train Shizuka sexually in sadomasochism to become the perfect wife.

Makoto was traumatized by his insane mother, who would do anything for money and because of her, he is impotent. But through the mysterious masochist Shizuka, he finally understands and overcomes his trauma.

This was one of the first times a major studio had attempted to explore the world of S&M. Nikkatsu's somewhat innocent approach inadvertently adds comedy, and lacks a perfect understanding of "top and bottom" dynamics, which results in a film that is wild, crazy, and entertaining. Author Dan himself was not very pleased with the film, but he and Nikkatsu managed to patch up their relationship to make more films together. Director Konuma would reunite with Naomi in 1974's *Ikenie fujin* (aka *Wife to be Sacrificed*).

In the very last scene in *Flower and Snake*, Shizuka smiles to her innocent young maid and says, "Would you like men to torment you? Men are so cute, aren't they?" The heroine, who was masochistically trained by men, was actually controlling them the whole time. To me, despite all the humiliations suffered by heroines like Naomi, this is the fundamental truth behind seventies-era Japanese sex films. (Izumi Evers)

☞ **Import only**

Pink Viole[nce]

Female Convict Scorpion—Jailhouse 41
Joshu sasori—Dai 41 zakkyobo

1973, Toei
Director Shunya Ito
Cast Meiko Kaji, Fumio Watanabe, Hideo Murota

The first film in the *Sasori* (Scorpion) series, 1972's *Female Convict #701*, plays majestically on the tried-and-true theme of mad love gone bad. Nami's detective boyfriend Sugimi betrays her, having her framed during a drug bust, after which she is gang raped as he looks on—he drops a series of small bills on her wracked body, quantifying her humiliation. The righteous anger of her lover's betrayal fuels Nami's grudge, propelling her through the set pieces of the female prisoner genre: the "meet the cellmates" sequence, the food fight, the shower scene, the "lights out" scene, the torture scene, the naked calisthenic scene, the catfight scene, various gore and splatter scenes, and the all-important fashion sequence—the "trying on the new uniform" scene. She encounters her nemesis, the evil warden, who makes it his personal mission to make sure she is punished. She finds and hunts down Sugimi and gouges out the eye of the evil warden, who is constantly surveying her with the long look of the law. As if there's any doubt he's a really unsavory father figure.

By the time the second film *Female Convict Scorpion—Jailhouse 41* rolled around in late 1973, in its unfathomable release as a new year's film, the cool and intense Nami has been established as a righteous and sympathetic character. But there is a tension in the film that sits oddly with the film's critique of male scopophilia, in the form of the pleasure that the evil warden takes in watching Nami's suffering. The hitch is that, in order to create her as a sympathetic and unkillable character in film after film, she has to be exposed on screen to a variety of tortures and violence, the obstacles necessary for her to transcend and attain the singular status of the Sasori. The spectacle of these ordeals as the slightly eroticized precondition for our sympathy is not without its own misogynist bent.

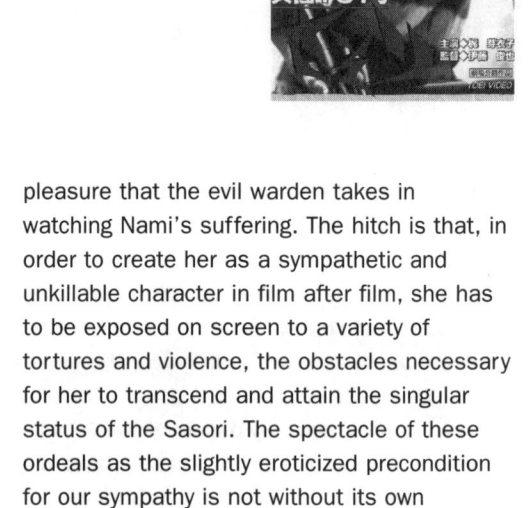

After the stock Toei logo appears, *Female Convict Scorpion—Jailhouse 41* begins with a haunting theme song, "A Woman's Grudge Song" (Onna no urami-bushi), sung by actress Meiko Kaji herself. The song sets out the chick-flick terms in simple stanzas, spelling out the lament of a "hard-headed woman." The language describing her grudge gets more excessive and supernatural, following the general development of the film itself. It turns from the pathos of decaying flowers to blood that flows every month, to tears that turn to blood or turn to wind once they leave the eyes, making men mad.

Cut to a fantastic, shrieking echo in a rare female voiceover, as the camera careens around a dank staircase, arriving at the dungeon where Nami is confined for bad behavior. She scrapes a spoon across the floor with her mouth, filing it down to a spike. Even the lighting that falls through the bars on the window above conspires to paint more

TOEI VIDEO
SASORI
乾いた女囚の冷たい表情に
一瞬よぎる恨みの殺意。
女囚
第41雑居房
主演◆梶 芽衣子
監督◆伊藤 俊也

SASORI
さそりは死んだ…。
だが、怨みの牙がまたキラリと光った。
けもの部屋
主演◆梶 芽衣子 監督◆伊藤 俊也

starkly the stripes on her prison uniform. She stares defiantly at the camera, looking pretty fresh for someone who has been underground for a year.

The evil warden tidies her up with a firehose and drags her out to display her to a big-shot official who is touring the prison. While the prison band plays an out-of-tune version of the national anthem, Nami lunges for the warden and almost gouges out his other eye. Not only is he hopping mad, but the other prisoners gleefully revolt, and the visiting official falls over in terror, in a puddle of his own streaming urine.

The warden regains control over Nami and her conspirators. He sends them to dig holes in the ground all day, in a landscape only slightly more pastoral than the moon. To ruin her status as prison idol, he orders her raped by guards in costumes that look something like ninja sock monkeys and has her strung up on a cross. Eventually the tables turn, and Nami and several others break free.

On the lam, they enter the territory of the fantastic, meeting a ghostly storyteller, the mother of all grudges, who relates the laments of Nami's co-conspirators. They also encounter a pack of marauding salarymen tourists. If there were any doubt that the tourists too were unimpeachably rotten—even before they gang rape an escaped prisoner and chuck her into a waterfall—the name of their tour bus is "Toa" tours, evoking the name of the colonial Greater East Asian Co-prosperity Sphere. On the bus, they reminisce about the good old days of rape and pillage in China. One describes how as a soldier he forced a woman into sex, "and I could hear my backpack clacking as we went at it."

In a 1999 interview, director Ito describes how Meiko Kaji's Nami is a role which says "no" to everything. He says he wanted this "no"-saying to inspire the everyman viewer to say "no" to state power. Let's set aside for a moment the weird glitch of Ito's 1998 love letter to nationalist wartime general Hideki Tojo in the film *Pride*. *Female Convict Scorpion—Jailhouse 41* gives us a chick flick that—even if it doesn't completely say no to thugs, and the pleasure they take in helping to prolong Nami's serial unkillability—does turn an eye toward questions of gender and power left in the dungeon by genre and art films alike. (Anne McKnight)

☞ **Available subbed on DVD from Image Entertainment**

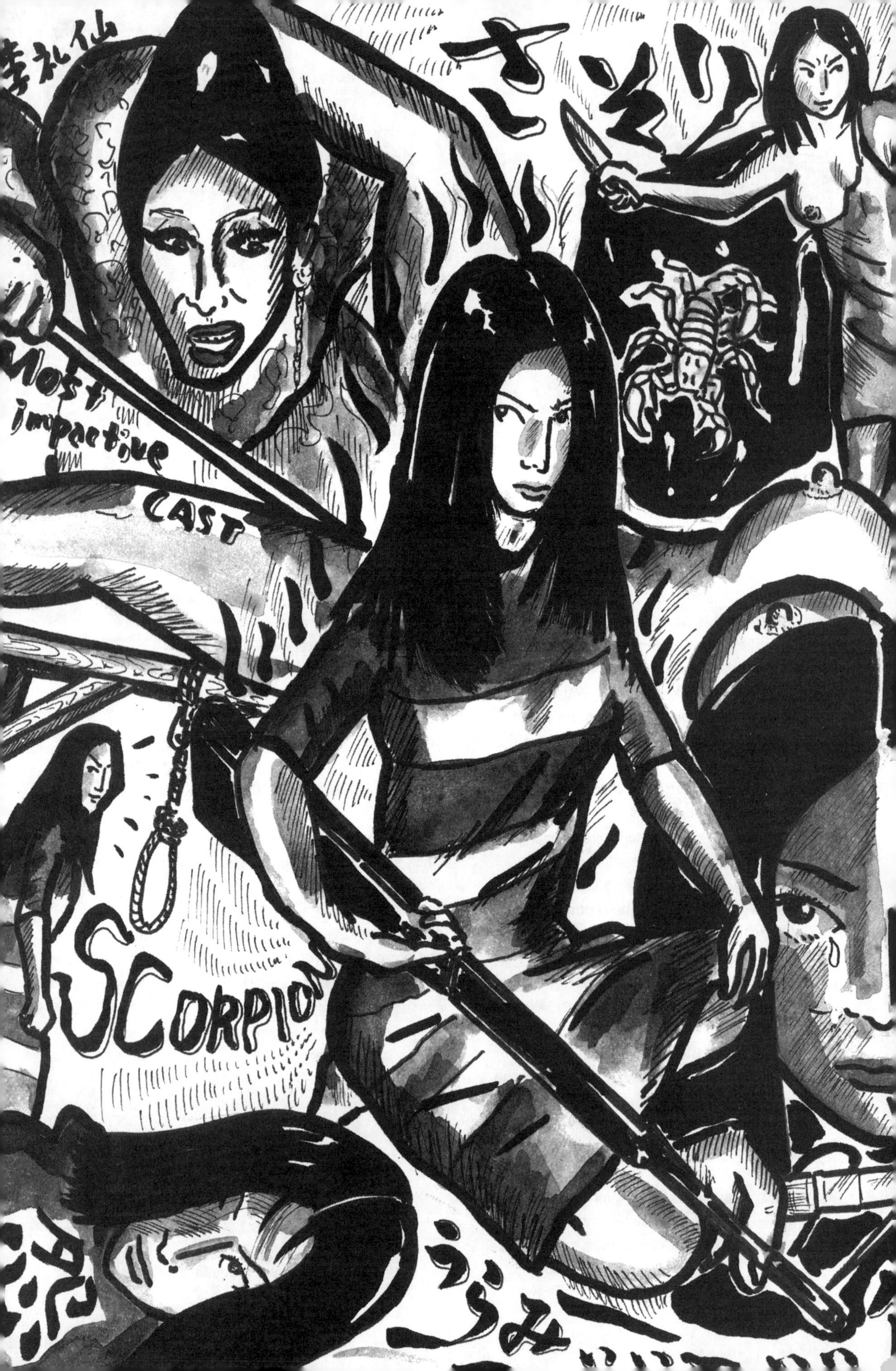
李れい仙
さそり
Most impactive CAST
SCORPION
うらみ

PROFILE

Nikkatsu's Roman Porno

日活

Nikkatsu kink! 1975's *Rose and Whip*.

Nikkatsu is Japan's oldest film studio. They have a long and distinguished history and were major players during the golden age of Japanese film. And yet they seem destined to be remembered best for being the major studio most associated with adult films. The famed name of their *roman porno* line has even become the all-purpose catchphrase for "Japanese adult film" overseas.

Founded in 1912, Nikkatsu was formed in a merger of three smaller companies—Yokuta, Yoshizawa, M. Pathe—and the Fukuda theater chain.

Nikkatsu's initial offerings were little more than filmed plays, but by 1922 they had hooked audiences with realistic melodramas about everyday people, then a revolutionary concept for Japanese films.

In 1954, Nikkatsu's new Chofu city studio was the largest filmmaking facility in Asia, and for the next fifteen years they churned out between sixty and eighty films annually.

Slowly, the old Nikkatsu style began to change. Instead of reflecting the lives and concerns of normal folks, "Nikkatsu Action" (and later "Nikkatsu New Action") was all about glamorous fantasy heavily influenced by American pop culture, to the point where Capone-styled gangster films and pistol-packing Westerns were common.

From the late fifties to the mid-sixties, nearly half of all top-grossing domestic films were Nikkatsu titles, and the studio's stable of young actors (Yujiro Ishihara, Akira Kobayashi, Ruriko Asaoka, and Tetsuya Watari among them) were the idols of the day.

Everything was going great until the late sixties. As Hollywood films and television seduced viewers away from theaters and the economy was hit by inflation, the Japanese film industry quickly descended into a major depression.

Nikkatsu downsized in order to stay afloat. Drastic survival measures had to be taken.

In 1971, with Takashi Itamochi acting as company president, Nikkatsu made the decision to focus on making adult movies, a genre that was already proving to be highly profitable for independent producers.

Under their *roman porno* (read: "romantic pornography") banner, Nikkatsu scaled the highs and lows of the sexual imagination with pit stops in the realm of S&M, rope bondage, rape, and alternative lifestyles ranging from time-honored courtesans (*joro ichiba*, "geisha market") to trendy wife swappers (*okashikko*, aka "community house"), and nearly everything else sandwiched somewhere in between.

While the average indie *pinku eiga* was an impoverished affair made by amateurs,

roman porno could boast handsome production values and well-trained professionals behind the camera. Each director seemed to have their own flavor. The films of Noboru Tanaka (1975's *Jitsuroku Sada Abe*, aka *A Woman Called Sada Abe*) were as sophisticated as they were erotic. Chusei Sone specialized in ribald tales from the past. Hasebe Yasuharu (*Boko kirisaki Jack*, "Assault Jack the Ripper") delivered frightening, raw, and violent images.

The facilities at the old Chofu city studio could lend a slick authenticity to period pieces, like the nine-film *Erogoyomi ohoku hiwa* series. Literary adaptations of works, such as those of erotic-grotesque nonsense king Edogawa Rampo (*Yaneura no sanposha*, aka *The Stroller in the Attic*) and contemporary S&M writer Dan Oniroku, were not uncommon. While single men and curious couples alike lined up for *roman porno* fare, film critics had no hesitations about singing their praises. Tatsumi Kumashiro's 1974 film *Yojohan fusuma no urabari* (Four and a Half Mats—Inside Paper of the Sliding Door, aka *World of the Geisha*) won the prestigious Best Film award from *Kinema Junpo* magazine while Nobuo Tanaka was voted Best New Director for *Jitsuroku Sada Abe*.

Along the way, Nikkatsu managed to periodically run afoul of moral watchdogs. The 1973 productions *Koi no karyudo* (Hunter of Love) and *OL Nikki—Mesuneko no noi* (Office Lady Diary—Scent of a Female Pussycat) were charged with obscenity by the Tokyo Metropolitan Police.

Undaunted, Nikkatsu continued to make erotic films until 1988. From there, further adult movies would be made strictly for the home video market, where Nikkatsu was also releasing cultish foreign titles like the Spanish-UK zombie flick *Let Sleeping Corpses Lie* and William Lustig's 42nd Street classic *Maniac*.

Sadly, Nikkatsu suffered the burst of the bubble economy badly and filed for bankruptcy in 1993, mostly as a result of some bad real estate investments in golf courses. Only a last minute merger with the Namco video game company bailed them out.

While Namco has publicly blamed the studio for recent profit losses, Nikkatsu still releases a handful of new features annually. Recent titles include Akihiko Shiota's *Sasayaki* (aka *Moonlight Whispers)*, and Takashi Ishii's *Freeze Me*. They also maintain a pair of satellite television channels and a healthy home video division. Also, Nikkatsu's tradition of breaking in young filmmakers is kept alive at the Nikkatsu Visual Arts Academy.

While current economic conditions in Japan do not bode well for Nikkatsu, the odds are they'll somehow manage to stay afloat by doing what they always have: whatever it takes. 東

ROMAN BOOKS
ENTERTAINMENT FOR MEN
Vol.1 No.13
ロマンポルノ写真集No.13
ロマンブックス

Nikkatsu also published a fine line of collectable photo books dedicated to their films.

PROFILE

Toei's "Pinky Violence" Abnormal, Sensational, and Shameless

1972's *Hot Spring Turtle Geisha*, directed by Norifumi Suzuki.

If you were single, urban, and male during the late sixties and early seventies, then Toei studios wanted dearly, desperately to be your best friend.

All for you, legendary Toei producer Kanji Amao created the *shigeki rosen* (Sensational Line), the *ijoseiai rosen* (Abnormal Line), and the *harenchi rosen* (Shameless Line).

Individually and collectively, they were wild-sex, and sometimes sex-and-action, films designed to play on the bottom half of double features with yakuza films in the top slot. And while Ken Takakura might extol the virtues of honor and humanity in the main feature, bathhouse geisha with fabulously talented lower regions (the *Onsen geisha* series), sexually perverted Tokugawa retainers (the *Tokugawa onna* series), or impossibly tough reform school girl gangs (the *Sukeban* series) would wreak havoc in the co-features.

Japanese film buffs today refer to the *shigeki, ijoseiai,* and *harenchi* lines as the era of "Toei Pinky Violence." And if the manga-style excess of "pink violence" seemed even a few degrees more manic and twisted than even Nikkatsu's *roman porno* films, that's probably owing to the conditions that they were created under. By manipulating contracts, Toei forced many of their directors to make sex films, frequently against their will. Consequently, nearly every Toei sex film seemed to be on a mission to subvert figures of authority. These films were as stuffed with hypocritical government officials and corrupt cops as they were with naked women.

It was director Teruo Ishii who really set the tone, establishing a queasy mix of comedy and torture in his 1968 films *Tokugawa onna keizu* (History of the Shogun's Harem) and *Onsen anma geisha* (Hot Spring Massage Geisha, starring key pinky violence siren Masumi Tachibana). From here, the gloves came off, and wild stuff started happening.

Toei began enlisting foreigners to play supporting parts in their sex films, such as French actress Sandra Julien (star of Max Pécas's 1972 film *I Am Frigid...Why?* and Jean Rollin's *Shiver of the Vampire*), who gave a memorable performance in Norifumi Suzuki's 1972's *Tokugawa Sex kinshirei—Shikijo daimyo* (Tokugawa Sex Prohibition—Lustful Lord), and Swiss X-port and singer Christina Lindberg. For 1974's *Shikijo toruko nikki* (Lustful Turkish Bath Diary), Toei flew in American porn star Sharon Kelley to copulate with actor Tatsuo Umemiya. (Umemiya plays Bunta Sugawara's best friend in the first *Jingi naki tatakai* film, but also has a reputation in Japan as the "King of Eros.")

As the sex in Toei films got more radical, so did the violence. Norifumi Suzuki's *Sukeban*

Pink & Violent

(Girl Gang) series imagined bare-chested, shotgun-packing chicks Miki Sugimoto and Ike Reiko getting into one catfight after another. Director Shunya Ito's *Joshu sasori* (Female Convict Scorpion) trilogy utilized amazing stylistic flourishes, made an unforgettable figure of ferocious tenacity out of actress Meiko Kaji, and turned the woman-in-prison genre on its head.

Director Teruo Ishii perhaps went the furthest out on the line with his *harenchi* films, which were almost unbearably grotesque catalogs of torture. Films like *Meiji-Taisho-Showa Ryoki Johanzaishi* (History of Bizarre Woman-Crimes—Meiji, Taisho, and Showa Eras) used a multistory omnibus structure and sometimes forgot about the sex entirely in lieu of *grand guignol* atrocity.

The end of the affair came in the late seventies, when Toei began phasing out the double-feature policy. Pinky violence sadly dried up like a wet spot, leaving a sweet memory behind. 東

女番長

Top: 1973's *Girl Gang—Woman Boss.*
Bottom: *Delinquent Anguish Group,* also 1973.

恐るべき非行実態を
暴くシリーズ最新作！
恐怖女子高校
不良悶絶グループ
成人映画
虫の好かない
学校でゴロ
祭り・買物と
悪いことなら
なんでもやる
軟派硬派の明け暮れさ！

NIKKATSU HYPERBOLE

Back in the eighties, Nikkatsu issued a series of glossy color brochures aimed at selling their roman porno *product to English-speaking countries. After discussing the illustrious history of their company (Nikkatsu was, after all, Japan's oldest motion picture company) and reassuring us that they also have produced "many serious features for adults and cheldren" (sic), the marketing department went overboard with the pervy movie hard sell. Printed here, with original misspellings and mangled grammar intact, are some of the highlights from these terminal documents, which often read like prison poetry (a feeling compounded by photos of directors that look like mug shots). Thanks to Mr. Chuck Stephens for providing the "hard" evidence.*

Lady Chatterly in Tokyo
(Tokyo Chatarei Fujin)
Skandal, they say, but kniking at fate and running! The white birch forest heard, the mountain hut saw! Panting depravity, ejaculations of ecstacy!
Directed by ...... Katsuhiko Fuji
Cast ...... Izumi Shima

The Girl With Pink Hips 2: Love Attack
(Momoshiri-Musume, Rabu Atakku)
How dumb to get pregnant! Can't wait to grow up! A city girl's cataclysmic experience!
Directed by ...... Koyu Ohara
Cast ...... Kaori Takeda

A Woman in Blue Films
(Shin-Danchizuma Burufirumu no Onna)
The dark past of a wife in an apartment complex exposed by a 8mm film! A couple's love-hate relationship! A glamorous-looking housewife becomes the target of the strong carnal appetites of men!
Directed by ...... Isao Hayashi
Cast ...... Rumi Tama

Butterfly Web
(Cho-no-Hone)
A caterpillar that turned into an alluring butterfly! Men Swarmed like ants around a honey Pot!
Directed by ...... Shogoro Nishimura
Cast ...... Yuki Nohira

Tangled Skeins of Love
(Hihon Muki-Tamago)
Early spring and convulsed with unquenchable longing for the touch of a velvety skin! The delicious tingle of fingers touching by chance!
Directed by ...... Shogoro Nishimura
Cast ...... Hitomi Kozue

Dewdrops on the Petals
(Kaben-no-Shizuku)
"Is there anything more heavenly?" The soliloquy of a frigid woman who gains fulfillment for the first time! "I hated sex until my doctor inserted a cork! Now, I cry for the very act I hated!" A once frigid wife's rebirth!
Directed by ...... Noboru Tanaka
Cast ...... Rie Nakagawa

Naked Paradise
(Toruko Maruhi Monzetsu)
Try a Japanese Turkish baths as an unforgettable experience! The world of naked men vs naked women half-veiled in rising steam!
Directed by ...... Isao Hayashi
Cast ...... Maya Hiromi

The Beasts' Warm Bodies
(Shinayakana kemonotachi)
Her passionate kisses made him break the gangster's code! A seemingly transient pastime lit the fires of true love!
Directed by ...... Akira Kato
Cast ...... Mari Tanaka

Love Me Tenderly, Love Me Wildly
(Motto Shinayakani, Motto Shitatakani)
Basking in sunny environments, the forces of nature make the bodies of women bloom! Also and elegy to youths who Endure nameless fears and hurts! Weary before their time, they do not know what they do!
Directed by ...... Toshiya Fujita
Cast ...... Junko Takazawa, Aiko Morishita

The Devil's Song
(Akai Boko)
The Rock Band of the Four Devils! Swooning fans! Virgins offering themselves at the altar of musical demigods!
Directed by ...... Chusei Sone
Cast ...... The Devils

Professional Specialists
(Kuro bara shoten)
This film is all about men who make pink films and how they search for loopholes in the law so that the law cannot catch up with them. These men are just as earnest as directors of regular feature films in their quest to please fans of their particular type of film.
Directed by ...... Tatsumi Kumashiro
Cast ...... Naomi Tani

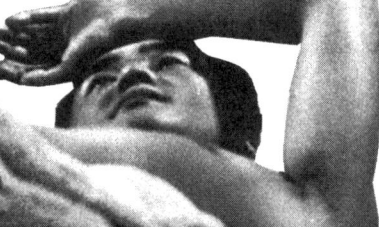

昭和館地下
上映中
女尻こすりあい
巨乳わしづかみ
昭和館地下劇場
Established in 1956
COME out from POSTER!
in
03-
③ Have a seat
You can chose any seats
お好きな席へどうぞ
② Don't hesitate to enter!
思い切って入ろう!
1本 約60-70分
one movie takes 60-70 mintes
You are Welcome
いらっしゃいまし
No performance
実演は
番組を調べよう
① Check weekly Showakan's program
by news-papers (sports)
ex Naigai times Tokyo Sports
年増好みだもんな…
I like middle-aged woman
My favorite is....
Telphone call to Showakan OK
Maybe, any weeks.
Showakan presents your favorite program
OPEN A.M 10:30
十時半開館
3本立 3 movies, everyday
fee: 1600yen
楽しもっ
④ Any way
Enjoy! Enjoy

和館地下劇場での
go to underground
WAKWAN-UNDERGROUND THEATER
ピンク映画の観かた
How to watch EROTIC Movies.
How you can be excited!
erotic SEXY
come come
⑥ At home after watching movies
You can still enjoy by your tention or imagination
家に帰っても まだ楽しめる
If you are single
独身の場合
Sure! masturbate and masturbate, Your imagination is growing up!
if you have a wife (wives)
妻帯者
oh! UTAMARO
Sure, make love with your wife more! more
Showakan makes your home happy!
注意
⑤ CAUTION
If you are excited, Don't Masturbate in the theater
せんずり禁止
It's important to keep your tension and imagination
余韻をのこして
Take a tea in break time
Vending machine in there
Coffee
Pop Corn
refreshment
It's OK only to make a tent
Don't escalate into masturbation
Take a break
Step
Pu

MESSAGE FROM SPACE

BY J-TARO SUGISAKI
TRANSLATION BY YUJI ONIKI

1

GOKUEI'S TOKYO STUDIO—

AKIHISA FUJIMOTO HAD BEEN AN ASSISTANT DIRECTOR AT GOKUEI FOR 18 YEARS. HE WAS IN **LOVE**...

...WITH...

OH... GOOD MORNING.

GOOD MORNING

...ANNA MOTOYAMA, GOKUEI'S NEW YOUNG STAR.

SINCE FUJIMOTO WAS AN ASSISTANT DIRECTOR, HE WASN'T PAID VERY WELL. ON TOP OF THAT, HE WAS PATHOLOGICALLY SHY WITH WOMEN, SO HE COULD ONLY STARE AT HER FROM A DISTANCE.

2

ONE DAY...

WHAT!?

YOU'RE PROMOTING ME TO DIRECTOR!?

YEAH, I WAS IMPRESSED BY YOUR PREVIEW FOR PREDATOR SWORDSMAN. WE'RE COUNTING ON YOU!

I'LL DO MY BEST!!

HE PLANNED ON HAVING ANNA MOTOYAMA AS THE LEAD ACTRESS IN HIS FILM, BUT...

WHAT!?

FUJIMOTO WAS ASSIGNED A FILM AVOIDED BY EVERYONE—A **HORROR PORN FLICK**.

Abnormal! Horrifying!
You'll want to turn your eyes from this world!
The debut film from newcomer Akihisa Fujimoto

The notorious inferno lynch

HORROR PUBIC HAIR INFERNO

CAST
Etsuko Mata • Mina Sotoyama • Yuya Kazato • Reiko Ichinose
Hiromi Fuji • Yoshio Igarashi • Takashi Noro • Terao Shirai
Kazu Komine • Seizo Fukushima • Kunimi Kitani • Masataka Iwaki
Taizo Hikita • Takezo Kawatani • Asahi Shioji

Panel 3:
SINCE THE COMPANY HAD BIG PLANS FOR ANNA MOTOYAMA, THEY WEREN'T ABOUT TO PUT HER IN **THAT KIND OF MOVIE**.

SO FUJIMOTO ENDED UP HIRING A HIGH SCHOOL PROSTITUTE.

HMMM...I WONDER IF THERE ISN'T STILL A WAY I CAN CONFESS MY LOVE FOR ANNA THROUGH THIS FILM..

SIR, THE CAMERA'S STILL RUNNING...

COME ON, JUST LEMME POKE IT IN.

HEY, STOP!

UNFORTUNATELY, THERE'S NO BEAUTIFUL LOVE STORY HERE...

SIR, THE CAMERA'S STILL RUNNING!

I'M COMIN' I'M COMIN'

Huh Huh

STOP IT! HEY DIRECTOR

I GOT IT!!

OH NO, HE CAME.

SHUP

I WAS A VIRGIN!!

Panel 4:
FUJIMOTO'S PLAN WAS TO USE **SUBLIMINAL MESSAGES**. HE WOULD CONFESS HIS LOVE —NO, HE WOULD **MANIPULATE HER FEELINGS**...

BY SPLICING IN FRAMES OF HIS LOVE FOR ANNA IN **HORROR— PUBIC HAIR INFERNO**.

THE FRAMES CONSISTED OF PHOTOS OF FUJIMOTO PASTED IN WITH **NUDE PHOTOS** OF ANNA.

SURELY THIS WOULD SUBLIMINALLY PROVOKE ANNA TO DESIRE SEX WITH HIM!

ANNA!!

I LOVE YOU!!

I LOVE YOU ANNA!!

ANNA-!!

Panel 5:
AWRIGHT! IT'S A WRAP!

CUT

AND SO HIS INSPIRED DEBUT FILM WAS COMPLETED!!

GOOD WORK.

BUT WHY WOULD ANNA GO SEE THAT KIND OF MOVIE IN THE FIRST PLACE?

OH MAN, THIS SOUNDS TOTALLY GROSS.

WHY DO THEY EVEN MAKE MOVIES LIKE THIS?

THUS ENDED FUJIMOTO'S LOVE—

ON TOP OF ALL THAT, THE FILM TANKED.

HEY!

LET'S SHAKE HANDS!

AS A RESULT, FUJIMOTO WAS REASSIGNED TO CHILDREN'S PROGRAMMING.

Panel 6:
THIS MANGA IS A COMPLETE WORK OF FICTION.

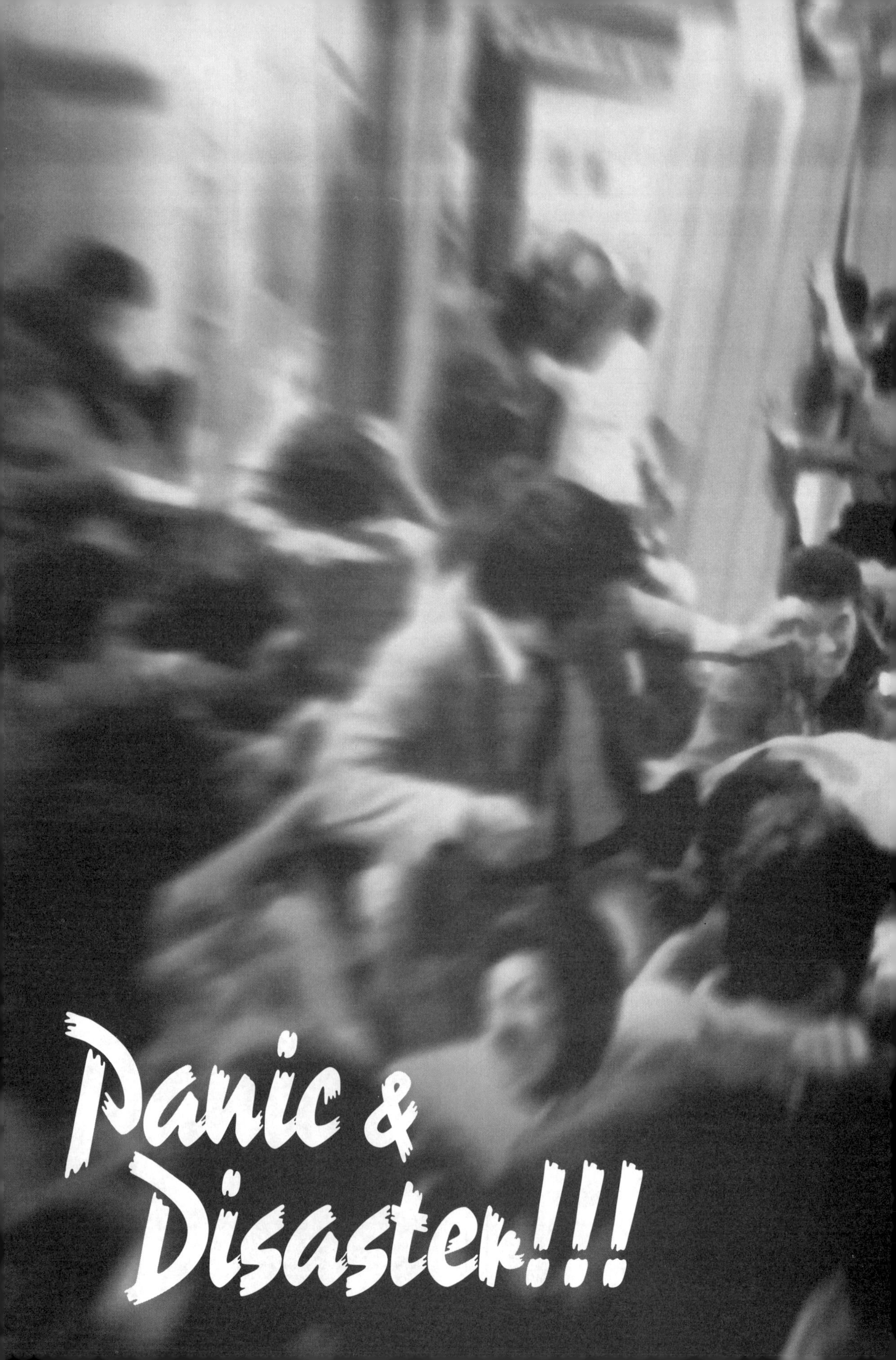

Panic & Disaster!!!

恐慌災害

Panic & Disaster!!!

PANIC & DISASTER

If super-sized servings of earthquakes, typhoons, tsunamis, and volcanic activity have achieved anything, they have made Japan the land not only of the rising sun, but also a specialist in panic and disaster.

One can add to the list a striking series of decidedly unnatural disasters: two atomic bombs, religious nuts armed with nerve gas, and a roller coaster for an economy.

It quickly becomes clear that Japan has had a surplus of real-time cataclysm. One would think that doomsday movies would be the last thing that they'd want to watch. Yet no one repeatedly destroys town and country with as much zeal as they do.

Consider the apocalypse as represented in any number of manga or anime, such as Katsuhiro Otomo's greedy *Akira*, which manages to both begin and end with big bangs. Godzilla, treasured national icon that he is, has done his bit to defend Tokyo from numerous threats, and yet proves to be most satisfying when destroying the city rather than saving it.

As for the origins of this seemingly suicidal impulse to depict megadeath, it would be easy to simply point to World War II, as C.G. Jung did in "Man and His Symbols," and say that Godzilla and other similar gestures of nation-razing are merely a case of guilt over the war writ large.

But the trail goes back even further. Some of the earliest Japanese films were disaster films. In 1923, right after the Great Kanto Earthquake, silent movies like *Daichi wa okoru* (The Earth Gets Angry) and *Daichi wa yuru* (The Earth Shakes), turned recent trauma into populist entertainment.

It was the Cold War that created the first end-of-the-world boom, adding a dash of cosmic awareness to Japan's doom-laden dreams. 1956's *Uchujin Tokyo ni arawaru* (Spacemen Appear in Tokyo, aka *Warning from Space*) had a United Nations-styled alien council sending a starfish-shaped emissary to Earth on a double mission to discourage a physicist from playing with a uranium-like substance and to spread the word about a runaway planet that was going to do a repeat performance of 1951's *When Worlds Collide*.

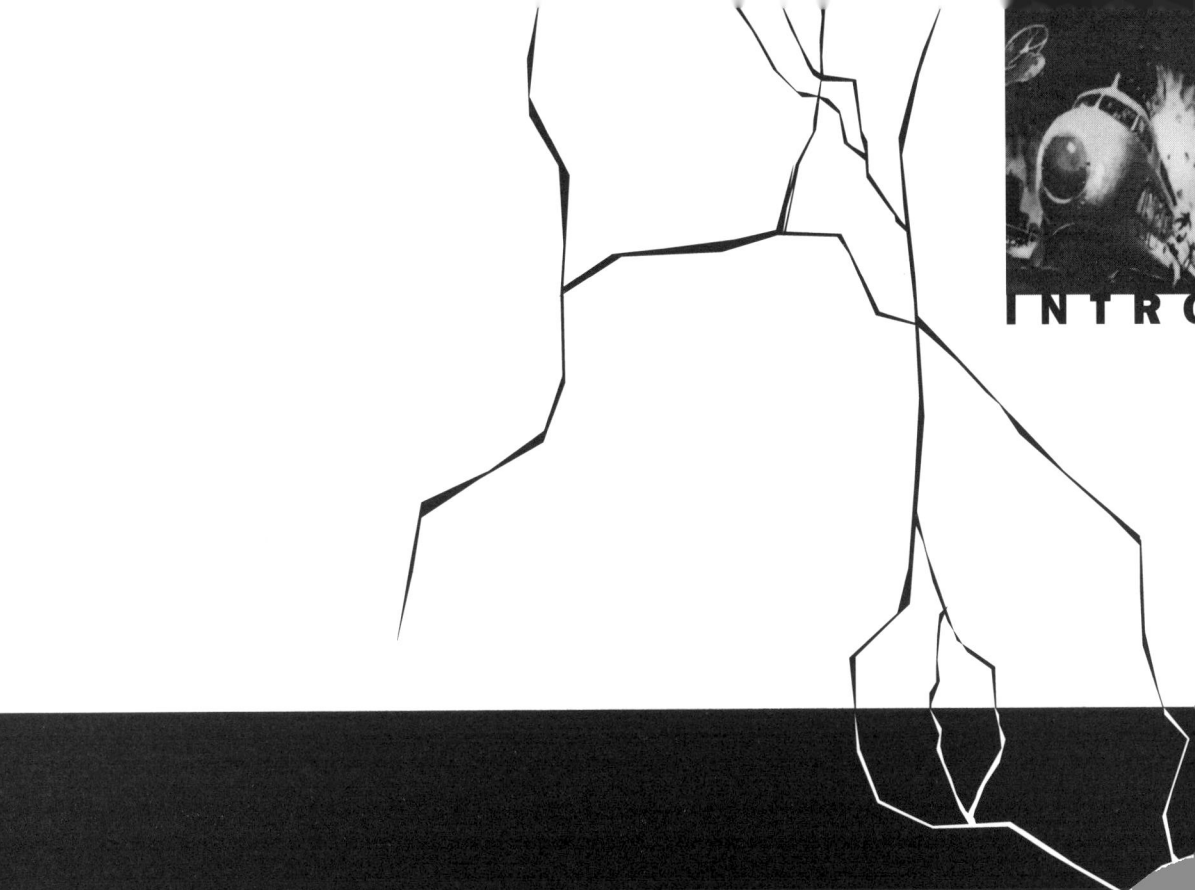

Demonstrators clashed in the streets over the US-Japan Peace Treaty in 1960, one of the most turbulent and violent years in Japan's modern history. Should East and West go to war with each other, Japan's destruction would be assured. There was a dark irony inherent in "anti-war" films like 1960's *Dai sanji sekai taisen* (aka *The Final War*) and 1961's *Sekai dai senso* (aka *The Last War*). The special effects techniques that depicted imaginary nuclear holocausts had been pioneered first through the making of wartime propaganda films. Yet the message now spreading out to the rest of the world was, "It must not happen again. We know. Trust us."

Progress was to be inseparable from pessimism. As Japan grew in postwar affluence, so did the need to drown it. Toho's 1962 *Gorath* showed Japan doing its part to save the planet from yet another close call from an object from space, but not until much damage had been done first. The film's concluding image of the Diet building adrift in a brave new sunken world has to be one of the greatest images in all of Japanese film. Daiei envisioned a tempest of biblical proportions for 1963's *Husoku nanaju-go meto* (75 MPH Wind), whose scenes of soggy ruin required fifteen tons of water to be poured on top of a miniature city, a deluge that wound up damaging the very soundstage they were filmed on.

Anthropomorphic monsters and alien menaces hogged special effects films from the mid to late sixties on. With no agenda other than fantasy, the tantalizing prospect of "The End" was constantly toyed with, but seldom did real doomsday result.

The turbulence of the early seventies put pure fantasy on the back burner in

Panic & Disaster!!!

lieu of more socially relevant subject matter. Unchecked industrial growth resulted in an increasingly poisoned environment. There was a noticeable dip in the economy as postwar growth finally began to slow down. War in the Middle East caused an oil and paper shortage, leading to inflation, scarcity, and harsh restrictions on energy consumption. The skyrocketing cost of film production contributed to the death of the studio system. Major talents and audiences continued their exodus to television en masse. Even Godzilla had to go on unemployment.

At the forefront of Japan's new prophets of doom was a seismologist named Hitoshi Takeuchi. Rife with radical ideas about mantle conversion and elastic rebound theory, Takeuchi was convinced that Japan was prone to experiencing sixty-year cycles of massive earthquakes. And since the Kanto quake of 1922 had been the most recent event of its kind, all people had to look forward to in the 1980s was the roof caving in on their heads.

Takeuchi acted as a scientific consultant to author Sakyo Komatsu as he penned his seminal novel *Nippon chinbotsu* (available in English from Kodansha as *Japan Sinks: A Novel*). Offering far more than just a killer quake, *Nippon chinbotsu* cycled through a series of catastrophic fires, tidal waves, volcanoes, and soap opera histrionics before climaxing with the entire island nation itself plunging into the drink.

Toho's movie adaptation of *Nippon chinbotsu* (aka *Submersion of Japan*) became the highest grossing domestic release of 1974. Sales of Komatsu's book eventually reached 3.5 million copies. And as a new *Nippon chinbotsu* weekly TV show appeared on TBS (complete with pre-show warnings that what viewers were about to see was only a simulation), a whole industry devoted to doom and gloom was doing knockout business.

The preeminent publication of these Last Days was a magazine called *Shumatsu kara* (After the End) which listed reams of scientific data for how, why, and when the world was going to end, be it by pollution, nuclear war, natural disaster, or economic meltdown. By all

End of the world: 1999!!!

accounts, it was a strange time to be alive.

If you rejected the hard-line science approach of Komatsu, Takeuchi, and co. then an equally attractive alternative came via psychic phenomena and the occult.

Journalist Ben Goto tapped perfectly into the need for answers in this uncertain zeitgeist with his book *Nostradamus no dai yogen*, which plundered the incredibly vague quatrains of France's top "all-knowing, all seeing" 16th-century oracle, Michel de Nostredame. Predicting World War 3 for the year 1999, it was yet another pessimistic and popular best-seller. Toho's 1974 controversial film adaptation of *Nostradamus no dai yogen* (aka *The Last Days of Planet Earth*) emerged as perhaps the ultimate mad, bad, and dangerous-to-know Japanese cult film.

Meanwhile the kiddies had their own child-sized apocalypse in the Toei 1974 anime short *Mazinger Z tai Ankoku Dai Shogun* (Mazinger Z vs. Great Shogun Darkness) which had a crazed Moses-like prophet convincingly screaming about the end of the world as major cities of the world succumbed to a robot army.

In spite of the economic doldrums, Toho could still boast of having the largest studio facilities in all of Asia. With such resources, only they could concoct such elaborate disasters as 1975's *Tokyo wan enjiyo* (Fire in Tokyo Bay, aka *Conflagration*), in which an oil tanker spilled flaming petrol on valuable real estate property.

Toei's genre pics were smaller in scale, but were high-energy, heavy-impact panic films. *Shinkansen dai bakuhatsu* (Bullet Train Big Explosion) and *Kurutaya jyu* (Crazy Beast) heralded the deeds of mad bomber terrorists and anti-heroic crooks and laid the real blame at the feet of polite society.

With the advent of the bubble economy in the 1980s, Japan reached the peak of prosperity. But for the shift of a few tectonic plates, it could all be broken like a breadstick in seconds. And with so much rampant greed going on and bad movies being made, why shouldn't a Sodom and Gomorrah be allowed to happen?

Studios had abandoned the old double-feature strategy and now concentrated on competing directly with Hollywood with

Panic & Disaster!!!

their own brand of big releases. Nuevo riche entrepreneurs, with no prior film experience, invested their earnings in the business of production. These risky strategies resulted in more than a few costly box-office flops and legendary bad movies. It seemed that films didn't have to be about flying warheads or wayward buses to be literal disasters.

Japan was a now a country strictly made for the young and moneyed to enjoy. The elderly and others who had been left behind by the ebullient economy now had little to look forward to but the end. Their own.

Tetsuro Tanba, a venerable actor who had played the sole authoritative voice of reason in *Nostradamus no dai yogen* and the Prime Minister in *Nippon chinbotsu* offered these folks a semi-religious movement spearheaded by a movie called *Tetsuro Tanba's Great Spirit World*. His was a merciful vision of an afterlife where happy, smiling ancestors greeted rejuvenated souls, images that flickered in movie theaters that reeked of abandonment and death immanent.

The time had come for a karmic balance. It came in the form of the 1995 Kobe earthquake. While not the knock-out Big One that had been predicted almost twenty years earlier, Kobe was a psychic blow that perfectly matched the burst of the bubble. More than a few survivors compared the experience to being an extra in a giant monster movie. As before, a movie restaging followed in short succession. *Dai jishin* (Big Earthquake) debuted in the direct-to-video market in that would-be fateful year of 1999.

Since then, the films of Kiyoshi Kurosawa, such as *Charisma* and *Kairo* (Pulse), routinely reach for the end of the world. Shinji Aoyama's *Eureka*, a mammoth 217-minute production, deals with the psychic aftermath of a homicidal busjacking and as such could be viewed as a companion piece of sorts to Toei's old *Crazy Beast*.

Still, time marches on. After all those Nostradamus movies and pleas by Tetsuro Tanba, it had to come as some kind of disappointment. But maybe the true nature of apocalypse is a simmering slow burn rather than a "now"—a single violent shattering event. The Japanese should know after all. 東

REVIEW

The Last War
Sekai dai senso (The Great World War)

1961, Toho
Director Shuei Matsubayashi
Cast Frankie Sakai, Akira Takarata, Yuriko Hoshi

"*The Last War* is our appeal to the world…It is our sincere hope that by producing and exhibiting this film we can serve the cause of peace." So wrote M. Shimizu, the President of Toho Co., Ltd. in a philanthropic sales pitch to international markets. The message being: *The Last War* wanted nothing less than to save the world and end the Cold War.

In truth, Toho's film played a key role in the Japanese apocalypse movie arms race. In 1960, perennial competitor Toei's *Dai sanji sekai taisin—Yonju-ichi jikan no kyofu* (World War 3—41 Hours of Fear, sold internationally as *The Final War*), featuring Tatsuo "King of Eros" Umemiya stumbling through the ruins, pulled in a nice profit despite being a modest 77-minute black and white film.

Toho responded with heavy artillery: a big-budget, all-star, color spectacular whose trailer screamed "The Annihilation of All Life!" "Destruction Goes Apace!" and perhaps most comfortingly, "This Could Happen to You!"

The melodramatic *Last War* plays like its own preview. Too over the top to really work as believable drama, it does successfully articulate the feelings of abject helplessness following the signing of the US-Japan Security Treaty in the summer of 1960. Should the Eastern bloc and the West go to war, Japan would surely be caught in the crossfire and *The Last War* would cease to be "only a movie…only a movie…"

Comedian Frankie Sakai (also seen in *Mothra* and NBC-TV's *Shogun* mini-series) is a happy-go-lucky chauffeur for the Tokyo Press Club. He isn't troubled much about the ticking of the doomsday clock in the background as "the Federation" (stand-ins for Americans, fittingly dressed like traffic cops) and the decidedly Communist "Alliance" escalate their hostilities. Frankie is more concerned with trying to buy a new house and seeing his daughter (Yuriko Hoshi) getting hitched to a handsome sailor (Akira Takarata). And a chorus of ever-present fresh-faced children and numerous speeches to the effect of "it can't happen here" keep him from feeling like he's ever out of step.

Too bad, because the fate of the world is in the hands of a bunch of mangy English-speaking *gaijin* actors with funny accents. And it's only a matter of time until the red light marked "Outbreak of War" goes on—when world landmarks start exploding, a giant mushroom cloud appears over Mt. Fuji, and the ground beneath the Diet building is reduced to a molten state. In other words, the last laugh is on funnyman Frankie. While the American edit of the film ended bizarrely with "It's a Small World" warbling away on the soundtrack, the Japanese closes with more fitting "it must never happen again" platitudes.

But it would! Eiji Tsuburaya's fantastic apocalyptic effects would be endlessly recycled in Toho films to come, even as late as 1977 for *Wakusei dai senso* (aka *The War in Space*). Toho's "Our Films Save the World" stance would return (along with more *Last War* stock footage) for *The Last Days of Planet Earth*.

☞ Import only

Submersion of Japan
Nippon chinbotsu, aka *Tidal Wave*

1974, Toho
Director Shiro Moritani
Cast Keiju Kobayashi, Hiroshi Fujioka, Tetsuro Tanba, Ayumi Ishida

Beginning with a God's-eye view of eons zipping by in seconds and the continental drift giving birth to the islands of Nippon, *Submersion of Japan*, based on the novel by noted sci-fi scribe Sakyo Komatsu, is a *big* movie.

With a whopping 140-minute running time, the film was backed by an enormous budget of three million dollars. By contrast a certain down-on-his luck lizard wandered like a hobo though *Godzilla vs. Megalon*. *Submersion*, of the same vintage, saw a fantastic variety of volcanoes, earthquakes, tidal waves, and other signifiers of mass destruction magnificently conjured out of Toho's special effects department.

Such a massive risk paid off handsomely. *Submersion of Japan* proved to be a huge hit at the box office, with the public and critics alike singing its praises.

A phenomenon of such magnitude could not help but attract Roger Corman, who cut the film down to 90 minutes, and managed to shoehorn *Earthquake* survivor Lorne Greene in there (which added another layer of meaning when he appeared as a guest on the *Pink Lady and Jeff* show). This unfortunate US variant, known as *Tidal Wave*, is a mere shadow of the genuine article which would prove to be incredibly influential on Toho's large-scale SFX films to come.

While investigating the disappearance of a series of small islands, a crotchety scientist and a young submarine captain (Hiroshi Fujioka, TV's original Kamen Rider) discover that Japan is resting on terra about as firma as cheap pie crust. The scientist tells it to a team of government officials and fellow scientists who quickly brand him a quack and an alarmist. Only after an enormous earthquake, which kills millions of people, is the interest of the Prime Minister (played by Mister Panic and Disaster, himself Tetsuro Tanba) finally piqued.

Owing to an unfortunate side effect of the expansion of the Earth's core, Japan is fated to rip apart and sink within two years, which spells plenty of global and personal intrigue in the meantime. A planned migration of Japanese folk to other countries goes badly. (Australia says, "If we have to accept things Japanese, I prefer them to be art objects rather than people." Ouch!) Hiroshi proposes marriage to his sweetie Ayumi Ishida. And PM Tanba wonders what is better, trying to save the Japanese race, or simply accepting extinction as par for the course.

Featuring some very tasty carnage candy, *Submersion* is also a remarkably graceful performance, somber and serious, lacking the manic, aggressive hysteria of both *The Last Days of Planet Earth* and *Deathquake*.

Upon the film's release, novelist Komatsu immediately promised a sequel tome that would further depict the global Japanese diaspora. It has still yet to materialize. There was also an all-new FX-heavy *Submersion of Japan* TV show which hit TBS airwaves in 1975.

Unlike the movie, it sank.

☞ **Import only**

年人類滅亡。
科学の粋と無限のイマジネーションを集めて鮮烈の映像化
大予言

The Last Days of Planet Earth

Nostradamus no dai yogen—Catastrophe 1999 (The Great Prophecies of Nostradamus)

1974, Toho
Director Toshio Matsuda
Cast Tetsuro Tanba, Toshio Kurosawa, Kaoru Yumi

In early 1974, Toho producer Tomoyuki Tanaka was still counting the beans from *Submersion of Japan*'s enormous box office success. Noting that a book on the prophecies of Nostradamus by author Ben Goto was then at the top of the bestseller list, an adaptation seemed a natural follow-up.

Submersion merely destroyed Japan. *Nostradamus no dai yogen* would aim to flush the whole planet down the crapper. Unfortunately, the film only shot itself in the foot, generating a storm of controversy and bad press upon its release. (Flip back to page 167 for that story.)

Directed by former Nikkatsu Action hand and *Space Cruiser Yamato* voice director Toshio Matsuda, *Nostradamus* is, simply put, a masterpiece of pure no-holds-barred overkill.

The end of the world comes from all directions at once, and the attack plan is outré, freaky, and frothing at the mouth.

There are giant snails in the junkyards, giant plants in the subway tubes, radioactive cannibals in New Guinea, widespread hallucinations, leather-clad motor-biking death cults, a big ol' hole in the ozone layer, food riots, snow on Egyptian pyramids, melting polar ice caps, nuclear power plant accidents, and the launching of a whole bunch of ICBM missiles.

All the while Tetsuro Tanba (playing a descendant of the guy who was persecuted for first bringing word of Nostradamus to Japan in 1835) wildly gesticulates, incorrectly quotes Nostradamus' *The Centuries,* and drives his points home with all the subtlety and charm of a flesh-eating virus.

Could this be the greatest movie ever made?

There are two of them actually: the original Japanese version, which plays it cool for the first thirty minutes like a good little lysergic before the bad trip kicks in. The heavily abridged and altered (but still priceless) American version known as *The Last Days of Planet Earth* goes right for the throat from frame one.

An Amazing Criswell-like narrator intones about how right on Nostradamus was about everything: the rise of Red Russia, world wars, the space race, and "that terrifying reality not yet upon us" (har har), the end of the world.

Cut to Tetsuro Tanba thinking aloud in abrasively dubbed English, "Sometimes I wonder if they have human brains." *They* of course are industrial and world leaders who stand by and do nothing, instead of waving their arms around shouting pronouncements of doom non-stop.

From here any synopsis would utterly fail. It would be easier to read a century's worth of supermarket tabloids.

Original author Ben Goto knew a good thing when he had it and continued to milk the Japanese fascination for Nostradamus which he helped to create. His 1991 book *Predictions of Nostradamus: Middle East Chapter* was yet another bestseller, dressing up the year 1999 for the outbreak of World War 3.

I wonder how well it's selling now?

☞ **Available on Paramount Home Video**

Bullet Train Big Explosion
Shinkansen dai bakuhatsu (aka Super Express 109)

1975, Toei
Director Junya Sato
Cast Practically everybody

It's one of those near perfect days on the Shinkansen, Japan's famed bullet train, as it travels from Shinjuku through the Kyoto area to the end of the line in Hakata.

All of a sudden…

"This is an announcement: a heartless person has planted a bomb on the train."

It's as if someone popped open a can of Instant Panic: a pregnant woman promptly goes into labor, passengers clash over the pay phone, and salarymen threaten to leap from the train in order to make their business meetings. Making matters worse, an amateur film crew on board rudely starts rolling their cameras, explaining they are "documenting the terror on a doomed train."

All aboard *Bullet Train Big Explosion*, a disaster-movie megaproduction with a superlative cast containing nearly everyone on the Toei payroll. Just to name the big 'uns: Takashi Shimura (the venerable leader of the *Seven Samurai* and Dr. Yamane in *Godzilla '54*) is the president of Japan's railway lines. Tetsuro Tanba is a hard-ass police inspector. Etsuko Shihomi is a briefly seen telephone operator. And Sonny Chiba is the bullet train's bug-eyed terrified conductor.

In his first turn as a terrorist, Ken Takakura and his ex-student radical pal (grungy Kei Yamamoto, seemingly always cast in films as a left-wing nut job) have rigged up a very inspirational bomb. If the bullet train should slow down to a certain, er, "Speed" then it will summarily detonate.

Few Toei movies ever really supported their local police force, and the pigs are truly despicable here. Rather than just forking over the ransom money, the cops seek to capture Ken out of foolish pride. Our sympathies fall instead to the downtrodden bombers, who have lost their livelihoods in typically bad Asian economic situations and only want some payback.

This "bombers=good, cops=bad" dynamic, perfectly suited to the seventies when the antihero was king in Japanese pop culture, is one reason why director and co-scripter Junya Sato (later to direct *The Peking Man*) had to make do with a miniature bullet train instead of the real deal. Japan Railways refused to lend support to a film where their pride and joy is held for ransom and rigged with explosives.

Crafted by producer Kanji Amao to celebrate Toei's triumphant survival at a time when rival studios were living on borrowed time and instant ramen, *Bullet Train* was hyped to the skies upon its release. It was parodied by black-comedy practitioner Yasuzo Masumura (*Blind Beast*). His 1975 film *Domiyaku retto* (Archipelago Artery) featured a lunatic threatening to blow up the Shinkansen unless it *slowed down* just so it wouldn't make so much noise.

Meanwhile over in France, a drastically edited version of *Bullet Train* became a smash hit. There, it played not so much as a showdown between Ken and the cops, but between the Shinkansen and France's own high-speed TGV trains.

Personally, we'll give the odds to the one with Sonny Chiba at the controls.

☞ **Import only**

REVIEW

Crazy Beast
Kurutaya jyu

1976, Toei
Director Sadao Nakajima
Cast Tsunehiko Watase, Jun Hoshino, Takumi Kawatani

Anyone who believes that Japanese filmmakers can't stage exciting car chases (a common complaint from foreign critics) deserves a nasty case of whiplash courtesy of *Crazy Beast*. This amazing perpetual motion machine, directed and co-scripted by Sadao Nakajima, runs full tilt on brazen death-defying auto stunts. While the similarly themed *Shinkansen dai bakuhatsu* (Bullet Train Big Explosion) of the same year was an all-star, big-budget affair, *Crazy Beast* is a low-budget B-movie, populated by B-list stars, and made so cheap and fast that there are few special effects and camera set-ups in sight—only wild hand-held camera and very real cars mashing into each other for our amusement. Running in real-time at a mere 78 minutes, it probably blew away whatever feature it was made to support.

Within moments of the opening credits, two bank robbers hijack a passing public transport bus. While the outraged passengers (a cross section of old people, philandering husbands, children, and street performers) shout and wail, cool Tsunehiko Watase sits calmly in the backseat clutching a violin case full of stolen jewels that he's ripped off from his former employer.

As news of the busjacking spreads, bumbling cops spread out across the Kansai area and Watase's leather-clad girlfriend races off, ala Marianne Faithfull, to find her man on her motorcycle. The elderly bus driver dies of a heart attack, causing the robbers to battle over who gets the wheel. After being tossed off the bus, beleaguered Watase gets right back on and eventually gains the upper hand, in spite of the fact that his lousy eyesight (which once caused him to wipeout during his pervious stint as a test car driver) renders him nearly blind. While a terrified cop clings to the back of the speeding vehicle, the wayward bus careens through barricades and chicken coops. Pursuing cars crash and burn. The cops try a kamikaze attack, launching a car directly at the bus in order to stop it. It doesn't work. Watase's lousy eyesight causes him to eat it. The bus tips over and the greedy passengers scoop up the jewels. The bank robbers get picked off by snipers and Watase dives into the bay to swim "to America" while his girlfriend dog paddles behind him.

As people on the street stand by with their mouths open and the rampaging caravan zooms by, it's clear that *Crazy Beast* was shot guerrilla style with little regard for sanity and safety. It is a panic film with both ends burning. Incredibly, Watase (said to have been nihilistically depressed over the dissolution of his marriage) does his own driving and stunts.

☞ **Import only**

Deathquake
Jishin retto (Earthquake Islands, aka Magnitude 7.9)

1980, Toho
Director Kenjiro Omori
Cast Hiroshi Katsuno, Toshiyuki Nagashima, Yumi Takigawa, Kayo Matsuo

Geologist Hiroshi Katsuno takes one look at the rising lava flow building up inside of Mt. Mihara and predicts a repeat performance of the Great Kanto Quake of 1922 in (cue overdramatic music) *exactly thirty days.* But try as he might to spread the warning (like the scientists of *Submersion of Japan* and *The Last Days of Planet Earth* before him), the prophecy only gets him branded a charlatan by his colleagues. Soon the government, led by a prime minister who practically has "Don't bother me, I'm golfing" tattooed on his forehead, tries to slap a muzzle on this Chicken Little lest he start a nationwide panic.

Hiroshi's hothouse private life isn't faring much better. His longstanding marriage to Kayo Matsuo is riddled with fault lines, owing chiefly to the fact that he spends his after hours with younger, prettier Yumi Takigawa (*School of the Holy Beast*) who is herself being continually pestered by TV journalist Toshiyuki Nagashima, who has sworn to win her heart any way he can.

Just as our principals begin to hash out their various affairs of the heart, the Big One finally hits, trapping Hiroshi in a flooding subway tunnel with his wife and leaving Yumi stuck in a towering inferno with lucky Toshiyuki. Meanwhile all the prime minister can do is sit in his bunker and watch cost-saving scenes of special effects and destruction from previous Toho disaster movies on his quakeproof big-screen TV.

Of all Japanese panic films, *Deathquake* probably comes closest to established Hollywood product. The script similarities to Universal's *Earthquake* (1974) are abundantly clear and the turgid soap opera theatrics are pumped up fierce with disaster-movie-strength Panavision and 4-channel magnetic sound (what? no Sensurround?). And just as Mario Puzo cashed in by writing the screenplay for *Earthquake*, Shindo Kaneto, the acclaimed screenwriter of *Onibaba* and *The Island*, lent oodles of prestige to *Deathquake*.

Despite some serious reservations in the drama department, and the flirtation with stock footage, *Deathquake* (whose film program came with irony-free ads for canned food and other earthquake necessities) hits the bullseye with the new bits of earthquake-fu: flaming cars flying off of damaged freeways and straight into people's homes, jumbo jets exploding on crumbling runways. Teruyoshi Nakano and the renowned Toho SFX department done right after all.

And in hindsight, maybe all the brassy melodrama wasn't so bad after all. *Deathquake* feels like the last stand of *atsui* (passionate) histrionics before the much mellower eighties and nineties kicked in, by which point everyone would be too busy counting money to worry about the sky ever falling down.

All of Hiroshi's stiff speechmaking about "the arrogance of Japan" would pay off bitterly when the Kobe earthquake finally hit in January 1995.

☞ **Import only**

REVIEW

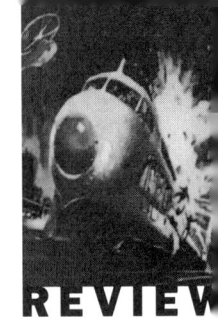

Tetsuro Tanba's Great Spirit World— What Happens after Death
Tetsuro Tanba no dai reikai—Shin dara do naru

1989, Shochiku
Director Teru Ishida and Tetsuro Tanba
Cast Yoshitaka Tanba, Evelyn Pringle, Tomisaburo Wakayama

Perhaps owing to all the death and destruction he had to endure in films like *Submersion of Japan*, Tetsuro Tanba devoted his later years trying to convince others that the afterlife was going to be swell. *Tetsuro Tanba's Great Spirit World* was one of three feature films that emerged from his popular quasi-religious *dai reikai* movement. Tanba himself narrates the film in play-by-play fashion. His dead-serious tone, coupled with a hastily stitched together hodgepodge of worldwide heaven and hell imagery, makes for a divine unintentional comedy.

Celebrated physicists Evelyn Pringle and Yoshitaka Tanba (Tetsuro's son), along with their pet poodle, are driving on a twisty mountain road while a maddening theme song consisting of the words "YOOOOUUUUUUU AND IIIIIIIIIIIIIIIII" repeats over and over on the soundtrack. But unless they pass a slow truck, they'll never make it to the "After Life World" conference on time. Yoshitaka changes lanes—only to crash head-on into a bus filled with a convenient cross-section of Japan's population (con men, prostitutes, politicians, blind kids).

Everyone goes over the side of a cliff. The only survivor is the poodle, who then promptly drowns while trying to pull Yoshitaka's body out of a rushing river. Yoshitaka's spirit, with dog in tow, floats through several layers of optical effects until they make it to a matte painting of purgatory and a long flight of stairs full of arriving dead folk, all of them suspiciously Japanese.

While Yoshitaka tries to find Evelyn, the obnoxious faction from the bus accident does nothing but complain about the bad service and disorganization. The goody two shoes on the other hand get their sight restored, their old bodies restored to youthful vigor, and are reunited with dead family members. A previously impoverished family imagines their bubble-economy dream house and it appears out of nowhere. As does a benevolent Tomisaburo Wakayama (*Lone Wolf and Cub*), cast as "The Great Spirit Person," who shows up just to remind everyone, in case they needed reminding, that they are dead.

As Yoshitaka ventures deeper into the Spirit World, he stumbles across a musical number where women reincarnate by flying back to earth on umbrellas. Then he falls into hell, a gravel pit where bad people get hit with sticks. He is rescued at the last minute by the Great Spirit World's cultural elite made up of (and no we are not making this up) white garbed Crazy Beast Tsunehiko Watase and Street Fighter Sonny Chiba! They decide to send Yoshitaka back to Earth to promote the Great Spirit World at which point the dog actually says the word "Sayonara" and the film stops cold.

☞ **Import only**
More: TETSURO TANBA p. 212

The Peking Man
Peking genjin—Who Are You?

1997, Toei
Director Junya Sato
Cast Tetsuro Tanba, Joey Wang, Naoto Ogata, Reiko Kataoka

Designed to be a family-friendly sci-fi adventure film on par with *Jurassic Park*, *Peking Man* instead turned out to be an artistic and financial apocalypse more akin to *Battlefield Earth*. While not a disaster film in concept, it proved to be one in execution. The resounding failure of this big-budget film silenced the careers of several of its stars and dragged Toei studios to the very brink of bankruptcy. If not for the success of a pair of *Neon Genesis Evangelion* anime movies released late in 1997, the ghastly yet still compelling-as-a-train-wreck *Peking Man* might have been the proverbial Last Movie.

Motivated by a Dr. Frankenstein-sized God complex, Life Science Laboratory president Tetsuro Tanba launches a space shuttle to conduct secret genetic experiments in zero gravity. His conceit pays off with a father-mother-son family unit of mangy cavemen culled from the DNA of a Peking Man fossil whisked away from China at the end of WWII.

Hoping to "shock the world" with his accomplishment, Tanba debuts his creations by making them enter running and jumping events at a track meet. This "so brilliant it's stupid" plan goes predictably awry when Peking Man, Jr. and his father are wooed away by a Chinese TV journalist (Hong Kong superstar Joey Wang, from *A Chinese Ghost Story*) who drags the pair back to their homeland in the name of national interest.

While the Cher-lookalike Mrs. Peking Man falls ill from the loss of her mate and child, Joey and the guys roll around in the dirt together until their ungodly grunts and groans summon a woolly mammoth that Tanba had tucked away in Siberia.

Though they've caused irreparable harm to Japanese-Chinese relations, the Peking Family is eventually reunited and, amidst much cringe-worthy dialogue from the principals about being free and living happily with the earth, ride off into the countryside on the back of the woolly (in more ways than one) mammoth. Pray that they never return.

Every frame of *Peking Man* plays like a Thing That Must Not Be. Plot threads begin and go nowhere. Characters, such as the intriguingly named "Lawyer Herman," are introduced only to vanish. Absurd situations—as when Tanba berates a scientist for not allowing the Peking Man to mate with her—are played without a perceptible trace of tongue-in-cheek. Simple embarrassment for the efforts of director Junya Sato (*Bullet Train Big Explosion*) becomes painful em-"bare-ass"-ment for the uncredited actors playing the hairy, naked, altogether grotesque Peking clan—who are, of course, supposed to warm their way into our hearts.

Peking Man is still too raw and painful to look back upon with any real affection, but generations to come may inevitably trace the devolution of Japanese film to 1997 A.D. and to the release of *Peking Man*.

☞ **Available subbed as a Region 3 DVD from Universe**

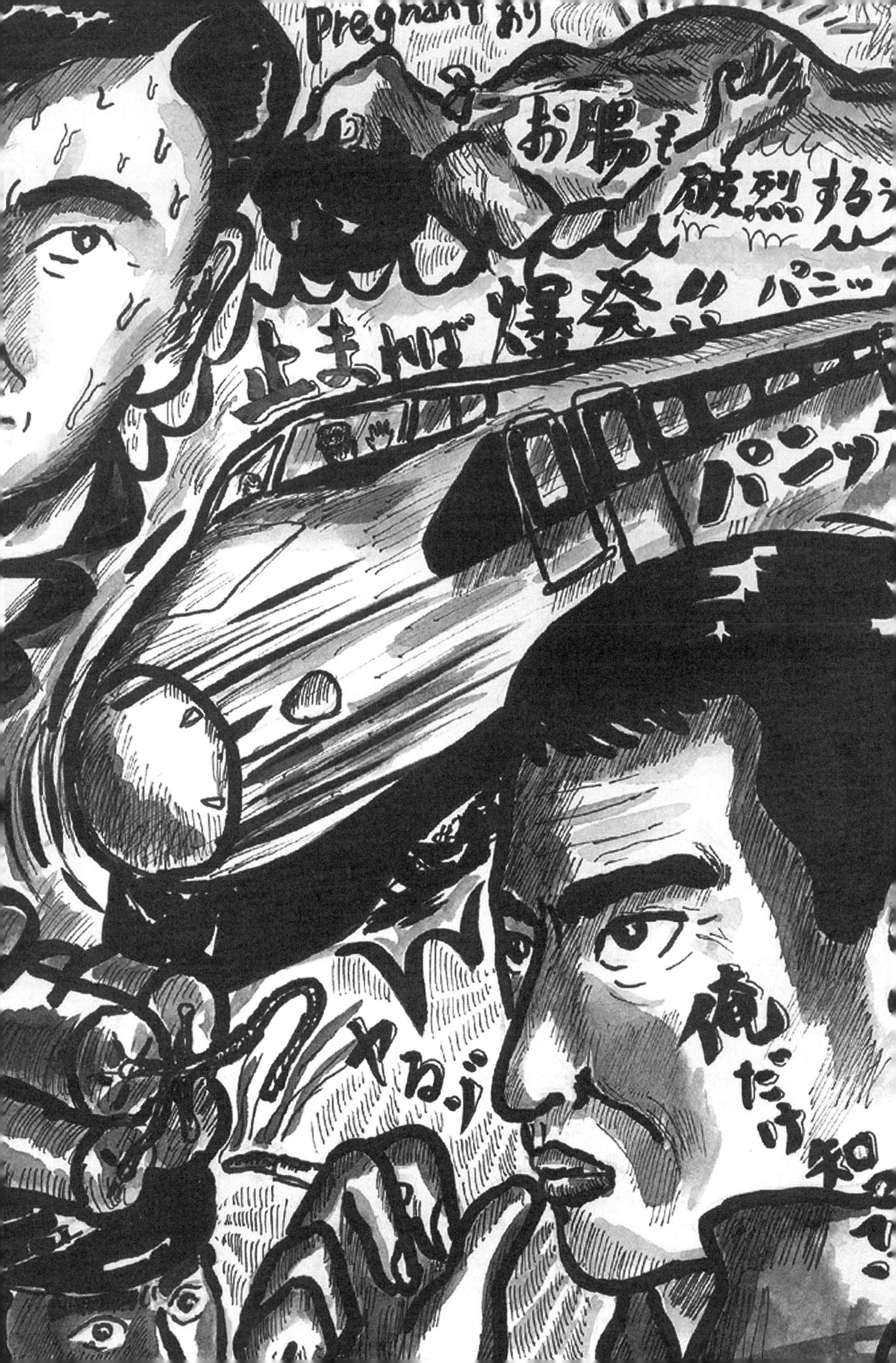
Pregnantであり
お腸も
破烈するぅ
止まれば爆発!!
パニッ
パニッ
やね
俺だけ知

Panic & Disaster!!!

Tetsuro Tanba
The Emperor

丹波哲朗

More of a beloved figurehead than a fully functional performer, Tetsuro Tanba is the Emperor of Japanese cult film.

Tanba surveys the entire breadth of his long acting career, which includes appearances in nearly 300 films, and in interviews has declared himself proudest of three facts:

- He has never turned down a role.
- He has never memorized a script.
- He has never seen a film that he's starred in all the way through.

Tanba (sometimes billed as "Tetsuro Tamba," an alternate pronunciation) is an immediately recognizable figure: forever poker-faced, reading off cue cards in a rich deep sonorous voice. His best known role may be that of "Tiger" Tanaka, the head of the Japanese Secret Service in the fifth James Bond film, *You Only Live Twice* (1967), but he's also appeared in films as prestigious as *Harakiri* and *Kwaidan*. Then there's the long and winding low road, which includes Teruo Ishii's *Porno Period Film—Way of the Outlaw Samurai* (1973) and the Hong Kong gore-fu classic *Riki-Oh: The Story of Ricky*.

To cast Tanba in your movie is to gain an instant illusion of prestige. Fittingly, he's most often cast in positions of authority—generals, prime ministers, scientists, battleship captains—roles that allow for podiums and reading prepared speeches rather than memorizing script pages.

Tetsuro Tanba was born on July 17, 1922 in Tokyo to a noble family. (The Tanba clan can trace their bloodline further back than the Imperial family. Tetsuro's father was also a personal physician to the Meiji Emperor.) The young Tanba attended Chuo University, but preferred to blow off studying to pursue what would emerge as lifelong pastimes: acting and womanizing.

Following World War II, Tanba's high society connections landed him a job as a translator for the Occupation forces. Although his English skills were extremely limited (read: nonexistent), he managed to earn his keep by showing US officials where the happening nightspots and gals were.

After attending a Shin Toho public audition in 1951, Tanba won a "New Face" contract at the studio. He made his film debut the following year in Hideo Suzuki's *Murderer Accused*.

Tanba's aristocratic background led to a somewhat sheltered life, which spelt trouble for his acting career. He had never quite learned how to be entirely polite to his superiors at Shin Toho who demanded that performers use only the most polite forms of Japanese language when working.

The studio brass was irked by Tetsuro's seeming defiance. They opted to keep him under contract, but rarely to give him any work. Yet by never kowtowing, Tanba wound up winning the lasting admiration of industry peers.

In 1959, Tanba wiggled out of his exclusive contract with Shin Toho and started working for other studios, including Toho, Toei, and Shochiku, where he played the heavy in many period films and crime thrillers.

His credentials as an interpreter helped him score the role of a Malaysian soldier in the

1964 British film *The 7th Dawn*. The film's producers were unaware of his limited bilingual ability. After all, his answer to nearly every question, such as "Do you speak English?" was "Yes."

Upon arriving in the UK, Tanba knew that desperate measures had to be taken to ensure his survival. On the first day of shooting, he worked his charm on a local English lass and found himself a new language tutor as well as a romantic liaison.

Three years later, Louis Gilbert, director of *The 7th Dawn*, cast Tanba in a role originally intended for Toshiro Mifune: "Tiger" Tanaka in *You Only Live Twice*. Some of Tanba's finest screen moments can be found here: downing sake with Sean Connery and lecturing 007 on the role of women in Japanese society as they enjoy an "all hands on deck" bathhouse scrub-down.

Tanba's Japanese TV and film roles continued to pile up with little regard for image or quality control. There was a stint on the hit Sonny Chiba TV show *G-Men '75*. There were numerous yakuza movies. In 1973, Tanba played the lead in *Human Revolution*, the life story of Josei Toda, one of the founders of the Sokkagakai Buddhist organization. What did it matter that Tanba was also starring simultaneously in the infamous Teruo Ishii's *Porno Period Film* at the same time he was playing a religious leader?

In 1974's *Nostradamus no dai yogen*, Tanba starred as a visionary scientist out to save the world from its own self-induced destruction. The messianic role mirrored a spiritual dimension dawning in the actor's life.

Decades prior, Tanba had sadly witnessed the pain and suffering of his friend, a terminally ill Shin Toho actor, who eventually succumbed to cancer.

Tanba began researching near-death experiences in search of definitive proof of an afterlife. His goal was to help end human suffering by eradicating the fear of death.

His findings resulted in the *dai reikai* (Great Spirit World) phenomenon of the eighties. Culled from different cultures and belief systems, *dai reikai* offered the elderly and the ill a comforting vision of a beautiful afterlife where the old became young again, the blind regained sight, and everyone was pleased as punch about being dead.

Tanba toiled over a ton of profitable *dai reikai* ancillary projects: books, lectures, amusement park attractions, and three theatrical films. While he was quick to point out that *dai reikai* was meant to be a scientific inquiry into the eternal mysteries, not a New Age religion, Tanba would periodically rent out his services as an advisor to several fringe cults.

Interest in *dai reikai* persists to this day. Tanba continues to lecture on matters of life and death, and a new phrase has even been coined for his philosophies: *Tanbaism*.

At no point has his acting output showed any signs of slowing down. Recent roles include Juzo Itami's *A Taxing Woman Returns*, and he's also reunited with director Teruo Ishii for a series of independent films, even reprising his role from *Porno Period Film* for Ishii's 1999 version of *Jigoku*.

A recent *Simpsons*-esque anime film from the popular *Crayon Shin-chan* series saw a giant monster attacking Japan and a cartoon Tanba trotted out for advice on how to deal with the situation. After all those authoritative film roles, his iconic image as a reliable know-it-all rests assured.

But perhaps the best example of Tanba's iconic celebrity is his nineties-era TV late night talk show *Tanba Club,* wherein members of the audience ask him a variety of questions ranging from romance to cooking to politics as Tanba sits Hugh Hefner-like among a throng of scantily clad women.

The Emperor. Enthroned at last. 東

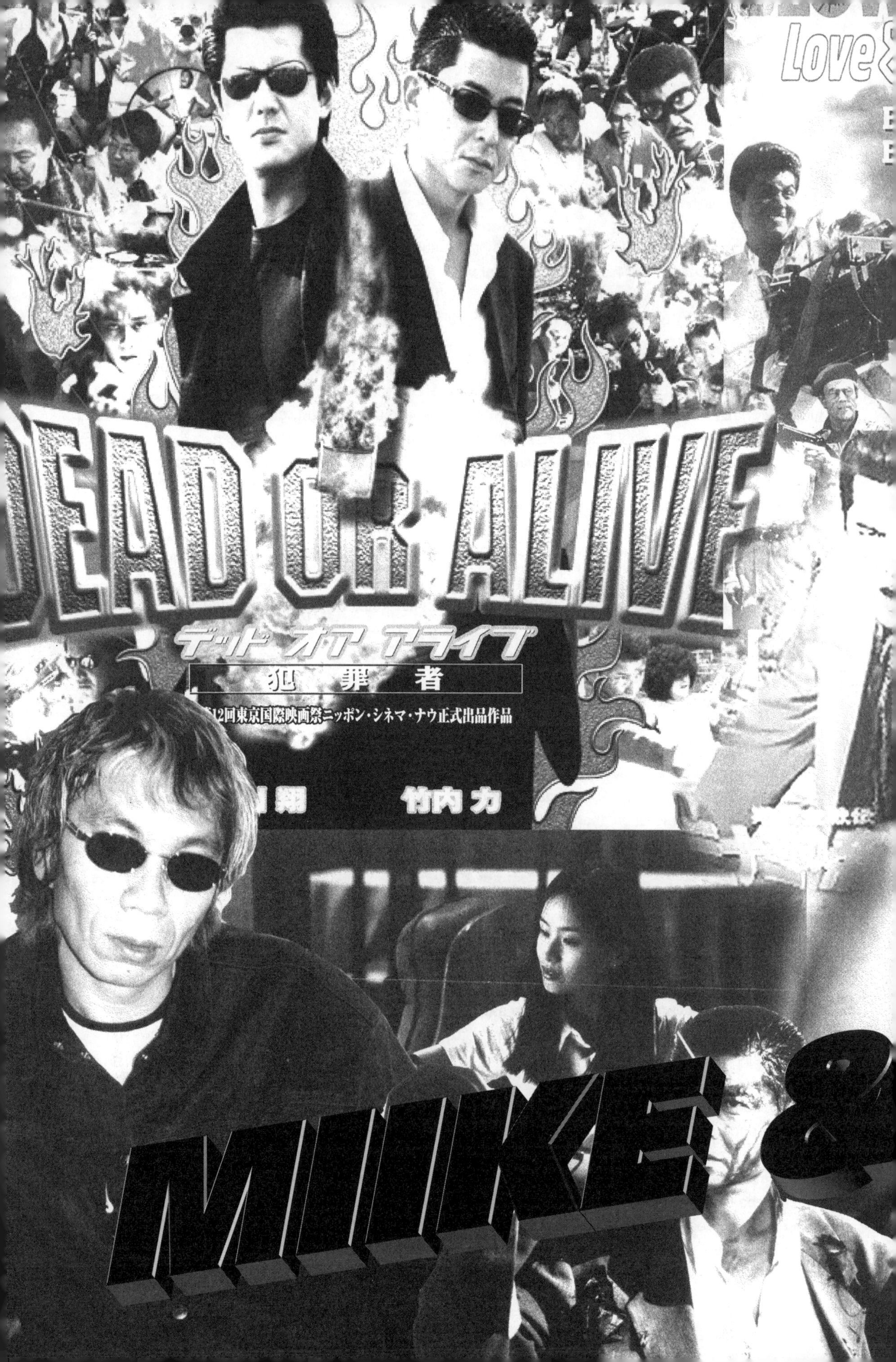
Love
EAD OR ALIVE
デッド オア アライブ
犯罪者
12回東京国際映画祭ニッポン・シネマ・ナウ正式出品作品
竹内力
MIIKE &

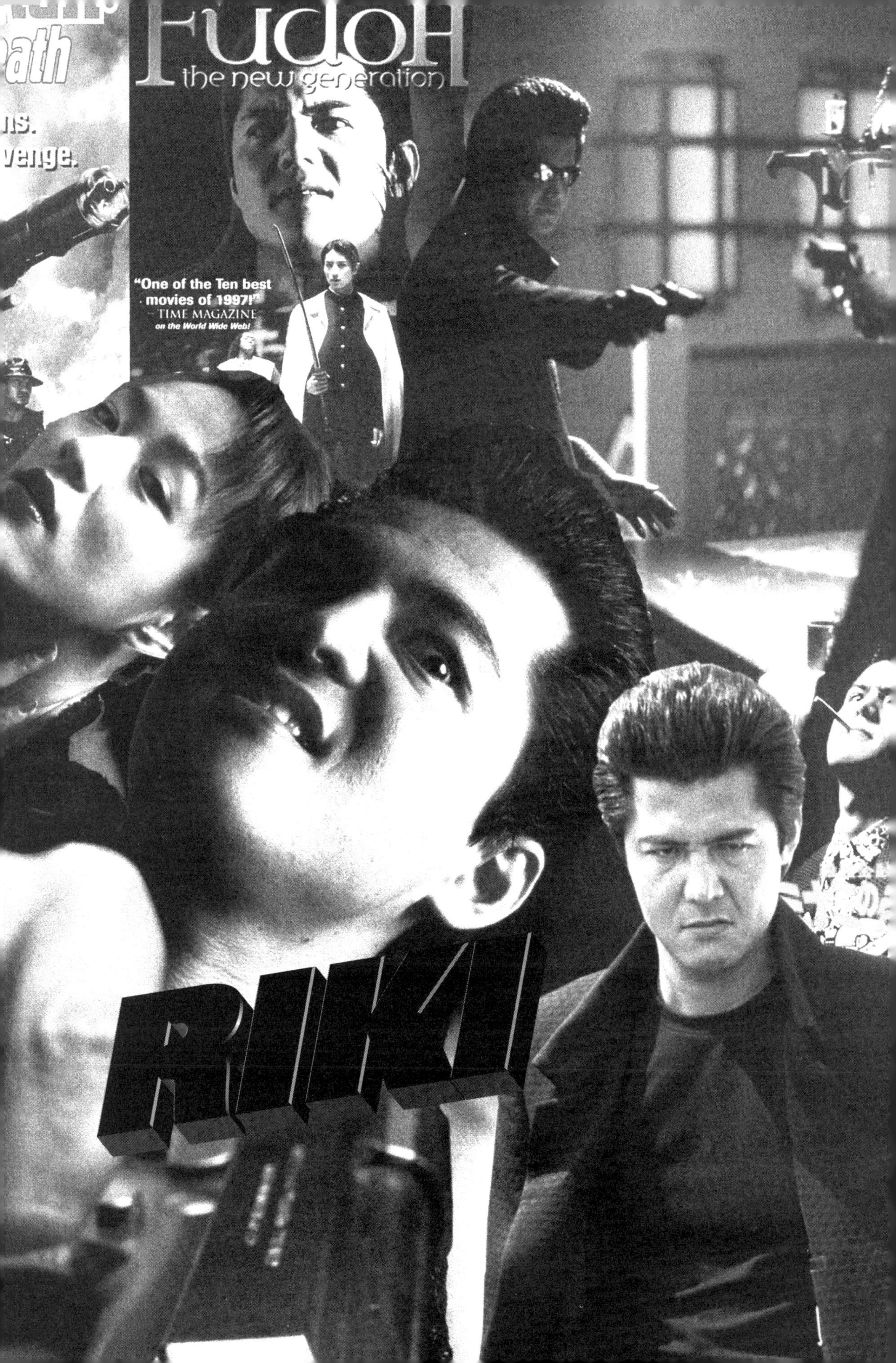

ath
ns.
venge.
Fudoh
the new generation
"One of the Ten best movies of 1997!"
– TIME MAGAZINE
on the World Wide Web!
RIKI

MIIKE

09/16/01

Takashi Miike is supposed to be at the Toronto Film Festival for a pair of midnight screenings of his latest film, *Kuroshiya Ichi* (aka *Ichi the Killer*). But the events of Tuesday the 11th have dramatically changed both Miike's travel plans and the state of things in general.

Owing to the attacks on the World Trade Center and the Pentagon, Miike has been diverted to San Francisco. Now, slightly hung over from almost empty, save for the employees, who have the disposition of the recently beat-up. There's no ignoring it. We are in one of history's periodic shitstorms.

"I got a call from Japan early on Tuesday morning," Miike says, his eyes hidden behind shades brimming with the rainbow colors of an oil slick. "I turned on the TV barely half awake. The situation was worse than I could imagine. This was real people. Real human beings with more stupidity, more violence, more sadness, and more pain than any movie could have. This improvise. Within 24 hours, he's made multiple appearances at local Bay Area screenings of his 1999 films *Audition* and *Dead or Alive*. His films are regularly playing at international film festivals. Short-run engagements are on the increase. Miike's come a long way since graduating from the Yokohama Academy of Broadcasting and his directorial debut with 1991's straight-to-video sex romp *Topu! Minipato tai—Eye Catch Junction* (Squall! Miniskirt Patrol Force). And after a decade of grinding out over forty TV shows, V-cinema productions and theatrical

"Love."

going to like," he replies. "If I try to make a film to satisfy everyone's needs, then it's going to be a boring film. As long as there will be some people who are deeply pleased, then I will be happy. Maybe it's a kind of self-centered desire to make films for these kinds of reasons, but if the world is going to allow me to do this, that's great. And that seems to be what's happening now."

While there's a good deal of diversity to be found in the Miike filmography, the real stunnas, which include 1996's *Fudoh—The New Generation*, *Audition*, and *Dead or Alive*, feature superlative outbursts of taboo imagery and sex-and-violence like you've never imagined. One often feels while watching a Miike movie that a) there are no rules and b) the person in charge must be a total and complete maniac.

"I'm just an ordinary guy with an ordinary life," he says reassuringly. "I have a family and parents who are very ordinary. I want my kids to go to a good school, and I'll be happy if they do. I don't want to create anything that will hurt them. However, I believe that I should have a lot of freedom. In other words, the freedom that you can't have in real life."

Now in his early forties, Miike's background clearly nurtured a desire for personal independence.

"I grew up in Osaka in the Kawachi district. It was pretty rough there. It's where they shot Shintaro Katsu's *Akumiyo* series [Bad Reputation, 16 films, 1961-74]. He was a local hero, and I liked him very much. Boys who grow up there love riding motorbikes and playing pachinko. You can imagine that guys like that are not exposed to a wide variety of movies. Of course, I'm speaking about myself here as well. So I didn't grow up being a film buff at all. I never had the time to watch videos. To this day, if I watch TV, I have to channel surf. I can't stay on one thing too long. It's not because I get bored easily. There are so many things going on at once inside of that box, the only way to have control over it is to surf. So there is a lot of stuff I don't know about film history.

"For me, film is something to bump into by accident. I like the feeling of chance encounters. Why did I meet this person? Why did I stumble across this film? If I started studying film, I would have to be more aggressive about it. So maybe I don't

217

really want to do that. I'd rather just keep bumping into them.

"I used to be an assistant director for Yukio Noda. He was working on a TV drama series for Shochiku. It wasn't an action show, so it wasn't his usual kind of project. I met him first in a working environment, and I didn't really know who he was. There was a lot of talk about him behind his back on the set. 'This guy used to make feature films, but now he can only get work on TV,' that sort of thing. After I found out about him, I secretly checked out his old stuff on video. I liked *Zero-ka no onna akai wapa* (Zero Woman—Red Handcuffs, 1974) and his *Furyo bancho* (Delinquent Boss) movies very much. Also, there's this amazing scene in his *Tokyo fundoshi geisha* (Tokyo Loincloth Geisha, 1975), a spectacle battle between women and men using sexual intercourse. When I saw that, I thought, all the cool stuff I wanted to do, this guy has already done it!"

Miike's films seem to draw attention to themselves for their own legendary excesses, their noise and sensation. After all, glimpses of bestiality and scatology can be awfully hard to ignore. Yet there is frequently more going on under the hood in Miike's films than a cursory glance can turn up. His loosely connected *Kuroshakai* (Black Society, 1995-1999) trilogy examined Chinese-Japanese race relations through the grimy haze of a multicultural Asian underworld. 2000's *Hyoryu gai* (Hazard City, aka *The City of Lost Souls*) unfolds in a variety of spoken languages which include Japanese, Chinese, Russian, and Portuguese. In some ways, Miike's films can be considered progressive as much as transgressive.

"The reality is that different kinds of people are in Japan, so naturally they have to appear in films. They have entered the world of the yakuza, so if you make a yakuza movie, they have to be represented. Tokyo and particularly Shinjuku are very remarkable places in the sense that so many people pass through the streets and buildings there. Different roads converge in the same place. You have ordinary people passing through who live in their ordinary world. You have the Chinese community passing through. The yakuza have their world there. And the women who work in the clubs have their own world there. And

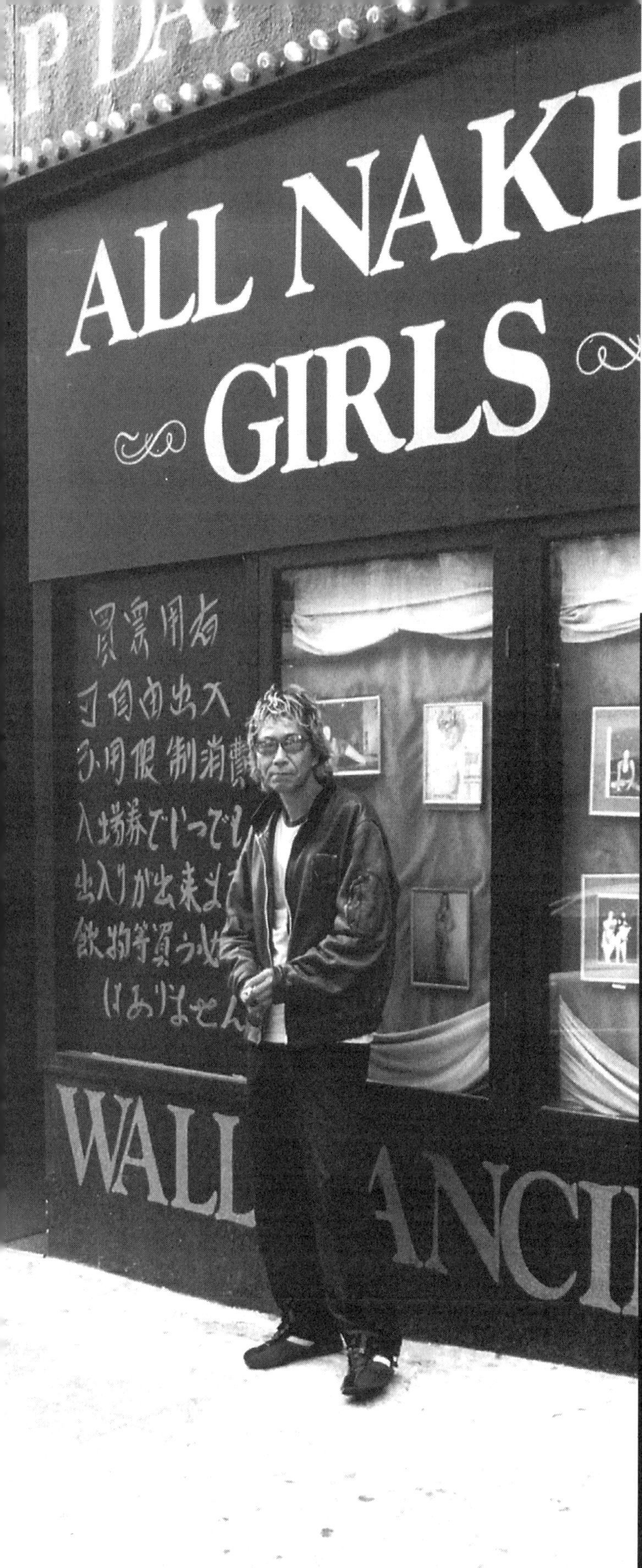
ALL NAKE
GIRLS
WALL
ANCI

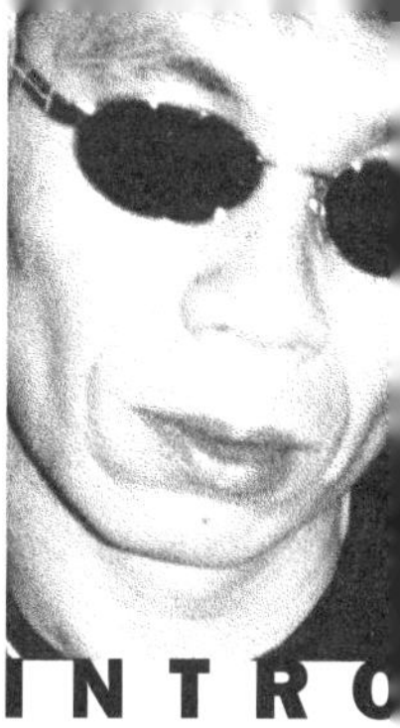

INTRO

these worlds all exist in the same place. Perhaps reality is even more remarkable than what we see in the movies. In some ways, the middle section of *Dead or Alive* is kind of a documentary in that I'm not trying to describe these guys as great men. I tried to make them ordinary. But even in the most boring life, there is always some kind of drama, like when people try to progress. Or people who just don't do well. I'm always attracted to that side of human nature."

This might be fine for ordinary guys or great men, but Miike's cinematic world can sometimes be a tough one for women. There's a nasty bit of breast mutilation in *Ichi the Killer*. A woman is actually drowned in her own feces in *Dead or Alive*. Meanwhile in *DOA*, cop Show Aikawa and crook Riki Takeuchi play out a kind of highly combustible love story amongst themselves.

"Well, men do like men! Even a little boy in Japan can fall in love with [Seattle Mariner] Ichiro. The feeling of longing can be the same for actors and music idols. It's not necessarily a physical kind of love. The problem with women in films is that they tend to bring with them a lot of logic, which requires reason and motivation. Too many logical things will destroy my films. Naturally, you still have to have women in films, mine included. But they get on my nerves. So it's my tendency to say 'let's get rid of them.'"

Such hard-line tactics can alienate the heck out of an audience. The final reel of *Audition*, for instance, inevitably sends people of both sexes fleeing for the exit.

"I counted twelve people who walked out of *Audition* last night," he notes, referring to the local San Francisco screening he just attended, not without some glee in his voice. "I usually predict that even more people are going to leave the theater than actually do. I can understand how those people feel. If there are going to be people who enjoy it, there will be people who won't. There is usually a balance on a case-by-case basis. But the people who actually make the motion to get up and leave tend to be very, very upset. You can tell by the way they walk. The people still seated become immediately aware of others leaving the theater. This makes the people that decide to stay realize, strongly, that they have chosen not to leave. 'I don't feel like those people feel.' I find it very interesting to watch."

Experiments in audience reaction are one thing, but how do you convince others to finance films that seem destined to scare away segments of the audience?

"The original manga of *Ichi the Killer* is itself very shocking and violent. It would be impossible and meaningless to make that kind of story into an accessible film—at least the violent aspects of the story. I felt like I had to go beyond the original manga, to make it more shocking, so it could still manage to have an impact. The philosophy with *Ichi* was that if we tried hard, then we could at least make back what we spent. We didn't have one single sponsor who put a heck of a lot of money into the project, expecting international sales and distribution. So the pressure to deliver a giant return isn't so great. Obviously one of the biggest weapons a filmmaker can wield is a big budget and lots of time to shoot. However, instead of getting those weapons, I'm getting a lot of freedom. The people who don't accept what I do are usually studio people. Recently I did a musical New Year's film for Shochiku (*Katakurike no kofuku*, aka *Happiness of the Katakuri Family*). New Years' films require a certain kind of handling. They are usually family films that anyone can watch, but I ended up making a crazy film. The Shochiku people saw it and were speechless. They said they don't know how they can show it or promote it!"

Musicals, yakuza films, gentle comedies (1998's *Bird People in China*), karate movies (three *Bodyguard Kiba* movies not starring Sonny Chiba), young adult dramas (1997's *Kishiwada shonen gurentai*, aka *Kishiwada Boy Soldiers*). Miike has worked in numerous styles and genres. Or has he?

"I don't have the common sense to acknowledge genres. Genres are for people who have to promote or critique films. As long as you are human, the bottom line of everything creative is simply to ask: why do we exist? Every theme seems to go back to that point, although I don't necessarily use that as the central theme in my films. To me, genre doesn't impose any meaning. I just want to experiment and create."

Nevertheless, in 2002, Miike will be setting his sights on one of Japan's most venerable screen icons: Zatoichi the blind swordsman, the role that Miike's childhood idol Shintaro Katsu made famous.

"People are probably thinking, 'If Miike does *Zatoichi*, it's going to be crazy.' But I want to betray those expectations by making something that's actually very subtle and very quiet. The character of Zatoichi himself is very simple and pure. Originally Takeshi Kitano wanted to both star and direct. But when you play Zatoichi, you can't see anything, so how is he supposed to direct? *[laughs]* So right now we are in negotiations with a younger actor. Zatoichi is my treasure for many reasons. It's something that I really want to do and do right."

Shintaro Katsu (1931-1997) acted in, directed, and produced films. By all accounts he lived a wild life of sex, drugs, and general misbehavior. It's not too hard to see why Miike might want to collaborate with him, even if only posthumously. Might they be kindred spirits of sorts?

"There's a lot of chaos, but there is also a need for balance in me. Once a year for the last three years, I've made films for the Kumamoto Department of Education. Because they are so far out in the suburbs, they haven't seen too many of my films. But the governor saw *Dead or Alive*, and he really liked it. One of his underlings said, 'Why does that bazooka come out of nowhere?' The governor said, 'You are so stupid! You have no sense for men's fantasy. If you really are a man, then you have a bazooka!' This gives me hope for the Japanese government, that they can understand this." Miike pauses to flash his teeth and smile broadly. Quickly though, he goes back to deadpanning utter sincerity.

"These films are made to help support the neighborhood through rough economic times. The stories are based on historical subjects and mythological characters native to the area. The next one will be about the collapse of the Yamato kingdom, only with an extremely cheap budget. We'll make a spectacle with dry ice and fire. We don't use village actors, we hire professionals like Renji Ishibashi and Ren Osugi. They'll be wearing animal costumes and masks. It's like a bunch of friends playing at making a movie. But I can't continue if we all act too much like friends. You don't want people to think that making a film is just for fun. There's a difference between enjoying it and just playing at it."

We walk out of the deserted hotel for a smoke break and snapshots. The intersection of Mason and O'Farrell street looks utterly unaffected by rumors and the reality of war. Tourists and street trash rub shoulders and avoid eye contact. Strip joints and massage parlors slumber behind closed daytime doors. Miike passes in front of a Japanese video store that stocks many of his films. For a moment he seems to be everywhere, except where he should be: back in Japan to wrap up post-production on *Dead or Alive 3*.

"If I can't get on a plane by tomorrow, I'll buy a cheap video camera and start shooting something right here. What do you think? Want to make a movie?"

SPECIAL WIDESCREEN EDITION
Fudoh
the new generation
"One of the Ten best movies of 1997!"
TIME MAGAZINE
on the World Wide Web
Original Japanese Dialogue with English Subtitles

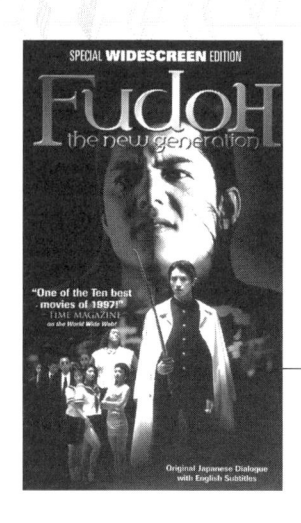

Fudoh—The New Generation

Gokudo sengoku shi—Fudoh (Rascal Civil War—Fudoh)

1996, Gaga Communications
Director Takashi Miike
Cast Shosuke Tanihara, Mihono Nomoto, Toru Minegishi, Riki Takeuchi

"A body becomes stiff unless you keep changing old blood for new," says high school student Riki Fudoh (Shosuke Tanihara), explaining why he's using an arsenal of child-age killers and lethal sailor-suited chicks as torpedoes in an underworld civil war whose implications are immense, stretching to North Korea and America.

A single family grievance is to blame. The preteen Fudoh was traumatized one night by the sight of seeing his dad (Toru Minegishi) kill his much adored older brother in a primal scene of father, son, sword, and blood. Now Fudoh seeks to bring down pop's organization and anyone who stands in his way—bad timing, since dad is planning a lucrative merger with a dangerous rival faction led by scowling Riki Takeuchi (sporting one of the screen's most spectacular-ever mullets). All the pieces have been set up. Now it's time for director Miike to knock 'em down.

After 1995's transitional *Shinjuku kuroshakai—China Mafia senso* (Shinjuku Black Society—China Mafia War), which marked Takashi's theatrical debut following numerous V-cinema productions, it was *Fudoh—The New Generation* that truly announced potential fulfilled. Like *Dead or Alive, Fudoh* was originally made for the direct-to-video market, but when the parent company saw what they had, an upgrade to theatrical release commenced. As if preparing for their future assault on *Battle Royale*, the Eirin ratings board, strongly objecting to the placement of children in violent situations, slapped the film with the equivalent of an NC-17 rating. Still, the good word managed to get out about the film, and it even wound up on *Time* magazine's online edition as one of 1997's best films.

Fudoh's episodic story unfolds at its own sweet pace, refusing to go into temporal overdrive, its tone alternating deftly between delusions of high drama (Miike has said that he'd like to do Shakespeare someday—one imagines it would be like Fudoh's opening reel) and gory jack-in-the-box surprises. The cast, verily, the royalty of V-cinema, proudly give it their all, be it Riki Takeuchi stubbing out his cigarette on old rockabilly star Mickey Curtis' severed head, or Mihono Nomoto doing an extended demonstration of her hermaphroditic powers still clad in her (his?) schoolgirl's uniform.

Utterly lacking the gritty documentary touches and racial focus that marks Miike's finest films, *Fudoh* is simple, honest, lowest-common-denominator entertainment. That doesn't stop the technical aspects from still being top notch, especially the cinematography by Hideo Yamamoto, one of the field's leading lights who went on to shoot Takeshi Kitano's *Hana-bi* (Fireworks) in addition to *Dead or Alive*. Two disappointing non-Miike V-cinema sequels to *Fudoh* followed, but they needn't have bothered. The old blood was replaced by the new blood the first time around.

☞ **Available on subtitled VHS from Tokyo Shock**

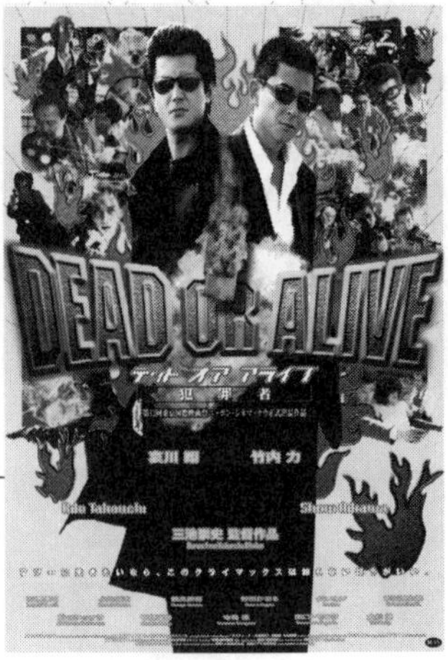
DEAD OR ALIVE

Dead or Alive

Dead or Alive

1999, Daiei/Toei Video
Director Takashi Miike
Cast Show Aikawa, Riki Takeuchi

Countdown "1...2...3...4..." Blast off for Japan. Tokyo. Shinjuku mean streets and Kabuki-cho cutups. Pow. Like, now. *Dead or Alive* doesn't begin so much as erupt in your face. Then it attacks your adrenal glands via the mucus membranes. The pulse quickens. The sphincter tightens. Riki Takeuchi materializes, like a god, out of nowhere. But there's no viewer identification with him, or even top rival Show Aikawa (118 V-cinema films to his credit and climbing), only with *DOA*'s denizens of excess. The slob slurping up bowls of noodles all sped up. The salaryman who huffs the World's Biggest Line, especially. Like him, we are somewhere high and mighty on Shinjuku *shabu*.

But like all kick-ass highs, the rush can't last forever. It would be impossible to even think so. Then, the more pedestrian mid-section of *DOA* kicks in. A bit of documentary, according to the director; a draggy hangover according to some viewers. With only occassional shocks to sustain the interest of the now hopelessly jaded, the head-scratchers miss out on the film's real best attributes. Even with a three-week shooting schedule, a script based on Michael Mann's *Heat*, and a strictly V-cinema conceit (Riki Takeuchi verses Show Aikawa at last!) Miike does real work in *Dead or Alive*, making observations on racial identity and the plight of immigrants and foreigners in Japan, speculating even that "signals from space" might have something to do with it all. Like the earlier films that made up his *Kuroshakai* series, meaning lingers in long takes and low-lit locations.

Then there's that ending, like so many of Miike's arrivals and departures, an unforgettable be-all-end-all. The irresistible force meets the immoveable object. It defies analysis, demands it. The facts: the director tossed the scripted ending out the window and, as would be the case with his later films, asked his buddies at NHK's CGI department to lend a hand. Tired of being asked to explain what it's all supposed to mean over and over, Miike now flatly refuses to discuss *DOA*'s ending anymore in interviews and Q&A sessions. Before you go and get that comforting sense of closure, and swear that you've learned your lesson and you'll never do it again, Miike has conjured up two seemingly impossible sequels to *Dead or Alive*, reuniting Show and Riki for more fun with guns and your head.

☞ **Available from Viz Films/Tidepoint Pictures**

REVIEW

Audition
Audition

1999, Omega/Daiei
Director Takashi Miike
Cast Ryo Ishibashi, Eihi Shiina, Matsuda Miyuki, Renji Ishibashi

So if it's really the case that Japanese horror boils down to some kind of fundamental fear of the fairer sex, then Miike's *Audition* (based on a novel by notorious *Almost Transparent Blue* novelist Ryu Murakami) could very well be the consummate modern Japanese horror film. Perhaps even the sum total of all that we've learned thus far, honed to razor-wire sharpness with which to snip off all excess genre baggage. The trouble is, *Audition* isn't really a horror movie. Even as disgusted audience members twitch and shout and dash for the exits during the black heart of the final reel, Takashi Miike flatly denies that he's even made a scare show.

"Genre is for people who have to market films to audiences," he's said in defense of any attempt at categorization. Still, some people have to do their jobs. And maybe an alternate way to sell *Audition* would be...a Love Story. A bit of boy-meets-girl and how, at least from the male perspective, everything falls apart from there. Someone tells a lie. Someone has an unpleasant past. Someone gets hurt. Maybe him. Maybe her. Maybe you.

"Words lie. There is truth in pain," says Asami (played by former Bennetton model Eihi Shiina), who makes her first appearance in *Audition* clad in a dazzling all-white dress, her face framed by long flowing black hair: a dead giveaway to anyone still clinging to Japanese genre motifs.

Widower and TV producer Aoyama (ex-rock star Ryo Ishibashi) is too lonely and myopic to see anything in Asami beyond his own needs for a romantic prospect. And he's such a nice guy, with such a nice son and a cute dog that we want it all to work out for him somehow. Heck, we'd probably like to take our grandma to this movie which so far has proven as sweet and low-impact as *Shall We Dance?*

But eventually, Miike violates the implicit trust that an audience lends its filmmakers. He loves to toy with us, and because that usually means entertainment, we are complacent.

In *Audition*'s final moments, Miike goes beyond the limits, brilliantly cutting off sympathies and expectations at the root. As the credits near, it isn't fear or pain that makes viewers bolt for the exits. After all, pain doesn't lie. The fact is that for the last 90 minutes or so, we've gone and given away the keys to the car and made a filmmaker our god. And like a revelation of Gnostic proportions, the peeling back of truth hurts even as it sets you free.

☞ **Available subbed on VHS and DVD from Vitagraph**

LOVE.
漂流街
THE HAZARD CITY

The City of Lost Souls

Hyoryu gai, aka The Hazard City

2000, Daiei/Tokyo FM/Tokuma/Tohokashinsha
Director Takashi Miike
Cast Teah, Michelle Reis, Koji Kikkawa, Mitsuhiro Oikawa

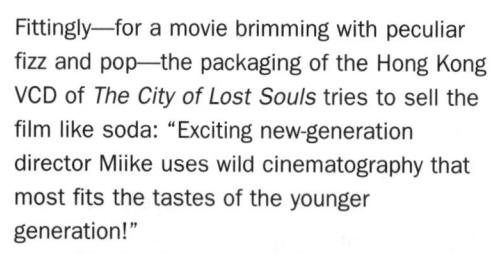

Fittingly—for a movie brimming with peculiar fizz and pop—the packaging of the Hong Kong VCD of *The City of Lost Souls* tries to sell the film like soda: "Exciting new-generation director Miike uses wild cinematography that most fits the tastes of the younger generation!"

Adapted from a novel by author Seishu Hase (also the author of *Sleepless Town*), *Lost Souls* opens with the daring rescue of Chinese hairstylist Kei (Michelle Reis) by her lover Mario (Brazilian soccer player Teah), just as she's being deported out of the country illegal-alien-style by an immigration bus. The intertitles tell us we are somewhere in boring old Saitama prefecture in Japan, but the screen shows a wide stretch of desert southwest of Los Angeles. Together, the lovebirds jump out of a chopper and land, Looney Tunes-style, smack in the middle of Shinjuku.

All throughout *The City of Lost Souls*, Miike tinkers with the surface of things: locations, interiors, exteriors. The hideout of the Chinese underworld (led by very Japanese rock star Mitsuhiro Oikawa) is literally in an underground cave. Displaced people from all over the globe replicate their old environs, grafting them to Japanese soil. Iconography abounds. Russians give impromptu demonstrations on how to imbibe vodka. Crucifixes and the Virgin Mary add a dash of old time religion. Dueling chickens reprise bullet time from *The Matrix*. The Chinese face down yakuza rivals in rigged games of ping pong.

When midgets start brushing their teeth with stolen cocaine and Miike starts framing shots from inside of turd-strewn toilet bowls, it begins to feel like *Lost Souls* has gone way beyond mere kitchen-sink mentality. The only thing that seems to be missing are actual characters. Kei and Mario (who was a pimp in the novel) are young and in love. That's about all we get to know. If Miike's previous gangland films come straight outta Shinjuku, then *Lost Souls* belongs to the fashion fair of the Shibuya ward and the area's mega-trendy 109 department store even makes a cameo in the Japanese poster.

On the other hand, Miike remains as dedicated as ever to giving us a wider conception of Japan's fragile race relations, even if only in cartoon terms. The Brazilians may write the word *LOVE* in colossal letters in their own blood, but the romance of Japan and China ends in a big wet male-to-male kiss.

Is this the taste of a new generation?

☞ **Available subtitled as a Region 3 DVD from Mei Ah**

A TAKASHI MIIKE FILM
ICHI THE KILLER
殺し屋

Ichi the Killer

Kuroshiya Ichi

2001, Omega/Emperor Multimedia/Star Max/Alpha Group/Spike/Excellent Film
Director Takashi Miike
Cast Nao Omori, Tadanobu Asano, Shinya Tsukamoto

The camera runs amok through the streets of Kabuki-cho, the most sleazy and violent place in Japan, while the staff and cast credits are scratched on the surface of the film. Finally, we focus on an apartment where a gigolo is blaming his trick baby for bringing home less money than before. While he beats her and deforms her face into something like Frankenstein's monster, a Peeping Tom jacks off while spying the torture. Then he cums and the camera gets close to the splash of his sperm. You can see a name oozing out on the surface of the drop: Ichi the Killer. It's also the name of a manga by Hideo Yamamoto (no relation to the cinematographer of the same name), which is actually banned in some prefectures for its violence. No wonder Miike's film adaptation is rated NC-17 in Japan.

Our hero (sort of) is Ichi (Nao Omori). He is timid, a wimp, and almost autistic, but when he breaks into tears, he turns into a one-man Texas Chainsaw Massacre! He is a deadly martial artist, and with a blade installed in his boot's heel, he cuts his enemies in half from head to crotch before the fool notices what's happened to him. What this means is that this movie is the biggest orgy of blood I've seen since Peter Jackson's *Dead Alive*.

Whoever makes Ichi cry shoots a fountain of blood from his throat, gets his face cut off like a Halloween mask, or gets sliced into mincemeat. Ichi butchers the men of Kakihara (Tadanobu Asano), the craziest yakuza in Kabuki-cho, one after another. Kakihara is even more dangerous than Ichi. He is a King of Pain. Like Bob Flanagan, supermasochist, he pleasures himself by piercing and scarring his body.

He loves to give pain to other people too. He tortures other yakuza by hanging them from ceilings with hooks, turning them into modern art objects. Kakihara is bored and tired of everything, including himself. So he is excited by rumors about Ichi and dying to face the faceless killer. He wants the ultimate pain that Ichi can give him, and this makes him want to live.

Ichi the Killer is an existentialist story about pain, or maybe a sado-masochistic homosexual love story (though for Kakihara, it's only one-sided). All the women in this film are treated like punching bags, literally. One gets beaten and kicked to death, another's ankle gets cut, and another's nipple gets pinched and cut. Ouch! Such painful and unbearable images are realistically embellished by special makeup and computer graphics created by NHK Enterprise, which was established for NHK's educational programs. And perhaps that's the strangest thing about this movie. (Tomo Machiyama)

☞ **Import only**

Non-Mike Riki Bonus!

竹内 力 主演 Riki Takeuch
HARD BOILE

Hardboiled

Hardboiled

1997, Maxam
Director Katsuji Kanazawa
Cast Riki Takeuchi, Mihono Nomoto, Toru Minegishi

Riki Takeuchi is perhaps the most unlikely candidate ever for a girls'-school bus driver, but there he is frowning behind the wheel while his noisy passengers say “cheese” and take snapshots. The flash of a camera distracts Riki, and he crashes into a local yakuza's car. Riki is beaten senseless, and the gangsters, demanding payoffs, quickly begin tormenting the hapless school officials.

Back at home, Riki's wife starts flashing him pricey real estate catalogs, dropping the hint that she wants to move out of their crummy apartment. Soon.

Riki is now A Man on the Edge. One day on the job, he simply stops driving and walks away from the bus, leaving his young charges miffed and confused.

Riki aimlessly wanders through the streets, gets mugged, and has his wallet stolen by a total stranger. Riki doggedly chases his attacker, who (admiring his strength) invites him up for a friendly drink. The thief is a down-on-his-luck boxer who can't afford a shot at a title match.

After an impromptu *Fight Club* session with the boxer, the newly invigorated Riki calls a meeting with his antagonists, who are proclaiming it's payoff time. But it's actually *payback* time, as Riki bashes the pastel-suited thug's head in. The mob boss (a horrifically dressed Toru Minegishi) then berates his boys and demands a pinkie chopping for allowing a frikkin' bus driver to get the better of them.

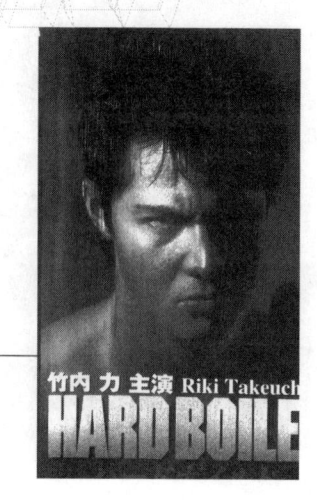

Meanwhile, in a sleazy nightclub, Riki teams up with prostitute Mihono Nomoto. Having both killed a couple of yakuza tormentors, they decide to flee the country, but not before coming up with a brilliant plan: rip off yakuza cash first!

Riki convinces the boxer to join them in the quest. Then he says goodbye to wife and child, kicking off a new outlaw existence by riding around on a motorcycle and groping his new sex partner Mihono.

The trio ambush the bag men in a messy shootout. The dough is theirs!

Having masterminded a successful heist, Riki's bunch decides to call it a day. But just as Mihono tries make it out of the country, she's nabbed by the surviving yakuza, dragged back to their office, and “fed” to a bald creepie.

Even though this is V-cinema, it's still a yakuza movie, and certain rules must be obeyed. Riki storms into the office like Ken Takakura in the old days. After a bloody gun battle (the girl gets it in the face), Riki and Toru engage in a clichéd duel with *dosu* knives.

Epilogue: the boxer gets his title shot, but he leaves the ring in a oxygen mask and a stretcher. Riki wanders around Tokyo Dome. Out of the corner of his eye, he sees his wife and child one last time. He shrugs, his thoughts impenetrable as the video-generated credits roll and the camera careens with random precision around rainy, nighttime Shinjuku.

☞ **Import only**

斬る
CUT!
He was only a driver.
what?what changed him!
Hardboild
Suddenly.
突然でんねん!
I'm bussy but..

竹内力

Riki Takeuchi
Superstar

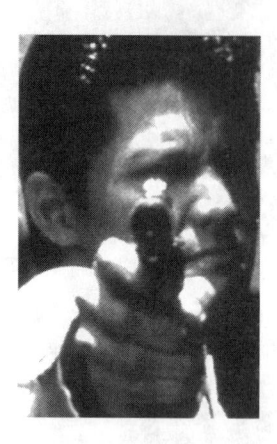

The collapse of interstellar clouds, the emergence of globules light years long, generating massive amounts of thermal energy: this is what occurs when a star is born.

The process down at your local Japanese video store is no less dramatic. Go look for some Bunta Sugawara or Ken Takakura oldies-but-goodies in the Yakuza or Action sections. You'll find that the reassuring chestnuts of old are rapidly being put out to pasture to make more room for tons of cheap straight-to-video potboilers.

All of which seem to star this one guy. This guy.

A sneering mug of mad, arrogant youth clad in a sour lime-green suit, so full of it he's actually wearing a bright yellow tie to compliment the sickly colored ensemble. There he is on the video box, sprawled out across the back of a limo, howling into a cell phone, or seated in front of a table covered in yen notes, his face a cockeyed sneer, legs spread "look-at-my-crotch" wide.

This is Riki Takeuchi, undisputed king and master thespian of Japanese V-cinema.

Riki was born Chikara Takeuchi ("Riki" means power—sounds cooler, huh?) on January 4, 1964 in Oita prefecture. His official bio tells us that the Rikster was a humble bank teller in Osaka before speeding away to a new life in Tokyo on the back of a 400cc motorcycle. There, Riki was discovered by a talent scout while working at an *izakaiya* bar, did some modeling work (just like Bunta!), and made his feature-film debut in *House* director Nobuhiko Obayashi's *Kare no auto-bi, kanojo no shima* (His Motorbike, Her Island) in 1986.

In addition to acting, Riki also currently designs a clothing line, runs a "boutique Riki Takeuchi" mail order service, and puts on cabaret shows for adoring lady fans. He lists among his hobbies "scuba diving and watching films," but it hardly seems possible that he could have a spare moment on hand.

After all, Riki has appeared in nearly 150 film productions in a 15-year time span. We repeat: 150 films in 15 years. Riki is an industry within the Japanese film industry. And at a time when the bloodless whelps of countless TV dramas have become the new media models for Japanese masculinity, scowling, howling Riki is a throwback to the hot-blooded yakuza heroes of yore.

Instead of replacing the old guard, as you might have initially feared, Riki is actually carrying on the torch with millennial multimedia gusto, even if that means he is more of a self-replicating virus than a trademark of quality.

With his workload and yakuza gestalt appearance, Riki has to be more than human, and perhaps no one since *Street Fighter*-era Sonny Chiba looks as much like a manga character escaped from pen-and-ink prison.

After all, many of Riki's movies are less like films and more like neverending volumes of *tankoban* graphic novels. At last count, his *Jingi* V-cinema series was up to number 27. Meanwhile, the *Minami no teio* (King of Minami) series, based on a serial in *Weekly Manga Goraku*, is up to (choke!) 32 installments.

And then there are the copious one-shots. Here's a box with a crosseyed Riki holding a gun up to his own head, the copy promising with Marvel Comics-like certainty, "Riki Dies!" Here's one where Riki is almost unrecognizably covered in blood and screaming. Go into other sections of the video store and you might find *Pachinko Game Drifter*, where grinning comedy good-guy Riki makes merry with little steel balls. Or perhaps he's playing a working-class antihero in *Hot Blood! 2nd Generation Shopping Center Owner*. When you make up to 27 films a year, subject matter is bound to be a variable. So is quality.

The devoted Riki fan puts up with it, to support him and simply to see him go through the moves. The whole phenomenon isn't unlike that of Elvis movies, only with pistol whippings and beat downs instead of musical numbers about clambakes.

Having taken over Japan in less than two decades, Riki is now invading US video stores as well, in the guise of dubbed/subtitled films of no fixed quality.

Asia Pulp Cinema's *Blowback: Love & Death* is actually 1990's *Blowback 2*, a three-way shotgun wedding between Sam Peckinpah, Spaghetti Westerns (Riki pulls a Gatling gun out of a coffin just like Django), and mind-numbing post-*Missing in Action*, shot-in-the-Philippines pyrotechnics. Fun enough as a day trip, but "old manga face" seems fundamentally more at home when wandering around Kanto and Kansai than the outskirts of Manila.

Asia Pulp Cinema has also released *Tokyo Mafia: Yakuza Wars*, a stunningly average Riki outing from 1995. The opening sequence, featuring Japanese and Chinese gangsters chopping each others' blocks off smack in the middle of crowded Kabuki-cho, is a gas, but from here the thrill is gone fast, despite the fun premise of Riki riding to the top of the underworld on the back of the illegal whale-meat racket.

Tokyo Shock struck next with 1999's *Wild Criminal*, which sadly is no great shakes either (notice a pattern emerging?). The "Riki is missing" plot means Our Man doesn't occupy the central position that he does on the box, but the film can boast of having actual characters (a pair of abused yakuza women, one of them Mihono Nomoto from *Fudoh* and *Hardboiled*, looking for some payback) and feels convincingly nasty in the key areas of misogyny and sadism.

Since it should be clear by now that Riki's V-cinema films are mostly steaming piles of crap any way, the very worst of them would have to be something special. Which brings us to *The Yakuza Way*, directed by Shundo Okawa (who also helmed 1999's *Nobody*, also starring Riki), produced by Simon Tse (*Message from Space*) and released in the USA by York Entertainment. Primo pompadour Riki invades Southern California, gets mixed up with suitcases of coke and dough, Mexicans and cops, and converses with the worst actors you've ever seen in unintelligible broken English. ("Where did you learn English?" someone asks Riki. "Prison," he answers convincingly.) In short, *The Yakuza Way* is a true trash film jackpot and a must see.

And if *The Yakuza Way*'s images of Riki brazenly smoking cigarettes at LAX and driving a muscle car down the 101 Hollywood Freeway aren't proof of a star now being born in our own backyard, maybe it's time to buy a better telescope. 東

Boutique Riki Takeuchi

By TDC Fujiki

This interview with Riki Takeuchi first appeared in Japanese in Eiga Hi-Ho *magazine during the theatrical release of* Dead or Alive *in early 2000. Translation by Andy Nakatani.*

In 1999, you were in about 18 films. There aren't many people who can do so many films.

Not many people do *[laughs]*. But compared to the previous year, or even the year before that, the number has become smaller. Two years ago I did 27 films, and last year I think it was 23.

How do you work so much? Does it affect your health?

I think I almost worked myself to death two years ago. That's why I really decreased the number of films I did in 1999. Next year, I'll do even less. Otherwise, I'll end up in some kind of accident or something and regret it.

Dead or Alive *has been getting a really great response. Even today people started to line up in front of the theater at noon.*

Are you sure they weren't lined up for pachinko? *[laughs]* I saw it with an audience at the Tokyo International Film Festival, and I was really pleased. It reminded me of seeing a movie in America, when I'm vacationing there or on location or something. You know, the audience over there gets into it like it's a concert or something. That's what it felt like. When Japanese people are in a movie theater they're pretty subdued. To make them react and get excited is something only Miike can do. That's entertainment baby!

Was *Fudoh—The New Generation* (1997) the last time you worked with Miike?

Yeah, I did *Peanuts* with him in '96, then *Fudoh*, and then *DOA*.

How was it working with Miike?

Same as always. Everything is up to him. You just do what he tells you to do. With other directors, I offer a lot of input, and try to think about what my character is doing, but with Miike you don't know what's going on, so you have to leave everything up to him. The script is always changing. You ask him what's happening in the scene, and he'll say, "Ummm, I'm thinking about it." *[laughs]* So it's better to just do as he says and try not to think too much about what's happening. But it's fun.

Speaking of diverging from the script, the crazy last scene in *DOA* where you pull that thing out of your chest—what was your take on that?

That was—*balls! [laughs]* But seriously, if you try to think too much about Miike's world you'll start getting really confused.

When I asked Miike what that was, he said, "That weapon is called Riki Takeuchi."

HA HA HA HA HA!!

When you take on the mafia in *DOA*, you use a pump-action shotgun. You also used the same kind of gun in *The Yakuza Way*. Do you like that type of gun?

Yes, I like it. I ride motorcycles and if you're

RIKI
RIKI TAKEUCHI
RIKI TAKEUCHIブランドの製品カタログを御希望の方は下記まで御連絡ください。
（有）アイビーアンドエス
TEL03-5619-4730
FAX03-5619-1538
RIKI Men's
R Lady's
RIKI TAKEUCHI ブランドの直営店 大阪に4月OPEN予定！

Advertisement for fashion a la Riki.

going to shoot that type of gun while on a motorcycle you have to ride with no hands. I like riding with no hands. So that type of action is suited for me.

In* The Yakuza Way *you shoot off five or six shots riding with no hands.

When they were writing the script I asked them to let me do a "no hands" scene.

You wanted to do that?!

Yes! We were shooting on location in Los Angeles and when we talked about that scene with the crew over there, they said it was too dangerous and wouldn't let me do it. In Hollywood they would use a stunt double. The guns they use in Japanese movies are toys, but over there they use the real thing—they're heavy. And the recoil is pretty heavy too. If you were riding at 80 kph and shot a gun like that, you'd probably go down. So they said it was too dangerous and wouldn't let me do it.

But you did do it.

I told them *"I'M DOING IT!!" [laughs].* So I rode in front of the stunt team and they applauded me.

Recently, at the ends of your films I've seen the credit "Boutique Riki Takeuchi."

I'm doing my own designs. We make everything for the *Minami no teio* [King of Minami] series. For now, its all mail-order. We have women's clothing too.

You're designing women's clothes?!

That's right. But women's clothing is difficult. I guess I'm not a woman, so I don't really understand.

I suppose clothes that women design for themselves and clothes that men design for women are going to be different.

Well, sure. But all I'm trying to do is create clothes that men want women to wear. If women want to wear it, fine. If not, then that's fine too. 東

EPILOGUE

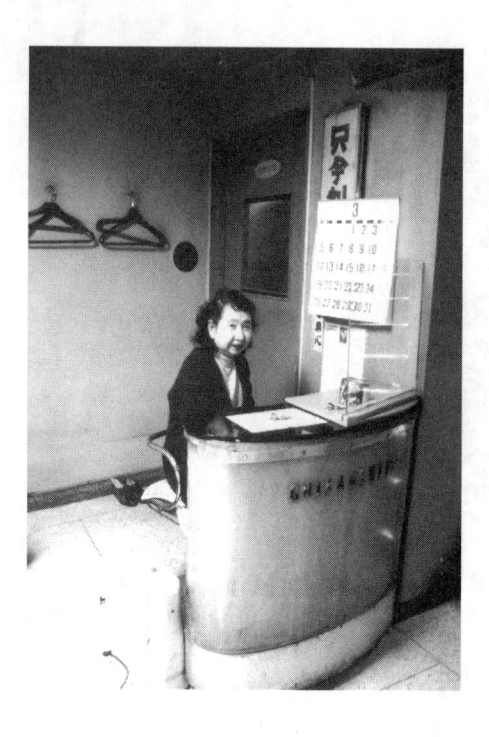

September 2000 on the border between East and South Shinjuku. Outside it's as hot as a urinary infection and as moist as you can imagine. The midday mix of rain and humidity is a quickly heralded call to get the hell off the street. Preferably to some place on the cheap with halfway decent air-conditioning. The Shinjuku Showakan nicely fits the bill. It ain't free, but at ¥1300 for a triple feature, it still beats blowing triple that on an hour of pachinko or breathing in second-hand smoke in a First Kitchen hamburger joint.

At least forty other guys have figured out as much, and they sit in the main floor like frozen stiffs. One *oyaji* has planted himself in the second row, his legs spread wide and draped over the seat in front. Looks like he's trying out the missionary position for a change. He's probably asleep.

It's almost besides the point, but there's actually a movie playing now, something called *Shinjuku junai monogatari* (Shinjuku True Love Story) which, although it begins with the Toei logo, sounds almost certain to be crap. And what the hell? Isn't this the place where they are supposed to play old school yakuza and *ninkyo eiga* from the sixties and seventies, like, all the time?

Sure enough, the pic starts on the offensive with two schoolgirls with cat in tow frolicking through East Shinjuku circa 1987. Soon enter our star, Toru Nakamura of *Be-Bop High School* fame, who's a bit like old youth Nikkatsu idol Yujiro Ishihara only now dressed to impress in a leather jacket that would make *Thriller*-era Michael Jackson drop the glove.

A case of Shinjuku true love-at-first-sight breaks out between Toru and now-forgotten actress Mina Ichijoji (although there are a couple of AV actresses currently operating under the same name). He goes out of his way to recover her lost cat, and, short on cash, he goes to the yakuza-owned "Wild Loan" company but winds up robbing the place on a whim and even stealing the boss's gold plated pistol. Local crooked cops take an interest after Toru shoots his pursuers in the train station. Once safe, the young couple pause to quietly talk it out tenderly while the cockroaches, sensing their cue, come out to dance around the seats in the theater.

The middle-aged cops hate Toru's young, rugged, handsome ass so they kidnap Mina and take her to a seedy hidden location. Toru mistakenly blames the yakuza for the deed, so he storms back to their office tossing Molotov cocktails before realizing that he's made a mistake, actually apologizing before he splits.

The karate-kicking yakuza boss breaks out the heavy artillery and soon Toru is being chased through the area by guys wielding preposterous weapons that would make G.I. Joe blush: Magnums with rifle sights, M-60 machine guns with laser scopes.

Maybe the moral of the film is supposed to be this: if someone is chasing you around Shinjuku with a flame thrower equipped with a grenade launcher attachment, it's probably a good time to take the next train to Harajuku. Instead, Toru climbs into a carpark elevator and takes the battle to the rooftops before descending down into the very bowels of the city.

But not before a mind-blowing moment of infinite reduction occurs, one that makes even the most poor, tired, huddled masses of the Showakan consider for a moment the fractal nature of time and space. Director Hiroyuki Nasu's camera records the unmistakable edifice of the Showakan as it was in 1987. The audience now ponders the same image inside the theater in the year 2000. Reality rips wide open. But the Showakan must go on.

With deft *Die Hard* moves, Toru blasts his way through the baddies (although, this being an idol movie, he never really kills anyone—suffice to say he only cripples them for life), but is still no wiser in locating his missing gal. That's when the cat comes back, leading the way to Mina's impending rape-torture at the hands of the wicked police. Toru comes crashing through the wall like the wrath of god with a machine gun in one hand, a flame thrower in the other, and that darn cat tucked away inside the flash jacket.

After the dust clears, Toru leaves Mina behind in the city and takes to the country with his one-time yakuza rival. They celebrate their new partnership by wearing matching Al Capone outfits and sharing a lovely swan-shaped paddle boat on a river. Who said this True Love Story was going to be hetero? Hey, this movie was pretty crazy after all. And now it's over.

Later, outside the Showakan, something dashes by on the quick. It's Mina Ichijoji's cat from the film, or at least a dead ringer for it, sneaking away into an alley after a second of brief eye contact. Is this low beast doing a Lassie and trying to tell you something important? Danger. Danger. Follow. Follow. And do you dare venture down the film-within-a-film-inside-a-movie-theater quantum rabbit hole tucked away behind the Shinjuku Showakan? On a day like this, what choice have you got? 東

Coming soon to the Showakan! Old movies from a bygone era.

AFTERWORD

This book is the bible of the Japanese film religion. It is a truly beautiful labor of love. Therefore, it is poison.

Oh Patrick, I sincerely congratulate you on the birth of this amazing book. I am honored to be a man who creates movies that are surrounded by Patrick's love. I am amazed at all types of specialists (weirdos), and you are also a great author. Thank you so much for this book. Your point of view will have a great impact on the Japanese film industry, and I hope this book will be distributed across the globe, so that the Soul of Patrick will guide our world to peace.

I declare: *I will definitely make a movie that will make Patrick cry for joy. Please wait patiently for it. I will repay my debt and gratitude to you. And thank you also for the belt buckle with the strange, old white guy snorting cocaine on it. I will treasure it for the rest of my life.*

So, hey everybody, take this book with you and go out into the city. And incidentally, please watch my movies.

Patrick Religious Group Tokyo Branch Chief
Takashi Miike

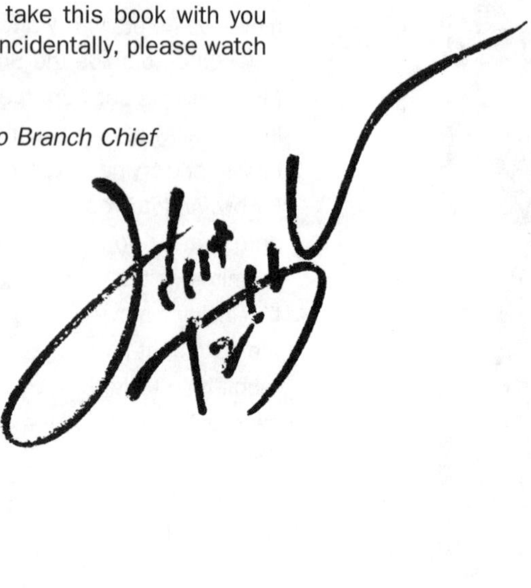

INDEX OF PERSONALITIES

A

Adachi, Masao — 180
Adachi, Nobuo — 74
Adams, Nick — 21, 22
Aikawa, Show — 103, 219, 224
Amachi, Shigeru — 75, 112
Amao, Kanji — 104, 189, 206
Ando, Masanobu — 145
Ando, Noboru — 101, 103, 105, 108, 109, 114–125, 129, 139, 140, 143
Asano, Tadanobu — 227

B

Banno, Yoshimitsu — 31–36
Bercovitch, Reuben — 22

C

Chiba, Jiro — 45, 49
Chiba, Shinichi "Sonny" — 11, 13, 38, 40–58, 77, 104, 107, 110, 112, 129, 134, 137, 140–142, 144, 169, 206, 209, 213, 221, 230
Corman, Roger — 62, 63, 66, 67, 85, 204

D

Dorsey, Willie — 58
Dunham, Robert — 137

E

Edogawa, Rampo — 48, 160, 166, 169, 188
Evans, Gibran — 64, 67
Evans, Jim — 63, 64, 66, 67

F

Fernandez, Peter — 56, 110
Fuji, Junko — 99, 120
Fujitani, Ayako — 25
Fujiwara, Tatsuya — 145, 146
Fukasaku, Kinji — 9, 10, 13, 42, 43, 45, 54, 56, 100, 102, 112, 132–158, 160, 164, 166
Fukushima, Masami — 35

G

Go, Eiji — 46, 48, 120
Gosha, Hideo — 102, 105
Goto, Ben — 167, 201, 205

H

Hamilton, Kipp — 22
Hasabe, Yasuharu — 99, 188
Hayashi, Isao — 191
Hayashi, Kaizo — 11, 57, 79
Higuchi, Shinji — 25
Higuchinsky — 82
Hijikata, Tatsumi — 166
Hino, Hideshi — 80
Hirata, Akihiko — 19
Hiromi, Maya — 108, 122, 123, 191
Honda, Ishiro — 16, 17, 19, 21, 22, 34, 76, 163, 165
Houston, Robert — 62–67

I

Ichijoji, Mina — 234, 235
Ichikawa, Kon — 10, 113

Ichikawa, Utaemon — 87
Ikebe, Ryo — 48
Ikegami, Kimiko — 78
Ikeuchi, Junko — 85
Imamura, Shohei — 11
Ishibashi, Masashi — 47, 50, 52
Ishibashi, Renji — 108, 120, 222, 225
Ishida, Teru — 209
Ishihara, Shintaro — 161, 174, 178
Ishihara, Yujiro — 99, 122, 161, 174, 187, 234
Ishii, Takashi — 188
Ishii, Teruo — 40, 48, 85, 104, 112, 128, 154, 162, 166, 169, 179, 189, 190, 212, 213
Itami, Juzo — 213
Ito, Daisuke — 96, 98
Ito, Jerry — 51
Ito, Junji — 73, 82
Ito, Kazunori — 25
Ito, Shunya — 10, 50, 184, 190

J

Jaeckel, Richard — 138, 165
Jissoji, Akio — 79
Julien, Sandra — 181, 189

K

Kaji, Meiko — 184, 185, 190
Kajiwara, Ikki — 46, 49
Kanazawa, Katsuji — 228
Kaneko, Shunsuke — 25
Kato, Tai — 98, 99

Katsu, Shintaro — 79, 98, 100, 217, 221
Kimura, Takeshi — 10, 22, 33, 35, 76
Kitano, Takeshi — 145, 146, 150, 152, 221, 223
Ko, Hideo — 77, 104
Kobayashi, Akira — 99, 105, 118, 187
Kohira, Yutaka — 50
Komatsu, Sakyo — 72, 200, 201, 204
Konuma, Masaru — 183
Kudo, Eiichi — 142
Kumashiro, Tatsumi — 188, 191
Kurahara, Koreyoshi — 178
Kurata, Yasuaki — 50
Kurosawa, Akira — 10, 11, 17, 18, 31, 87, 155
Kurosawa, Kiyoshi — 11, 13, 88, 89, 202

M

Machida, Masanori — 26
Maeda, Ai — 25
Maeda, Sadao — 40
Magatani, Morihei — 164
Makino, Masahiro — 98, 128
Makino, Shozo — 70, 87
Masumura, Yasuzo — 178, 206
Matsubayashi, Shuei — 203
Matsuda, Toshio — 167, 205
Matsukata, Hiroki — 100, 103, 104, 106, 110, 129, 141, 142
Mifune, Toshiro — 44, 85, 212
Mihara, Yoko — 164, 179
Miike, Takashi — 11, 13, 46, 173, 216–227, 232, 236
Minegishi, Tor — 24, 223, 228
Misumi, Kenji — 30, 62

Mizoguchi, Kenji — 10, 87, 155
Mizuno, Kumi — 21, 22, 76
Moritani, Shiro — 204

N

Nagabuchi, Tsuyoshi — 55
Nagata, Masaichi — 20, 97
Nagisa, Mayumi — 140
Nakagawa, Nobuo — 13, 70, 75, 85, 87, 169
Nakahara, Ko — 178
Nakajima, Sadao — 102, 106, 117, 128, 129, 207
Nakajima, Yoshio — 49
Nakajima, Yutaka — 107
Nakamura, Kinnosuke — 99
Nakamura, Toru — 234, 235
Nakano, Teruyoshi — 33, 208
Nakata, Hideo — 11, 81
Namiki, Kyotaro — 85
Narita, Mikio — 49, 52, 96, 144
Nasu, Hiroyuki — 235
Negishi, Akemi — 163
Nishimoto, Tadashi — 85, 87
Noda, Yukio — 11, 45, 51, 57, 141, 218
Noguchi, Haruyasu — 23
Nomoto, Mihono — 223, 228, 231

O

Obayashi, Nobuhiko — 55, 78, 230
Okabe, Nobuya — 26
Okamoto, Akihisa — 107
Okawa, Shundo — 231

Okura, Mitsugu — 5, 70, 84–87, 164, 169, 173, 176, 179
Omori, Kazuki — 24
Omori, Kenjiro — 208
Omori, Nao — 227
Oniroku, Dan — 183, 188
Onoda, Yoshiki — 164, 179
Oshima, Nagisa — 10, 11, 85, 178, 180
Osugi, Ren — 82, 222
Oyama, Masutatsu — 41, 49
Ozawa, Shigehiro — 40, 42, 47
Ozu, Yasujiro — 10, 11, 155

S

Sabu — 13
Sahara, Kenji — 22, 76
Saito, Mitsumase — 57
Sakai, Frankie — 203
Sanada, Hiroyuki "Duke" — 42, 52, 54, 81, 144
Saperstein, Henry G. — 22
Sato, Hajime — 77
Sato, Junya — 42, 51, 100, 117, 118, 129, 206, 210
Sato, Makoto — 48, 56, 144
Sekizawa, Shinichi — 33, 165
Shihomi, Etsuko — 42, 50, 52, 55–57, 144, 206
Shimada, Kyusaku — 79
Shimura, Takashi — 19, 206
Shiota, Akihiko — 188
Shishido, Jo — 48, 99, 113
Sholder, Jack — 110
Sone, Chusei — 188, 191

Sugawara, Bunta — 10, 85, 100, 102–105, 107, 110, 112, 113, 119, 128, 129, 137, 140–142, 153, 154, 164, 179, 189, 230

Sugimoto, Miki — 181, 190

Suzuki, Akinari — 30

Suzuki, Norifumi — 10, 49, 52, 54, 56, 98, 113, 181, 182, 189

Suzuki, Seijun — 143, 176

T

Takahashi, Koji — 24

Takakura, Ken — 51, 94, 97, 99, 110, 128, 129, 142, 169, 189, 206, 228, 230

Takami, Koushun — 145, 149

Takamori, Tatsuichi — 45, 46

Takarata, Akira — 19, 163, 165, 203

Takashima, Masahiro — 57

Takechi, Tetsuji — 175, 176, 177

Takeuchi, Riki — 103, 219, 223, 224, 228, 230–233

Takigawa, Yumi — 49, 143, 182, 208

Tamblyn, Russ — 22

Tanaka, Kunie — 102, 107

Tanaka, Noboru — 108, 120, 122, 129, 188, 191

Tanaka, Tomoyuki — 18, 31, 35, 167, 205

Tanba, Tetsuro — 48, 56, 85, 100, 105, 114, 128, 129, 137, 144, 167, 179, 202, 204–206, 209, 210, 212, 213

Tani, Naomi — 183, 191

Tsuburaya, Eiji — 25, 36, 76, 165, 203

Tsuchiya, Yoshio — 21, 76

Tsuge, Yoshiharu — 32, 169

Tsuruta, Koji — 51, 97, 98, 116, 134, 139

U

Umemiya, Tatsuo — 45, 100, 106, 110, 113, 117, 120, 129, 141, 143, 189, 203

Umezu, Kazuo — 78

W

Wakamatsu, Koji — 176, 177, 180

Wakamatsu, Setsuro — 12

Wakasugi, Kazuko — 75, 85

Wakayama, Tomisaburo — 98, 106, 112, 134, 139, 209

Watanabe, Fumio — 182, 184

Watari, Tetsuya — 106, 108, 136, 143

Watase, Tsunehiko — 108, 110, 118, 207, 209

Weisman, David — 62–64, 66, 67

Woo, John — 51, 128

Y

Yamada, Goichi — 47

Yamaguchi, Kazuhiko — 49, 56

Yamaguchi, Yoko — 121, 122

Yamamoto, Kei — 34, 206

Yamashita, Kosaku — 110

Yamashita, Tadashi — 57

Yoshida, Teruo — 77, 104, 112, 166

Yuasa, Namio — 120, 125

Yuasa, Noriaki — 20

Yumi, Kaoru — 167, 205